# FOOD PROCESSING AND AGRO BASED INDUSTRIES

# FOOD PROCESSING AND AGRO BASED INDUSTRIES

Written By :
**EIRI Consultants and Éngineers**

&

Compiled By
**Sudhir Gupta**

**ENGINEERS INDIA RESEARCH INSTITUTE**

4449, Nai Sarak, Main Road, Delhi-110 006 (India)
**Ph. :** 91-11-23918117, 23916431, 45120361
**Fax :** 91-11-23916431, 23918117
✶ **E-Mail :** eiribooks@yahoo.com
✶ **Website :** www.eiriindia.org

**Sole Distributor :**
**EIRI PROJECT CONSULTANTS & PUBLISHERS**
4/54, Roop Nagar, Delhi-110007

Printed and Published by :

**ENGINEERS INDIA RESEARCH INSTITUTE**

4449, Nai Sarak, Main Road, Delhi-110 006 (India)
**Ph. :** 91-11-23918117, 23916431, 45120361
**Fax :** 91-11-23916431, 23918117
* **E-Mail :** eiribooks@yahoo.com
* **Website :** www.eiriindia.org

**Distributed by :**

EIRI PROJECT CONSULTANTS & PUBLISHERS
4/54, Roop Nagar, Delhi-110007

2nd Edition


**ISBN : 9788186732120**
Printed in New Delhi (India)



**₹ 975**

---

Printed and Published by Sudhir Gupta for
"Engineers India Research Institute", 4449, Nai Sarak, Main Road,
New Delhi-110 006 and Printed at Swastik Offset, Delhi

# Preface

Food Processing and Agro Based Industries now-a-days are flourishing industries and having bright future scope. The book on Food Processing and Agro Based Industries is are potentially useful book. Agro Based Industry is the largest determinant of Gross National Production in our country. The Food Processing sector in India is a high priority area. Currently, the industry contributes nearly 18 per cent of the total output of the industrial sector and provides employment to 1.5 million.

This sector has an enormous potential for growth given the fact that india is among the largest producers of fruits and vegetables in the world. With a long coastline and a large livestock population, opportunities abound in this sector.

India is home to an enormous variety and range of fruits and vegetables. Popular Indian fruits are the mango, banana, papaya, orange, mosambi, grapes, apple, pineapple, sapota, lichi, walnut and guava. Grapes are an important item of export from India.

The vegetables grown in the country include potato, onions, garlic, lady's finger, tomato, brinjal, peas, beans, celery, cabbage, cauliflower, etc. India's vegetables are popular in the Middle East and South East Asian markets.

The processed food sector in India has grabbed a large share of foreign direct invest in the last few years. Currently, India has been able to export roughly 10 per cent of its processed food output, to the international market. With the on-going moderniisation, technological upgradation, as well as fresh investments in this sector, coupled with the tie-ups with world leaders, it is expected that the export of Indian processed foods will record a major growth in the coming years.

The book which is in your hand is covering 31 detailed and exhaustive chapters including dairy, confectionery, fruit juice, chocolate, frozen desserts, honey, chewing gum, tomato products, jams and jellies, chutney, dehydration of fruit and vegetables, packaging of food & allied products, new development in technologies for food processing, aseptic packaging of food and beverages, packaging of dairy & milk products, bread, buns, pies, pasta products, cakes, biscuits and other allied bakery products. Among all the project profiles on different food products are also incorporated in this book. Apart from the above informations the most valuable chapter named directory section which is fully covered with the addresses of plant and machinery suppliers for all the fruit & vegetables, dairy, confectionery and bakery products.

**Director**
**ENGINEERS INDIA RESEARCH INSTITUTE**
**Nai Sarak, New Delhi.**
Fax : 91-11-291 6431

# CONTENTS AND SUBJECT INDEX

| Chapters | Page No. |
|---|---|

| Chapters | Page No. |
|---|---|

| Chapters | Page No. |
|---|---|

| Chapters | Page No. |
|---|---|

| Chapters | Page No. |
|---|---|

| Chapters | Page No. |
|---|---|

| Chapters | Page No. |
|---|---|

# Chapter - 1

# *New Developments in Technologies for Food Processing*

## TECHNOLOGY AND MARKET

The technology and market are very much complimentary to each other as far as food processing industry is concerned. Market pull necessitates continuous technology inputs while Technology push necessitates continuous market for new products and both drag each other.

Technology is a tool by which a perceived market need in translated into an actual product to meet the potent creations of :

1. New Possibilities
2. New Applications or
3. New opportunities that the unrevealed market wants

For example, a couple of years ago nobody has though about fruit juice varieties in tetrapacks, two minutes instant noodles or instant soups to flood the Indian market. Retort pouches or Microwaves are examples of technology push.

## TECHNOLOGY UPGRADATION

Technology upgradation in food processing is directed on the following important aspects.

1. Development in processing technology
2. Effective use of modern technology
3. New product development
4. Increased impetus on R & D
5. Development in packaging systems

## Development in Processing Technology

It started from batch processes, developed into semi continuous and finally to continuous process or in producing the same product better, easier and at low cost. Though the food processing industry in India is still groping in the dark, in order to keep ourselves abreast of the modern techniques, following new sectors have been upgraded with the introduction of modern processes.

(a) In preservation techniques, the Autoclaves, sterilization, quick freezing and vacuum freeze drying.

(b) Automation in filling in can, jars or polypacks of frozen products to vacuum drying and vacuum freeze drying.

(c) In snack food industry which has captured enormous volume, with extrusion technology, development of spinning, extrusion and steam texturing processes for soya protein.

(d) Agglomeration process like potato & milk agglomerates

(e) Fluidised bed process techniques

(f) Hypobaric techniques (low temperature, pressure, high humidity, ventilation) for extending life of perishable products in storage & distribution.

(g) Ultra high temperature (UHT) processing and aseptic packaging for milk; now applied to other products also.

(h) Micro processor controlled processes to enable both production and quality assurance with increased efficiency and fool proof performance.

(i) Introduction vending machines with particularly very significant application of microprocessor technology...

## Effective Use of Modern Technologies

New products may not necessarily depend on new technology, but there could be a combination of known technologies. These technologies may be used in an imaginative way which complies with the needs of changing market.

## New Products Development

Major New Product Development may Include :

(a) A product entirely new in character like instant soups, vacuum freeze dried products.

(b) A product ostensibly similar in many respect to some existing brands but with distinguishing features with extra consumer appeal, like Bisca instant noodles against Maggie two minutes noodles.

(c) A product similar to one already in the market but new from a manufacture, like Tree Top that followed Frooty, Apply and Great shake etc.

(d) A product novel in kind, made by novel process or through novel ingredients, like vacuum freeze dried coffee & instant meals, Retort pouches ready meals.

(e) A product resulting from substantial modifications of the character of one of the company's existing products, with change in nature/proportion of ingredients or processing methods or conditions or packaging system, like Tang, Juice-C against Rasna etc. or packed Sausages etc.

*Minor New Products : e.g. to improve sales message*

(i) Change in flavour e.g. cola, orange, lemon etc.
(ii) Range extension : Fruit flavour, Dessert mixes
(iii) Change in pack size/addition of new packs

The product development starategy undergoes through metamorphic sieve as is a result of the decision of multifunctional project team who prepare the workplan and include the following functional inputs.

- Commercial brain (Marketing)
- Technical brain (Product Development)
- Financial brain (Finance & Cost Accountancy)
- Muscle Power (Production)
- Nervous System (Food Control)

## Increased Impetus on R & D

*This is necessary for :*

(a) Increasing stability and shelf life of food products
(b) New products to provide health and nutrition at affordable price with low cholesterol, low sodium may be enriched with bran, cereals or other cheap nutritional products.
(c) Studies on water-binding properties of meat, electron microscopy studies in tissue of fruit, vegetable, meat fish and fine structure of food stuffs.
(d) Behaviour and instruction of hydrochloride gel systems.
(e) Combination of food preservation systems
(f) Studies on nature of behaviour of food emulsions
(g) Studies on food powders like juices & soups etc.
(h) On extrusion cooking technology
(i) Enzymes responsible for food deterioration
(j) Improved means of inactivating enzymes or inhibiting their effects
(k) Research in enzymes that produce desirable effects
(l) Quest for newer processes of preservation
(m) Studies on genetic engineering to produce new food materials.

All this R & D is relevant to potential future products of commercial viability. Unifortunately our R & D institutions under auspices of CSR suffer from lack of funds, facilities and infrastructure while R & D facilities of the industry have the sole purpose of enjoying income benefits in its name. Time has come when we can not shy away from the importance of this programme in a serious way.

## Developments in packaging systems and materials

This field has undergone a revolution while the further development continue to be a day to day affair.

(a) The influence of packaging is widespread (i) Technological aspects like oxygen barrier and moisture barrier involved in packaging can be taken care of by using plastic films & laminates which further offer the following R & D exercise.

(b) Plastic films that stand up to boilint water for boil-in-bag frozen foods and instant snack products reconstituted with boiling water in PP/Styrofoam pots (BISCA)

(c) Moulded PVC Polypot for product not subjected to heat like yoghurt, cottage cheese, chilled desserts, chilled salads and short life delicacies.

(d) Overable board for microwaves

(e) Retortable laminated pouch, which is a phenomenal success in Japan, USA and Europe.

Various modern processes and advancement in food processing industry are dealt with in detail under the following heads :–

1. Quick Freezing
2. Accelerated Freeze-Drying
3. Cryogenic Pulverization
4. Dehydration
5. Sterilization
6. Concentration/Evaporation
7. Ohmic heating

## QUICK FREEZING

During the past three decades in the western world the growth of the frozen industry has been greater than any other segment of the food industry. The food processing system is changing rapidly. In processing the predominance of frozen vegetable which can be kept for a longtime is estimated with more emphasis on nutritional quality.

Freezing can preserve many foods in a form comparable to the fresh product. Frozen foods are essentially prepared without the application of any preservatives unlike in canned and other pre-cooked foods. Frozen foods are convenient because they will be available around the year. These are convenient foods because they are cleaned, trimmed and cut to a size which can be used for cooking readily. Frozen foods are hygienic and healthy because they are blanched and frozen at - 40°C temperature where the biological activity is completely stalled. The frozen foods are convenient as they can be brought and stored in bulk for a long period in comparison to the fresh vegetables, which have to be brought frequently as their shelf life is very short.

## Principle involved in Quick Freezing

*There are two main principles involved in the preservation of foods by freezing these are:*

(i) All types of change that cause decay, whether due to living micro organisms or to enzymes naturally present are slowed down at low temperature.

(ii) Water present in the fresh foods is withdrawn from the food during freezing and is almost considered to have been dried.

Further it is also believed that rapid withdrawal of heat, during quick freezing, leads to the conservation of the watery fraction of the food into very small crystals which do much less harm to the structure of the commodity frozen than the large crystals produced when the rate of freezing is slow.

## FREEZING PROCESSES

*Five types of freezing processes are used in modern food technology:*

### 1. Immersion Freezing

The foods to be frozen immersed directly into a very cold solution. Previously brine was employed particularly for freezing whole fish. The brine freezing system was generally used in freezing special products requiring immediate freeze, e.g. bonito, to protect the product from bleaching. Freezing was accomplished by immersing the product in 20 or 25°C brine. Alternative freezing liquids that have more recently come into use are invert sugar solutions, particularly for fruit and vegetables. A variation of immersion freezing is the indirect contact system in which the food is placed in a metal container and the container then immersed in a bath of refrigerated brine or some other freezing solution.

### 2. Convection Freezing

This system involved the use of a blast of cold air which, when directed on the foods, quickly freeze them. This is again of two types.

#### (i) Semi Air Blast Freezing

This system is utilized primarily for quick freezing products of comparatively large size. It is one of the most popular types of freezing marine foods both on board the fishing vessel and at onshore facilities.

### (ii) Air Blast Freezing

Air blast freezing is used primarily for freezing big quantities of large size products. This system consists of a unit cooler having a large capacity with lower evaporative temperature. In case of freezing large size products at slaughter houses hanging rails are provided in the freezing room, considering good circulation of chilled air.

The vegetables are also frozen in air blast tunnel (chamber freeze) in which cold air at 40°C is rapidly moved around the product giving it a cryogenic shock and freezing it instantly. This type of freezing results in the product free roplling and not clotting into lumps. This process is also called individual quick freezing (IQF). The frozen vegetables & fruits are packed into polybags and printed cartons for consumers.

## 3. Crygenic Freezing

This method involves the exposure of food to a cooling medium at a very low temperature. Liquid nitrogen at a temperature of - 195.8°C has been used successfully on a commercial scale. The principle may be used in number of ways. For example, strawberries immersed into liquid nitrogen for 30 seconds can be cooled from 72°F (23°C). Alternatively, the food to be frozen can be exposed to a spray of liquid nitrogen or to a blast of the very cold nitrogen gas. The rapid freezing achieved by these processes can give product of particularly good flavour.

## 4. Multiple Freezing

This is a cabinet with a number of hollow shelves which form the freezing surface. The food to be frozen is placed between the shelves, which press together onto the items to be processed. This is also called contact plate freezer and is one of the most popular types of equipment for freezing packed foods or small items. In recent years the manufacture and use of pressure type multiple units has expanded considerably to meet the demand for a flat, well formed frozen package that will stack compactly in retail cabinets. The product freezing rate in a contact plate freezer varies with the size of the packages, the type of product, and the packing material utilized.

## 5. Fluidized Bed Freezing

In this process, a blast of cold air is blown upwards through a bed of the food to be frozen in such a way that the portions of food bounce up and down in the air flow and the entire mass behaves almost as if it were a liquid. If the bed in slightly sloping, the mass of food will flow along supported on the air steam without the need for conveyor belts which may give mechanical trouble and require cleaning.

## ACCELERATED FREEZE DRYING

The principle involved in accelerated freeze drying is that natural moisture present in the product during freezing is turned into ice which will evaporate directly as vapour without ever turning back into moisture when heated or placed under high vacuum.

If a food stuff is frozen so that the natural moisture in it is turned into ice and under high vacuum ice evaporates directly the phenomenon is known as accelerated freeze drying. Frozen food is dehydrated because its moisture is immobilized as ice crystals. It retains its stability so long as it is kept frozen. Food which is subjected to accelerated freeze drying and from which the ice crystals have been removed by evaporation will remain stable so long as it is kept dry and protected from air. Structure and quantity of food is also well maintained. When such food is unpacked and moistened again it becomes a food of high quality and good flavour.

The main disadvantage of accelerated freeze drying is that it requires quite elaborate machinery and is consequently expensive. It also requires a high degree of technical competence from the people who operate the process. Accelerated freeze drying has been very successfully applied to meat, fish particularly shrimps fruit & vegetable of various sorts. It has recently been applied successfully on a large scale to eggs.

The foods is placed in a freeze dryer in moderately large portions. The plates of the freeze dryer are arranged so that pressure can be exerted on the food and at the same time a very high vacuum capable of producing an atmosphere of about 1 mm of mercury is applied. Raw meat subjected simultaneously to a light applied plate pressure and a high vacuum has been successfully frozen by the loss of heat produced by the high rate of evaporation of moisture.

## CRYOGENIC PULVERIZATION

Cryogenic pulverization process is a good method of food stuff manufacture. The principle of cryogenic pulverization involves the use of the cryogenic brittleness of materials for the pulverization process. It has been known for sometime that this process has several characteristics that are superior to those of conventional normal temperature pulverization, for example its ability to provide finer particles or the quality of the initial material is minimally degraded. However, this process has bee applied to only a very limited part of processed foodstuff manufacture. Pulverization conditions must be observed very closely and strict quality control measures must be reviewed and adapted to this process.

This technology produces foodstuff with improved flavours and other features by pulverizing food materials, which cannot be pulverized easily in conventional normal temperature pulverization process. By this process new types of foodstuff can be produced by effectively using raw materials which have not been used in the past due to their value.

In this process, food materials such as rice, soyabean, meat, vegetable, seasonings, favourite non-nourishing food and spices, prepared for a size suitable to be fed into a pulverizer are frozen using liquid nitrogen (196°C) as a refrigerant. The frozen material is introduced into a pulverizer and pulverized while the temperature is maintained at a predetermined level by the liquid nitrogen. The particle size of pulverization is controlled by regulating the opening of the slit plate in the pulveriser. Process such as heating, mixing and/or drying, are used with the particles, depending on the material, resulting in a form of powder, granule or paste.

*Following tables shows some examples of products made by this process and usage of these products.*

| | *Produce* | *Example of usage* |
|---|---|---|
| 1. | Rice powder | Rice cake, rice bread |
| 2. | Alpha rice powder | Thickener of instant pottage soup |
| 3. | Soyabean powder | Additive to TOFU, (beancurd), health beverage |
| 4. | Coffee bean powder | Flavour for instant coffee |
| 5. | Chocolate nuts paste | Confectionery |
| 6. | Baby food granule | Food for weaning babies & the sick |
| 7. | Resoluble gelatine powder | Instant jelly |
| 8. | Powder of crab meat & shell | Crab meat flavour for KAMABOKO (boiled fish paste) |
| 9. | Chicken meat & bomb granule | Instant soup |
| 10. | Orange paste | Spice for confectionery |

Cryogenic Pulverisation has definitely got added advantages over the conventional normal temperature pulverization. These are as follows : When food materials are pulverized in a normal-temperature pulverization method, the material easily degrades due to the heat and oxidation at the time of pulverization. It is also difficult to pulverize a material containing much of fat or moisture. For example, since the particle size of rice starch is the finest among all cereals, and the particles have a very strong mutual integrity, it is impossible to pulverize rice down to single particles. The best obtainable are lumps of particles. Therefore, the rice powder lack in flavour, and use is limited since it cannot be evenly mixed with other food materials.

Cryogenic pulverization process has the following good effects.

1. Since cryogenic brittleness is utilized for the pulverisation, materials can be pulverised into fine particles (not greater than 0.06 mm in the case of rice) and palatable processed foods can be made.

2. Food materials that cannot be easily pulverized at normal temperature,

such as those containing much far (meat) or moisture (meat, vegetables) or those having a low softening point (chocolate) can be pulverised by this process, providing opportunities of producing new processed foods.

3. The use of liquid nitrogen prevents food materials from being degraded by the heat and oxidation at the time of pulverization and prevents the flavour from diffusing.

## DEHYDRATION

The latest process of dehydration consists of the removal of moisture from foods by the application of heat usually in the presence of a controlled flow of air. Fresh fruits & leafy vegetables perish faster than potatoes etc. For longer life the water contents of the food products should be reduced by drying or dehydration. Ideally the moisture content may be reduced to a level below that at which micro organisms can grow.

### Dehydration Operations

Before and after there are various other important operations carried out in the dehydration of fruits and vegetables. A general scheme of processing of fruits and vegetables is presented below.

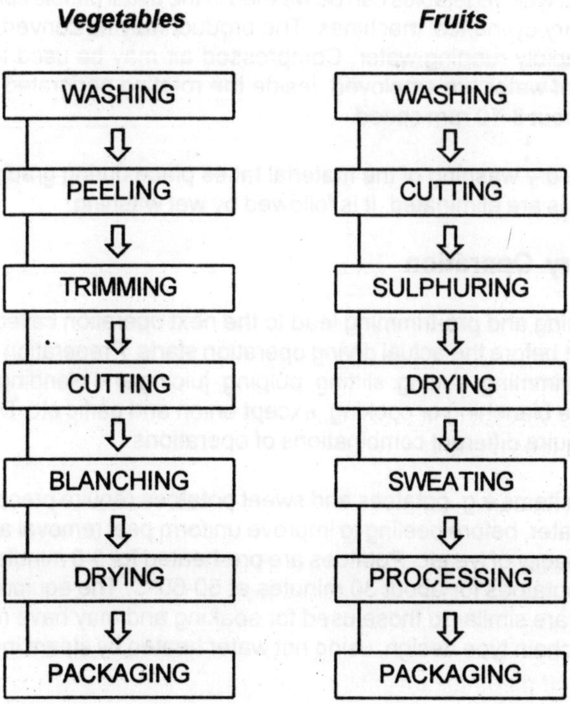

## Storage

Processing of fruits & vegetables is carried out as soon as the raw material is received at the plant but due to some unavoidable circumstances such as early arrivals, non availability, market price which changes according to time etc., they may have to be stored prior to processing. During storage products continue to mature, loss of water by chemical and physical breakdown taken place. The loss of sugar during storage also results in loss of flavour, sweetness and general excellence. During storage especially at high temperature and humidities all fruits & vegetables my be susceptible to mold and other diseases and some vegetables can become hard. Thus the storage area should be well ventilated to dissipate the heat generated. Shade, water, baths, per-cooling and even cold storage when available should be used.

## Washing

Washing is carried out to reduce the dirt and mucilaginous coating present in the raw materials. Washing removes further any spray residue that has been left on the product. Clean water is used for washing and when parts or tanks are employed for this purpose, the water must be changed regularly to ensure through clearing. The type of wash depends upon the type of product being cleaned. For large quantity processing mechanical agitation is employed.

All root type vegetables can be washed in the usual paddle conveyor washers or in rotary cylindrical machines. The product may be converted through a current of rapidly running water. Compressed air may be used to agitate the water. Jets of water are employed, inside the rotating perforated drum, which rotates at about 8-10 rpm speed.

Some dry washing of the material takes place during grading. Where in dirt and debris are eliminated. It is followed by wet washing.

## Preparatory Operation

Washing and pre-trimming lead to the next operation called preparation is carried out before the actual drying operation starts. Preparation involve peeling, coring, trimming, cutting, slitting, pulping, juicing and blending etc. All solid foods require blanching or cooking, except onion and garlic etc. Different commodities require different combinations of operations.

Some items e.g. potatoes and sweet potatoes require preconditioning or heating in water, before peeling to improve uniform peel removal and yield, and improve capacity of lye etc. Potatoes are pre-heated for 5-6 minutes at 55-70°C and sweet potatoes for about 30 minutes at 50-60°C. The equipment used for pre-heating are similar to those used for soaking and may have rotary, screw, belt or drag chain type design, using hot water heated by steam injectors.

## Peeling

The skin or outer covering of some fruits and vegetable must be removed in the preparation process. It should be efficient to prevent excess loss of useful products. Peeling losses should be controlled to minimum.

*There are following types of peeling.*

## Abrasive Peeling

In this method the vegetable are rotated against rough surfaces such as carborandum, which rub off the soft peel. Losses may amount to as much as 30% but by careful control may be kept down to about 15 per cent. Batch type abrasive peelers consist of a drum coated internally with carborundum and a rotating base plate, also carborandum covered continuous peelers consist of a number of rows of abrasive covered cylinders which rotate at high speed and are arranged to give forward and side-ways movements to vegetables. In all the compartments loosened peel is washed away with water sprays.

## Lye Peeling

Hot lye solution is used in the lye peeling process. This method has got both advantages and disadvantages. It completely treats even the deep seated lye vegetable effectively, permits rapid handling of the product and reduce the loss frequently ecountered in other means of peeling. Disadvantage being the danger of handling the hot caustic soda solution. Lye peeling is frequently used on peaches, sweet potatoes, potatoes, apricots, carrots etc.

*This peeling operation involves*

1. Preliminary dusting and water wash in standard equipment
2. Short immersion in a hot caustic soda solution in the lye peeler itself,
3. Vigorous water rinse and tumbling in a washer to remove all skins and the caustic.
4. Acid neutralisation bath in sometimes used
5. Hand trimming and cutting

The usual lye concentration is about 4 to 10 per cent. Lye peels be batch or continuous type depending on the plant capacity. Rotary or wheel type peeler consists of a perforated steel drum with internal valves. A steam coil keeps the lye hot. Draper type continuous lye peeler is also in use. Copper, bronze, brass, aluminium, lead, zinc, cadmium and tin etc. are not used as material of construction of a lye peeler as material of construction of a lye peeler as these are attacked by the Caustic. Rotary type lye peeler which can also be used as a pre-heater blancher is shown below.

## Flame and Radiant Heat Peeling

Rotary type furnace with refractory lining is employed in this method. Vegetables are brought either in direct contact with live flame or subjected to high radiant heat temperatures. The skins are charred or blistered by the action of direct gas flames. Radiant heat method, using temperatures as high as 100°C and above are considered more satisfactory for peeling potatoes since the lyes of the potatoes are also burnt out. After this treatment the vegetables are subjected to a high pressure water spray which remove the charred skins. In this method peeling losses are very low.

## Steam Peeling

This method is very popular now and operation be either batch or continuous. Batch type vessels are chambers, closed by quick acting lids, mounted on swivels. Continuous steam peeler usually consists of a cylinder containing a helical conveyor, fed and discharged by a rotary valve mechanism at either end. Steaming temperature (ore pressure) and time depend on the nature and condition of vegetables, thus potatoes can be peeled at 6 kg/cm$^2$ steam pressure for 30 sec. After steaming the vegetables are washed with high pressure jets to remove the loosened peel.

## Trimming, Shelling and Coring

Some commodities require special steps during the processing. Carrot, onion and other root vegetables are topped and rooted; cabbage is cored and outer leaves are removed. Steam-ends, husks etc. are removed. Onions are topped and rooted also. These are kept by hand on a rotating turret and are conveyed between two circular saws which cut off the top and root ends. Coring machines are available which can core fruit automatically. After peeling a final hand trimming is required to remove residual skin, eyes, roots, cuts, discoloured areas and other defects.

## Cutting, Pulping and Reducing

The peeled and trimmed product is cut into cubes, slices, rings, strips etc. It may also be pulped, juiced or homogenised cutting is performed to get the product in a desired shape and also to facilitate bleaching and drying. Potatoes and carrots are cut in 1/4" to 1/2" cubes and pieces and 1/5" to 1/3" thick strips. Cutting machines are used for making slices, strips, cubes etc. The prepared commodity is fed into the rotating slicing shell and is forced against the slicing knife. The commodity is cut into slices and then into cubes in one pass. Cut material is washed with water before blanching.

Pulping is a process used to breakdown such products as pumpkin, apples, tomatoes, sweet potato etc. The product is steamed to soften it for pulping, using a steam retort. The material is cut into uniform pieces to ensure uniform steaming. After steaming the product is passed through a sieve where the skins, seeds, core and fibrous materials from the pulp are removed.

After products such as pumpkin have been pulped it is frequently desirable to evaporate the liquid from the pulp mass, to the desired consistency, by heating in a steam-jacketed kettle. Reducing improves the texture of the product, improves soup stock flavour and decreases the number of cans required for a given volume of the initial product.

## Blanching

Blanching or scalding is an essential step in dehydration of almost all food products. Blanching is carried out with a purpose to inactivate the enzymes present that cause discoloration and loss of flavour during drying and storage. It improves texture, of the product and assists in preservation of vitamin viz vitamin C. Onion, Garlic and the seasoning materials and fruits that are sulphured before drying are not blanched. Thus when the products of enzymes catalysed reaction in foodstuffs are undesirable, blanching is used to eliminate enzymes. When the products of enzyme catalysed reaction are desirable as in onions and garlic, blanching is not used before dehydration.

Blanching refers to the practice of heating raw foods for short time at almost the boiling point of water. Blanching may be done in water or steam, or by microwave heating. To obtain effective enzyme inactivation all parts of the product should attain a temperature of at least 90°C thus blanching time shall be longer for thicker pieces. Water or steam may be used as blanching medium. Water blanching requires less time as compared to steam blanching due to faster heat application in liquid medium.

## Water Blanching

Water blanching is carried out at about 99oC for 2-3 minutes. Over-blanching should be avoided to prevent mushiness and drying difficulties. For certain vegetables addition of sodium sulphite or meta-bisulphite during blanching improves colour, storage life and vitamin C retention. Some leaching of solutes takes place and the concentration of soluted in the liquor should be allowed to build up to minimise leaching. Excessive concentration also effects, adversely the quality and storage life of the product. Ideal concentration is 3 percent for carrot, 1.5 per cent for cabbage and 1 per cent for potato. During blanching the pH of liquor falls hence in the case of cabbage some sodium corbonate is added to maintain the pH at 7.3 to 7.8 to avoid degradation of chlorophyll. Phosphate may be added whose discoloration by iron-tanin reactions appears e.g. in some varieties of carrots.

## Steam Blanching

This method of blanching is preferred over water blanching due to the smaller leaching losses. Root type vegetables require 2 - 4 minutes in steam at

100°C when cut into small dics, slices and strips; about 5 - 15 minutes for chunks etc. and 15-20 minutes for quarters of potatoes for making flakes, granules etc. Leafy vegetables require only 1/2 to 2 minutes exposure. Steam blanching may pose difficulty in deep beds and the outer layers of the commodity may get over-cooked.

## Microwave Blanching

In this method heat is generated in the food by exposing it to microwave or high frequency radiation. It is a new but high cost and low output method but there occurs no leaching of solutes, and hence losses of flavour and nutritive value are kept at a minimum.

## Blanchers

Blanchers may be batch or continuous type, and their design depends on the output, type of commodity and blanching procedure etc. In simple batch blanchers, baskets of prepared commodity are immersed in vats of hot or boiling water or placed in steam chambers. Leafy vegetable like cabbage which cannot withstand transfer from the blancher and spreading on the drying surface are blanched directly on the dryer trays.

Continuous blanchers may be belt or rotary type. In rotary water blancher a perforated rotating cylinder with an internal helical scroll is kept half immersed in water heated with steam. Rotating cylinder should preferably be supported on external bearings, rather than on trunnions below the water level, which could cause metallic contamination in the liquor.

In continuous conveyor type steam blancher vegetable is spread in a thin layer on the conveyor. It is taken through a tunnel into which steam is injected. Wire mesh belt is preferred as the conveyor. Belt blanchers vary in size, 50-175 cms. in width and 10 to 20 metres long. Rotary continuous blanchers may consist of a helical screw conveying prepared vegetable along a covered trough in which steam is injected through the sides or the hollow screw shaft. For water blanching water may be kept in the trough, heated by steam. In this equipment the liquor needs frequent replacements. Screw blanchers are available in a variety of sizes from about 20 cm in dia. by 3 meter long, to 60 cm x 10 meter for steam blanching and 60 cm x 5 meter to 1 meter x 6 meter for water blanching.

Perforated drum type rotary continuous blancher similar in design to peeler is also in use.

Pipe blancher is suitable for peas, beans and diced vegetable. They are carried by a steam of water in a column or table, the water being maintained at the blanching temperature. Means are provided to withdraw a constant proportion of liquor, from which the blanched vegetables are separated, the liquor is returned to the circuit.

The blancher parts that come into contact with food products should be made of stainless steel, though sometimes black iron and galvanised iron may also be used. Use of stainless steel is a must where sulphiting solutions are used before blanching or are sprayed into the product during blanching.

## Sulphiting

Sodium sulphite and sod bisulphite in equal proportions are added to the blanching liquor in 0.2 - 0.5 per cent concentration (as $So_2$). Or, otherwise this solution is sprayed on the commodity in the blancher during or after the operation. Vitamin C, citric acid and sodium chloride etc. are also sometimes incorporated to retard enzymic browning or oxidation during processing. Borates can be used to inhibit oxidative enzymes in apples. After blanching a spray of hot starch solution improves the storage characteristics of carrots.

## Cooling

Blanching is followed by cooling. It is necessary to cool the vegetable after blanching and before drying. The pieces are spread on the drying trays to stop the cooking effect. When the rotary blanchers are used the vegetable from the exist slides down a spreader on to a stainless steel mesh belt passing through a chamber where a cooling air steam cools it. In the case of potatoes cooling is done with water sprays which removes the adhering gelatinised starch also. This methods is not applicable for other fruits & vegetables. Clean water should be used in all the operations.

## Drying

The products are dried using different types of dryers and their selection is made according to the commodity required to be dried. Apart from air drying, osmosis, dispersion, microwave, centrifugal buds and superheated vapours are also the modes employed in drying process. The equipment necessary to accomplish the desired results must be designed and operated to make optimum use.

Some dryers commonly used in food processing are discussed here.

## Cabinet Dryers

Cabinet or chamber driers consists an enclosed chamber fitted with heater/ electric or steam coils) and fan for air circulation with airflow deflectors. The product is loaded on trays which may be located either on guide rails fixed to the inside of an insulated frame. The flow of the air is either parallel to the trays, or vertically through the trays. Air flow is maintained in the range of 150-300 M/min. It is usual to recirculate a certain percentage of air, according to humidity required in the chamber.

In cross-drought flow, the material on the upstream trays dry earlier than those on the downward side. In some driers the cabinets are arranged in series, so that trolley loads of trays pass from one to the next.

## Continuous Conveyor Dryers

Foodstuffs are subjected to heat while being carried along on a stainless steel belt. Hot air is blown through the perforated belt and the material such as apple, beet, carrots, onion, potatoes and sweet potatoes etc. are dried by the air circulation in tunnel driers. Material is loaded on the belt at one end using a spreader twice, in 3-6" thick layer. The width of the belt and the drier varies between 2/3 metres and the length above 10-20 metres. Belt moves slowly so that when the material the other end, it had achieved the desired lowering of the moisture content. The conveyor drying is terminated while the moisture content is still as high as 10-15 per cent, to be dried further to desired extent. Total residence time of product in the conveyor driers may be as short as 2.5 hours. A drier of this kind with a belt width of 2 m. and length 25 m. When loaded at the rate of 45 kg/cm$^2$ shall have a capacity of drying about 20 tonnes (wet material)/ day.

There are 2-stage driers wherein speeds of belts carrying the foodstuffs along with it for drying move at varied speeds. The use of two stages makes it possible to discharge the partly dried material at the end of the first stage, mix it, and repile it in a thicker layer for the second stage. This gives more uniform product and reduces the drier width in the second stage.

## Belt-Trough Dryer

The belt-trough drier is a continuous through-flow drier. It consists of an endless wire mesh conveyor belts, supported and transported by roller chain sprockets carried by three parallel drive shafts. Between the drive shafts the belt forms a trough, the bottom of which rests on a flat surfaced air gate which slopes upwards in the direction of motion of the belt. Heated air is forced upwards via the air gate and through the belt. The foodstuff is fed on to the trough, in a direction parallel to the drive shaft, and is raised by the movement of the belt towards the lip of the trough, tumbles back, and so in a series of spiral like movements travels along the drier towards an adjustable discharge weir at the exist end.

## Tunnel Dryers

Tunnel driers combine high capacity and high quality of product. It is a semi-continuous process where truck loads of freshly prepared material are removed at intervals into one end of the long, closely fitting enclosure, the whole string of trucks is periodically advanced a step, and the dried truck loads are removed at the other end of the tunnel. Foods in pieces of any size and shape can be dried in tunnel driers. Material to be dried is loaded on the drying trays stacked one above another on a low bed truck and are designed so that when they are properly stacked a clear air passage is left between trays. A single tunnel may contain 5 too 15 trucks, a maximum working length of 15 metres, space for fan and recirculation port etc. shall take up further 5 m length. Modern direct heated tunnel driers are almost invariably built of fireproof material such as hollow concrete block, hollow tile, sheet metal or asbestos-cement sheeting.

## Heating System

Air is passed over steam heated coils or furnace gas heater coil and it becomes hot. Alternatively heating of air can also be carried out by mixing with the products of combustion from the furnace. Airflow system is further maintained under different designs which strongly influence the drying characteristics. Air flow can be concurrent, counter, transverse or a combination of concurrent and counter.

## Recommended drying and blanching practice for some common varieties of vegetables

Blanching and drying practice for vegetables are carried out under some controlled parameters for which certain standard are recommended. These standards are presented in the following table.

| Vegetable | Form for drying | Steam blanching time | Max. drying temp. | Approx yield of dry product per 100 kg of fresh | |
|---|---|---|---|---|---|
| | | | | from prepared | from unprepared |
| Beans, Lima | Shelled beans, green | 10 | 68°C | - | - |
| Cauliflower | Flowers broken apart and sliced in half | 5-10 | 60°C | - | - |
| Carrots | Sliced or diced | 5-15 | 70°C | 11-14 | 8-12 |
| Celery | Sliced thin or 0.5" length | 1-3 | 63°C | 6-9 | 4-8 |
| Cabbage | Trimmed & shredded | 2-6 | 65°C | 8-12 | 6-10 |
| Corn | Precooked or cob. cut from cob | 15-20 | 70°C | 25-28 | 8-12 |
| Garlic | Peeled, sliced | Untreated or 1-2 | 65°C | - | - |
| Green beans | 0.25" to 1" length | 15-20 | 69°C | 10-13 | 8-12 |
| Peas | Shelled | 3-10 | 65°C | 18-22 | 9-14 |
| Potato, white | Peeled, sliced or diced | 5-7 | 65°C | 22-25 | 17-21 |
| Potato, sweet | Peeled, sliced or diced | 6-8 | 70°C | 32-35 | 24-28 |
| Pumpkin | Peeled and sliced | 3-8 | 68°C | 7-9 | 4-8 |
| Spinach | Trim and wash | 3-5 | 65°C | 7-11 | 3-6 |
| Sprouts | Washws, cut in half | 5-8 | 65°C | - | - |
| Tomatoes | Scald, peeled, sliced | Nil or 2-3 | 65°C | 5-8 | 3-7 |
| Turnips | Peeled, sliced & diced | 3-10 | 68°C | 10-12 | 7-10 |

# STERILIZATION

## Sterilization by Radioactivity

Ionizing radiation emitted by radioactive isotopes (e.g. gamma rays from cobalt 60) or generated by electrical machines producing electron beam or x-rays are absorbed by all forms of matter. Their energy appears as chemical change and, to a lesser extent, as heat. Living cells are particularly sensitive to these kinds of irradiation which can, therefore, be used to kill micro-organisms, to damage the reproductive mechanism of insects, their eggs and larvae, and to destroy actively growing cells such as those in the sprouts of potatoes or the hearts of onions. Unfortunately, the use of radioactivity to sterilize foodstuffs poses two major drawbacks.

(i) Too large a dose has a harmful effect on quality: butter is bleached; salmon loses its red colour; meat becomes darker; and a burnt off flavour, described as wet dog odour.

(ii) It demands a very heavy capital investment if it is to be applied to bulk quantities of food.

The Units of absorbed irradiation is a red, which is equivalent to the absorption of 100 ergs/g of the absorbing substance.

*Some of the processes explored so far in the use of radioactivity are:*

### a) Complete sterilization

To obtain absolute sterility in a foodstuff requires the use of 10 million reds (10 M red). This damages the quality and flavour so seriously that the food becomes uneatable.

### b) Cold sterilization

To obtain a lever so sterility approaching that obtained in normal canning process, 3 to 5 M red is employed. It kills most types of harmful bacteria. Even, this level causes unacceptable harm to flavour and quality. Some improvement has been achieved by partially cooking the food before it is irradiated or by keeping it well below freezing point during irradiation.

## Treatment of spices etc.

Irradiation from 1 to 3 M red has been applied in treatment of spices and seeds, which may be quite heavily contaminated with micro-organisms. This level of treatment has also been suggested as a means of reducing the bacterial content of sugar which is used during canning.

## Pasteurization through radiation

Certain pathological micro organisms in frozen whole egg and particularly the salmonella that cause food poisoning are subjected to 0.1 to 1.0 rad irradiation treatment for pasteurization. Meat can also be treated the same way. This method and level of treatment have also been found to increase the storage life of such products as sausages and fish. Irradiation flavour is difficult to be avoided in this treatment. Radiation pasteurization cannot be used for fruits or vegetables because it appears to damage the cells.

## Disinfestation

Grain and dried fruits when prepared for long storage are exposed to 0.02 M rad of radiation. It destroys insect eggs and renders the insects themselves incapable of breeding. To be effective, a thin layer of food stuffs must be exposed to the radioactivity. Capital cost of an installation sufficiently large to deal with materials in bulk is very high.

## Sprout Inhibition

Actively growing cells of living being are most susceptible to radiation. So to inhibit sprouting even quite a small dose of radiation (say about 0.01 M) can destroy the cells which grow into sprouts. The use of radioactivity in food stuffs is still not very popular. Efforts are underway to establish whether these possess advantages over more conventional methods sufficient to justify the cost of the necessary installation.

## Retort Sterilization

Retort thermal sterilization is one of the latest methods of food preservation. Retort packages are utilized in wide range of food fields, as they have the following characteristics in comparison with conventional canned foods.

1. Product image is enhanced, as container shape can be formed at will by processing and it is possible to effect sterilization without breaking shape of the product.

2. It is handy, simple and easy to dispose of packaging.

3. Sterilization is a short time is possible and it makes the quality of food better.

## Equipment

Retort sterilization equipment is available both in batch and continuous models. Hot water system and steam system in batch system retorting are available. In hot water system there are rotation system furnished with rotation device. Among these systems, retort sterilization equipment of batch system, hot water system is most largely employed.

## CONCENTRATION/EVAPORATION

The most common and convenient form of concentration employed on fruit juices is vacuum evaporation. The conventional method of concentration liquid foods by modified evaporators is now becoming obsolete. Common types include the vacuum pan, the calandria evaporator, and side-arm evaporators with either natural or forced circulations. Such evaporators are customarily operated under vacuum and are combined into double-and tripple-effect systems for better heat efficiency. Stainless steel is the common material of construction. Tubular, plate type, centrifugal and heat pump type evaporators are available. Now-a-days mechanically agitated film evaporator or wiped-film evaporator has come into prominence particularly for making concentrates that become very viscous at high solids concentration and contain substantial amount of pulp or fibre.

Concentration of milk and fruit juices is often necessary to save storage space and to reduce transportation costs. The most common method for concentration is by evaporation ad more recently by the use of memberanes.

Plate type evaporators are ideal for heat sensitive products to prevent heat damage, as this is greatly reduced by low product contact times and excellent heat transfer characteristics.

There are many plants producing high quality orange and apple juice concentrates of up to 72 per cent total solids. Other concentrates which can be produced include grapeful, lemon, lime, pineapple, mango, guava and passion fruit. A very important consideration with fruit products is the recovery of volatile aromas and essence which are removed during evaporation. These must be recovered from the vapour and added back, otherwise important flavour components will be lost.

### Membrane Concentration

In recent years we have seen the introduction of membranes for concentration of milk and fruit juices. These systems do not cause any flavour damage and have the advantage of low energy costs. Products which can be concentrated include milk, citrus and apple juices and tomato juice.

### Wiped Film Evaporator

The body of this evaporator is a cylinder which may be straight or tapered in either direction with respect to fluid flow, depending upon the flow characteristics of material in process. The units may be mounted vertically for downflow or horizontally for cross-flow of feed, again, depending upon the nature of the feed material. The body of the evaporator is surrounded by a jacket for circulation of the heating medium. In the straight body type, fixed clearance blades are mounted on a shaft passing centrally through the cylinder, constructed to clear the heat transfer surface by as little as .03". In the tapered body type, adjustable blade clearance can be provided by longitudinal movement of the shaft. The rotor may be fitted with hinged wiper blades which contact the heat transfer surface, if required by the material in process. When the central shaft is driven, the rotor blades continually agitate and reform the film of product passing down the walls of the evaporator.

## OHMIC HEATING

A very recent development in heating food products. This is a novel approach to the continuous aseptic processing of viscous and particulate food products. The heater applies the effect of resistance heating within the flow of an electrically conducting liquid and is able to handle food products containing particulates of up to 25 mm cubes. Apart from the feed pump there need be no other moving parts, so damage to the product is minimised.

Examples of particulate food materials which have been processed with minimal structural damage, include those containing meat chunks, prawns, diced or sliced carrots, potatoes and sliced mushrooms. Fruits such as diced apple and whole strawberries have also been successfully heat treated. Processed particulate food materials have been aseptically filled and will, therefore, have a prolonged shelf life, without the need to store under refrigerated conditions.

## PROCESSING OF SOME SELECTED FOOD ITEMS

Foodstuff such green vegetables, potatoes, meat, fish, milk and eggs are processed incorporating all these steps discussed earlier.

## CABBAGE AND OTHER GREEN VEGETABLES

### Blanching

Green vegetables including cabbage etc. after necessary washing and shredding are blanched. During blanching enzymes become inactive when foodstuff is scalded for a brief period. This helps in retaining vitamin C content, colour and flavour intact. In commercial practice as discussed earlier, 0.125% of Sod. Sulphate is added to the scalding water used for blanching. This is formed to protect the colour and vitamin C contents of vegetables and fruits.

### Cooling

Vegetables are cooled in a current of cold air before drying in order to prevent their becoming soft and mushy due to over blanching.

### Drying

During the early stages of drying, the evaporation moisture prevents the temperature of vegetables rising unduly. A current of air at 90 - 95°C (194-203°F), is at first used. As the drying proceeds the temperature is reduced to 55°C (130°F) to avoid producing a scorched flavour. Moisture contents are also reduced to a final value of less than 5% within about five hours.

## PROCESSING OF POTATOES

Potatoes can be dehydrated to produce a useful and attractive material. They may either be peeled or cut into strips, blanched and dried very much as described above for green vegetables. Drying of potatoes is improved if 0.05% of calcium chloride is mixed in at this stage.

### Conditioning

The mashed potato is first partially dried until its moisture content falls to 50%. It is then allowed to cooled for about 2 hours. This conditioning process enables a finer powder to be produced subsequently when the material is fully dried.

### Slaving and Drying

The cooled partially dried potato is sieved to a fine powder and the dried fully to less than 5% moisture on trays in a cabinet or tunnel.

### Reconstitution

The dried mashed potato can be readily reconstituted if three and a half to four parts by weight of water, containing 0.5% of salt and at a temperature of 96°C (203°F), are stirred into one part of the powder. The water should not be boiling or the mashed potato will have a pasty consistency.

## MEAT PROCESSING

### Cooking

Meat give the best quality dried product if, before it is dried, it is first cooked. A convenient process is to cut it into pieces and steam it at 100°C (212°F) for 40 minutes.

### Cooling and Mincing

Meat is cooled and minced through a screen containing apertures of about small size. If the liquid that runs out during the cooking process is separated from fat, concentrated to small volume and returned to minced meat before it is dried, the flavour of the final products is improved. Meat dries more rapidly and gives a more satisfactory dried product if its fat content is below 35%.

### Drying

A suitable type of drier of meat is one in which the minced meat is in trays over which a current of warm air is passed. During the initial stages of drying, the temperature of the meat remains low due to evaporation of moisture regardless of temperature of the drying air. In the later stages care is taken to avoid the meat temperature to exceed 70°C (159°F).

The best results are obtained if a dry matter content of 96.8% is achieved within four to five hours.

## PROCESSING OF FISH

Fresh, good quality, low fat fish, such as cod, haddock, whiting and others available in Indian subcontinent, can be dehydrated to produce an attractive and readily reconstituted article.

### Preparation

The fish is washed, skinned, filleted and minced in a machine to give pieces about 7 mm to 15 mm cube.

### Cooking

After preparation fish is spread on perforated trays and is cooked in the steam at about 2 lb. pressure for about 30 minutes.

### Mincing

After having been cooked, the fish needs to be reduced once more than shreds by being passed through the mincer. This time through still finer holes of 4 mm to 8 mm in diameter.

### Drying

As with meat, drying should be completed within four hours. An initial air temperature of 85°C (185°F) should be reduced to 65-70°C (149-158°F) as the fish approaches its final dry matter of 90%.

## Dried Milk and Dried Egg

### (i) Dried Milk

The high nutritional content of milk - its specially nutritious protein, its calcium, the group B-vitamins and the vitamins A and D from its butter-fat can most conveniently be preserved by drying it. Dried milk also forms useful and potable culinary ingredient.

### Roller-Drying

It is the simplest method where in milk is caused to run, either as whole milk or after having been condensed on to a heated roll. The film of milk is dried almost instantaneously and is scrapped off as the roller slowly turns. Roller-dried milk, however, is a food of excellent nutritional value.

### Spray-Drying

Spray drying is another method for drying milk which is superior to roller drying. The milk is injected as a fine spray into a chamber through which a stream of hot air is blown. The droplets of milk are immediately dried and fall at the bottom as powder. Spray dried milk, efficiently manufactured, does not suffer from the partial insolubility which is a weakness of roller-dried milk and its protein is also of slightly higher nutritional value. On the other hand, the spray-dried powder and the cost of packing, storing and transporting is, therefore, somewhat higher. Steps involved in spray drying are pre-heating, condensing and spray-drying.

### Easily reconstituted powdered skim milk

Lactose, the sugar naturally present in milk, is not very readily soluble when it is entirely freed from combination with water. The wetability of powdered skim-milk is greatly improved if, after it has been initially dried, it is damped and then redried. This restores the 'water of hydration' to the lactose and makes it much readily soluble.

### Storage of Dried Milk

Dried milk is packed in air tight drums or cans in an atmosphere of nitrogen and at a moisture content preferably hot exceeding 3%, but certainly not above 5%, and preferably be stored in a cool place.

## (ii) Dried Eggs

Spray drier used for the milk spray drying is also used for the eggs spray drying. The production a high quality article of good flavour is not altogether easy since it is obviously undesirable to use too high a temperature in the drying process. Where the dried egg is to be used for confectionery, sugar may be added to the liquid egg before drying since it has been found that the dried egg reconstitutes easier when water is added. The moisture content of the dried eggs must not exceed 5%. Stability is obtained by adjusting the pH of the liquid egg to 6.5 and then dry to less than 1% moisture.

# Chapter - 2

# *Packaging of Food & Allied*

*A packaging must provide*

a) Complete protection of the packed material against, light, dust, air, foreign odours, pests, corrosion and microbes.

b) Strength and stability during storage, handling and marketing.

c) Size, shape and appearance to promote salability of the product and convenience in use.

d) A packaging material suitable for use in contact with food stuffs, and its cost must be compatible with the value of the contents and the degree of protection needed.

## PACKAGING MATERIAL AND CONDITIONS

Foodstuffs are packed in sacks, bags, drums, bins, cartons, cans, bottles, jars, pouches etc. The weight, size, economy, durability, dispensibility, permeability, shelf life and interaction between food and packaging material should be taken into consideration while selecting a packaging material. Tin and glass containers made of plastics are in use now while paper containers are also used in a number of applications. Clear films to opaque rigid containers of acrylic, styrene, polyethylene, cellophane, polypropylene, vinyl etc. are mainly in use nowadays. Re-usability of empty containers may also be taken into consideration.

Some dehydrated products require packaging in inert gas. The gassing operation is done on specially equipped semi-automatic can closing machines with large vacuum pump; the vacuum is relieved with nitrogen. When vacuum packing is resorted to, the container should be able to withstand the pressure differential without leakage. Very low moisture dehydrated products are sometimes packed with a small envelop of desiccant included in the container. This envelop is called IPD or in-package desiccant, which is permeable to moisture but does not allow contamination of the product with desiccant.

## Tin Cans

*Canning in tin has many advantages over canning in glass, viz.*

a) Tin cans are easy to handle because there is no danger of breakage
b) There is no leakage of liquid as they are always tightly sealed before processing
c) Processing period is shorter
d) The containers by immersion in water. This permits better control of cooking times.
e) Being lighter in weight they are easy to transport

When tin cans are used, the cans, lids and gaskets should not be damaged in any way. Bent edges will not give a good seal. Hot dipped cold reduced 1.5 lg coating tin plate of 1 to 1.5 lb coating electrolytic tin plate may be used for making open top sanitary cans. Cans are available in various sizes. Can supplying companies may supply cans with bottom attached and with top separate, or to reduce transport costs can bodies may be supplied as flats along with end pieces. Cans are made readily at the factory by using a set of machines consisting of a can body reformer, flanger and double seamer. Cans after fixing the bottom end should be stored upside down in a clean dry place.

It is difficult to coat steel plate uniformly with tin during the process of manufacture. Small micro-scopic spaces are always left uncoated, although the coating may appear perfect to the eye. The contents of the can may react with these exposed parts and cause corrosion of the plate and discoloration of the product, resulting in black stains of iron sulphide. This can be eliminated by lacquer coating of the inside of the can. Acid resistant enamel (AR lacquer or R-or sanitary enamel) cans are used for acid foods especially red-meated fruits and vegetable to prevent bleaching of colour while sulphur resistant enamel (SR or C-enamel) cans are used for non-acid foods. C-enamel cans should not be used for acid foods, otherwise enamel shall pell off.

## Glass Containers

Glass containers viz. bottles and jars have assumed great importance in packaging of food products. The use of glass has many advantages, in particular impermeability , cleanliness, durability and rigidity. It is not susceptible to moul growth and is impremeable to gases, odours, vapours and liquids. Thus almost all products can safely be stored in glass. These properties together with its hard, smooth surface and its ability to withstand hot processing, enable bottles and jars to be washed and sterilised effectively.

*Glass jars have a number of advantages over tin cans.*

a) Glass jars may be reused as long as they are not damaged
b) Food packaged in glass jars are attractive since the product can be seen

c) Some highly corrosive products, such as rhubarb and strawberries react with tin even when it is enamelled and tend to lose their colour. These products may be safely canned in glass.

*Disadvantages of glass jars*

a) Glass jars weigh more than tin cans
b) Glass jars are subject to breakage
c) Glass jars have slower heat penetration and cannot be cooled as rapidly as tin cans.
d) Product canned in glass jars generally must be stored in dark places as light tend to discolour some products.

Glass containers are rigid and robust and can steadily withstand high speed filling and sealing process. There is an infinite variety of shapes available for the glass containers. They can be made in a variety of colours which in many cases save to protect the food production from light rays. Some of the glass containers are reusable e.g. milk bottles, beer bottles and some bottles for carbonated drinks.

## Closure of Glass Containers

Various types of closures are available for glass containers. Majority of closures are made of metal or plastics although other materials such as paper, rubber, glass or their combinations are also used. The metals most commonly used are tinplate, aluminium or its alloys; the plastics are usually based on phenol formaldehyde or UF resin or one of the thermoplastics such as polyethylene, PVC or polystyrene.

These closures are rigid or semi-rigid, compressing an interposing wad which acts as a cushion against the sealing edge of the glass container. The wads may be made of cork, paper board, rubber synthetic materials. Some of the important varieties of closures are described below.

## External Screw Caps

These are made from metal or thermosetting plastics. A variation is the rolled on closure where instead of a preformed screw cap, an aluminium blank shell is supplied complete with liner, and sealing pressure is applied.

## Lug Cap

There are four luge, equally spaced on the circumference of the cap. When the cap is turned, corresponding lugs are engaged. It is generally used for packing powders and viscous materials. This closure can be tightened or released very quickly.

## Crown Cork

It is a popular type of closure for glass bottles. A series of flutes around the skirt of the cap are closed by a capping chuck under a ring on the bottle finish. This is suitable for bottled drinks to be sealed against internal pressure.

## Snap-on Cap

The rim of this cap, which can be metal or plastic, fits over a ring on the neck of the bottle. One metal type with a series of lugs on the circumference engages the undesirable of the ring on the glass finish by pressure around the edge, and is detached simply by pressure on the centre.

## Vacuum Seals

These closure are generally applied to wide mouthed jars where the quick filling of the semi-solid viscous products is involved. Several types are available, including a light gauge aluminium cap which is crimped under the neck ring and sealed by a flowed-in gasket and a more rigid tin plate course with a rubber rind side seal.

## Flexible Packaging Materials

As the name indicate these materials made containers flexible in nature. They are cheap and when empty easier to transport, handle and seal. After use these containers are simply discarded. The most important property of flexible packaging material is the degree to which they are able to resist the passage of gases and vapour. In the case of paper based materials e.g. kraft paper to glassine and pores. In the case of homogeneous plastic films e.g. cellulose, polythylene, and cellulose acetate etc. the gas or vapour very slowly flows by the activated diffusion process. In the case of aluminium foil, the transmission is entirely due to pinholes in the foil.

*Table following gives the permeability index of various plastic material used in packaging on next page.*

## Premeability of Various Plastics

All flexible packaging materials are creased to a greater or lesser extent during fabrication into packages. These creases reduce the barrier properties i.e. increase the gas and vapour diffusion.

The packaging material is selected to get the desired performance at the minimum cost. Importance of seal should also be kept in mind. Unless an efficient seal is made the protective value of the complete package may be considerably reduced. Plastic packages are usually heat-sealed, this gives a good efficient seal.

| *Film material* | ***Permeability*** (px $10^{10}$ cc/cm$^2$/mm/sec/cm/Hg) | | |
|---|---|---|---|
| | $N_2$ | $O_2$ | $H_2O$ at 25 °C 90% RH |
| Polyvinylidene chloride | 0.01 | 0.05 | 14 |
| PTFE | 0.03 | 0.10 | 3 |
| Polyester (Mylar A) | 0.05 | 0.22 | 1300 |
| Polyamide (Nylon 6) | 0.10 | 0.38 | 7000 |
| PVC, unplasticised | 0.40 | 1.20 | 1560 |
| Cellulose acetate | 2.80 | 7.80 | 75000 |
| Polyethene d=0.954 - 0.960 | 2.70 | 10.60 | 130 |
| Polystyrene | 2.9 | 11 | 12000 |
| Polypropylene (d=0910) | - | 23 | 680 |
| Ethyl cellulose (plasticised) | 84 | 265 | 130000 |

## PAPER BASED PACKAGING MATERIALS

Flat, gusseted, self opening satchel and rose-bottom bags, made of paper, are available. These bags are available in various size, weight and designs to be used according to the product while kraft paper bags are used where strength is important. Grease proof, vegetable parchment or glassine paper bags are used where resistance to grease or fatty foods is required. These materials give some resistance to vapour also. Waxed paper is also used, particularly where mild resistance to water vapours is required. For good moisture barrier due attention has to be paid to the closure and the seams of packing.

Glassine is the densest and most compact form of paper made and is extensively used for food packaging because of its outstanding protective properties. If during the formation of glassine paper super calendering is omitted grease proof paper is obtained. Both papers are highly resistant to the passage of oils, fats and grease. These wrappers maintain the inherent flavours and aromas of the contents, but being untreated they are not moisture-proof. The smooth, non-porous, non-absorbent surface of glassine is ideal for wax coating and laminating. Coating improves gas, odour, water vapour and water resistance and gives an ability to heat seal. Wet strength glassine is also available. This can also be coated suitably. These papers are suitable for packaging of meat, dairy and frozen foods.

Grease proof paper or imitation parchment is cheaper than vegetable parchment and is much inferior in whiteness, bulk strength and grease proof nature. Vegetable parchment paper is used in packaging of fatty biscuits and other baked goods, butter, margarine, cooking fats, dried milk, cheese, ice cream, fish products, poultry, meat products, cakes etc. Tea and coffee packs often contain parchment as the intermediate wrapper. It has wet strength also, i.e. it retains strength after soaking in water. Apart from its use as a wrapper it is made into bags, corrugated paper and board and is often printed.

## Multi-wall Paper Sacks

These sacks re made from 2 to 6 plies of paper depending on the material to be packed and degree of protection required. Plain crepe, extendible or waxed kraft, polyethylene coated paper and sometimes kraft union paper are used for food products. When the product is somewhat sensitive, high cost of requires long shelf life, then laminated plies including plastic film or foil are used. Most popular sacks are with open mouth and are usually stitched and sometimes pasted. The piles should be well ousted inside one another to distribute the total load over all the plies together during handling.

Wet waxed and dry waxed papers ar available. Wet waxed papers are made by passing the paper through the molten wax while the dry waxed paper is made by applying the molten wax on the paper. Thus the wet wax paper exhibits better barrier properties. Straight paraffin wax is brittle and the water vapour permeability increase sharply on creasing; incorporation of micro-crystalline wax, polyisobutylene, polyethylene (low M. Wt.) increases gloss, flexibility and heat sealability.

Now-a-days synthetic polymers are being extensively coated on paper to get the desired strength handling properties and barrier properties. These coatings may be applied to the paper by various methods, e.g. - (a) from aqueous solutions, (b) from solvent solutions or lacquers, (c) from aqueous dispersions, (d) as hot melts, and (e) as extrusion coatings.

Use of lacquer coating including resins and plasticizers is also quite popular.

**Properties of Common Flexible Packaging Materials**

| | Polythene | PVC | PVDC copolymer | Polyester (mylar) | PT Cellulose | Cellulose acetate | Kraft paper | Sulphite paper | Glassine paper | Wet waxed paper | Waxed glassine | Polythene coated paper | PVDC coated paper | 0.009 mm Al. foil |
|---|---|---|---|---|---|---|---|---|---|---|---|---|---|---|
| Durability, toughness | 6 | 8 | 9 | 10 | 2 | 4 | 4 | 3 | 2 | 3 | 2 | 6 | 4 | 1 |
| Convertibility | 6 | 6 | 4 | 4 | 10 | 10 | 10 | 10 | 8 | 6 | 6 | 8 | 8 | 4 |
| Printability | 6 | 5 | 5 | 6 | 10 | 8 | 10 | 10 | 10 | 10 | 10 | 8 | 8 | 6 |
| Heatsealability | 6 | 4 | 4 | 2 | 0 | 0 | 0 | 0 | 0 | 5 | 4 | 7 | 8 | 6 |
| Water vapour resistance | 7 | 2 | 10 | 4 | 0 | 0 | 0 | 0 | 0 | 5 | 4 | 7 | 8 | 6 |
| Gas transmission resistance | 3 | 5 | 8 | 6 | 6 | 0 | 0 | 0 | 3 | 2 | 5 | 3 | 8 | 7 |
| Odour resistance | 3 | 5 | 8 | 8 | 6 | 2 | 0 | 0 | 3 | 2 | 4 | 3 | 8 | 7 |
| Water resistance | 10 | 9 | 10 | 10 | 0 | 6 | 4 | 4 | 2 | 8 | 5 | 6 | 6 | 10 |
| Oil and grease resistance | 5 | 8 | 8 | 8 | 10 | 6 | 0 | 0 | 4 | 5 | 6 | 5 | 8 | 10 |
| Chemical resistance | 10 | 6 | 8 | 10 | 3 | 3 | 0 | 0 | 2 | 5 | 4 | 7 | 7 | 5 |

**Grading from 0 -10 while 10 is the highest grading and 0 signifies the quality is non-existing**

## Plastic-based Food Packaging

There have been some significant development in the field of food packaging throughout the world. In the field of food packaging, plastic have been a relatively recent entry compared to traditional materials like glass and metals. However, during the last two decades, with the increasing availability of variety of plastic raw materials coupled with change in the concept of packaging, plastics are increasingly being used in various forms for packing foods and allied products. Because of economy, they are progressively replacing conventional materials like paper, metal and glass. Besides, many plastic based coatings are also used on glass and metal containers. In India many of these developments are being introduced and some research organisations are engaged in R & D efforts to improve the packaging of food products for more attractiveness and improved shelf life for the internal and export market. In the direction, plastic packaging is becoming are popular in recent years due to logistic advantages like low cost, functionality, light weight and saving in freight charges, strength, chemical resistance, flexibility, excellent barrier properties and aesthetic appeal.

The impact of plastic has been so significant particularly in food packaging that they have revolutionized the art of packaging. Such as unparallel versatility of plastics is due to a host of important characteristics of which most important is their capability to provide a host of combinations and provide end use properties which is not possible with other materials. After declaring the food products as a thrust area activity this trend of plastic packaging is increasing in our country in quantitative and qualitative terms. A large number of plastic packaging materials are consequently available is various forms like sheets, bottle, jar, jetty cans, sachet and containers of all shapes and sizes for good packaging. Common plastic raw material generally used for food packaging are :

1. Polyethylene
   a) Low Density Polyethylene (LDPE)
   b) High Density Polyethylene (HDPE)
   c) Linear Low Density Polyethylene (LLDPE)
2. Polyvinyl Chloride (PVC)
3. Polystyrene (PS)
4. Polypropylene (PP)
5. Thermoplastic Polyester (PET)
6. Polyvinyldene Chloride (PVDC)
7. Nylon 6
8. Polytetrafluroethylene (PTFE)
9. Ethylene Vinylacetate (EVA)
10. Nitrocellulose (NC)
11. Biaxially Oriented Polypropylene (BOPP)
12. Acrylonitrile Butadiene Styrene (ABS)
13. High Impact Polystyrene (HIPS)
14. Ionomer resins
15. Ethylene Acrylic Acid copolymers (EAA)

The use of polymeric resins have certain special advantages besides the traditional requirements of food packaging industry as given below.

1. Maintenance of aseptic conditions
2. Barrier properties as per product requirement
3. Flexibility of rigidity could be introduced as per produce requirement
4. Possibility of transparency for customer appeal
5. Package is sterilizable according to requirements
6. Attractive printing
7. High strength to weight ratio
8. Substantial weight saving compared to other forms of packaging
9. Size and shape can be made according to variable requirements
10. Unique forms and shape possible for packaging of different food products and convenience of display
11. All forms of packaging are amendable to automated production techniques
12. Problems of corrosion and metal reactions are eliminated

The polymeric resins tested above distinguished themselves by their ability to protect and isolate the raw and processed food products from a hostile environment.

## Other Requirements of Food Packaging Materials

In addition to usual requirements because of perishable nature, the materials used for packing food stuffs, have to fulfil other requirements, viz:

1. Protection during handling, transport and storage
2. Protection against water, moisture air, heat, cold etc.
3. Protection against attack from insects, mold, bacteria termites etc.
4. Protection against pilferage, adulteration etc.
5. Should be non-toxic and should conform to statutory regulations.
6. Should have good printability, good customer appeal, ease in packaging and package forming etc.

A number of plastics meet most of these requirements and so ar being widely used either separately or in combination with other materials.

## NEW TRENDS OF PACKAGING

Some of the raw trends in packaging of food products are based on plastics. A few of them are the following.

### Co-extruded Flexible Packs

These may be obtained by either blown film process or by flat die technique. In these processes two or more polymeric materials from different extruders are fed to the common die and the films of different materials emerge as single flexible composite layer by being united in the die head.

With an extruder system it is possible today to produce a five layer composite structure, wherein the merit of individual materials can be united to form a composite in a single operation thereby eliminating secondary processes. The structural layers are normally based on LDPE, LLDPE, HDPE and the barrier layer is usually PVDC, EVOH and Polyamides. The bonding/tie layer is usually a copolymer based on polyolefins or ionomer.

The use of five layer co-extruded structure in flexible packaging of food enables the thickness of the barrier layer to be reduced by 30-40%. In addition the curling of the composite structure is considerably reduced due to the symmetrical structure with improved barrier properties. These films are mainly used for snack food, cheese, sausage, cold cuts, fish, meat, pre-cooked meals etc.

Co-extruded BOPP with a sealing layer based on terpolymer of PP has resulted in increasing the sealing range and reduction in head initiation temperature thus giving a versatile film for using in different types of form filling machines for packing snacks foods, tobacco etc.

Biaxially oriented nylon co-extruded with LLDPE seal and layer offers extended shelf life, flexicrak and abrasion resistance, high level of seal integrity, consistency and puncture resistance for food products to be distributed over long distance.

Improved matellizing techniques have enabled development of metallized OPP and very low light transmission. Shelf life of potato chips packed in this type of metallized OPP has been improved from 6 months to 9 months. Established applications of metallized film include packaging of coffee, tobacco, snack foods, ice cream, yoghurt, biscuits, cakes, deep frozen foods, milk powder, cheese, ketchup etc.

## Co-extrusion Coatings

Like co-extruded films, multilayer coatings consisting of 4-5 layers is increasingly becoming popular. The advantages of such systems are :

1. Selection of wide range of base material including paper, foil and cello phane
2. Possibility of reverse printing for better seals appeal
3. For the same conventional requirements co-extrusion coating are more cost effective
4. With the development of coating technology, it will be possible to replace foil, glassine paper and cellophane with other plastic films in the laminate structure.

## Semi-Rigid Containers

Multilayer sheets are normally used for manufacturing semi-rigid containers by thermoforming. The structural layer used for these sheets are PP, HDPE, HIPS, while the barrier layer is either PVDC or EVOH.

Controlled Atmosphere Packaging (CAP) can be done in co-extruded sheets based on PS/EVOH/PE of 0.6 mm thickness used for thermoforming trays while the top lid/film may be of Aluminium Foil/PE, PE/PVDC, PE/EVOH/ Metallised PET. Meat, Poultry, Vegetables, Salad, Pastry etc. are packed under specified gaseous atmosphere for maintaining their freshness and having a prolonged shelf life. Such containers are also replacing metal cans.

In case of aseptic packaging containers from co-extruded sheets of PS/ TIE/EOH/TIE/PE are used for thermoforming trays while a lid of lacquered foil is used for packing products like fresh food, cream, processed cheese etc. for shelf life up to one year. Aluminium foil, PP and paper board combinations are also used for aseptic filling of fresh juices, milk and other non-carbonated beverages. PP/EVA/PP structures are also used for hot fill aseptic barrier applications.

Pasteurization and retort sterilization applications are finding use of PVDC barrier containers in form of PP/PVDC/PP as synermetrical co-extruded structure.

In case of retortable packing, thermoformed containers are manufactured using co-extruded structure of PP and PVDC with a seamed easy opening aluminium top for packing delecatessan meat and fish gas, water and odour of the product. Combinations of their materials are also used along with PET, EVOH etc. to give specific properties to retortable pouch. Some of the suggested specific applications are :

| | | |
|---|---|---|
| OPP/ EVOH/PE | - | Dehydrated fish |
| LDPE/EVOH/LDPR | - | Mayonnaise |
| HDPE/EVOH/HDPE | - | Salad Oil |
| LDPE/PVDC/PS | - | Butter |
| PS/PVDC/PS | - | Fruit Juices |
| PET/PVDC/PE | - | Snacks |
| PP/EVOH/PP | - | Hot filled liquids |

## Rigid Containers

Stretch blow moulding technique has been developed in the recent past to biaxially stretch containers made from PVC, PET and PP which increases their strength and improves their properties such as stiffness, tensile, impact resistance, gas and vapour resistance, burst strength and transparency etc. This technology leads to reduction in weight and wall thickness. Such containers are very useful for carbonated drinks, beverages, wines, edible oil, etc., where oxidation of the product has to be prevented and flavour of the products has to be retained. Hot fillable PET containers are also being developed, which can stand up to 195°C.

Use of multilayer blow containers for packing of foods and beverages is now becoming quite popular in developed countries. The structure layer is mainly of Hdpe, LDPE, PP, PVC, and PET and the co-extrudable barrier layer is based on Nylons, EVOH, PVDC etc. Such multilayer composite materials have a large number of applications for packing of processed foods.

A new area of applications is the packed food which could be heated in the packaged form in a microwave or in ordinary oven. For such applications thermoformed trays made from sheets of crystalline PET, polymide and polycarbonate structure are normally used.

The increasing awareness amongst the consumer on the need for assurance on quality, standard weight changing lifestyle has accelerated the process of giving packaging modes to a large number of food products. The advanced composite structure and packaging technology for packaging of different raw and processed food products is poised for high growth rate during the ensuring years and polymeric products would play a vital role in giving a new thrust to the food processing industry in our country.

## CLASSIFICATION OF PACKAGING MACHINERY

Considering the point of convenience, the packaging machinery can be classified in the following ways :

### 1. Primary Packaging Machinery

These are packing machinery which are used for manufacturing container/packages/caps, closures, tageers, foil etc. Here, the basic materials are choosen and run on the packaging machinery so as to convert them into some shapes, forms and thus make them purposeful for packaging functions.

### 2. Secondary Packaging Machinery

These are machines which help in handling the packages before and till filling and sealing/closing. Such machines are normally erecting, folding, filling, closing, sealing, sterilizing, capping, form, fill and sealing systems/aseptic packaging etc.

### 3. Tertiary Packaging Machinery

These are machines which are required to scan packages, cleaning, sterilizing, stacking, unstacking, cartoning, handling etc.

Besides, these also include those machines which are required to maintain and test the quality of the packages.

## Types of Processed Food Industries and Their Products

*The processed food industries which turns out a wide variety of products, such as :*

1. **Bakery**
   Bread, Biscuits, Cake, Pastry, Bun etc.

2. **Beverages**
   Ready to serve beverages (mango, guava, orange, grape, apple,)

3. **Breakfast Cereals**
   Corn flakes

4. **Concentrates**
   Concentrate from Pineapple, Orange etc.

5. **Confectioneries**
   Hard boiled Sweets, Sugar Coated Sweets, Centre Filled, Traditional Sweets (Sandesh, Burfi)

6. **Canning Plant**
   For fruits (Pulp, Juice, Marmalade, Puree etc.), For vegetables (whole, chunks etc.), Meat & meat products (chunks, minced meat, Ham, etc.), Fish & fish products (whole, with gravy, chunks etc.)

7. **Coffee making Unit**

8. **Dairy**
   Fresh milk

9. **Extruder Plants**
   Ready to eat snacks, noodles, macaroni & spaghetti etc.

10. **Fruits Processing Plants**
    Jam, Jelly, Juice, Squash and Ketchup, Pickles etc.

11. **Fast Foods**
    Idly, Dosa, Samosa, Bhelpuri, Paubhaji etc.

12. **Ice-cream making unit**
    Ordinary, noble etc.

13. **Milk Based products Unit**
    Baby foods, Curd, Shrikhand, Butter, Ghee

14. **Malt Based products Unit**
    Infant foods (cerelac), Beer

15. **Papad Making Unit**
    Cereal based

16. **Spices Unit**
    Whole, Powder, Mixed, Powder form

17. **Snack Foods**
    Potato chips, Banana Chips

18. **Tea**

19. **Vegetable Oil Extrusion**
    Oil, Hydrogenated oil (Vanaspati)

## STATUS OF PACKAGING MACHINERY INDUSTRY IN INDIA

Fortunately, India has a number of packaging industries and several kinds of packaging machinery, technologies and other auxiliary systems have already been established in the country. There are more than 3000 packaging machinery manufacturers in India. One finds packaging machines which are manually operated, semi-automatic or fully automatic. These machines are versatile in speed, application and can handle a variety of products be they granular, pasty, liquid, solids, chemicals, pharmaceuticals etc.

Though, there is a wide gap between the Indian Packaging machinery systems vis-a-vis those developed in overseas countries, the country has developed a remarkable packaging technology infrastructure. The following systems are available in our country.

a) Filling Machinery
b) Blister Packaging Machinery
c) Wrapping
d) Canning
e) Cartoning
f) Shrink Wrapping
g) Thermoform Container Making Machinery

There are a few hundred large enterprises also which are involved in similar products or slightly improved version which are governed under the industrial development and regulations act of the Government. Some of them have links with international giants like Continental Can, American Can etc. The composition of the India Packaging Industry appears in the table on next page.

## Composition of India Packaging Industry

| | Item | Estimated No. of Units |
|---|---|---|
| 1. | Metal Containers | 4,000 (130) |
| 2. | Plastic Packaging | 2,400 ( 17) |
| 3. | Paper & Board Packaging | 2,000 (121) |
| 4. | Wooden Containers | 1,500 ( 44) |
| 5. | Jute Packaging | 100 ( 86) |
| 6. | Glass Containers | 200 ( 33) |
| 7. | Packaging Machinery | 450 ( 20) |
| 8. | Miscellaneous Items | 400 ( 30) |
| | **Total** | **11,500 (481)** |

* Figures in brackets show the number of units in the organised sector.

The development of packaging machinery industry can be termed to be a development of the 70s. Here, again the number of large producers are few but the small ones are many. The total number units exceeds 450.

## The structure of the Indian Packaging Machinery Industry

| | Machinery | No. of Manufacturing Units |
|---|---|---|
| A. | **Packaging** | |
| 1. | Filling and Closing - all types | 60 |
| 2. | Complete packaging lines of ampoules, vials, tubes and bottling | 15 |
| 3. | Form-fill & seal | 15 |
| 4. | Labelling | 30 |
| 5. | Strip Packaging | 15 |
| 6. | Shrink Packaging | 6 |
| 7. | Vacuum Thermoforming | 10 |
| 8. | Bagging | 10 |
| 9. | Wrapping | 15 |
| 10. | Capping | 20 |
| 11. | Canning | 15 |
| 12. | Carton Forming & Cartoning | 3 |
| 13. | Capsule Filling and Sealing | 4 |
| 14. | Systems Packaging | 4 |
| 15. | Tying and Strapping | 15 |
| 16. | Others | 63 |
| | **Total** | ***300** |
| B. | Package Manufacturing | *180 |
| C. | Package Testing | 20 |
| D. | Package Handling | 50 |
| | **Total Number** | **450** |

* About 100 units are common

## PACKAGING MATERIAL AND PACKAGING MACHINERY FOR MAJOR PROCESSED FOOD PRODUCTS

The processed foods are categorised under some convenient heads in the following table. Packaging materials and relevant packaging machinery are shown against each item.

| | Food Products | Packaging Materials | Packaging Machinery |
|---|---|---|---|
| 1. | Bakery Products | Waxed Papers<br>Polyethylene bags<br>Cellophane Pouches<br>Aluminium Laminate | Wrapping machine<br>Bagging machine<br>Cartoning machine<br>Waxing machine |
| 2. | Beverages | Glass Bottle<br>Paperboard/polyethylene Laminated Carton | Bottling Plant<br>Aseptic Filling machine |
| 3. | Fish Products | Tinplate Container<br>Vacuum Plastic Pouch | Canning Unit<br>Labelling machine<br>Cartoning machine<br>Palletising machine<br>Vacuum Packing<br>MAP |
| 4. | Processed Fruits & Vegetables | Tinplate container<br>Paper based carton<br>Plastic Pouch<br>Blister Pack | Canning Plant<br>Aseptic<br>Form-fill-seal machine<br>FFS machine<br>Blister packaging machine |
| 5. | Tea | Lined carton<br>Plastic pouch<br>Carton | System Packaging<br>Pouch making m/c<br>Cartoning machine |
| 6. | Coffee | Glass Bottle<br>Lined carton | Automatic filling m/c.<br>System packaging |
| 7. | Milk based products | Cartons<br>Thermoform container<br>Paper cups | Cartoning machine<br>Thermoforming m/c<br>Cup making unit |
| 8. | Ice-cream | Waxed board cartons & cups | Cartoning machine |
| 9. | Vegetable oil/ vanaspati | Tin container<br>Plastic pouch<br>Plastic container<br>Plastic bottle | Automatic filling m/c<br><br>FFS machine |
| 10. | Edible Ghee | Tin container/<br>Plastic pouch | Filling machine<br>FFS machine |

## Important Indian Manufacturers of Packaging Machines

| | Name of the Company | Item of Manufacture |
|---|---|---|
| 1. | Vulcan Laval Ltd.<br>Mumbai | Automatic carton filling machines<br>Tube filling machines |
| 2. | Larsen & Turbo Ltd.,<br>Mumbai | Automatic packaging machines<br>for foodstuff cans |
| 3. | Metal Box Company of India<br>Ltd. Calcutta | Automatic packing machinery<br>for foodstuff cans |
| 4. | Hindustan Lever Ltd.,<br>Mumbai | Packaging machinery<br>(mainly for captive use) |
| | Hindustan Level Ltd.,<br>Calcutta | " |
| | Hindustan Lever Ltd.,<br>Ghaziabad | " |
| 5. | Rollatainers Ltd.,<br>Faridabad | Carton filling and<br>packaging machinery |
| 6. | Brook Bond India Ltd.,<br>Calcutta | Tea packaging machinery<br>(for captive use mainly) |
| 7. | Reed Medway Co. of India<br>Pvt. Ltd. New Delhi | Automatic bag sealing & filling<br>machine, bag closing m/c., sprouts etc. |
| 8. | Lipton India Ltd.,<br>Calcutta | Packing machinery<br>(mainly for captive use) |
| 9. | Molins of India Ltd., | Razor blade packing & strip packing m/c |
| 10. | Wimco Ltd.,<br>Mumbai | Packing machinery |
| 11. | Engineering systems (P) Ltd.<br>Bangalore | Bag filling, weighing machinery |
| 12. | Ravalgon Sugar Farms Ltd.,<br>Mumbai | Packing machinery<br>(Biscuit wrapping machinery) |
| 13. | Enexco Engineering Pvt. Ltd.<br>New Delhi. | Bag Packaging machinery,<br>screens, spares |
| 14. | Lohic Starligner P. Ltd.,<br>Kanpur | Circular Weaving machines<br>(circular looms) |

## MECHANISMS OF CERTAIN PACKAGING MACHINERY

### Filling Machinery

#### Pouch/Carton System

These machines can be used for filling milk, soyamilk, juices and beverages. The packaging film in roll form is mounted, the roll is progressively unwound under constant tension control. On entering the aseptic cabinet, the film passes through a sterilizing batch of hydrogen peroxide. Under aseptic conditions, the pouch is formed, filled and sealed. Pouches can be filled from 250 cc to the 3 litre pouch.

#### Semi-automatic and automatic filling machines

These are for vanaspati, oils, juices, etc. Sealing is possible either with impulse sealer or hot bar sealer.

#### Volumetric powder filling machinery

This can take up antibiotics, instant coffee, dyes, caustic detergents, cocoa, spices, insecticides, food powder (egg powder) milk powder, chemical powder etc. Table gives an idea about the production of selected liquids and powders

#### Form-fill-seal machine

This is a king of systems packaging. There can be horizontal or vertical form fill and seal machines. Pouches made of multi-layer laminated films, from 10 ml to 75 ml. or higher sizes are formed, filled and sealed as continuous process. Pouches depending upon sizes and product, can be filled from 20 to 60 numbers. Up to 1,200 pouches per hour are possible with indigenous machinery.

#### AR-Espresso Systems

These are used for food and non food powders are granules, tea, coffee, milk and milk food derivatives, frozen foods, ice-cream. Espresso machines are capable of packing volume ranging from 150 cc to 3000 cc. In this system, cartons are automatically formed and bottom flaps are folded out. After the bottom membrane is heat sealed to the bottom flaps are tucked in after filling the product, the top membrane heat sealed to the top flaps which are tucked in. These are more or less small sizes bag-in-box systems.

### Tube Filling

Tube filling machines are available for ointments, pastes, creams and liquids of far ranging viscosities for the cosmetics, pharmaceuticals and food industries. These machines can handle tube diameters from 10 mm to 40 mm and Length from 40 mm to 200 mm. These can tighten cap automatically, attached with tube cleaning device, tube infeeding is automatic; filling pumps are adjustable with various volumes. Machines are made in such a manner that contact parts are corrosion resistant. Tube registration is done photo-electrically which facilitates automatic positioning of tube decor orientation; 80 to 120 tubes per minute can be filled. Tube filling machines can also have optional attachments like cream stirring device, heating device, jar filling attachments, tube transfer devices, counting devices, flange connection in place of hopper etc.

## Blister Packaging Machines

This technology has proved of immense use to mankind. This machine is normally used for packing of pharmaceuticals products. But now-a-days, this machine is extensively used for the packing of processed food products like jam, jelly, pickles, butter etc.

Normally, PVC with PE or PVDC films are used in blister packaging. These films are opaque or transparent, thermoformable and non-toxic. In operation, PVC base film web is drawn off from a reel and fed into the blister forming assembly where blisters are formed on continuous basis. The web is then led into the sealing area over guide track. The product is filled into the blisters by filling machines or unit before the web enters the sealing assembly. Aluminium foil or other film combination is drawn off from a separate reel and is fed to the sealing unit where it is sealed with the base web, thus enclosing the product hermetically. The web trim is sheared off to allow collections. Machines may have speed output from 150 packs to 240 packs and so on.

## Shrink Packaging Machinery

The process is to envelop the product or group of products into a specially manufactured film, which has undergone a stretching and cooling process during its manufacture. This causes an orientation in the film and introduces built in shrinkage which can be released by hot air so that the film shrinks in area and increases slightly in thickness. After shrinkage the film is cooled. The shrinkage force reached its maximum during this cooling stage and is maintained for a long period thereafter. These applications are specially suitable for final packaging of processed food products where in India packing is presently done in jars (pickles and jams), bottles (ketchup or squashes), cans (vegetables or fruits), tins (milk powder baby food ghee edible oil), bottles and cans (beer or liquor, p n masala, cartons of frozen foods such as meat, fish, poultry), tetra packs ( ilk, fruit juices), etc.

# Chapter - 3

## *Milk*

Milk is the normal secretion of the mammary glands for the feeding of young mammals and it is the fundamental requirement of body to survive.

An infant needs mother's milk to fulfil the quench of the body-thrist to extract the basic nutrients of its body. This is the food, which is required since birth till the survival.

The composition of milk is rather complex and of Moisture, Fat, Minerals, Carbohydrates, Energy/Calories, Calcium, Phosphorus and Iron. Though the percentage of these constituents vary in different types of milk. The figures mentioned below would highlight the percentage of these constituents in different kinds of milk derived from different cattles:

| Sl. No. | Constituents | Milk derived from | | | |
|---|---|---|---|---|---|
| | | Buffalo | Cow | Goat | Liquid Skimmed Milk |
| 1. | Moisture (gm) | 8.100 | 87.50 | 86.80 | 92.10 |
| 2. | Protein (gm) | 4.30 | 3.20 | 3.30 | 2.50 |
| 3. | Fat (gm) | 6.50 | 4.10 | 4.50 | 0.10 |
| 4. | Minerals (gm) | 0.80 | 0.80 | 0.80 | 0.70 |
| 5. | Carbohydrates (gm) | 5.00 | 4.40 | 4.60 | 4.60 |
| 6. | Energy/Calories (Kcal) | 117.00 | 67.00 | 72.00 | 29.00 |
| 7. | Calcium (mg) | 210.00 | 120.00 | 170.00 | 120.00 |
| 8. | Phosphorous (mg) | 130.00 | 90.00 | 120.00 | 90.00 |
| 9. | Iron (mg) | 0.20 | 0.20 | 0.30 | 0.20 |

All these constituents of milk are responsible our bodily needs, at different stages of life. As per Recommended Daily Allowance (RDA), one year old child needs around 1000 Kealories per day, a 3 year child needs around 3000 to 5000 Kealories a day. A normal child needs at least 3 servings of milk or milk poducts per day. The amount of milk/milk product consumed, yields the norishment to our body through milk exchange and Fat Exchange processes. These are nutritional needs of the body to keep the person healthy and fit.

Milk Exchange is the substitution of alternatives in the form of other items, besides milk products, to fulfil the nutritional needs of the body. In other words, the milk exchange is a serving of food equivalent to I cup milk, retaining its energy and nutritional contents. One milk exchange contains the substantial amounts of Carbohydrates and Proteins and about 80 Kealories of energy. Here the milk exchange programme and fat exchange programme shall be highlighted, enabling the reader to procure the awareness pertaining to Nutritional needs of the body. Since the milk exchange has already been defined, let us take fat exchange into consideration. Although it is most prevalent idea that the fat contents of any product are responsible for the formation of Cholesterol in the body. So it is utmost to take this aspect into consideration. Although the regular exercise and by burning fat, one can prevent the formation of Cholesterol in our body.

A whole milk adds 2 fat exchange, whereas I cup of fortified milk with 1% fat, adds 1/2 fat exchange. One cup of the fat fortified plain/unflavoured Yogurt made from 2% of fortified milk adds 1 fat exchange. A cup of milk contains 12 gm of carbohydrates and 1 gm of carbohydrates is worth 4 Kealories. 48 Kealories are derived from carbohydates and 32 Kealories are derived from protein. Cream and butter are not milk exchange because they contain little or no carbohydrates and insignificant amounts of other nutrients, important in milk. They simply contain fat and are responsible fot the fat exchange process.

This is the significance of milk pertaining to the human body, but the other living creatures other than human beings, who need the body nutrients for the infants' body, need no education in regard to this. It is the nature and the bodily needs which teach them every thing, as per the demand of the time. A human body has a brain which understands the logic and reacts accordingly, but an animal is almost brainless and is governed and nurtured by the nature as per the timely needs of the body. But above all, the milk is the basic and utmost need of any living creature, besides human beings. No matter the creatur is on the earth, under earth or in the sea.

The Breast milk of human or the human milk, which is sufficient enough to keep the infant healthy and fit to generate the body resistance to fight the diseases and illness, throughout the life, is no less than the nature's miracle. The human milk/breast milk of the human being is consisted of the following ingredients and the percentage:-

The human milk is consisted of 88.0 gm of moisture, 1.1 gm of Protein, 3.4 gm of Fat, 0.1 gm of Minerals, 7.4 gm of carbohydrates, 65 Kealories of energy, 28 mg of calcium, 11 mg of Phosphorus and insignificant amount of Iron. This is the drink which is responsible to form a dirm base of an infant till its death. The fundamental nutrients are extracted by an infant in the womb and after taking birth, the human milk is responsible to create the body resistance to curb and fight the different kind of diseases and sickness. Besides human beings, even the animals also need the mothers milk in any form or the other to form a solid base to erect the building of a strong and healthy survival. The food habits in India are confined to a little limited sphere of milk consumption, in the form of milk or its derivatives, but in the other parts of world also, it is the milk or the milk products which are consumed as a culture in their lives. Keeping in view the comparison, it is apparent, that India needs a lot of modification and the development in the field of Dairy. It may be in regard to the Cattled Breeding or the maintenance of the cattle providing us the milk. We must overcome the discrepancies pertaining to the quality and standards of the milk procured from the cattle. These setbacks are well apparent, although, not admitted. The present conditions of the milk yielding cattle are pathetic despite the Government trying to complement many a regulations.

Precisely, the cow is considered to be a holy creature among the animals, mythologically. But the present scenario is well descriptive to reveal the truth, in practical manner. The stray cattle, abandomed by the owners, are responsible for many a road hazards and accidents in the metro cities like Delhi. The eating habits of milk yielding animals, especially cow, are really pathetic and unhygienic.

The presently prevailing conditions reveal the poor quality of milk derived from such animals,, precisely cow, a holy6 creature, mythologically. It means that to procure the best quantity and quality of milk, fundamentally, the milk yielding animal has to be maintained well. Its food habits, the sheds etc., must be kept clean and hygienically intact to procure the best quantity and quality of the milk to keep the whole generation of the national to fight the odd future despite the age of advancement. Entering in the 21st century would require a lot of enlightenment and awareness with regard to present scenario, to cope up with the developing or developed countries. In this era of globalisation and liberalisation, we Indians have to mould ourselves to sustain in the International market, to fight the stage of competition inthe International market. It may concern the field of Exporters to abide by the buyers' specifications as per the International norms. If we do not improve the quality of our products, we may fail and left behind in the International market. To ascertain the quantity and the quality, we have to learn a lot, to cope up with the International market, to sustain ourselves. Not only this, if we do not improve, the Foreign Investors may conquer us and our freedom may be in danger. Besides this, as already highlighted, we may earn a lot of foreign exchange to nourish our country, otherwise for a better placement in the International Survival.

To fight the present scene of inflation, due to which, even the biggest capitalist like United States of States of America, is longing to have the Japanese collaboration to sustain in the International market. Why can't we become like Japanese, who sacrificed every thing in the Second World War, but still have a name in the International market to keep their survival safe.

# Chapter - 4

## *Indian Buffaloes*

**Buffaloes** have been classified into two main categories namely riverine and swamp depending upon variation in their habitat and genome. The swamp buffaloes are stocky animals with marshy land habitats and have 48 chromosomes. They are found primarily in south east Asian countries but few animals are also available in north-eastern states of India. These animals are used for draught power in paddy fields and haulage and are also used for meat production. River buffaloes are massive in size mostly with curled horns and prefer to enter clear water and have 50 chromosomes. Though these two distinct breeds have been successfully interbred, yet they maintain a separate genetic identity.

**World's** buffalo population has undergone demographic change over a long period of time in different countries. Out of the total buffalo population of 147 millions about 142 millions are predominantly found in Asia and the pacific. The trend of global population change indicates almost 3 times faster rate of increase per annum (2.04) during 1950 to 1970 (0.64 per cent). The average rate of change from 1950 to 1992 being 1.47 per cent per annum.

**India** continues to be the leading most buffalo populated country having 78 million heads, most of which are riverine. Buffaloes in India are primarily maintained by farmers in more than 570 thousand villages in the herd size of 2 to 3 animals. Large herds are also available in milk shed areas of metropolitan and big cities where dairying is considerd as an industry and intensive system of management is followed. Besides, there are approximately 60-70 Govt. institutional farms for research and developmental activities in the country.

The picture with regard to buffalo **milk production** is very encouraging as is evident from the fact that about 95% of world buffalo milk (45.3 million tons) is produced in Asia and the Pacific, while 64.4 per cent is produced in

India (FAO, 1992). From the data for trend in milk production from 1950 to 1992 it appears that milk production in the world increased by 4.26%. Except for Italy, all other buffalo owning countries in Europe have shown downfall milk production mainly due to the larger emphasis on buffaloes for meat production. However, significant improvement in lactation milk production have been reported for riverine buffaloes (mainly imported from India) in Bulgaria, Italy and Egypt. The all round increase in buffalo milk production is an indication of increasing importance and preference of Indian buffaloes over cattle in India as well as in other countries.

**The percent of total bovines slaughtered** in the world during the last decade has remained almost constant i.e. 17.1 to 17.4 per cent. However, in India the number of animals going to abattoir has doubled during the last 10 days whereas the overall increase in the world is just 0.22 per cent. Similarly, the total quantity of meat produced has increased at the rate of almost 15 per cent per annum in India which is much higher than the percent increase in Asia (6.6%) and the world (1.6%) per annum over the last 10 years.

**The increasing trend of buffalo population** is most of the Asian countries and in Brazil and Italy is indicative of the fact that buffalo will continue to play a vital role in the economy of the developing countries for the supply of milk, meat and draught power for lung time to come.

## BREEDS

**India posseses** some of the best milch breeds of the world e.g. Murrah, Nili-RAVI and Surti. Some other breeds of this type found in India e.g. Meshing, Jaffarabadi and Bhadawari also have high potential for milk and fat production besides being used for work.

**Buffaoles of different breeds** have been classified into various group types depending upon their phenotypes and geographic locations. It classified all buffaloes of river type into following two sub-groups.

1. The sub-group in which the *horns are curled* and set close to the head and are down swept e.g. Murrah Ravi, Mehsana, Jaffarabadi and Sambalpur.

2. The sub-group in which the **horns are sickle shaped and un-swept** e.g. Bhadawari, Kalahandi, Kanara, Manda, Nagpuri, Pandharpuri, Surti, Tarai and Toda.

Indian buffaloes have also been classified on the basis of their well defined characters into five major groups. Indian buffaloes and classified below on the basis of their group type and breeding tract of each of the breed is also indicated.

**Breeds buffaloes of Indian origin and their breeding tracts.**

| *Group* | *Breed* | *Breeding Tract* |
|---|---|---|
| **Murrah type** | Murrah | Rohtak, Jind, Hissar, Bhiwani, Sonepat District in Haryana. |
| | Nili Ravi | Ferozepur District in Punjab. |
| **Gujarat** | Surti | Kaira and Baroda districts. |
| | Jaffarabadi | Kutch, Junagarh and Jamnagar districts. |
| | Mehsana | Mehsana, Sabarkantha & Banaskantha distt. |
| **Uttar Pradesh** | Bhadawari | Bhadawari estate and Bah tehsil in Agra, Gwalior and Etawah district. |
| | Tarai | Tarai region of Uttar Pradesh. |
| **Central India** | Nagpuri | Nagpur, Akola and Amraoti districts. |
| | Pandharpuri | South Maharashtra, West Andhra Pradesh and North Karnataka. |
| | Paralakhemundi | Ganjam, Koraput and Plateau region of Orissa. |
| | Kalahandi | Hilly region of Andhra Pradesh & Orissa. |
| | Sambalpur | Bilaspur district |
| **South India** | Toda | Nilgiri hills |
| | South Kanara | West Coast in Kerala |

All riverine breeds are primarily good milk producers though majority of them are dual purpose animals exhibiting good meat and draught characteristics, however, their potentiality for meat remains unexplored and unexploited. Of the breeds listed above only Murrah, Nili-Ravi Surti have been studied extensively for production and reproduction characteristics in India. However, most of the buffaloes of the Indian sub-continent fall into the non-descript group which are designated as desi (undefined buffaloes) and cannot be categorised in any of well defined above breeds. The large population of desi buffalos in India is primarily because of the lack of organised breeding activities. In the farmers buffaloes such as breed improvement societies. As process of development programmes, migration of stock from within and between breeding improvement societies. As process of development programmes, migration of stock from within and between breeding tracts and grading up of non-descript population in various states, large distinct breeds are available even in their respective breeding tracts.

Buffaloes found in the north-eastern states and in the eastern coastal region of India and in China and South-east Asian countries e.g. Philiippines, Thailand, Malaysia, Vietnam, Sri Lanka, Burma, Laos, Kampuchea,

Bangladesh etc. have been classified as swamp buffaloes on the basis of their genetic constitution (2n=48) and natural habitat. The breeds included in this group in India and Manda and Parlakhemundi.

## PRODUCTION PERFORMANCE

## GROWTH :

**The average birth weight** in Indian buffaloes have been reported to be as low as 21 kg in Surti reported from Sri Lanka as high as 41 kg in Indian Murrah and higher in male calves than in female calves born. Significant effect of season, year sex, sire and sequence of calving have also been reported. Information on body weight at birth, 6 months, 12 months, 24 months and at maturity in various breeds is presented in table 1.

**Growth curve from birth to 36 months** of age in Indian buffaloes follows a linear trend with average daily gain of 548 g between 3-6 months and 404 g between birth to 36 months of age. Body weight as first calving in different breeds (Table 1) range from 367 kg in Dharwari to 531 kg in Nili-Ravi buffaloes. Buffalo calves at Central Institute for Research on Buffaloes, Hisar has shown growth rate of more than 500 g per day from birth to one year of age. Some calves have body weight as high as 290 kg at one year of age/ Under free choice feeding system calves weaned at birth showed higher body weights than unweaned calves.

**The comparative growth rate** in riverine and swamp breeds of different origin reported by Moran (1986) indicate higher growth rate in riverine breeds than in swamp buffaloes. Buffaloes of the European and Australian origin had higher growth rate than buffaloes of Asian origin primarily due to the fact that buffaloes in Australia and Europe have been reared for meat while in India they have primarily been reared for milk production. For milch type of animals growth rate ranging from 400 to 500 g per day upto the age of 18 months and 300 to 400 g per day from 18 months to first calving is highly remunerative.

## MILK PRODUCTION :

Average lactation milk production and range of lactation milk yield reported in different breeds is presented in Table 2. Milk production as reported from different sources indicate averge lactation milk production in Murrah (1850 kg) and Nili-Ravi (1765 kg) buffaloes. However, the average from elite herds have been reported as high as 2850 kg in Murrah and 2808 kg in Nili-Ravi buffaloes from NDRI Karnal and PAU Ludhiana respectively.

**In India the average first lactation milk yield** in Murrah buffaloes varies from 1540 to 1868 kg (Bhalaru and Dhillon, 1978; Patro and Bhat, 1979;Reddy, 1980). First lactation yield in Nili-Ravi (1707) is almost equal to that of Murrah, however, the averages for first lactation milk yield for Bhadwari (1165 kg), Nagpuri (1026 kg) and Surti (1364 kg) are lower than Murrah and Nili-Ravi breeds. The average lactation milk yield in elite herds has been reported to be as high as 2808 kg in an average lactation length of 305 days (Tiwana, 1990) and some buffaloes yielding as high as 4000 kg of milk in a lactation with recorded peak yield as high as 20-25 kg per day.

**Heritability estimates for first lactation milk yield** in Murrah buffaloes range from 0.08+ 0.04 to 0.19+0.08 which are slightly lower than the 0.28+0.20 for Nili-Ravi buffaloes. The heritability of second and subsequent lactation milk yield (0.22) is higher than that of first lactation milk yield (0.16) with unadjusted data (Acharya, 1988).

Studies on genetic aspects of monthly and cumulative monthly milk yield and components of lactation curve has revealed that heritability estimated for part lactation records is higher than those of total records.

## LACTATION LENGTH :

Average lactation length and the range of average reported by different sources for various breeds are presented in Table 2. The first lactation length in Murrah buffaloes is around 300 days and in Nili-Ravi it is slightly higher (323 days). In Bhadawari, Nagpuri and Surti it ranges between 276 and 295 days for the first lactation as well as for the overall lactations.

## MILK CONSTITUENTS :

The average fat and solid not fat percentage at different stage of lactation in Murrah buffaloes at CIRB Hisar is presented in the table. The fat percentage in Murrah and Nili-Ravi is comparable however, the SNF constituents in Murrah buffaloes reported from NDRI Karnal are slightly higher than Nili-Ravi breed reported from Pakistan. Though the fat contents increase significantly with the advancement of lactation but the SNF percent remain almost constant throughout the lactation. Fat and total solids percent has been found statistically different among pregnant and non-pregnant buffaloes at the same stage of lactation. All the three constituents have been reported to have low repeatability estimate of 0.167+0.014, 0.087+0.016 and 0.10+0.017 respectively.

## AGE AT FIRST CALVING:

The average age at first calving in different breeds is presented in the table 2. The average age at first calving in Murrah buffaloes range from 39.9 months to 54.6 months which is higher than 37.6 months of age reported in Bulgarian Murrah. In Bhadawari and Nagpuri buffaloes the age at first calving is slightly higher (44.3 - 54.2 months) than Surti (41.4 months) and Nili-Ravi buffaloes (41.4 months). However, Nili-Ravi buffaloes in Pakistan are reported to have higher (47.3 months) age at first calving than Indian Nili-Ravi. Swamp buffaloes have been reported to have the highest age at first calving (51 months) and the average from different sources range from 37.0 to 74.0 months.

## DRY PERIOD:

The approximate average and the rage of dry periods reported for various breeds is presented, which range from 95 days to as high as 288 days. In India the average dry period in Murrah, Nili-Ravi, Dharwari and Bhadawari breeds range from 148 days to 198 days. Dry period in Nagpuri buffaloes over different lactation ranged from 95-155.

## REPRODUCTION PERFORMANCE

**Most of the buffaloes are considered to be seasonal breeders** with maximum calvings taking place from July to November in almost all breeds. Rierine breeds exported to various other countries also show the similar trend of seasonal calvings from October to January in Egypt from July to October in Italy. The above findings suggest that the buffaloes in general come in oestrus during the cold months and are subfertile during the hot months.

The cause of sub-fertility has been reported as poor thermoregulation in buffaloes and also poor nutrition during summer months when green fodder is almost negligible and only lingo-cellulosic material e.g. straw/dry roughages are mainly available for feeding and poor heat symptoms resulting in low heat detection rate. Investigations on management practices to overcome the problem of sub-fertility in summer months have revealed that in summer months wallowing or water sprinkling during the hot hours of the day helps in maintaining the reproduction efficiency in breedable buffaloes.

## SERVICE PERIOD:

The average service period in different riverine breeds reported in India varies from 90 days in Nagpuri to 211 days in Nili-Ravi from Pakistan. The overall service period in Nagpuri and Dharwari breeds has been reported to be lower than the other riverine breeds, however, in swamp buffaloes this trait is reported to be higher than in riverine bred. Service period in all the breeds needs further investigation since this is the key reproduction trait which needs to be improved, through appropriate reproductive management.

## CALVING INTERVAL:

The average first calving interval for Murrah, Nili-Ravi, Surti and Bhadawari breeds is slightly higher than the overall calving interval for almost all the breeds. The swamp buffaloes show much higher calving interval than riverine breeds.

## MEAT PRODUCTION PERFORMANCE

**Meat production potentialities** of riverine buffaloes of Indian origin has been undertaken more extensively in some of the european countries and in Brazil as compared to India mainly due to the meat production emphasis in those countries. Mediterranean and Egyptian buffaloes which are also of riverine type have been bred for beef production due to their excellent muscle confirmation. Swamp type of buffaloes mainly found in South-east Asian countries and in China which are extensively used for work in agricultural fields, are also usd for meat production as well.

**Experimental evidence** for raising buffalo calves for meat production shown body weight gain as high as 635 g per day in Murrah buffalo calves between the age from 8 to 11 months. In non-descript Indian buffaloes growth rate of 469 to 607 g per day has also been reported. Under group and individual feeding systems of management body weight gain of 541 and 534 g respectively was achieved in Murrah buffalo male calves. Average DM intake per 100 kg body weight was also higher in individually (3.17 + 0.06) than in group fed calves (3.11 + 0.04) at CIRB, Hissar.

In Trinidad and Brazil, Indian breeds like Murrah, Surti, Jaffarabadi, Nili-Ravi and Bhadawari have been crossed with local buffaloes to raise crossbred progeny for beef production. An average finished weight of 476 kg at 2 years of age was attained in these crosses giving a daily weight gain of 512 g. Higher rates of gain between 900 and 1150 g per day was achieved in China and USSR and the dressing percentage between 52 and 62%.

**Dressing percentage** in buffaloes range from 55 to 64 per cent depdending upon the level of protein and energy intake. In Egyptian buffaloes percentage in well fed buffalo steers weighing 435 kg was reported to be 59 per cent.

**Buffalo meat is richer in protein** and amino acids than the meat of other species. Water buffalo carcass is lean with low percentage of fat deposition, has rounded ribs, a higher proportion of muscle and less fat. Flavour is comparable to that of beef in steaks as well as in processed meat products. Buffalo meat is superior to beef in palatability and tenderness.

Of the total buffalo population in India about 30 per cent are young calves of which half the number are male calves. These calves with appropriate feeding can raised upto 18 months to achieve at least 300-350 kg weight. This can result into quality meat production from buffaloes. With future trends of biotechnology and genetic selection, Indian buffaloes have great potential as red meat producers.

The potentialities of river buffaloes as meat support the present and future requirements of rapidly growing population deserve special attention, because of its capacity to convert coarse roughages and other cereal by-products into meat economically. There is an urgent need for the development of feed lot and feltering by upgrading the non-descript buffaloes with males of elite breeds available in the country for developing the stock for quality meat production.

## GENETIC IMPROVEMENT PROGRAMMES

For genetic improvement in buffaloes systematically selective breeding in milch breeds and use of high pedigreed bulls in non-descript buffaloes has been undertaken. Progeny testing have shown some genetic improvement over number of generations in a few institutional and organised herds.

## PROGENY TESTING:

Progeny testing in India has been undertaken at Military Dairy Farms, State Govt., farms and various institutional and research herds. These herds are now the elite germplasm resource for Murrah, Nili-Ravi and Surti breeds of buffaloes and will continue to make genetic progress for wider dissemination of genetic material developed at these institutions.

**Results of progeny testing** at various military dairy farms have revealed that 13% of the bulls had a breeding value of more than+100 kg and only 4 bulls out of 98 tested bulls had breeding value above 10% of the population mean. With the average generation interval of 7 years, the genetic improvement per years was upto 0.37 per cent over the population mean as against theoretically expected improvement of 1.0 to 2.0 per cent per annum at heritability estimate of 0.25 and average phenotypic standard deviation of 400 litres. The slow rate of improvement indicates that the programme needed systematic approach for implementation. Other non-additive factors which cause the genetic drift also contributed to relatively low progress.

**The All India Co-ordinated Research Project on Buffaloes** was as started by ICAR in the year 1970 at 4 different centres. The results revealed some significant observations at Karnal and Ludhiana for Murrah (Heavy) bred but at the other two centres namely Vallabhnagar and Dharwad the asprogramme showed a very slow pace. The results of progeny testing at Karnal in the first 6 sets of bulls showed superiority of the top ranking bulls selected over the contemporaries in each set between 7.53% (4th set) to 19.99% (3rd set) showing annual genetic gain in milk production from 0.28 to 0.67%. Results of 7 sets of 8 bulls each at Ludhiana revealed sire index of proven bulls as high as 2224 (2nd set) on daughters performance resulting in annual genetic gain of 4.5 kg milk yield averaging 0.27% of the herd average.

**Buffalo Improvement Projects** were taken up at several state and Central Government farms, e.g. Alamadi farm, Chennai; govt. Livestock Farm, Banawasi, Government Cattle Breeding Farm, Anjora; Government Livestock Farm, Dhamrod, for Surti breed. Most of these farms have not shown any impact of the progeny testing programme.

**Progeny testing programme** at Central Institute for Research on Buffaloes, Hisar was intially sponsored by the Government of India with an object to evaluate Murrah bulls on the basis of the performance of their daughters and distribution of progeny tested bulls to various breeding and farms. The number of bulls in each set ranged from 7 to 9 and the average duration of use from 26 to 36 months. The sire index based daughters contemporary comparison method ranged from 1803 in the first set t 1434 in the 3rd set with declining trend upto the 8th set.

The possible causes of slow rate of genetic improvement were the small herd size at the all centres, slow intensity of selection and non-availability of good quality bulls since at all the centres a sort of close system of breeding was followed.

## CROSS BREEDING:

During the past two decades attempts have been made in several countries e.g. Malayasia, Thailand, Philippines. China, Vietnam and other countries to cross swamp buffaloes with riverine breeds e.g. Murrah, Nili-Ravi and Surti besides crossing among the riverine buffaloes in India to produce crossbreds with higher potential for milk, meat and draft power.

The origin of Mehsana and Godavari is said to have been evolved from crossing of Surti and local buffalo cows with Murrah bulls respectively. In an experiment at NDRI, Karnal significant increase in milk yield and improvement in reproduction traits was observed in Murrah X Surti crossbred buffaloes (Sharma and Basu, 1984). In terms of efficiency of milk production (milk yield per day of calving interval), the crossbred (3.4 kg) were even reported to be better than the Murrah (3.2 kg).

In Bulgaria, Murrah buffaloes were reported to the superior than Bulgarian buffaloes both for body weights and milk yield while the Murrah & Bulgarian crosses were close to Murrah for body weights at different age groups. The milk yield and total fat in the crossbred were close to the mid parent value.

There is genetic diversity among river and swamp type buffaloes. Inspite of the genetic diversity among the two types of buffaloes, crossbreeding between the two has resulted in fertile hybrids (FI) with diploid number of chromosomes equal to 49 as a result of 4/9 tandom fusion of long metacentric chromosomes. The experimental evidences in back cross and F2 progenies indicate buffaloes with diploid number 48, 49 and 50 however, Ranjhan, 1987 reported only two populations with 2n=49 and 2n=50 speculating the possibility of early phasing out the population of 2n-48 from the normal theoretical expectation of 1:2:1. However, these results are based on very small population and hence needs further confirmation. Since hybrids have been found to be fertile and there is manifold increase in the production characteristics of crossbreds therefore crossbreeding of swamp buffaloes with various breeds of river buffalo has been undertaken in Philippines, Vietnam, China, Indonesia, Malaysia, Brazil and several other countries.

## GENETIC AND PHENOTYPIC TRENDS:

Phenotypic performance of the daughters of the bulls under progeny testing at the erst while Progeny Testing Farm, Hisar (CIRB) and the herd averages from 1970 to 1986 indicate declining phenotypic trend of about 15 per cent in daughters performance and 22 per cent in the overall herd performance. Data on 209 records of first lactation traits in Murrah buffaloes at National Dairy Research Institute, Karnal indicated significant change in phenotypic trend in first lactation milk yield and 305 days milk yield. However, genetic as well as environmental trends were non-significant for all the traits. At military dairy farms the estimated genetic gain was reported as 15.88 kg (0.9%) per annum of the population mean. The esimates of annual genetic in lactation yield reported from Egypt were 0.04 to 0.80%.

These estimates are lower than the estimates of % reported in temperate breeds of dairy cattle. In most of the herds selection was effected for sires based on their pedigree performance either on single trait basis or multi trait selection.

Based on the date from Mathura, Madhuri-Kund, Babugarh and Chak-Ganjaria in Uttar Pradesh from 1967-1983 it was found that selection index incorporating age of first calving, first lactation.

## STRATEGIES FOR ENHANCING GENETIC IMPROVEMENT ASSOCIATED PROGENY TESTING:

To overcome the problem of small herds in progeny testing the concept of Associated Herds Progeny Testing has been introduced in India where several herds with common technical programme will work together to achieve the objective. This programme has been undertaken under Network programme for the improvement of Murrah and Surti breeds of buffaloes at Central Institute for Research on Buffaloes. Hisar under the coordinating unit of Network. The model of network project on Murrah buffaloes has been prepared which elucidates the concept of Associated Progeny Testing while came in operation from July, 1993.

### 1. Participating Institutions and population size

| | Test Herd | Elite Herd |
|---|---|---|
| CIRB, Hisar | 316 | 18 |
| PAU, Ludhiana | 193 | 26 |
| IVRI, Izatnagar | 5 | 99 |
| CIRB, Sub Campus, Nabha | 3 | 72 |
| CCS HAU, Hisar | 18 | 92 |
| CBBF, Alamadi | 3 | 125 |
| NDRI, Karnal | 75 | 125 |
| | 147 | 1022 |

**(i) Population size has increased** from mere 150-200 animals in each herd to 1022 buffaloes for test matings and 147 elite buffaloes for nominated matings.

**(ii) Selection of proven sires:** From the progeny tested bulls available at various institutions 5 top proven, bulls with sire index ranging from 2224 to 1826 kg were selected for nominated matings with the 147 elite buffaloes. At the end of each cycle 4-5 proven bulls need to be selected from among the tested bulls which shall be used for elite matings.

**(iii) Selection of elite dams and nominated matings:** From the total population of all the centres 147 buffaloes were selected using either of the following criteria -

a) Best lactation yield > = 2500 kg
b) First lactation yield > = 2300 kg
c) Breeding value >'= 1950 kg

List of elite dams needs to be updated every quarter on the basis of information on their milk production and after every calving fresh allotment for nominated mating shall be made.

**(iv) Selection of test bulls:** 15 bulls were selected for the 1st set on the basis of following criteria -

a) Sons of elite dams
b) Semen freezability
c) Murrah characteristics
d) Sons of proven/recognised sires.

This criteria will be used in future for selection of 15 test bulls in each set.

**(v) Semen freezing from test bulls and storage of semen:** Selected bulls are maintained at the respective institutions from where it is selected. About 6000 doses of semen are frozen from each bull, 1000 doses for testing mating and 5000 doses for future use till the bull is evaluated.

**(vi) Selection and rearing of young males:** All the male calves born out of elite matings stand primarily selected as future test bull. These male calves are reared at the respective centres and final selection is made on the criteria as laid above for selection of test bulls. Besides growth pattern at periodic interval is also imposed for selection of bulls.

**(vii) Test matings:** All breedable females identified in the test herd at the respective centres are inseminated with the frozen semen of test bulls in such a manner that mating system is randomised for all the bulls. Test mating for each bull in the set is performed simultaneously for a cycle of 18 months in order to obtain at least 60 to 70 pregnancies from each bull. About 16-20 recorded daughters per bull are expected to be obtained from all the centres.

**(viii) Data Recording:** Information on various parameters concerning inseminations, pregnancies, daughter born to each bull, monitoring the growth of each calf till maturity and subsequently milk yield is to be collected for evaluation of the sires.

**(ix) Sire Evaluation:** Daughers 305 day 1st lactation milk yield will be used for estimation of sire indices. Bulls will be ranked on the basis of sire index and top 20 to 25% bulls will be selected for elite mating.

## RANGE OF AVERAGES FOR BODY WEIGHT AT DIFFERENT AGE IN DIFFERENT BREEDS OF BUFFALOES.

| | Birth weight | Age (Months) | | | |
|---|---|---|---|---|---|
| | | 6 | 12 | 24 | Maturity |
| Murrah India | 29 - 32 | 112 - 127 | 185 - 213 | 376 | 447 - 500 |
| Murrah Italy | 29.6 | 166 | 294 | - | 546 |
| Nili-Ravi India | 31.0 | 134 - 145 | 219 - 243 | - | 510 - 531 |
| Nili-Ravi Pak. | 29.4 - 37.8 | 94.4 | 132.4 | - | 436 |
| Surti India | - | 70 - 80 | 109 - 135 | 205 - 318 | - |
| Surti Sri Lanka | 21 | - | - | - | - |
| Dharwai | - | - | - | - | 367 |

## PRODUCTION PERFORMANCE OF DIFFERENT BREEDS OF BUFFALOES

| | Age at Ist calving (months) | | Lact. Yield (kg) | | Lactation length (days) | |
|---|---|---|---|---|---|---|
| | Av. | Range | Av. | Range | Av. | Range |
| Murrah | 43.0 | 39.9 - 54.5 | 1850 | 1476 - 2515 | 315 | 267 - 365 |
| Nili-Ravi | 42.0 | 41.4 - 47.3 | 1765 | 1596 - 2808 | 309 | - |
| Surti | 39.0 | 26.5 - 45.0 | 1364 | 1304 - 1693 | 313 | 300 - 373 |
| Bhadawari | 46.0 | 44.3 - 54.2 | 1181 | - | 276 | - |
| Nagpuri | 48.0 | 44.3 - 55.6 | 1103 | 926 - 1175 | 270 | - |

# Chapter - 5

# *Co-Operative Role in Dairy Development*

**Milk** production assumes second priority after rice cultivation in Indian agriculture. The village economy is incomplete for even marginal farmers if they lack one or two bovine animals. The fact that about 75% population of India is engaged in agricultural activities has put the organised milk production on the prime priorities of Government and other organizations. In this context operation flood and consequent thresh-hold of white revolution has come through the cooperative pattern of milk production management. Consequently more than 5 million farmers are today organised into about 0.5 lac of village milk cooperatives and the total turnover of Dairy sector has reached to Rs. 30,000 crore per annum.

The milk production in Indian set up is largely a source of supplementary income to the farmers who produce milk basically for self consumption and may spare the surplus for the market. The problems of Dairy Industry in the Indian context are unique in the sense that through India accounts for probably the largest bovine population in the world yet it contributes only five percent of the total world milk and milk products. The main impediment in the Indian Dairy has been the low intensity dairying based on poor yielding cattle fed on crop residues and labour intensive management.

However, with the efforts of different agencies in various states, the development of cooperative systems in the sector which has tried to integrate both technology of milk production and its subsequent marketing had led to steady growth of five percent per annum. Since the cost of production per litre of milk has been found to have inverse relationship with the productivity, the aim of cooperative movement in India has been to upgrade the productivity alongwith the efficient marketing management so that a fruitful source and sink relationship is maintained to the benefit of even marginal farmers.

The cooperative and organised milk production gained momentum only after the independence. Earlier Dairy activity was limited to household activity only except for a few trading cooperatives of milk and ghee in some isolated cities. These cooperatives and trading societies represented and interest of trading merchants only till late fifties. In the post independence era the orientation of cooperatives started changing towards the utilization of surplus to market orientation, integration of producers into cooperative systems with upgradation of Dairy production from subsistence to commercial production. Thus during the las two decades one can see that the marketable surplus of milk in rural areas has increased manifolds both in absolute and relative terms. The immediate effect of this enhancement in marketable surplus has been the direct supply of milk and milk products to the consumers both in the urban and rural areas. However, one can see declining trend in processing of surplus milk to ghee, khoa, etc. in rural areas, which does not commensurate with the increase in milk production. Cooperatives with a thrust on direct marketing of milk, played a major role in this respect.

The Dairy processing in India can be divided into private, cooperative and Govt. agencies besides, the traditional unorganised sector. At present all the aforesaid components of organised sector use modern methods technologies and management systems. The cooperative sector is examplified by the Anand Pattern of dairy cooperatives. The cooperatives being welfare oriented; production systems of the society have multifaceted activities and attention is given to all the finer aspects from maintenance of cattle to the utilization of end product i.e. milk. Broadly speaking, nine different activities are involved in dairy economy. Most of these activities are now being looked after by the cooperatives as compared to private, government or the unorganised sector.

| | Traditional/ Unorganised | | Modern/ Organised | | |
|---|---|---|---|---|---|
| | Private | Coop. | Private | Coop. | Govt. |
| 1. Trade in cattle buffaloes and bullocks | ***** | | | | |
| 2. Procurement and marketing of liquid milk | **** | * | * | **** | ** |
| 3. Marketing of ghee, khoa & other indigenous products | **** | * | ** | *** | |
| 4. Marketing of butter baby food | | | | **** | |
| 5. Production and marketing of pelleted cattle feed | | * | *** | **** | |
| 6. Supply of veterinary cover | ** | | **** | ***** | |
| 7. Supply of A land other breeding Services | | | | **** | |
| 8. Supply of indigenous feeds | **** | | | | |
| 9. Lease markets/costracts for bullocks | **** | | | | |

Adopted from shah et al., 1995 * Degree of significance

At present milk cooperatives represent the major share of organised milk production. These are functionally multipurpose societies organised on principle of federalism. Besides, there are various levels of control at village, district and state level. The whole structure is based on "Milk Producers Cooperative Society" at village level. The milk producers cooperative society is managed by elected representatives amonst the milk producers and look after the interest of milk producers; through providing marketing facilities and the key inputs like fodder seeds, loans upgradation of cattle veterinary facilities etc. so that the milk production is enhanced. At district level, about one thousand village cooperatives are clubbed into a "District Cooperative Milk Union". The main objective of District cooperative union is to process the pooled milk in a dairy plant and its subsequent marketing. The District level cooperative is managed by a Board of Directors elected from amongst and chairman of Dairy cooperative socities. A modern distinct cooperative milk union employs professionals like Dairy Technologies and Managers. This becomes more pertinent in view of the multifareous activities like manufacture of milk powders, butter, cheese, milk beverages etc. for effective marketing purpose. The district level union also undertakes transfer of improved technologies in Animal Husbandry practices, promotion and arrangement of quality feed and fodder to primary societies. The different district milk cooperative unions ultimately culminate into milk federation of respective state. It regulates the marketing of milk and milk products at inter and intra state levels through National Milk Grid.

The cooperative dairy movements has gone a long way in utilization of dairy surplus and make it accessible to public both at rural level during the past decades. At the rural level the cooperative system has brought awareness amongst the villagers towards an aggressive dairy farming instead of traditional sustenance based milk production. This attitude has further geared the villagers towards community development through organizational set ups in other sphere also. The interaction brought by cooperatives for production and collection of milk amongst the villagers and different communities in a village on a common plateform has also helped in mitigating the cost barrier in may areas. The cooperative movement at village level envisaged facilities in terms of inputs like improved feeds, veterinary services, dairy plants etc, and above all inculcation of general and collective responsibilities for successful and viable running of the cooperatives. Therefore, dairy cooperative movement has proved to be an instrument of social and economic change at village level. The cooperative movement has thus exposed the villagers to processes of development, modern scientific ideas and creation of infrastructure.

The cooperatives, in initial stages have played a significant role in livestock trading and its productivity enhancement. Nevertheless, the role of Govt. agencies is of equal importance. An impetus was provided for the improvement of livestock through improved breeding, feeding and management. No doubt, this vaccuum was catered to by Govt. and now by other commercial sectors.

The success of cooperatives can be judged by the amount and scale of patronage and allegiance they command from the basic milk producer members in the villages, on one hand and the consumers particularly in the urban areas on the other hand. This development of source and sink relationship by the cooperative movement has resulted in the circulation of money to the tune of several crores with economic benefits at various levels besides, creating employment opportunities. The dairy cooperatives system over a period of time has succeeded in offering to their members or the milk producers remunerative prices and a dependable market for their surplus; However, since the cooperatives has been sluggish in providing efficient technical inputs and in many cases due to poor management practices, the economic impact is not going to very significant in the context of present day competitive market economy.

There has been a change due to cooperative movement for subsistence dairy enterprise to market oriented one by providing a perpetual regenerating, and a remunerative market for milk round the year. This has resulted in enhancement of the memberships of cooperatives on one hand and also a desire on the part of members to increase their productivity of livestock by proper scientific breeding, quality feeding and management practices. The overall impact at various levels is indicated in the table.

As a result of successful Operation Flood programmes under the co-operative movement the house hold economics of producers increased over the past years resulting in enhancement in their house-hold income and expenditure and thereby increasing their living standards particularly in respect of their nutrition. Owing to the success of cooperatives, there has been an unprecedented incresae of milk production in the country. The near self sufficiency and self reliance in milk production is also reflected by the fact that India refused commodity aid in this sector for the first time. The success of "Anand Pattern" milk cooperative movement was appreciated worldwide and a ministerial level meeting of six Asian Countries comprising Vietnam, Indonesia, Philippines, China, Pakistan and India resolved to replicate the same pattern in their respective countries and establish an international Centre at anand for sharing the experiences of operation flood.

One of the main contributions of operation flood at the national level has been the development of infrastructure in milk processing and marketing. The National Milk Grid alongwith well organised milk supply schemes working in different parts of the country has made it possible to swiftly collect process and transport the available surplus milk and despatch it under hygenic conditions to the consumers in milk scarce area. As a result the milk market has expanded manifolds catering to about 300 million consumers at present in different parts of the country.

The network of cooperative institutions created through the operation flood programme now comprised about 70,000 dairy cooperatives in 170 milk sheds, encompassing 8.4 million milk producer families. Average milk procurement by these cooperatives has now reached some 12.3 million kg per day, of which 8.2 million litres are marketed as liquid milk, while the remainder is converted into products such as milk powder, butter, cheese, ghee and a wide range of traditional milk products. Milk processing capacity of approximately 15.6 million litres per day, chilling capacity of 6.5 million litres per day and milk powder production capacity of 726 tonnes per day have been established through the programme. One of the challenging aspects of dairy development in a tropical or subtropical country is the movement of milk over long distances. In operation flood, this has been made possible through the operation of about 140 insulated rail milk tankers, each with a capacity of 40,000 liters, supplemented by another 25 rail tankers of 21,000.

| | Pre Cooperative Stage | A young but effective cooperative | The Cooperative matures: So does the dairying in the village. | A modern coopertative with infrastru- ture to sustain cross breeding on major scale |
|---|---|---|---|---|
| | ***Main Characters*** | ***Main Characters*** | ***Main Characters*** | ***Main Characters*** |
| a) | High draft power orientation | Increase in the feeding of cattle feed, grain and green fodder. | Increase in ratio of animals in milk to bovine holidngs. | Intensive campaign is launched to introduce A.I. |
| b) | Low yield/animal low ratio of animals in milk to livestock holdings. | Increase in yield/ animal. | Culling of un productive animals begins. | Largest possible number of local animals to be covered by A.I. with semen of properly chosen exotic species. |
| c) | Bulk of milk output used for self consumption. | Increase in pro- portion of milk output sold. | Longer lactation lengths shorter calving patterns increase in breed ing efficiency. | Elaborate support structure enable farmers to raise cross-breds. |
| d) | Low real cost of milk production | Buffalo emerges as main dairy animal. | Emergency of lease markets for bullocks. | Economics of dairying under- goes major cha- nge. Use of land to support live- stock increases. |
| e) | | Economics of dairying and opportunity costs of feeds became important | Constraints impo- sed by traditional milk production technologies begin to be felt by producers. | Real cost of milk production falls. |
| f) | | | | Milk procurement by coop. rises rapidly with salutary effects on its economics. |

Adopted from Shah et al., 1995

liters capacity, Approximately 1,000 other insulated road milk tankers operate throuoghout the country as well. This has enabled the operation of a national milk grid, balancing regional fluctuations in milk procurement and bridging demand and supply gaps resulting from concentrated production of liquid milk in selected milk sheds. To balance, seasonal variations in milk supply and demand caused by low milk production during the summer months, a large milk powder storage capacity has been created for buffer stocking.

The cooperative movement has also encouraged the development and establishment of milk producing units on small scale level providing regular source of income to the farmers. The expansion of cooperative movement has resulted in increased demand of dairy equipments, feed industry and indirectly the milk product industry also. India is now exporting the dairy equipment machinery. The milk production in the country has increased from 20 million MT to 60.8 million tonnes, milk powder production has risen from 22,000 MT in 1969-70 to 1,60,000 MT in 1992-93 per capita availability of milk which had declined consistently during the two decades between 1951 and 1970, drooping to 107g at the start of operation flood, is now 187 g per day; despite a substantial increase in population as a result of the awareness generated among producers by the cooperative movement in all facts of dairying.

Although till recently cooperative dairying has proved a bone for small producers particularly small farmers and landless labourers by providing livelihood and security to such segments of society but now with the advancement of technology and its incorporation in the cooperative and other organised sectors, there is a tendency of more benefits to large units only. Unless proper remedial measures are taken, the present day capital intensive dairying involving high technology may ultimately ease out the small producers from advanced cooperative systems. In this aspect exposure of the rural small producers to scientific improvement of livestock and management at village level is of utmost importance. The need of the hour for the cooperative is to come face to face in the aforesaid challenges so that the cooperative movement is rejuvenated for rural human resource development and upliftment of marginal farmers.

# Chapter - 6

## *Increasing in Milk Protein by Feeding*

Milk composition affects the price received. Although the pricing basis used initially rewarded fat content more than protein, in the last few years the balance has swung in favour of a higher milk protein analysis.

Therefore, the cow feeding strategies applied by the producers today seek to keep milk volume-or 'yield' - and fat within quotas limits, while maximising the protein. A BSAS report from nutritionists at the University of Reading and Trident Feeds noted that these goals are not easily reconciled. It is relatively straightforward to control the milk fat content by nutritional means, but feeding for more protein is more difficult and certainly less predictable.

### SODA GRAIN FOR PROTEIN BOOST

However, some quite significant improvements have been obtained from giving the cows a supplement which is rich in energy. Several studies have shown a valuable protein increase results from processing feedstuff starch sources to change the nature as well as the amount of carbohydrate in the diet.

One example of how that has been put into practice in the UK concerns an ingredient known locally as soda grain. Proving increasingly popular in feeds on British dairy farms, this ingredient takes the form of whole wheat treated with caustic soda (sodium hydroxide or NaOH) to reduce the rate of degradation in the rumen.

A typical soda grain treatment described to the BSAS meeting involved adding 30 kg of sodium hydroxide per ton of wheat, plus water to bring the total drymatter to 700 g/kg and storing for 5 days before feeding. The use of soda grain was said to be associated with consistent improvements in milk protein content observed on a number of farms.

In one recent test the caustic treated material was compared with wheat that had been milled through a 3 mm screen, both being employed to provide increasing amounts of wheat starch to Holstein cows which were also allowed grass silage to appetite. The study, by the ADAS farm advisory service, confirmed that a higher intake of dietary starch from either source was able to raise milk protein. But it also shows an essential difference between the wheat ingredients, in that only in the case of the ground wheat was the greater starch intake per day also accompanied by a lift in the milk yield.

Positive benefits on milk protein content from feeding NaOH-treated or rolled wheat have been established by a Reading University experiment. Soda grain was compared with 50:50 mixture of rolled wheat and sugarbeet feed, for Friesian dairy cows in their early or middle lactation. The cows received there as supplements to their ad libitum access to grass silage, including wheat in their diet significantly enhanced the protein level of their milk. However, although both supplements gave the same response for milk protein, the rolled wheat-sugarbeet feed mixture differed from soda grain in also leading to an increase in milk yield and milk fat.

## ALTERNATIVES FOR EXTRA RUMEN BYPASS ENERGY

An alternatively grain treatment for reducing rumen degradability was discussed by animal production specialists from Finland's agricultural research centre in Jokionen. They outlined promising results from cooking the barley, before mixing it with sugarbeet pulp and rapeseed meal into a concentrate to accompany grass silage.

In their studies the basal concentrate was a 2.8 mixture of sugarbeet pulp and either untreated or cooked barley, which for some cows supplemented using untreated or treated rapeseed meal. This protein addition did increase both total yield and protein yield, but the treatment of the rapeseed meal obtained no extra response.

By contrast, cooked barley proved better than the raw cereal despite apparently depressing the cows' daily intake of silage and of total drymatter. Both milk yield and protein yield were maintained; the milk contained less fat besides having slightly more protein.

Combinations of barley or unmolassed beet pulp with rapeseed meal were reported by IGER grassland research institute scientists in Wales to give an acceptable concentrate for feeding at low levels to dairy cows given high-digestibility grass silage. But replacing the rapeseed in the concentrate with a 1:3 blend of whitefish and soyabean meals had the effect of elevating protein and fat in the milk white reducing yield.

Energy-rich supplements can be produced using root starches as well as cereal sources, University of Newcastle investigators pointed out. They fed Friesia-Holstein cows during lactation with concentrates of the same 180 g/kg crude protein value, in which manioc (cassava or tapioca) replaced all or part of the barley-wheat cereal present. Interestingly, neither the all-cereal nor the all-root starch option resulted in the best cow performance. For yields of protein, lactose and milk fat this came from a 0.25:0.75 cereal-root mix. At the other end of the scale was the blend of 75% cereals with 25% manioc.

Across all combinations, however, there was no significant effect of dietary treatment on the proportion of protein in the milk. It required the extra daily milk production on the 25%-75% concentrate to obtain the appreciable rise observed in milk protein yield.

What degree of milk protein manipulation is possible by these feeding techniques?

The result from Findland, for Finish Ayrshire cows, pointed to protein content of 31.4 g/kg when the cows received simply grass silage and uncooked barley. Adding the rapeseed meal and cooking the barley raised this to 32.2 g/kg. The Holsteins in the British ADAS test provided 32.9 g protein per kilogram of milk where soda grain was giving them a daily starch intake of 1.9 kg, rising to 34.5 g protein on a 4.6 kg/day intake. For the Friesians at Reading University in the UK, the 30.1 g/kg protein results of unsupplemented controls rose to a peak 33.2 g/kg after feeding soda grain. Completely replacing barley and wheat with tapioca in the concentrates given Friesian-Holsteins at Newcastle University reduced their milk protein proportion from 30.8 g/kg to 30.1 g/kg.

# Chapter - 7

## *Aseptic Packaging of Food and Beverage*

**Aseptic** packaging is neither a major breakthrough technology that will revolutionise all food business nor a mature or declining technology whose future has been shattered by regulatory disapprovals. Further, concepts of aseptic processing and packaging which are somewhat removed from the core of the original technologies are gradually being adopted to both said and pumpable foods for extended shelf life refrigerated distribution.

The classical technology encompasses independent sterilisation of product and package and assembly under sterile conditions to deliver food capable of being distributed under ambient temperature conditions. In this manner, much lower thermal inputs may be imparted to reasonably homogeneous pumpable food, usually beverage, and its packaging. Thus, heat sensitive foods such as milk may be effectively stabilised. Further, because of the ability to sterilise the package by one of several methods not necessarily involving high heat means that virtually any size, shape, or composition package may be the container.

Today, the most widely used systems are those of Sweden's Tetra Pak using chemical sterilization and paperboard/plastic/aluminium foil composite brick-shaped packages. But more than forty different supply companies offer aseptic packaging systems of various types ranging from fractional mililitre bottles to 2000 litres or larger size bulk flexible bags.

### DOLE ASEPTIC CANNING

Dole canning lines employ superheated steam as the sterilant for metal cans ranging in size from 100cc to 400cc, with reliable results. Dole systems seem to have fallen into a category of beginner's aseptic packaging, with food companies starting with these very high speed units and eventually converting to plastic cup and tub packaging whose variable costs tend to be lower than for metal cans. Oddly, the capital costs for Dole lines are lower than for systems using chemical sterilants.

Just to demonstrate their continuing viability, a number of new Dole aseptic canning line have been recently installed for packging dietary type milk-based liquid meals which were introduced in the American market with modest success. The packages are 340cc two-piece steel cans. The products are distributed in the traditional manner of aseptic packages, i.e., under ambient conditions.

## PLASTIC CUP LINES

A pharmaceutical company is aseptically packaging some of its nutritional liquid diet using the FMC

Freshfil performed cup deposit/fill/seal system. Developed by the United Kingdom's Carnauld Metal box, the system employs multilayer high oxygen barrier cups and heat sealed flexible lamination closure materials with hydrogen peroxide spray as the sterilant. Also using the Freshfil system is a major breakfast cereal company for its portion size precooked and ready-to-microwave-heat oatmeal cereal. Again, the packages are performed coextruded sthylene vinyl alcohol/polypropylene closed with aluminum foil flexible laminations. Earlier, these systems were used to aseptically package cheese sauce/dips in barrier plastic cups.

All of these products are or were low acid homogeneous or nearly homogeneous fluids. They may be readily heat sterilised in continuous heat exchangers and transferred into the packages by reliable fillers without finite risk microbiological recontamination.

## THERMOFORM/FILL/SEAL: LOW ACID FLUID FOODS

Milk puddings and analogous dairy foods are aseptically packaed on French ERCA or German Bosch thermoform/fill/seal systems beginning with roll stock multilayer barrier sheet. Both systems use a traditional polystyrene/polyvinylidene chloride (PVDC) sheet material for ease of in-line thermoforming. Sterilisation on the Bosch system is with hydrogen peroxide immersion. The ERCA system employs a complex process of relying on the heat of plastic extrusion to effect the sterility of the material followed by protecting the clean surface with an added film that is removed immediately prior to filling. The ERCA system avoids any hint of residual chemicals.

Both systems are relatively expensive to acquire and install, but offer the benefit of low material costs, and so far packagers with high output requirements, total systems costs can be the lowest of any aseptic cup system. Output speeds can be in the range of hundreds of 50cc to 250cc cups a minute.

German Hassia thermoform/fill/seal equipment is unique in that it uses high pressure temperature steam to both sterilise the package materials and to thermoform the base plastic sheet into cups.

Both Hassia and Bosch thermoform/fill/seal equipment are being used for aseptic packaging of unit portion size liquid coffee lighteners. This trend is away from the use of irradiation sterilised preformed polystyrene cups on Purity and Portion Packaging deposit/fill/seal equipment, due largely to the higher output and lower total system cost for larger packagers.

## THERMOFORM/FILL/SEAL: HIGH ACID PRODUCTS

The application of thermoform/fill/seal aseptic packaging systems for low acid foods does not in any way preclude their employment for high acid foods which are much less concern from a microbiological safety perspective. Thus, ERCA systems have been successfully used for aseptic packaging of juices and other fruit beverages, apple sauce and, with modification, fruit pieces. In both Australia and the United States, ERCA thermoform/fill/seal equipment has integrated hot filling under aseptic conditions coupled with post filling cooling to deliver ambient temperature shelf stable fruit pieces in unit portion size plastic cups.

Aseptic thermoform/fill/seal systems are being applied for tomato type sauces and pastes in Australia.

## DEPOSIT/FILL/SEAL SYSTEMS

Refrigerated milk puddings and fruit flavoured gels in unit portion size multilayer barrier plastics have expanded significantly, increasing the primary market for convenient-to-eat desserts. Packages are usually performed high barrier multilayer plastic cups with heat sealed flexible aluminium foil structure closures. Packaging is on machines such as German Hamba or Gasti which are engineered and operated in aseptic modes, but whose mechinsms are not regarded as truly aseptic by some regulatory agencies. In those territories, the product output is classified as ultra clean but not sterile. The product is distributed under refrigeration, a factor that helps to retain its flavour attributes as well as ensure its microbiological safety.

An increasing number of products are being processed and packaged under aseptic conditions to significantly prolong their refrigerated shelf lives. Apple, cranberry and blended fruit sauces for desserts and garnishes are, of course, high acid products. Such products are stabilised by thermal processes and aseptically packaged for ambient temperature distribution in high barrier plastic cups and trays. High oxygen barrier is important for fruit products because of their oxygen sensitivity. Packaging is in preformed coextruded polypropylene/ethylene vinyl alcohol cups, in the case of those packaged on to Crosscheck system. This system is unique among all aseptic packaging systems because it was engineered specifically for acid fluid foods. It uses a non-invasive sterilisation system and eliminates oxygen from the package before filling. Sterilisation on the Crosscheck system is with hot water.

Fruit sauce products are also aseptically packaged on thermoform/fill/seal on ERCA or Bosch systems. Juices are aseptically packaged in unit portion sizes on Hassia thermoform/fill/seal equipment using superheated steam as both the sterilant and the thermoforming pressure source.

## ASEPTIC PACKAGING IN BOTTLES

In both North America and Europe during 1993 and 1994, aseptically packaged fruit beverages have appeared in polyster bottles in sizes are large as 1800cc and as small as 454cc. The aseptic technologies employed are the French Serac in which the premade bottles are washed with mixtures of aqueous chlorine and oxonia and rinsed with distilled water prior to aseptic filling. An analogous system from France's Remy is used to aseptically package flavoured water in polyester bottles.

For perspective, however, most ambient temperature shelf stable polyester bottles of fruit beverages are hot filled rather than aseptically filled. Hot filling requires the employment of special bottle structures that permit the walls to collapse inwardly damaging the bottle as a result of the vacuums developed from steam condensation upon cooling. Shelf life in polyester bottles is not as long as it is with coextruded multilayer barrier bottles, but is evidently acceptable in several territories.

At least two American packagers are delivering fruit flavoured high acid drinks in high density polyethylene bottles whose sterility is achieved by employing aseptically blow mold/fill/seal technologies from suppliers such as Germany's Rommelag or the United States Automatic Liquid Packaging. The primary bottles are fabricated from high density polyethylene which is a low barrier material, and so the gas barrier is built into a coextruded ethylene vinyl alcohol-based shrink film package.

A similar type of packaging is offered by Japan's Kogyo which preforms the containers under sterile conditions and transfers them under clean conditions for aseptic packaging.

## FLAVOUR SCALPING FROM ASEPTIC PACKAGES

Increasingly, juice and fruit beverages companies are employing technologies to significantly prolong the refrigerated shelf lives of their products packages in gable top barrier papaerboard cartons and plastic bottles. More than seven weeks of chilled quality retention is now commercially achieved for pasteurised fruit beverages and four weeks for unpasteurised, all employing aseptic packaging. Accompanying the long shelf life, however, has been scalping or removal of desirable flavour components from the contained product by the interior polyolefin layer. This problem has been largely overcome through the incorporation of ethylene vinyl alcohol on the interior layer in gable topo cartons, an International Paper development, or nylon used by other suppliers. Nylon has also been the interior layer choice for coextruded polyethylene bottles for pasteurised and unpasteurised juices, also, of course, for chilled distribution. The relative interness of polyester with contained fruit beverages obviates any need for an extra layer on the interior of aseptically packaged polyester bottles.

## ASEPTIC PACKAGING FOR CHILLED FOODS

Aseptic technologies are being integrated with product formulation, reduced water activity, high pH and chilled distribution to deliver foods with excellent initial quality for extended periods. Chilled puddings cited above fall into this category, but in Japan, precooked rice has emerged as another important class. Rice is a true particulate product, and so the aseptic packaging of this product represents a most intriguing advance from the classical technology. Control is achieved by water activity control, mechanical removal of oxygen and by insertion of oxygen scavenger sachets. Shelf life is limited not by microbiological problems but rather by biochemical degradation of the rice starch itself.

## BULK ASEPTIC PACKAGING

Probably the greatest growth in aseptic packaing has been in the realm of bulk packaging of high acid fluids foods in barrier flexible pouch packages. The best known are those produced in preformed pouches incorporating valves through which the valve areas cleaned with chlorine compounds immediately prior to filling. Companies such as Scholle and Liqui Box are supplying the complete systems which are applied for high acid pumpable foods such as tomato ketchup and sauces.

For bulk packaging of low acid pumpable foods such as cheese sauces and dips, aseptic vertical form/fill/seal systems for Bosch are employed. These systems employed roll stock high barrier transparent multilayer films which are sterilised in-line by liquid hydrogen peroxide. Some of the sauces incorporate small particles which do not necessarily retain their integrity during the sterilisation process.

## PAPERBOARD COMPOSITE BRICK & BLOCK PACKAGING

It is important to note that, despite scant mention of paperboard composite systems such as those from Sweden's Tetra Pak, Germany's Combibloc and Japan's Fuji, these constitute the largest category of aseptic packaging systems by any measure of number of installations, volume packaged, number of units packed, etc. The overwhelming majority are applied for milk, with fruit beverages as an increasingly stronger second. Among the recent developments in this packaging system class have been larger sizes for the Combibloc and easy open and reclosure featuers for both Tetra Pak and Combibloc.

Recently, Tetra Pak has been testing silica coating as the primary barrier for its brick packages. By replacing aluminiuum foil in its paperboard structures, a similar barrier is effects with material that can then be more readily recycled. Combibloc is experimenting with ethylene vinyl alcohol as the primary barrier material in its paperboard structure.

## ASEPTIC PROCESSING

Little commercial aseptic packaging of significant sized particulates is underway because of the continued difficulty of thermally sterilising discrete particulates in continuous flow. This paucity of commercial installations has not deterred development.

Ohmic or electrical resistance heating of foods to sterilisation temperatures is under intensive study with a prototype system capable of sterilising large particulates. The resulting sterile product can be as high quality as minimally processed foods (for example, blanched vegetables) provided the electrical conductivity of the solid food matches that of the liquid carrier fluid. Ohmic sterilisation is reportedly being used in Europe for sterilisation of pet foods, followed by aseptic packaging in brick paperboard composite packages and for aseptic packaging in fruit in Japan.

Although not Ohmic heating, Raztek high frequency electrical resistance thermal sterilisation of liquid eggs is being performed commercially. The eggs are packaged aseptically in gable top paperboard cartons, but distributed under refrigeration.

In a longer term development, Maxwell Laboratories' joint venture company Foodeo in the United States is developing pulsed electrical discharges to sterilize food in depth, another variant on the basic electrical resistance heating principle. Ohmic and pulsed electricity represent potential technologies to heat sterilise solid products without excess thermal damage.

In another technology development from the Maxwell Laboratories group, pulsed high-intensity light is being developed to sterilise surfaces such as those of package materials before aseptic packaging. If it works, non-thermal, non-chemical technology for surface sterilization will be available.

# Chapter - 8

# *Technology/Processing of Dairy and Milk Products*

## MILK SHAKE

Milk shake, a product of Western origin, is obtained by freezing mix very similar to soft serve icecream mix and speed mixing the frozen product in a mixer to make it pourable and generate foam in it. It has lower fat and sugar contents and higher milk solids-not-fat (msnf) content than icecream. In view of the increasing popularity of milk based frozen products, a study was undertaken to standardize the method of manufacture of milk shake. The study was also extended to obtain the product in a powder form which could easily be reconstituted by housewives.

## COMBINATION

Of the various combinations studied, the one with fact and msnf levels of 4 and 13% respectively, was found to be the most acceptable with respect to the whipping ability of mix and foam stability and sensory evaluation of the milk shake prepared therefrom.

## STEPS IN PROCESSING

The ingredients required i.e. whole milk, skim milk powder, sugar and stabilizer (sodium alginate) were weighed and mixed as follows. Sugar (at the rate of 10%) and stabiliser (at the rate of 0.4%) were dry-mixed first. The milk was warmed upto 40° C and the skim milk powdet was slowly added to it with continuous stirring. The temperature of the mixture was then raised to about 70°C before adding the sugar stabilizer mixture. After thorough mixing. After thorough mixing, the liquid was filtered through muslin cloth and while at about 60°C it was homogenized in two stages first at 175 kg $cm^2$ and seemed at 35 $Kg/cm^2$ pressure. The homogenized mix was pasteurised at

70°C for 30 minutes. The mix was then cooled to about 10°C and aged for 2-3 hr at 6°-10°C. Following the aging, the milk shake mix was frozen in a soft-serve ice-cream freezer using strawberry flavour (0.1 ml/ltr). The drawing temperature varied between -2°C to -6°C. The frozen mix was blended in a mixer for 90-120 sec to produce milk shake.

## DRIED MILK SHAKE MIX POWDER

The milk shake mix was also spray dried and powder contained 3.3% moisture; 15.1% fat, 17.7% protein and the rest being carbohydrate and ash. Its solubility index was 0.45 mi, and bulk density 0.44 g/ml (loose) and 0.59 g/ml (packed).

The dried milk shake mix powder could be reconstituted by mixing calculated amount of crushed ice (to adjust the solids level at 28% in the final product) and blending in a mixer for 9C-120 sec. The reconstituted product when subjected to sensory evaluation was found to be quite acceptable. However, it scored slightly less than fresh milk shake, on account of slight chalkiness and too large ice crystals. Aging of the reconstituted milk shake for 2 to 3 hours in refrigerator prior to mixing in a mixer would, however, help improve the accetability of the product.

## STERILISED CREAM

Economic utilisation of seasonal and regional surpluses of milk is of great importance to the dairy industry and while the solids-not-fat content is used for the manufacture of dried milks, the surplus fat is used for the production of ghee. Preparation of sterilised cream would be a very profitable proposition for the utilisation of surplus milk fat and can fetch a much higher return by nearly 100% per unit weight of fat as compared to ghee. The product can be made either on a small scale or on large scale depending on the demand, in any dairy equipped with the usual facilities for milk handling.

## COMPOSITION

The product has the following approximate composition

i) Fat - 20-21%

ii) Milk SNF - 6%

iii) Stabiliser - 0.2 to 0.3%

iv) Water - 72.7 - 73.8% (by difference)

## STEPS IN PROCESSING

i) Adjustment of the fat level of cream to 20% (minimum)

ii) Forewarning to 85° C and holding for 15 minutes.

iii) Homogenisation at 65-67°C at a pressure of 175 kg/s.cm$^2$ for the 1st stage and 35 kg/s.cm$^2$ for the 2nd stage.

iv) Addition of trisodium phosphate as a stabiliser @ 0.2% by weight of cream.

v) Canning the cream in suitable size containers and leak detection

vi) Sterilisation at 114±1°C for 14-15 min. and rapid cooling.

vii) Testing the final quality of the product.

## ADDITIONAL REQUIREMENTS OF EQUIPMENT

i) Homogeniser

ii) Can filling and seaming equipment

iii) Steriliser.

The cost of the equipment depends on the proposed capacity of handling.

The product has an acceptable shelf life to about six months and can be used in beverages like coffee, tea and fruit-cream etc. The contents of the tin are to be shaken thorough before opening.

## DAHI FROM SWEET CREAM BUTTERMILK

Buttermilk is the fluid portion left behind after churning of cream or 'dahi' during butter manufacture. Since buttermilk is largely defatted cream, its composition is much like that of skim milk. It is estimated that 1.5 million tonnes of milk is annually used for the production of creamery butter and therefore nearly 8,000 tonnes of buttermilk solids are available for utilization. While a small portion of the by-product thus obtained is utilized for the manufacture of infant food, skim milk powder etc., a major portion does not find economic disposal, and is merely wasted.

This investigation was undertaken with a view to evolve a suitable technique for the manufacture of dahi from sweet-cream butter milk. Dahi is used as a part of diet in this country on account of its virtues from the nutritional standpoint. It has been resorted that nearly 7.8 per cent of all milk produced in the country is used for dahi manufacture. If an acceptable quality of dahi could be made from buttermilk, not only it will open a way for its utilization but may also release part of milk currently used for dahi for other uses.

## COMPOSITION

Dahi was made with cow and buffalo buttermilk using cultures such as *Str.lactis, Sir.diacetilactis*. **L.F-40** and *Str. Thermophilus* and *L. bulgaricus* (1:1) with or without increasing total solids content by the addition of skim milk powder. The dahi thus made was analysed for total solids, fact, total nitrogen, non-protein nitrogen, per cent lactic acid, curd tension and diacetyl content, and sensory evaluation by a panel of judges, and compared with skim and whole milk dahi.

It was observed that dahi of acceptable quality from sweet cream buttermilk could be prepared by subjecting the buttermilk to cream separation (if desired) at 55°C, (optionally adding 1 to 2 per cent skim milk solids) and heating it to 90°C for 30 min. before cooling to 30°C, inoculating with one per cent of a culture of *Sir. Lactis* (for cow butter milk) and 0.5 per cent of culture of *Str. Diacetilactis* (for buffaloe buttermilk) and finally incubating in for 16 and 12 hours respectively.

## ACIDOPHILUS MILK

Acidophilus milk is a sour milk product that have been allowed to ferment under conditions that favour the growth and development of a large number of lactobacillus, acidophilus organisms. Acidophilus milk differs from Indian dahi in that the milk used in the preparation and the type of micro-organisms involved are different. The final product differs from dahi in body, texture, consistency, flavour, chemical composition and in antibacterial activities.

### Uses

Products of mixed fermentation such as acidophilus yeast milk being rich in alcohol and carbon dioxide excite the respiratory and central nervous systems. This improves the process of oxidation and reduction in the organisms and hence there is an increase in the oxygen flow to the lungs. In the Soviet Union, acidophilus yeast milk is widely used in treating tuberculosis.

The recent emphasis on feeding lactobacilli is attributed to the side effects of antibiotics. Antibiotics damage the intestinal microflora and intentinal discomforts caused by flatulence and diarrhoea. Induction of *Lacidophilus* into the intestine accelerates return to normalcy in the intestinal microflora. A Rumanian strain of *L. acidophilus* is claimed to have been produced for treatment of gastrointestinal disorders but also produces a feeling of general vigour and health. It has been reported that acidophilus milk products combind with chemo-therapeutic preparation can also be used effectively for several disesaes, such as typhoid, para-typhoidpsoriosis, osteomyelitis, pneumonia, migraine and urological infection. Experiments have revealed that the body weight of a hild, or an animal increases when fed with acidophilus milk preparations.

## Preparation

*L. acidophilus*-based fermented products differ in the type of starter culture and milk used for their preparation. Acidophilus sour milk, as the name indicates, is a sour milk beverage made out of standardized milk, acidifying it by means of pure culture of acidophilus rods (*L. acidophilus*). Milk culture of *L. acidophilus* has the therapeutic value described earlier but does not possess the buttery acetaldehyde flavour of the regular fermented milk products such as dahi and yoghurt.

The procedure for the preparation of acidophilus sour milk has been standardized. The milk used for the preparation of acidophilus sour milk is standardised to 3.5% fat and 8.5% SNF content. For this preparation standardized milk is sterilized and is cooled to 40°C. The milk is inoculated with 24 hours old pure starter culture of *L. acidophilus* at the rate of 2 to 3% and filled into 200 ml glass or plastic container and incubated at about 39°C for 8-12 hrs. the product is then cooled and stored at 5-8°C till it is consumed.

The product so obtained is sout with 1 to 1.2% lactic acid (pH 3.7-4.0). The product should contain more than 2000-3000 million viable *L. acidophilus* organisms/ml which possess satisfactory antibiotic effect against I; coli as well as other pathogenic and non-pathogenic undesirable bacteria of the intestinal tract. The viability of the organisms is of primary importance in the use of acidophilus milk. The acidophilus sour milk can be preserved upto a week below 5°C.

# FLAVOURED TYPE OF MILK BEVERAGE FROM CHEESE WHEY

In most of the cheese producing countries utilization of cheese whey has become a problem, on the other hand it is an excellent source of protein "ranks high in nutritive value only next to egg protein", lactose minerals and water soluble vitamins. Utilization of cheese whey for the manufacture of flavoured type milk beverage is a most logical use of return to the human food chain in a palatable form, in the light of growing global food shortage.

To standardise the method of manufacture of flavoured type milk beverage, a base material (prepared by taking whey 4.5% skim-milk acidified with HCL heated to 90° C followed by filtration through muslin cloth) was obtained in the form of curd. This curd was mixed with part of separated whey in a proportion so as to obtain 3.0% protein level followed by neutralizing with 10% sodium hydroxide solution, preheating to 65°C, homogenization at 2.000

and 500 psi. pasteurizing at 75°C and finally cooling it immediately. The product with 6% pineapple or rose flavour had a good acceptability. It has shelf life of about 7 days under refrigerated conditions.

## YOGHURT FROM BUFFALO MILK

It is an undisputable fact that the enormously increasing popularity of yoghurt, now becoming available throughout the world, is primarily based on the cultural and biochemical performance of lactic cultures namely *Streptococcus thermophulus* and *lactobacillus bulgaricus*. These are the corner stones upon which the success or failure of yoghurt processing hinges.

Although our knowledge regarding the growth and biochemical performance of yoghurt lactic cultures in cow milk has been well established there is paucity of information on this aspect in milk of other species like buffalo. Attempts have been made to obtain information on the ability of lactic cultures in the preparation of three types of yoghurt namely, plain yoghurt, fruit yoghurt and sweetened yoghurt by the procedure indicated in the flow sheet.

### Processing

Cow and buffalo milk samples are individually steamed for 30 min. cooled to a temperature of 43°C and then inoculated at 3% level with *Sir thermophulus* and *l.b. bulgarous* an equal proportions (I:1). The contents are mixed thoroughly and filled in glass bottles covered with lids or aluminium foil caps, transferred to water bath maintained at 42°C±0.5°C. After incubation for 3.0-3.5 hrs when the coagulum is formed, the bottles are removed from water bath, cooled at 30°C for 1/2 hr and transferred to refrigerator for overnight storage.

**Fruit/Sweetened Yoghurt** — **Plain Yoghurt**

**Milk (cow buffalo) (Perform compositional test)**

**Standardisation (A-C)** — **(A) Adjust fat (2-3%)**
**(B) Add NFDMS (2%)**
**(C) Add Gelatin (0.5%)**

**Stir**

**Homogenisation**

**Heat Treatment** — **(Steaming for 30 minutes)**

**Stir**

**Add Sugar (5-6%)- Inoculation with Yoghurt starter (3%)** — **S.thermophilus+1.. bulgaricus (1:1)**

**Stir**

**Add Fruit Pulp (15-20%)**

**Stir**

**Incubation** — **(45°C for 3.5 hrs.)**

**Cooling (20°C) & quality evaluation (1-2)**

**1. Subjective Tests (Sensory Evaluation)**
**A. Body**
**B. Texture**
**C. Flavour**

**2. Objective Tests (Laboratory Analysis)**
**A. Chemical**
**B. Physical**
**C. Microbiological**

**Storage at 5°C**

## PROCEDURE FOR THE MANUFACTURE AND QUALITY EVALUATION OF PLAIN/SWEETENED/FRUIT YOGHURT

## CHEDDAR CHEESE FROM COW MILK

Cheese is one of the most important dairy products in the world market. The growth rate in production of cheese is increasing steadily the world over. It provides one of the best methods of conserving and preserving milk solids. The standard method for its production is as follows:

### Manufacturing Method

1. Selection of milk : Fresh, good quality milk, free from antibiotics and preservatives.
2. Selection of starter : A good, active and uniform starter is essential.
3. Clarification and Standardization of milk: Casein/fat ratio (CF)-0.7.

4. Pasteurization : 63°C 30 min or 72°C 15 sec.
5. Cooling to 30°C.
6. Adding starter (LF-40) at 30 C: 1% by wt....0.
7. Adding rennet when titratable acidity of milk incresaed by 0.01 to 0.02% : 2.5g/100 lit. 45-60 min.
8. Cutting the coagulum whey acidity 0.1% 30 min.
9. Cooking : start at 30°C 15 min.
10. Cooking/stirring : finish at 38° C 90 min.
11. Draining, when whey acidity is 0.13-0.16% or about 0.02% than cutting acidity 10 min.
12. Packing the curd, after piling, acidity of whey should be 0.17 to 0.20% 10 min.
13. Cheddaring periodical turning of blocks and piling and repiling till whey acidity reaches 0.45 to 0.5% 2 hrs.
14. Milling............................. 10 min.
15. Salting : 2% by wt. of curd, in three applications. 30 min.
16. Hooping : After the salt has dissolved completely. 10 min.
17. Pressing : Max. pressure of 2 kg/cm² to be applied slowly. 30 min.
18. Dressing the cheese : The hoops are removed from the press, cheese cloth is pulled to remove all the wrinkles and pressed again overnight. 10 min.
19. Removing cheese from press, when the rind becomes free from openings. 12-24 hrs.
20. Drying the cheese : Dry at 10-15°C till dry, clean and bright surface is obtained. 2-5 days.
21. Paraffining : Dip the cheese in paraffin heated to 105° C.
22. Ripening at 8-10°C 4-8 months

## CHEDDAR CHEESE FROM BUFFALO MILK

In the manufacture of cheddar cheese from buffalo milk, the basic steps remain the same as applied to cow milk, however, certain modifications have to be introduced to get desirabe product. Out of the three methods recommended (Czulak, Burde and Presalting) the last one results in superior product. The salient features of Presalting method are described as below:

1. The standardized (C/F, 0.7) and pasteurized (63° C/30 min) Buffalo milk is cooled to 28°C followed by addition of common salt @ 1% with thorough mixing.

2. After 15 min. an active starter culture (LF-40) is added @ 2.5%. Supplementation of regular culture with 0.5% *Lcasei* enhances flavour development. After about 10 min. Hansen's calf rennet powder (2.5 g/100 lit) is dissolved in tap water (20 times) and added to milk with thorough mixing. Substitution of calf rennet with microbial rennet, viz. Modilase, Noury and Marzyzme have stimulatory effect on flavour development.

3. After setting (50-55 min.) the curd is cut with 1.4 cm knife. Precaution should be taken to judge the exact cutting time. Delay in cutting results in a tough coagulum which hampers uniformity of the cubes and higher losses in whey due to breaking up into small particles.

4. The stirring is started after 10-15 min. of cutting and the curd is cooked to 35-36°C in 40-45 min. After proper cooking the curd is left in whey undisturbed for 5-10 min. and then whey is drained. The curd expels moisture at a very fast rate and even a delay of 10 min. in drainage of whey was found to result in excessive drying and hardening of cubes, which ultimately led to tough body and mechanical openness in the pressed cheese. Hence, draining has to be quick and cooking time of 1 hr to be critically observed.

5. Higher piling during cheddaring helps obtaining good texture at the end. It is essential to develop a good texture resembling chicken breast type during cheddaring to ensure proper milling, salting, pressing and rind formation.

6. After pressing, green cheese blocks are transferred to cold storage for drying. The temperature of cold storage should be maintained preferably between 10-15°C. After proper drying generally in 2-3 days, the cheese blocks are paraffined. It is recommended to ripen the cheese for about 3 weeks followed by completion of curing at 8-10°C.

## MOZZARELLA CHEESE

Mozzarella cheese originated from buffalo milk in Italy. It is a soft, white, unripened, plastic curd cheese with bland but mildly acidic flavour. It has special melting and stretching characteristics. It is mainly used in preparation of bakery products like pizza. Recently, the production of mozzarella cheese is increasing in our country. Its manufacturing method is shown as below :

1. *Selection of Milk* : Fresh, good quality milk, free from antibiotics and preservatives. Buffalo, Cow or mixed milk can be used. Originally made from whole raw milk, it can now be made from pasteurised milk, partially skimmed milk.

2. *Selection of Culture* : A good, active, uniform culture containing, *S. lactis*

*S. thermophilus* and *L. bulgaricu* is often used. Also *S. thermophilus* and *L. bulgaricus* in the ratio of l:l can be used.

3. Clarification and standardization of milk to any desired fat level, mostly 3.2%.

4. Pasteurization : 72°C/16 second.

5. Cooling to 31-23°C.

6. Addition to starter at the rate of 0.5-2.0%.

7. Addition of rennet @ 20 ml. or 2.5 g/100 lit. after the acidity has in creased by 0.02% to give a coagulation time of 25-30 min.

8. The curd is cut and left undisturbed for 10-15 min. followed by cooking slowly upto 38-39°C for 30-45 min.

9. Whey is drained off and the curd is allowed to ripen to an acidity of 0.65 to 0.70%.

10. The curd is cut into pieces and stretched in hot water (82-85°C) for proper development of body and texture.

11. The curd is moulded by filling hot, plastic curd into hoops.

12. The moulded cheese in water at 10°C for 1/2 to 1 hr for hardening.

13. The cheese blocks is then transferred to a 16-20% brine solution at 8 10°C for sufficient time to allow 1.6% salt in cheese.

14. Dry off the cheese for about an hour and pack in PVDC film or laminated pouches (moisture and airtight) preferably under vacuum.

## COTTAGE CHEESE

Cottage cheese is a soft, unripened variety made from skim-milk to which cream and salt may be added. It is pleasant, mild in flavour. It is a good sourceof quality protein and low in calories which is highly suitable to those conscious of over weight. Its manufacturing method is shown as follows :-

1. Selection of milk: Fresh, good quality milk, free from antibiotics and preservatives.

2. Selection of starter : A good, active and uniform starter is essential.
3. Standardization of milk : SNF of milk to 9.0% by fortifying with skim milk powder.
4. Pasteurization 63°C/30 min. or 72°C/16 sec.
5. Cooling : 30 ± 1°C.
6. Addition of Calcium Chloride @ 10g/100 lit.

| | | |
|---|---|---|
| 7. Addition of starter culture @ 6% | | 0 |
| 8. Addition of rennet @ 0.04g/100 lit. | | 75 min. |
| 9. Cutting of curd at whey acidity 0.5% | | 240 min. |
| 10. Cooking start | | 15 min. |
| 11. Washing of curd : | First wash Temp. 27°C. | 10 min. |
| | Second wash Temp. 17°C | 10 min. |
| | Third wash Temp. 8°C | 10 min. |

12. Creaming of curd with dressing containing 18% fat.

## PROCESSED CHEESE

Processed cheese is made from natural ripened cheeses. Cheese of different age is blended together and processed into a final product with pleasant flavour and smooth body and texture. The basic objective of processing is to blend natural cheese, water emulsifying salts into a homogenous mixture and pasteurise to obtain an end product which has sufficient fluidity for convenient packging and which posseses long keeping quality. As per PFA process cheese should contain not more than 47% moisture, not less than 40% fat on dry matter basis and not more than 3% common salt and emulsifiers. Its manufacturing technique is as follows :

### Manufacturing Method

1. **Selection of Cheese** : The selection is determined chiefly by age, acidity, flavour, body, texture and composition of lots of cheese available. It is recommended that in order to obtain best quality product, the cheeses should be at three different stages of ripening :

a) Current these 25% not over 1 month old.

b) Short held cheese 50% about 3 months old.

c) Aged cheese 25% 6 months or more.

2. **Cleaning, Shredding and Mixing** : The paraffin and other non-edible portion of natural cheese is trimmed off. The trimmed cheese is then ground.

3). **Selection of Emulsifier** : Emulsifying agents are used to prevent the separation of cheese into its three main Constiuents (fat, protein and water) during processing and also to improve the body and texture of finished product. The most common emulsifiers used are sodium citrate and disodium phosphate. Normally they are added at the rate of 2%. They may be added to the cheese during grinding or melting.

4. **Processing** : The purpose of actual processing is to blend the cheese and added substances into a homogenous mixture, to pasteurise it and to attain sufficient fluidity for convenient packaging. This is accomplished by heating and stirring and by addition of suitable emulsifying salt and water.

The cheese is pasteurised in a steam jacketed kettle fitted with double action agitator. The ground cheese remains crumbly until a temp. of abour 49°C is reached. Beyond this point the cheese becomes sticky, stringy and plastic and may effectively retain or reincorporate the fat without the addition of emulsifying agent. The heating and stirring are continued until final temp. is reached (75°C) followed by packaging in presterilized containers. The sealed tins are gradually cooled to 22°C. The packages should not be kept under refrigeration until they have attained this temperature.

## SURTI CHEESE

Surti cheese is a form of cottage cheese popular in Western India. So far this delicious cheese has been made only under cottage industry using indigenous utensils and wicker baskets. The present technique is described for commercial production of Surti Cheese and make possible to utilise and surplus milk in market milk plants more economically while ensuring the quality of Cheese comparable to that made by the indigenous process. The major production steps are as follows :

## Steps in processing

**Steps in Processing for surti cheese**

↓

Standardised raw milk 1:0.7 casein fat ratio

↓

Pasteurised 71°C/5 min.

↓

Inoculated Culture 0.04% at 35-36°C

↓

Rennet added 7.5/100 lit. milk

↓

Incubated 30 min. at 35-36°C

↓

Set Curd Cut

↓

Salt added 2.5%

↓

Whey drained

↓

Curd cubes filled in hoops

↓

Applied pressure by weight

↓

Turn curd block every 1.2 hr.

↓

Turn 2 times

↓

Remove weight

↓

Cut into slices and pack with whey

↓

Stored at 4-6°C

## Composition

Average Composition of Surti Cheese : Fat 13% Moisture - 72% TS 28%

## SOFT CHEESE

### Steps in Processing

Varieties made from cow milk are quite popular in Western countries. In the context of popularising this type of highly nutritive dairy product in India NDRI has studied and standardised one soft sweet cheese variety. The major steps for the production of sweet cheese are described below:

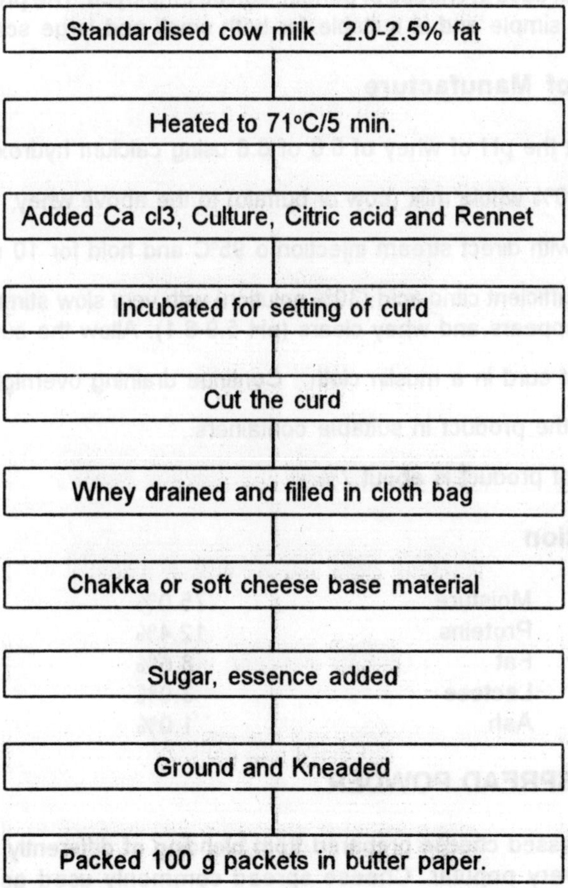


### Composition

The composition of Sweet Cheese may range from fat 12-16%, TS-35-40% moisture - 60-65%. Sugar 25-30% by weight of soft cheese and essence 1 ml per kg of mix.

## RICOTTA CHEESE FROM DIFFERENT WHEY SYSTEMS

Ricotta cheese originated from Italy is a soft, granular variety having a bland taste. Its physico-chemical characteristics are midway between those of Chhana and Khoa. Ricotta cheese in its fresh formis quite suitable for the partial replacement of Chhana and Khoa for the manufacture of a number of sweets (such as Sandesh, Burfi, Gulabjamun, etc) and Indian culinary dishes (such as stuffed potatoes, tomatoes, etc). No special equipment is needed for the manufacture of Ricotta. In fact, the same equipment which is used for production of case in cheese or paneer, can be employed. The process involved is relatively simple and is suitable for both small and large scale handling

### Process of Manufacture

1. Adjust the pH of whey of 6.6 of 6.8 using calcium hydroxide.
2. Add 10% whole milk (cow or buffalo) to the above whey,
3. Heat with direct stream injection o 95°C and hold for 10 minutes.
4. Add sufficient citric acid (30% solution) with very slow stirring till granular curd appears and whey clears (pH 5.9-6.1). Allow the curd to settle.
5. Collect curd in a muslin cloth. Continue draining overnight.
6. Pack the product in suitable containers.
7. Yield of product is about 7%.

### Composition

| | |
|---|---|
| Moisture | 75.0% |
| Proteins | 12.4% |
| Fat | 8.6% |
| Lactose | 3.0% |
| Ash | 1.0% |

## CHEESE SPREAD POWDER

Processed cheese prepared from blending of differently aged cheese varities is very popular. Cheese spread commonly used as a paste for sandwitches, is another cheese based product. However, certain sections of the population in India are not used to strong cheese flavour. Taking into consideration the requirement of mild flavoured and smooth textured cheese product, a method for the manufacture of cheese spread powder has been developed.

## Steps in Processing

The cheese spread was prepared by blending equal proportion of young (2 months old) and fully ripened (7-8 months) lots of buffalo milk cheddar cheese. Minced cheese alongwith predetermined amounts of moisture, butterfat, salt and emulsifying agents (trisodium citrate and trisodium orthophosphate in the ratio of 5:1) at 2.0% were mixed thoroughly in a cheese processing kettle. Gelatine (0.3% in dissolved form), flavouring agents like tomato juice, onion juice etc (optional at 5.0% of the blend) were added at 60°C. The temperature was raised at 71°C with constant stirring and preservations (nisin or scorbic acid) were added at the rate of 0.02%. The hot slurry was then homogenised in a single stage homogeniser at 100 kg/cm$^2$ and collected in presterilised lacquered tin cans, covered with lids and seamed immediately. The seamed cans were kept in hot water at 80°C for 5 minutes and then kept at room temperature for 24 hours and transferred to cold store.

Besides the ready to use form, cheese spread was also prepared in the free flowing powder form. For this purpose, the homogenised cheese slurry without any added preservatives was adjusted to 35% total solids and then spray dried at an inlet air temperature of 160°C and outlet air temperature of 100°C. The dried product was packed in lacquered tins under nitrogen packing.

## Composition

| Particulars | Cheese spread | Dried cheese spread |
|---|---|---|
| Fat | 21.50% | 56.00% |
| T.S. | 42.50% | 96.50% |
| Moisture | 57.50% | 3.50% |
| Salt | 1.00% | 2.00% |

The samples of cheese spread powder were acceptable upto 6 months storage at room temperture.

## PANEER

Panner is primarily acid coagulated milk solid used as an ingredient in cooking of vegetables in Northern India. Mostly, buffalo milk is used for the production of paneer. The best quality product is made from milk of 6.0% fat content. Packed paneer could be stored for 3 days without any loss of freshness when refrigerated.

## Steps in Processing for Paneer Manufacture

Standardised buffalo milk 6.0%

↓

Heated to 82°C/5 min.

↓

Cooled to 70°C

↓

Coagulated by 1% citric acid.

↓

Whey drained out.

↓

Milk solids filled in hoops.

↓

Pressed by weight

↓

Weight removed

↓

Cut into pieces.

↓

Dipped in chilled water for 1-2 hrs. at 4-6°C.

↓

Chilled water drained out.

↓

Packed into desired weight and stored at 4-6°C.

### Composition

The average composition of paneer may be fat - 26% moisture 55% and T.S. 45%.

## CHHANA MAKING

It is recognised that good quality chhana for rossogolla cannot be made from buffalo milk as the balls do not swell during cooking as those made from cow milk chhana. The rossogollas prepared from buffalo milk chhana also showed shattering during cooking and dark colouration.

The comparative study of the physico-chemical properties of chhana from cow and buffalo milk and their admixture was carried out to develop an appropriate technology for production of good quality chhana from milk and to minimize losses of milk solids in whey. The factors studied in this investigation included kind of milk-type of coagulant and temperature and pH of coagulation.

### Steps in Processing

The coagulation of cow milk at pH 5.7 resulted in very soft chhana with high moisture and increased losses of milk solids in whey while at pH 5.1, channa was soft and cohesive with minimum losses of milk solids in whey. Buffalo milk followed a similar trend although the effect was less pronounced. Temperatures above 70°C caused grainy texture and increased hardness while lower temperature produced highly sticky chhana which was difficult to drain. Compared to lactic acid, citric acid produced more cohesive chhana with lower losses of milk solids in whey. Best quality chhana from cow milk was obtained by coagulating milk at 70oC at pH 5.1 using 2% citric acid solution as coagulant. This combination of factors for buffalo milk coagulation produced less cohesive chhana. Treatment of buffalo milk with 0.05% sodium citrate before boiling, dilution of milk with 25% water, and coagulation with 1% citric acid solution improved the softness and product can be comparable with cow milk chhana.

## DRIED CHHANA

Chhana, also called paneer in some regions of the country, is an Indian whole milk product which constitutes an important base for sweets like Sandesh and Rossogolla. However, it is mostly prepared on small scale by the disorganised sector of dairy industry for obvious reasons of its low shelf life and difficulties in transportation. Since, it was felt that drying of chhana and consequent increase in its shelf life would help in the growth of this product a method for production of dried chhana, as detailed below, was standardised. The dried chhana is suitable for preparation of Sandesh.

### Steps in Processing

Raw cow milk is standardised to 4% fat, given first boil in the coagulation vessel and then lowered to 80±5°C. The emulsifier tri-sodium citrate @ 0.02% of milk is added as an aqueous solution. The milk is kept covered and left undisturbed for 2±1 hrs. Then coagulating acid (1-2% solution of lactic or citric acid) is added to milk with gentle stirring. At the end of coagulation (pH-5.4), the contents are poured over a piece of muslin cloth stretched over another vessel. The coagulated milk solids stay on the top of the cloth while the whey passes through it.

The Chhana is transferred to milk can and calculated amount of water is added as to give 19-21% total solid in the slurry. After premixing with the held of a plunger, the mix is further passed through micro-pulveriser to give a smooth slurry. The slurry is dried in a spray-drier using an inlet air temperature of 195±5°C and an outlet temperature of 100±2°C. The dried product is promptly removed from the drying chamber, cooled, packaged and stored at room temperature.

## Composition

The average percentage chemical composition of dried chhhana is: Moisture 3.5%, Fat 41.6%, Protein 46.3%, Lactose 4.2% and Ash 4.4%. The storageability of chhana powder is 2 and 4 months at 20±2°C under air tight and nitrogen gas packing respectively. The powder is dehydrated back to chhana for preparation of Sandesh.

## PREPARATION OF SANDESH FROM CHHANA

The channa is first kneaded, then ground sugar added @ 30% of chhana and mixed with it. The mix is baked on a very slow fire, stirring all the time. Crushed cardamon, if desired, is added towards the end. When mixture starts forming balls, it is poured into tray and left for cooling and setting. It is then cut in desired size and decorated with pista and silver paper.

## FROM DRIED CHHANA

The dried chhana is rehydrated with warm milk in the ratio of l:l of weight, left for 15 minutes, then Sandesh is made from this chhana as above.

## SRIKHAND

Srikhand is a fermented and coagulated delicacy popular in the Western part of the country. The technology of Srikhand begins and the production of Dahi, from which whey is drained out and a semi-soft material is produced after mixing sugar and essence.

## Steps in Processing to make Srikhand

Standardised raw milk (3.5-4.0% fat)

↓

Heated to 71°C/10 min.

↓

Cooled to 25-30°C

↓

Innoculated with Culture @ 1%

↓

Incubated 15-16 hrs. at 25-30°C

↓

Dahi

↓

Whey drained out by hanging in a cloth

↓

Srikhand base or Chakka

↓

Sugar and cardamom added

↓

Sieving and Kneading to a smooth paste

↓

Cooled and stored at 4-6°C

## Composition

The composition of Srikhand may range from : fat 5-15%, moisture 40-45% and sugar 45-55%. The product is expected to keep at least for two weeks when refrigerated.

## KHOA

The dairy plants in India usually face the problem of using surplus milk during winter. It has now been demonstrated that the organized dairies can profitably divert part of this surplus milk and some of the standard quality milk for the manufacture of Khoa. The problem concerned with limited shelf life of Khoa due to microbial spoilage and chemical deterioration was the major impediment in the adoption of this product by the organised sector. Small scale sector engaged in the manufacture of Khoa was also confronted with the limited shelf life of Khoa leading to uneconomic marketing situations. Investigations were, therefore, conducted to standardise a process for the manufacture of Khoa with long shelf life using readily available packaging materials and permitted chemical additives.

### Increasing the Shelf Life

The non-availability of tin sheets and prohibitive costs of tin containers warranted us to find out a suitable substitute. The flexible packaging materials such as food grade polyethyene, parchment paper, and laminated pouches were used. Khao samples packed in sterilized four ply laminates afforded the same protection as tin containers. The product kept in good condition upto 13 days at 30°C. Khao should be lifted while hot (70°C) in these containers and sealed employing all the aseptic precautions.

The shelf life of Khoa was increasded to 75 days at cold room temperature of 7°C. Incorporation of 0.02% butylated hydroxy anisole (by weight of fat content in Khoa), addition of 0.2% potassium sorbate and mixing of nisin (100u/gm) improved the shelf life of Khoa upto 20 days at 30°C and 125 days in the cold stores. The studies showed that incorporation of potassium sorbate and nisin considerably enhanced the shelf life of Khoa without impairing its flavour and other marketable characteristics.

## UTILIZATION OF BUTTTERMILK & SOYABEAN FOR THE MANUFACTURE OF SOFTY ICE-CREAM

Buttermilk is an important by-product of butter industry. It is estimated that nearly 0.92 million tons of buttermilk is produced annually in the organised dairy sector. There is, however, little evidence of its economical utilization. The composition of buttermilk is quite similar to skim milk, except for little higher concentration of fat, mainly phospholipids. The utilization of buttermilk for popular frozen desserts such as softy ice-cream will conserve the solids of milk.

Buttermilk powder is considered to be an excellent replacement for the skim milk powder in the ice-cream mixes, Soyabean is unique, in that it produces more protein per acre than any other protein source and its protein contains, in nearly optimum proportions, all the essential amino acids except sulphur containing AA's. Two kgs of soy flour contains as much protein as 14 litres of milk. Soyabean acts as a moistrue retainer, emulsifier, stabilizer binder, as well as enhances the shelf life of products and improves product appearance. It helps food processors to produce generally high quality food at comparatively lower production cost.

The present study was, therefore, undertaken to develop a softy ice-cream using buttermilk and soyabean. It was expected that the product would not only be cheaper but also nearly equal in nutritional value.

## Steps in Processing

The process, as standardized, entails in presoaking the soybean overnight in sodium bicarbonate solution, blanching and dehulling. The cotyledons thus obtained were ground in various ratio with buttermilk. Fat and sugar were then added and the mixture was pasteurised and homogenised. The mix was cooled and aged, and then frozen in a softserve ice-cream freezer.

## Composition

In order to get the most acceptable product, various combinations of soybean: buttermilk solids were tested, such as 1.1:1, 1.3:1, 1.5:1, 2:1 etc. The first combination was liked most and the second was the next best. Amongst additional source of vegetable oils, three oils/fats locally available were tried, these were coconut, groundnut oil and hydrogenated vegetable fat. Of these, the last did not impart any of its own flavour to the product and, therefore, was found to be the most acceptable. Softy ice-cream was thus made using 1.3:1 of soybean and buttermilk solids, using hydrogenated vegetable fat for subsequent trails. By varying the fat, SNF and sugar concentration, the most acceptable combination was found which was respectively, 9%, 12% and 15%.

It was observed that addition 0.1, 0.2 or 0.3% sodium alginate brought about unusually large increase in the viscosity of the mix, which was not appreciated by judges. It was then felt that there was no need for addition of a stabilizer in the soybean-buttermilk softy ice-cream.

The final softy ice-cream mix was spray dried and stored in tin (packaged with/without nitrogen) and polyethylene containers and stored at 30°C±1°C and 5°±2°C to assess the shelf life of the product. From this storage study, it was observed, from physico-chemical and sensory properties (of reconstituted, softy ice-cream) that the product packaged in tins could be stored for 9 months at 30°±1°C and more than 12 months at 5°±2°C. While in polyethylene bags, the product had acceptable quality for 5 months at 30°±1°C and 9 months at 5°±2°C.

## COFFEE/TEA WHITENERS

In metropolitan cities, a large amount of milk is used for the preparation of coffee/tea. Use of coffee/tea whiteners for this purpose will encourage the use of fluid milk for other purposes, such as feeding children, elderly group of people, etc.

Method has been standardised for the manufacture of two types of coffee/tea whiteners - one which is low in fat content(LFCW), is specially meant for the group users, who like to restrict calorie intake and other with high (HFCW) which is meant for the replacement of cream for whitening of coffee/tea.

### Equipment Used

1. Mixing vats
2. Plate heat exchangers
3. Homogenizer
4. Spray drier
5. Packing equipment

### Steps in Processing

1. Various ingredients (cream, sodium caseinate, glucose syrup, GMS, CMC, Trisodium phosphate and sodium citrate) are mixed in the desired proportion as indicated in the table. Total solids are adjusted to 35 per cent.

2. The mix is preheated to 80°C/10 min. and then homogenised (1st stage 175 kgs/cm$^2$ and 2nd stage 35 kgs/cm$^2$).

3. This mix is spray dried, employing drying air inlet temperature of 210°C and outlet temperature of 95°C. The moisture content of the dried product should be about 3 per cent.

4. The percent is packaged under nitrogen and stored preferably below 15°C.

## Composition

| Constituents (%) | LFCW | HFCW |
|---|---|---|
| Fat | 12.4 | 48.6 |
| Sodium caseinate | 37.0 | 20.8 |
| Glucose syrup | 37.0 | 20.8 |
| GMS | 5.6 | 3.8 |
| GMC | 1.2 | 0.7 |
| Tri-sodium phosphate | 1.2 | 0.7 |
| Tri-sodium citrate | 2.5 | 1.4 |

## GULABJAMUN MIX POWDER

The existing method for the preparation of gulabjamun is suitable at cottage scale. Khoa is generally used as a base which causes wide variations in flavour, texture and chemical composition of the sweet. Good quality khoa may not be available all the year round in different parts of the country. In order to overcome these difficulties, a ready-to-form gulabjamun mix powder formulations based on skimmed milk powder with six months shelf life has been developed.

The formulated mix consists of skim milk powder (roller) 434 g; butter-fat/vanaspati 150 g; maida 260 g; suji 150 g; baking powder 15 g and powdered cardamom 0.1 g (alternatively 2 cup SMP, 3/4 cup maida, 1/3 cup butterfat, 1/2 cup suji, 1 tea spoonful baking powder and a pinch of cardamom). All these ingredients are properly blended and packed in a polyethylene bag. The mix powder stays well for about 6 months at room temperature and can be conveniently used in the preparation of gulabjamun at any time.

The production of gulabjamun starts with the preparation of sugar syrup. Equal proportions (on weight basis) of water and sugar are boiled till a syrup of about 60% concentration (one thread consistency) is obtained. The dirt and impurities gathering at the surface are removed with the help of a perforated laddle and the syrup strained through a nylon/muslin cloth.

For the preparation of dough and balls, mix instant gulabjamun mix with required quantity of water (50-55 ml for 100 g mix) and knead well until smooth body is obtained.

Normally 100 g instant mix yields 13 balls. The performed balls are covered with a wet cloth to arrest evaporation of moisture and case hardening until they are transferred to the frying pan. Deep fry the balls in refined vegetable oil or hydrogenated fat (Ghee optional) at 125-130°C for 20 minutes till the colour becomes brown. Drain the excess fat from the surface of the fried balls and finally transfer them into the sugar syrup maintained at 60°C. Soak for atleast 2 hours. Pack the sweet in presterilised polystyrene containers and serve hot.

## BUTTER POWDER FROM BUFFALO MILK

Free flowing butter powder (80% fat) could be manufactured (see flow sheet) from buffalo milk solids. The product having the most desirable characteristics is made by taking buffalo milk cream and mixing in it reconstituted skim milk powder so that the final total solids content including 1% each of sodium citrate and glycerol monoste rate is 40% and contains 80% fat and 16.5% SNF (on dry basis).

The mix (optionally containing 0.015% BHA) is heated (65°C), homogenised (141 & 35 kg/cm$^2$), pasteurised (75°C for 1 min), ripened with LF-40-a mixed lactic starter culutre (at the rate of 1%) to obtain 0.12 to 0.16% lactic acidity and spray dried at 82°C outlet and 175°C inlet air temperatures. The butter powder should be immediately cooled (to 50°C) and coarse sieved to break any lumps culture, the butter powder could be dry blended with 0.5% fine sod.aluminium silicate to increase the flowability if desired. The finished butter powder contains 80% fact, 193.% SNF and 0.7% moisture.

In order to obtain a butter spread for the powder, 19% moisture (i.e. approx. 4 parts powder +1 part water) need be added and the powder reconstituted to a semi solid homogenous mass. If salt is desired in the spread, it should be added to the water before reconstituting the powder. To achieve the desirable colour and flavour, 0.5% annatoo butter colour and 4 drops of Butardol per 100 g spread respectively may be added.

When stored in tin cans or polyethylene bags, the butter powder keeps well for over one year at refrigeration (5°C).

## FLOW SHEET FOR THE PRODUCTION OF BUTTER POWDER FROM BUFFALO MILK

| Added / Remarks | Process | Added |
|---|---|---|
| Skim milk powder | CREAM | |
| Dispersed in water | Blending | Emulsifier, anti-oxidant, sodium cirate |
| | Total solids adjusted to 40% | |
| | Preheating (65°C) | |
| | Homogenization (141+35 kg/cm²) | |
| | Pasteurization (75°C for i min.) | |
| Starter culture | Ripening (to 0.12-0.16% LA) | |
| | Spray Drying (82°C outlet, 175°C inlet air temp.) | |
| | Cooling | |
| Free flowing agent | Dry Blending | |
| | Sieving | |
| | Packaging | |

## UTILIZATION OF SOUR BUFFALO MILK FOR THE MANUFACTURE OF EDIBLE CASEIN

Various process parameters for the manufacture of edible casein from fresh 0.2, 0.3 and 0.4% T.A. buffalo milk have been standardized. Optimised processes are : Neutralize the sour milks with $NaHCO_a$ to 0.063-0.090% T.A. Heat the fresh and neutralized sour milk to 50-60°C and separate them once through the triprocess machine. Pasteurise the skim milk from fresh milk byHTST method and that from neutralized sour milks by heating to 80°C. Precipitate the skim milks from fresh, 0.2, 0.3 and 0.4% T.A. milks at 35-36, 36-37, 38-39 and 40°C and 3.7, 4.0, 4.2 and 4.6 pH respectively. Give three washings to the precipitates, each 15 min. contact time with wash water at 35-37°C. Maintain the pH of wash water for first two washings at 4.0 and of last one at neutral. Press the washed precipitates overnight and shred them uniformly in trays. Dry the product in cabinet tray dryer with hot air circulation at 60-65°C. All the edible casein samples met ISI standards. Yield on skim milk basis from fresh 0.2, 0.3 and 0.4% T.A. milk was 2.83, 2.59, 2.53 and 2.40% respectively. All the samples graded good to excellent on flavour evaluation. PER of fresh milk edible casein was 2.49 and that of sour milk products, 2.02-2.15. All the casein samples showed 12 months of storageability at 30°C in polyethene bags. Sodium and calcium caseinates were also prepared from different edible casein samples. Edible caseins from different acidity milks did not significantly affect pH, solubility index, sinkability and wettability significantly of sodium and calcium caseinates. Calcium caseinates had significantly greater solubility index, sinkability, flowability and bulk density compared to sodium caseinates. Emulsifying and whipping properties of sodium and calcium caseinates were observed to be unaffected with the different acidity milk edible caseins. Sodium caseinate was observed to possess better emulsifying properties and whipping ability than calcium caseinate.

## FROZEN YOGHURT FROM SOYABEAN & BUTTER MILK

The fermented milk products like acid philus milk, Bulgarian buttermilk, Mazum, Kefir, Kusiss, Yoghurt and other related products occupy important place and are consumed regularly all over the world. Popularizing frozen yoghurt that too from soyabean and buttermilk in India will not only help to improve the nutritional status of the Indian population but also would be a possible substitute for ice-cream which is luxury item due to its high cost.

The balanced soyabean cotyledons were ground with buttermilk to get slurry havying soy-colids to buttermilk solids ratio 1:1. The slurry (11% T.S.) was homogenised at 175 and 35 kg/cm$^2$ at 65°C, pasteurised at 85° C and inoculated with L. Bulgarians+S. Ther. @ 3% after addition of gelatin as stabilizer. It was then incubated at 40°C for about 5 hours. The curd so obtained was added with 12% sugar in the form of syrup and synthetic pineapple flavour then mixed well and frozen. The product was hardened and stored. The product had protein 4.45% fat 2.4% ash 0.48% carbohydrate 18.26% and T.S. 25.6% and a good acceptability.

## ICE CREAM POWDER

Ice cream is a delicious, wholesome, nutritious, frozen dairy food. It has occupied a unique place in the diet of the people in the West and is gaining steady in popularity all over India.

In India near16 60 per cent of milk production is from buffaloes. In the lean season, raw milk is in short supply and most of the surplus milk available in the flush season is used for preparing butter, ghee and skim milk powder. There is considerable demand for ice cream in the summer season (incidentally it is also the lean season of milk production) which can be coveniently met by driversifying a part of the milk during the flush season for the manufacture of ice cream powder.

Use of gelatin as stabilizer in the manufacture of dried ice cream mix yields ice cream having coarse body and texture characteristics and foam melt-down. Moreover, use of gelatin hurts the sentiments of a majority of the people who are vegetarians. Ice cream powder prepared using polysaccharide stabiliser of vegetable origin, and which on reconstitution with water yields ice cream of smooth body and texture characteristics has been developed recently at NDRI, Karnal.

## Steps in Processing

The ingredients used are fresh milk/skim milk, skim milk powder, pregelatinized potato starch as stabilizer and Tween 80 as emulsifier. The composition of the ice cream mix is adjusted so that is contains only 25 per cent of the total sugar before spray drying. All the ingredients are weighed so that the mix contains 17.1 per cent fact, 14.2% SNF, 5.3% sugar, 0.7% pregelatinized potato starch and .07% Tween-80. Pregelatinized potato starch is mixed with little amount of sugar and added to milk/skim milk and heated, agitation. The required amount of cream is adjusted to 50°C. Skim milk powder mixed with the remaining sugar (to facilitate dissolution of powder particles) is added to the mixture with vigorous stirring.

The contents are filtered through a muslin cloth and Tween-80 added to the mixture. The temperature of the contents is raised to 70°C and the mix homogenized at 176 kg/cm$^2$ and 35 kg/cm$^2$ on the first and second stage respectively. The mix is then pasteruized at 68°C/30 min, cooled to 5-10°C, aged for 16 hours and spray dried using an inlet air temperature of 73°C and an atomizer speed of 16500 r/min. The powder obtained is dry blended with refined sugar in the ratio 100 parts : 41 parts (by weight). The finished product contains 1.75% to 1.96% moisture, 24.84% to 25.13% SNF, 31.04%, 31.43% fat, 40.60% to 41.2% sugar, 1.3% pregelatinized potato starch and 0.13% Tween-80.

The powder has a shelf life of 9 months when packed in laminated polyester/polyethylene packages and stored at 30°C.

For preparation of ice cream ; one part of powder should be mixed with 1.6 parts of potable water at 45°C cooled and frozen in a batch freezer to about 100% over run. 1 kg of powder then reconstituted in 1.6 kg of water yields 36 cups (125 ml) of ice cream.

The powder can be advantageously used by the industry and small scale manufacturer to cater to the demand for ice cream in the summer season. Small scale manufacturers who need to invest in a homogenizer and pasteurizer can prepare ice cream having the desired body and characteristics at a reasonably low cost.

## AN IMPROVED INFANT FOOD FORMULA

An industrial process has been developed that permits manufacture of an infant formula which resembles human milk in the ratio of protein : fat : carbohydrates. The protein content in formula is adequate to fulfill the entire nutritional requirements of infant during the first year of the life, but without overloading the renal functions (which the presently available infant formulae do). This also permits extension of available bovine milk for the manufacture of higher quantities of infant foods, as well as reduce costs. Further modification also permits adjustment of whey protein to casein ratio, thus stimulating human milk more closely.

The fat content has been modified so as to incorporate nutritionally superior middle chain glycerides from vegetable sources. Significantly, this aspect has both nutritional and cost advantages. Process has been also standardised for the manufacture of malto dextrins through starch hydrolysis suitable for incorporation into the formula in order to adjust the ratio of calorie contributing nutrients.

Another outstanding feature of the formula developed relates to the bifidus stimulating property. Animal bioassay as well as clinical studies carried out under medical supervision have demonstrated *Bifidobacterium bifidum* can be implanted in the intestinal tract through feeding of formula developed. In this manner, the improved formulation is expected to favour superior utilization of minerals, synthesise "B-Complex" vitamins in intestine, play a detoxification role in chronic liver diseases and provide protection against interopathogenic infection.

## INCREASING THE SHELF LIFE OF GHEE

Ghee (Clarified butter oil) is the most important indigenous dairy product of India. About 33% of the total milk produced in India is converted into ghee. This product undergoes oxidative deterioration at ambien temperature. The oxidation of unsaturated fatty acids producers hydroperoxiders and their subsequent breakdown products viz. aldehydes, ketones, low molecular weight acids and oxyacids, cause the development of off-flavours in ghee. To prevent oxidation, the Food Adulteration Rules as amended in 1976, allow the addition of 0.02% by weight of butylated hydroxy anisole (BHA) and butylated hydroxytoluene (BHT) either singly or in combination in ghee. The continuous use of chemical antioxidants has been reported to cause taratogenic and carcinogenic effects in small animals and primates. In ancient times, edible vegetable sources such as betel and curry leaves were added to butter during clarification into ghee for unknown reasons. It is likely that they would improve the shelf life and flavour of ghee besides being safe to the health of the ghee consumers. An attempt was made to study the effects of betel and curry leaves with butter during clarifications at different concentration on flavour and antioxidative properties of ghee. Ghee samples treated Bha+BHT at 0.02% concentration curry leaves at 0.5, 0.8 and 1% and betel leaves at 0.2, 0.5 and 1% were stored at 30 Degree C and the samples were examined for peroxide value, iodene value, free fatty acidity Butyrorefractometer reading and flavour.

## Changes during Storage

The initial peroxide value of ghee (0.00) did not increase up to 30 days of storage at 30°C. The control samples without antioxidants showed a steep rise in peroxide value after 60 days of storage. Ghee samples prepared with 1% curry leaves were most resistant to oxidation upto 135 days of storage and betel leaves at 1% level were second most potent as natural antioxidant. However, ghee samples treated with betel leaves at 1% concentration proved to be most acceptable and stable even after 147 days of storage at 30°C.

The extent of hydrolysis of ghee during storage was measured by titration for free fatty acidity. After 30 days of storage, there was a progressive increase in the free fatty acid contents of all the ghee samples. The control sample of ghee after 147 days of storage of 30°C showed an increase in FFA by more than 100%. Betel leaves at 1.0% conc. provided maximum protection against the hydrolysis of ghee. Sunderajan obseved that plant leaves contain phenolic compounds like hydroxychavicol, eugenol and some amino acids like, Aspargine, glycine, serine, aspartic acid, glotamic acid, threonine, alanine, proline and tryptophan. It is quite likely that these compounds might have served as potent antioxidants.

Although all the samples of ghee during storage showed varying degree of peroxide formation and increase in free-fatty acidity, only slight reduction in iodine value of treated ghee samples was observed. The initial iodine value of 35.9 in control sample of ghee got reduced to 35.6 after 147 days storage. The changes were non-significant in samples treated with higher doses of betel and curry leaves. Ghee samples treated BHA and BHT also offered similar benefits.

Ghee samples prepared with betel and curry leaves inhibited lower B.r. value. It is possible that the natural compounds which get dissolved in ghee during clarification might have lowered the B.R. values. Ghee samples were also evaluated for appearance, texture and flavour. All the samples of ghee were rated excellent at the beginning of the experiment. The judges preferred ghee samples treated with betel and curry leaves. These samples were awarded highest scores for flavour and colour. The samples treated with BHA and BHT were rated as ordinary.

**It can be concluded that betel leaves and curry leaves at 1% concentration can easily act as replacers for BHA and BHT for extending the shelf life of ghee.**

## THE CHEMICAL COMPOSITION OF MILK HUMAN, COW, BUFFALO, GOAT AND SHEEP

| | Human | Cow | Buffalow | Goat | Sheep |
|---|---|---|---|---|---|
| Fat | 3.75 | 4.9 | 6.6 | 4.5 | 6.0 |
| Total solid | 12.57 | 13.7 | 15.8 | 13.5 | 16.3 |
| Solids-not-fat | 8.82 | 8.8 | 9.2 | 9.0 | 10.3 |
| Lactose | 6.98 | 4.1 | 5.2 | 4.7 | 4.9 |
| Total Protein | 1.63 | 3.4 | 3.9 | 3.5 | 4.8 |
| Ash | 0.21 | 0.7 | 0.7 | 0.8 | 0.8 |
| VitaminC mg/100ml | 40.00 | 2.5 | 2.8 | 3.5 | 5.5 |
| Vitamin A(I.U.)/100ml | 189.90 | 148.9 | 175.6 | 137.4 | 189.7 |

## STATUS OF MAJOR MINERALS IN BUFFALO MILK & COMPARISON WITH COW MILK*

| Sr. No. | Minerals | Concentration (mg/100g) | | Soluble % (Through rennet coagulation | |
|---|---|---|---|---|---|
| | | Buffalo Milk | Cow Milk | Buffalo Milk | Cow Milk |
| 1. | Calcium | 175.50± 1.15 | 123.3 | 20.93± 0.939 | 35.0 |
| 2. | Magnesium | 19.25± 0.381 | 11.1 | 50.64± 0.843 | 70.9 |
| 3. | Sodium | 44.63± 0.402 | 58.0 | 95.10± 0.439 | 94.0 |
| 4. | Potassium | 103.00± 0.913 | 140.0 | 95.15± 0.322 | 96.2 |
| 5. | Phosphate | 97.60±1.28 | 95.1 | 32.98±0.657 | 44.10 |
| 6. | Citrate | 163.60±2.60 | 176.0 | 85.72±1.52 | 91.5 |
| 7. | Chloride | 62.84±0.933 | 104.5 | 99.51±0.454 | 100.0 |

* Results on cow milk from Davies & White (1958, 60)

## STANDARDS FOR DIFFERENT CLASSES AND DESIGNATIONS OF MILK AS PER P.F.A.

| Class of Milk | Designation | Locality | Minimum Milk fat | Percent Solid not fat |
|---|---|---|---|---|
| Buffalo Milk | Raw, Pasteurised, Boiled, Flavoured & Sterilised | Haryana | 6.0 | 9.0 |
| Cow Milk | Raw, Pasteurised, Boiled Flavoured & Sterilised | Haryana | 4.0 | 8.5 |
| Goat or Sheep milk | Raw, Pasteurised, Boiled Flavoured & Sterilised | Haryana | 3.5 | 9.0 |
| Standardised Milk | -do- | All India | 4.5 | 8.5 |
| Recombined Milk | -do- | All India | 3.0 | 8.5 |
| Toned Milk | -do- | All India | 3.0 | 8.5 |
| Double Toned Milk | -do- | All India | 1.5 | 9.0 |
| Skimmed Milk | Raw, Pasteurised, Boiled Flavoured & Sterilised | All India | not more than 0.5% | 8.7 |

## STANDARDS OF VARIOUS MILK PRODUCTS AS PER P.F.A.

| | | |
|---|---|---|
| 1. | Cream | Milk fat 25.0% (Minimum) |
| 2. | Dahi or Curd | Dahi shall have the same minimum percentage of milk fat and milk solids-not-fat as the milk from which it is prepared. |
| 3. | Paneer/Channa | Moisture 70.0% (maximum)<br>Fat - 50.0% of the dry matter (Minimum) |
| 4. | Skim Milk Paneer/Channa | Moisture - 70.0% (Max.)<br>Fat - 13% of the dry matter (max.) |
| 5. | Cheese (Hard) | Moisture 43.0% (Max.)<br>Fat - 42.0% of the dry matter (Min.)<br>Stabiliser/emulsifier/NISIN - 0.1%. |
| 6. | Processed Cheese | Moisture - 47.0% (Max.)<br>Fat - 40.0% of the dry matter (min.)<br>Salt - 3.0% (Max.) |

| | |
|---|---|
| | Stabiliser/Emulsifier - 4.0% (max.) or Sorbic Acid - 0.1 or NISIN - 0.1% |
| 7. Ice Cream | Fat - 10% (min.) 8.0% (min.) if containing fruits or nuts<br>Protein - 3.5% (min)<br>T.S. - 36.0% (min)<br>Emulsifier/Stabiliser - 0.5% (max.) |
| 8. Milk ices/Lollies | Fat-2.0% (max.)<br>Protein - 3.5% (min.)<br>T.S. - 20% (min.)<br>Stabiliser/emulsifier - 0.5% (max) |
| 9. Condensed Milk Unsweetened Evaporated Milk | Fat - 8.0% (min)<br>Total Milk Solids - 26.0% (min) |
| 10. Condensed Milk Sweetened | Fat - 9.0% (min)<br>Total milk solids - 31.0% (min)<br>Cane sugar - 40.0% (min) |
| 11. Condensed Skimmed Milk Unsweetened (Evaporated Skimmed Milk) | Total Milk Solids - 20.0% (min)<br>Milk Fat - Not more than 0.5% by weight |
| 12. Condesned Skimmed Milk Sweetned | Total milk solids 26.0% (min)<br>Cane Sugar 40.0% (min)<br>Milk fat - Not more than 0.5% by weight |
| 13. Whole Milk Powder | Fat - 26.0%<br>Acidity - 1.2% (L.A.) Max.<br>Solubility 98.5% (Spray) 85% (Roller), S.Index 2.0(ml) spray & 15.0 ml (Roller),<br>Moisture - 5.0% (Max.),<br>BHA - 0.01% Coliform 90/g. S.P.C. 50,000 (g) Sod. Citrate 0.3. |
| 14. Skimmed Milk Powder | Milk Fat - 1.5% (max.)<br>Moisture - 5.0% (max.), Max/S.P.C. - 50,000/g.,<br>Acidity-1.5% (max) E.Col. =90/g.,<br>Sod. Citrate-0.3%<br>S.P.C. =50,000/g. Coliform - 90/g. |

The minimum Solubility Index of the Product

| | Roller Dried | Spray Dried |
|---|---|---|
| Solubility percent | 85.0 | 98.0 |
| Solubility Index | 15.0 ml | 2.0 ml. |

15. Partially Skimmed Milk Powder

| | | |
|---|---|---|
| Moisture | - | 5.0% (max.) |
| Fat | - | It should be between 1.6 to 24.0% |
| Acidity | - | 1.5% (I.A.) (max.) |
| Sod. Citrate | - | 0.3% |
| BHA | - | 0.01% |

The Minimum Solubility Index of the Product

| | Roller Dried | Spray Dried |
|---|---|---|
| Solubility percent | 85.0 | 98.5 |
| Solubility Index | 15.0 ml | 2.0 ml. |

16. Khoa — Moisture - 28.0% (max.); Fat - 20.0% (min.)

17. Table Butter — Fat-80.0% (min); Salt - 3.0% (max); Curd - 1.5% (min); Diacetyl - 4.0% ppm (max)

18. Deshi Butter (Cooking): Fat - 76.0% (min)

19. Ghee — Butyro-refractomer - 40.0 to 43.0 reading at 40°C Min. Reichert value-28.0% of free fatty acids as 3.0 Oleic acid (max. limit) % of moisture (max. limit) 0.5.

20. Infant Milk Food — Moisture - 5.0% (max); Fat - 18.0% (min); 28.0% max. total carbohydrates - 35.0% (min); Milk proteins - 20% (min.) Ash - 8.5% (max); S.P.C. - 50,000/gm.; S.I.-2.0 ml (Spray)

21. Soy-Whey Food — Fat - 12%; Protein - 23%; Carbohydrate - 50.5%; Ash - 5.0%; Moisture - 1.5%; (Fortification with Vitamins & iron).

22. Coffee Complete — Instant coffee - 7.2%, S.N.F. - 20.0%; Sugar - 39.0%; Water - 25.0%; Total solids - 75.0% Milk Fat - 8.5%

23. Tea Complete — Fat-13.0%; S.N.F. - 31.5%; Sugar - 39.5% Tea solids - 14.0%; Moisture - 2.0%

## BACTERIOLOGICAL STANDARDS FOR GRADING MILK

| Grade | Standard plate count per ml/g | Methylene blue reduction time (Hr. Min.) | One hour Resazurin Disc No. | Presumptive coliform test |
|---|---|---|---|---|
| **Raw Milk** | | | | |
| Very good | Not exceeding 200,000 | 5 and above | 4 or higher | Absent in 0.01 ml |
| Good | 200,001 to 10,00,000 | 3 and 4 | - do - | - do - |
| Fair | 1 to 5 million | 1 and 2 | 3.5 and 1 | - do - |
| Poor | Over 5 million | 1/2 | 0.5 to 0 | Present in 0.01 ml |
| **Pasteurised Milk** | | | | |
| Satisfactory | Not exceeding 30,000 | - | - | Absent in 0.01 ml |

**(Acceptance Standards for raw milk for pasteurization based on MBR time). This is a suggestion to be followed**

| | |
|---|---|
| Summer | over 1 hr |
| Winter | over 2 hr |

**Recommended standards for payment of bonus for high quality raw milk based on MBR time.**

| | Summer | Winter |
|---|---|---|
| Payment of bonus | Over 2.5 hr | Over 4.5 hr |
| Penalty or reduction in price | Less than 1/2 hr | Less than 1 hr |

## Bacteriology Standards of Milk Products

| Product | Standard for satisfactory quality | | | |
|---|---|---|---|---|
| | SPC per ml/g (maximum) | Coliform count per ml/g (maximum) | Other tests | |
| 1 | 2 | 3 | 4 | 5 |
| 1. Sterilized milk | - | - | Spore count<br>Change in Titratable acidity | Max. 5 per ml<br>Max after incubation for 7 days 0.02% at 37°C |
| 2. Flavoured milk | | | | |
| a) Pasteurized | 50,000 | 10 | Phosphate test | negative |
| b) Sterilized | - | - | Spore count; | Max: 5 per ml |
| 3. Cream | | | | |
| a) Raw | 2,000,000 | 100 | - | |
| b) Pasteurized | 60,000 | - | Phosphate test | negative |
| c) Sterilized | - | - | Incubation at 30°C for 14 day | No change in flavour or appearance |
| 4. Ice Cream | 250,000 | 90 | Phosphate test | negative |
| 5. Butter | - | 10 | Yeast and mould count | Max 50/g |
| 6. Condensed milk (sweetened) | 500 | - | Yeast and mould | Max 10/g |
| 7. Evaporated milk | - | - | Incubation of tins for 14 days at 30°C | No bulging due to gas production |
| 8. Processed cheese | - | - | -do- | -do- |
| 9. Milk Powders | 50,000 | 90 | - | - |
| 10. Infant milk foods | 50,000 | 10 | - | - |
| 11. Malted milk foods | 50,000 | 10 | - | - |
| 12. Processed cereals weaning foods | 50,000 | 10 | - | - |

| | | | | |
|---|---|---|---|---|
| 13. Casein (Edible quality | 50,000 | 10 | Yeast & mould | Max. 50/g |
| 14. Vegetable protein infant food with milk, flavoured milk, malted skim milk food. | 50,000 | 10 | - | - |
| 15. Dried ice creaim mix sweet cream butter milk powder, partly skim sour milk powder | 50,000 | 90 | - | - |
| 16. Burfi | 30,000 | - | Yeast & mould | Max.10/g |

## Equipment Standards for satisfactory sterility

| | Max. standard plate count/litre of capacity (Rinse method) | Max. standard plate count/900 sq. cm. of surface (Swab method) | Frequency of checking |
|---|---|---|---|
| 1 | 2 | 3 | 4 |
| 1. Milk can/pail | 1,000 | - | One in every batch of 50 |
| 2. Milk bottle | 1,000 | - | Four bottles just before the addition of fresh lot of detergent |
| 3. Milk receiving tank/vats | - | 5,000 | Once every day immediately after the preparation of equipment for operation. |
| 4. Weighing bowl/ pan | - | 5,000 | Once every day immediately after the preparation of equipment for operation. |
| 5. Storage/holding transport tanks | - | 5,000 | -do- |
| 6. Batch Pasteurizer | - | 5,000 | -do- |
| 7. Plate heat exchanger | - | 5,000 | -do- |
| 8. Surface cooler | - | 5,000 | -do- |
| 9. Cotton filtercloth | - | 5,000 | Once every week |
| 10. Evaporator | - | 5,000 | Every time the equipment is cleaned for operation. |

| | | | |
|---|---|---|---|
| 11. Roller drier | - | 5,000 | -do- |
| 12. Bottle filler (Circulation method SPC of first litre of rinse coming out) 25,000 | | - | Coliform count not more 10 per litre. |
| 13. HTST Plate pasteurizer | -do- | - | -do- |
| 14. Homogenizer | 25,000 | - | Every time the equipment is cleaned for operation. Coliform: Max. 10/lit. |
| 15. Cream separator clarifier | -do- | - | -do- |
| 16. Spray drier | -do- | - | -do- |
| 17. Ice cream freezer | -do- | - | -do- |
| 18. Walls, floor etc. | - | - | Free from visible dirt and mould growth. |
| 19. Milk crates | - | - | -do- |

## Recommended Programme of Bacteriological Quality Control at the Dairy Plant

| | Name of test | Frequency of testing | Remarks |
|---|---|---|---|
| | **A. Raw milk supplies at the receiving platform** | | |
| | *(i) Unchilled milk* | | |
| 1. | Organoleptic quality (Smell) | Each can or lot of milk daily | Unsatisfactory lots to be rejected or segreated |
| 2. | Titratable acidity | Unsatisfactory and doubtful samples | For confirming the results of (1) above. |
| 3. | Sediment test | Each individual milk supply to be tested once a week | Provides information about hygienic quality of milk for encouraging better quality by payment of bonus. |
| 4. | Methylene blue reduction test. | | |
| 5. | Standard plate count | Each individual milk supply to be tested at least once a fortnight. | Information regarding source of contamination for advisory work. |
| | *(ii) Chilled milk* | | |
| | (Test 1 to 6 as above) | -do- | -do- |
| 7. | Temperature | Each supply of milk daily | Information regarding conditions of storage. |
| 8. | Psychrophilic count | Each supply of milk once a fortnight | -do- |

## B. Pasteurized milk

### *(i) Pasteurised milk before despatch*

(At least 3 samples of bottled and 2 samples of can milk selected at random)

| | Test | Frequency | Remarks |
|---|---|---|---|
| 1. | Temperature | Daily | Information regarding condition of storage. |
| 2. | Phosphate test | Daily | To test efficiency of Pastcurisation. |
| 3. | Coliform test | Daily | To test post pasteurization contamination. |
| 4. | Standard plate count | Daily | To check general quality of pasteurized milk. |
| 5. | Keeping quality at room temperature. | Daily | -do- |

### *(ii) Returned milk (one or two bottles taken at random)*

| | Test | Frequency | Remarks |
|---|---|---|---|
| 1. | Temperature | Daily | As above |
| 2. | Standard plate count. | Daily | As above |

## *C. Line testing (once a fortnight)*

***Test samples of milk drawn at the following stages for standard plate count.***

1. Raw milk (Dump tank)
2. Freshly pasteurized milk
3. Storage tank
4. Bottle filler
5. Bottle of milk) Before despatch
6. Cane of milk) -do-

## *D. Other tests*

1. Testing detergents for alkalinity
2. Testing chlorine solution for available chlorine
3. Checking temperature of pasteurization (Thermograph).

# Chapter - 9

## *Packaging of Dairy & Milk Products*

With substantial increase in India's milk production, which is likely to be around 60 million tonnes in 1995-96, the availability of milk and dairy products is rapidly increasing. Most of this increased milk production has been in the rural pockets of the country, while the major markets markets for dairy products are in the cities. So, the need for its transportation over long distances has become a necessity. Milk, being a highly perishable product, utmost care is needed on its preservation during storage, handling and transportation. This is also true of dairy products like butter butter, ghee, yoghurt, dairy sweets, etc..

Milk spoils fast at high ambient temperature in the presence of oxygen and other contaminating agents present in the atmosphere. Similarly, other dairy products also have a relatively short shelf-life, and major factors responsible for their spoilage are temperature, oxygen and bacteriological activity. Hence primary requirements of preservation of most the dairy products are to store it under as cool a temperature as possible, hygienically handle it and protect it from oxygen and bacterial contamination.

Organized milk marketing in India made its beginning in 1950 with bottling of milk in Mumbai, followed by Calcutta and other cities. Glass bottle is a multi-trip package for milk, and on an average each bottle performs as many as 91 trips to the consumer before it goes out of circulation. Bottles are filled on automatic filling machines at a speed of 90 bottles per minute approximately and sealed with aluminium foil. Use of multi-trip glass bottles makes prior cleaning of bottles filling necessary. Weight of empty glass bottle is also high, resulting in higher frieght cost. It is estimated that cost of bottling milk in glass bottles is around 35 paise per litre.

Today, though bottling of milk is still prevalent in many dairies, it is fast being replaced by plastic pouches. This was a new concept in that unlike multi-trip reusable bottles, plastic bags were single trip containers. Economics worked in favour of these pouches as it saved need for returning the empty containers to the dairies and its subsequent washing and cleaning before refilling for the next trip. In Mumbai, the Aarey Dairy was the first in the country to experiment with plastic pouches more than two decades ago. Today, even in smaller cities, milk pouches have become due to the convenience it offers. A good consumer response to milk pouches paved the way for the technological changes needed in the industry. Initially, the form-fill-and-seal (FFS) machines used for packaging of milk in pouches were imported but these machines are now manufactured indigenously by a number of units in the country. Availability of plastic films needed for the pouches also increased during this period, with a large number of entrepreneurs taking up the production of multi-layer films for milk packaging.

## Form Fill and Seal (FFS) System

In this technique, raw materials i.e. milk and plastic film (commonly LDPE) are fed into the form-fil-and-seal (FFS) machine. First, the plastic film is formed into a tube, sealed along its length and then at bottom, thus forming a pouch. It is filled with the milk and then sealed at the top. All these steps constitute a single continuous operation in the same machine and thus, milk is handled more hygienically. The use of ultraviolet light inside the filling cabinet of the machine minimises bacterial contamination. The machine runs at a speed of about 40-60 pouches a minute. The cost of a one litre pouch ranges between 40-50 paise.

For sweetened milk, multilayer LD/LD film is also used with outer film being opaque and inner one in black colour, which helps in reducing transmission of light inside the pouch. Co-extruded multilayer LDPE/LDPE film is becoming more popular, as it helps in material saving due to its better barrier properties. Generally, 65 micron thick film is used, as against 75 micron of monolayer film. The cost of FFS machines ranges from Rs. 1,00,000/- to Rs. 8,50,000/-.

It is estimated that for a new dairy which needs to distribute 1.5 lakh litre/day of liquid milk, it is more economical (70 per cent in capital investment) to set up LDPE pouch filling system than glass bottle filling equipment. Also, in terms of operational cost, LDPE pouches are economical. A one litre pouch costs approximately 30-40 paise. In 1994-95, about 45,000 tonnes of film was used for packaging 15 million tonnes of liquid milk.

## Aseptic System :

This system has converted a highly perishable product like milk into a grocery item. The Tetra Paks are now available even with a grocery store. In this package, milk remains good for more than ten days without a need to store it in a refrigerator. This has become possible because of ultra high temperature (UHT) treatment at 140°C for 2-3 seconds of milk prior to packaging and then aseptically packing it in a carton. The packaging material (carton) is also sterilized with hydrogen peroxide. The sterile material is first formed into a tube shape, filled with milk and sealed in tetrahedron/brick shape, all done in aseptic conditions.

The machinery needed for this system is more capital intensive. The package used is LDPE-coated paperboard made locally. The tetra pack uses 170 gms paperboard laminated with 10 micron LDPE from outside and 70-75 micron LDPE from inside. The cost of 1000 ml. Tetra Pak is around 200 paise. Though this is higher than the bottle and plastic pouch system, consumers particularly in cities find it more convenient since they can buy their milk requirement once in a week or use it as an emergency stock due to its extended shelf-life.

## Bulk Vending Booth

Some dairies are trying a system where milk is store in FRP (Fibre Reinforced Plastic) tanks with automatic dispensing device. This system is catching up as it reduces milk distribution cost.

To facilitate wide distribution cost, wide distribution and to reach different economic groups, milk is sold through bulk vending FRP tanks, bottles/ sachets, tetra pack, etc. In 1985-86, the Delhi dairies alone distributed on an average close to 9 lakh litres of milk per day through 300 bulk-vending booths, 340 insulated containers, 245 polypack milk retail outlets and two unrefrigerated mini booths. Data on latest status is not available till date of the time of writing of this book.

## Packing of Shrikhand :

With the increased availability of milk, need for marketing milk related products have also grown. Though many of these products have been traditionally made in most of the Indian homes, their commercial availability became a reality one due to the emergence of better packaging techniques. The Baroda Dairy has installed a machine in which High Impact Polystyrene (HIPS) sheets are heated and formed into cups or trays and then filled with shrinkhand which is heat-treated in order to extend its shelf life prior to filling. Sealing of the cup or tray with polystyrene film or aluminium foil coated with paper and wax follows immediately to give a continuous flow of nicely packed and sealed cups of shrikhand. The entire process of forming, filling and sealing is done as a single continuous operation, thus minimising the risk of contamination.

Plastic cups are moisture-proof, leak-proof and convenient to use. Weight of the HIPS varies from 5 gms to 35 gms and thickness between 0.3mm and 0.65 mm. These cups have capacities between 100 ml to one litre and cost in the rage of 35 paise to Rs. 2.50 with two colour printing.

## Butter :

It consists primarily of about 80 per cent milk fat, 15 per cent moisture and in table butter upto 3 per cent common salt. Because of high moisture content, butter is susceptible it mould growth. Mould growth is inhibited by exclusion of air while packaging by tight wrapping or by avoiding head space in teh container. Packaging must protect the product for preservation of its flavour, body, texture, appearance, moisture and colour. Packing of butter therefore should have resistance to fat, oxygen, moisture, foreign odour and light. In India, butter is packed in bulk as well as retail packages. For bulk packaging there is no standard method, and stainless steel and in plate containers are used. For retail packaging, there is some degree of standardization.

There is an Indian Standard (IS: 2034-1961) which gives specifications for tin cans of 200 gms and 400 gms capacity. It specifies tinplate thickness of 0.24 mm and 0.17 mm respectively, and minimum tin coating of 17 g/m$^2$, besides many other requirements. Tinplate containers are the best for product protection, but owing to their increasing cost, very little quantity of butter is packed in the tin containers.

Flexible packaging materials like vegetable parchment paper or grease proof (GP) paper, aluminium foil, and folding board cartons which together give similar protection to the product are more commonly used. There is an Indian Standard: 7161-1973 which gives specifications for vegetable parchment paper has a good wet strength which is in contact with butter. Generally, paper of 45 gsm and above and aluminium foil above 0.009 mm thickness are used.

Butter being highly susceptible to foreign odour, one has to be very careful while choosing adhesive and printing inks used in the manufacture of the laminates. There is also another IS: 8113 - 1976 for primary cartons for packaging of 100 gms, 200 gms and 250 gms butter slabs.

Cartons protect butter while handling, after packaging in primary wrapper, in the distribution system. Since butter is stored in the refrigerator, cartons may be waxed with about 10 gsm wax on each side or laminated with a plastic film, though it is not mandatory. As most plastics have poor fat resistance, plastic films are not recommended for long term storage. However, for short term storage and packaging, many vendors of butter use LDPE or HDPE film, along with a paper overwrap.

## Ghee

It is usually 100 per cent fat, obtained by boiling butter at 110°C till all water is evaporated. For long term storage, stainless steel containers or tinplate cans are desirable. Multilayer co-extruded films of LDPE/HDPE are being increasingly used for short term storage. Nylon/Surlyn based laminates are also being experimented. Generally, pastic pouches are filled on automatic FFS machines. However, if the sealing surface is contaminated with the product, sealing of the pouch becomes difficult. Packaging material should have good fat resistance and barrier properties against oxygen and moisture. IS: 11352-1985, specifications for flexible packs for the packing of edible oils and vanaspati could be a useful reference.

## Cheese

Is essentially a product with high fat and moisture content. Therefore, package used for cheese should prevent moisture loss and ingress of oxygen to prevent oxidation and mould growth. It should also have fat and grease resistance and be able to prevent growth of micro-ogranisms. Oxygen is eliminated by packing cheese in hermetically sealed containers in vacuum or in inert gas atmosphere. Processed cheese is usually paked in aluminium foil in cubes with different shapes. Tinplate cans are used for 200 gms and above quantity. PVDC coated plastic films are suitable for cheese packaging as the provide good oxygen and moisture barrier properties.

## Dried Milk Powders :

Since whole milk and infant milk powders are rich in fat (20-30 per cent), packaging material should provide protection against oxygen and moisture. Generally, tinplate cans are used, and packaging is done under nitrogen cover to replace air by nitrogen in the headspace of the tin cans. Skim milk powders have very low fat content and as such a good moisture barrier material is adequate for short term storage. Multiwall papers sacks with one polyethylene liner (IS: 1165-1975) is used for bulk packaging. Lined cartons are used for retail packaging. The multiwall bags can be tested for their transport worthiness according to IS: 7028. Recently, some skim milk powder has also been sold in polyethylene bags of 1 kg. Even plastic bottles of HDPE are being tried for 200 gms and 400 gms of powder.

## Ice Cream

Is made by mixing milk cream, sugar, stabilisers and flavours. Since ice-cream is stored at very low temperatures, packaging material used for ice-cream should have low temperature stability. It should also provide protection against contamination, ease of opening, case of disposal, and it should also be amenable to attractive printing. Wax coated paper board is commonly used in the form of cups and cartons. IS: 7162-1973 gives specifications for waxed cartons for packaging of 300,500 and 1000 ml of ice-cream. The standard also covers packing of 100 ml chocobars. Generally, paperboard made from virgin chemical wood pulp, coated with wax, is used. Bars are generally wrapped in vegetable parchment paper. High impact polystyrene (HIPS) cups are also becoming popular.

The empty plastic cup does not support the growth of bacteria like paper packaging. Further, their comparative strength and rigidity lend themselves to its use in automatic filling equipment which is especially true of small packs of 50 and 100 ml, required in large numbers.

From the marketing point of view, possibility to get white, translucent or even transparent cups with lids or sealable closures makes it more attractive. It terms of cost effectiveness, small sizes of plastic cups are approximately 20 per cent costlier than paper cups. However, taking into account, the obvious advantages of thermoformed containers, with hygiene, extended shelf life and attractive package, the plastic packaging will get increasingly popular.

## Packaging of Indigenous Products:

Pedas are first wrapped in grease proof paper and then placed in cartons lined with GP paper. Products like lassi (sweetened butter milk) in 200 ml plastic pouches packed on FFS machine is a recent introduction in the Indian market. Sweet curd is packed in HIPS cups, while local vendors used LDPE bags for loose sale of fresh curd. There is not much of organized packaging of Khoya, and materials used vary from banana leaves to grease-proof paper and polyethylene films.

# Chapter - 10

## *Bread Making*

Bread is a mixture of wheat, flour, sugar, shortening, salt and water made into doughs, raised by the action of the added yeast, followed by fermentation and final baking. It is used as a staple food in many countries and varies in size, shape, texture, taste and composition from one country to another. The name of the variety therefore, denotes either the area of itss origin or the presence of certain sspecial ingredients e.g. French, Italian, Vienna, Dutch, Crunch, Raisin, Rye etc.

In India the most popular bread is usual white sandwich bread; and some other varieties e.g. milk bread, brown bread, spiced bread, fruit bread and sweet bread are being produced in a few large cities that too in very small quantities. In this chapter the mainly white sandwich bread will be described which rules the Indian markets followed by some discussion about some special breads also

**Figure Bread Sliced and Packed**

## PROCESS OF MANUFACTURE

The very first step is the making of dough. The various ingredients are correctly weighed or measured ass per the formulation and then the dough is prepared. the following composition may be used for a 400 gms. loaf of bread :-

| | |
|---|---|
| Flour | 271.42 gms. |
| Sugar | 4% of flour |
| Salt | 1.5% of flour |
| Dry yeast | 0.75% of flour |
| Vegetable oil | 1.5% of flour |
| Mixi | 0.33% of flour |
| Bread Improvers | 0.32% of flour |

*Another formulation for preparation of bread dough as follows :-*

| | |
|---|---|
| Flour | 100 kgs. |
| Water | 64 kgs. |
| Sugar | 4 kgs. |
| Salt | 2 kgs. |
| Shortening | 4 kgs. |
| Dried baker's yeast, or | 0.5 kg. |
| Compressed yeast | 1.2 kgs. |
| Skimmed milk powder | 4 kgs. |
| Mineral yeast food or dough conditioner | 350 gms. |

### Dough Mixing

The ingredients as per the formula are mixed by hand or machine e.g. Kneader. For best results ingredients should be mixed in certain order and thoroughly. There are two methods for mixing viz. (**1**) Straight Dough Method (**2**) Sponge Dough Method. In the Straight Dough Method the ingredients are mixed at one time. The dry ingredients are mixed with the liquid until thoroughly dissolved, thhe flour is also mixed in until most of the liquid has been absorbed and the lumpy mass is formed. The yeast solution prepared separately is added, and the dough mixing is completed. If a small amount of fat is also used then it is added after the yeast is mixed in and the dough is allowed toi develop. If oil is used, it should be added at the begining of mixing with the water. Mixing is continued until the mass becomes smooth and the back of the bowl is cleared of dough. the machine speed should be medium. The mixing operation usually takes about 20 to 30 minutes.

In the Sponge Dough Method, two mixing periods and two fermentation periods are used. In the first mixing period a sponge is prepared with 50 to 75% of the flour to be used, 60 to 70% of the water, malt if any, part of the sugar and added minerals or yeast food. The sponge is placed in a warm place to rise; in large plants a special fermentation room is used. Sponge time will vary with water temperature, amount of yeast, and shop temperature; usually it varies between 3 to 4.5 hrs. Sponge ready when it starts falling after maximum rise. At this drop point the structure of the sponge becomes extended to such an extent by the gas produced during fermentation, that it breaks and part of the gas escapes. The sponge is then mixed with remaining ingredients in a machine and sponge dough is thus obtained.

## Fermentation

The mixed dough is placed aside for allowing the dough to ferment. The fermentation room should preferably be a separate one being maintained at about 32°C and 75% relative humidity. In small factories this control may not be possible, then the dough should be kept covered so that evaporation of moisture from the dough is eliminated thus crust formation does not take place. The dough should not be too warm or too cold, and should be protected from air drafts. In cold weather the amount of yeast in the dough should be increased. Also fermentation will have to be increased. In hot weather yeast amount and fermentation time are reduced. During fermentation part of sugar gets converted to the form in which it can serve as food to the yeast. Starches are converted into sugar that produce carbon dioxide gas and alcohol. This expands the dough. Enzymes condition the gluten and make it mellow. Acidity increases due to the conversion of part of alcohol to acetic acid. Combined effect of alcohol and acid make the gluten elastic. Gluten forms thin walls which retain the gas. The dough matures until it reaches maximum spring and elasticity.

When the dough has risen, it is tested by inserting fingers into it; if the finger marks close very slowly the dough is ready for punching. In punching the ends and the sides of the dough are folded from one side of the trough to the other; it ensures even temperature throughout the dough, release of excess carbon dioxide, introduction of fresh oxidation resulting in better fermentation, and mechanical development of gluten. The first punching is done about 50% fermentation, and second after 80% fermentation has taken place. Punching and knocking back are the same thing.

## Sealing or Dividing

After punching or knocking back the dough is in a fully inflated condition as it approaches optimum ripening. The dough is divided into uniform pieces of the desired weight, because for uniform baking the size and weight of each loaf must be the same. Dividing may be done by hand also using scrappers and weighing the pieces to the required weight. Dividing should be done quickly and accurately otherwise dough pieces will become overfermented, as fermentation is continuing. This operation is also called scaling because the pieces of dough are scaled to the exact weight desired. Hand scaling takes much time, in larger plants a Dividing Machine is used for this purpose which is adjusted to produce dough pieces of desired weight. During baking about 12 to 13% weight loss occurs due to evaporation hence for a 400 gm. loaf the dough piece should weight about 450 to 455 gms.

The divided dough pieces have irregular and raw edges and will give irregular shaped breads. Hence they are rounded by tucking in the edges. This provides a skin around the dough to hold the gas in, eliminate the stickness of the dough and also reduces the quantity of dusting flour required during shaping into loaves.

## Intermediate Proofing

The period of time, usually 8 to 12 minutes, allowed to the rounded piece of dough between the time it is divided and the time when it is put in pans is called Intermediate Proof. This period relaxes the dough. During this period fermentation continues and the pieces become gassy and the gluten relaxes making the dough handling easier.

## Moulding

Each dough piece is shapped properly so that it can rise in the pan giving desirably shaped loaf of bread. This gives better crumb structure also. This may be done by hands or with help of a machine known as moulder. Pressure put on the dough during moulding should not be too little and also should not be so high as to tear or damage the dough structure. Too much dusting flour should not be used in this operation otherwise it will result in separation of the rolled dough and will lead to open seams, which will open in baking resulting in cripples on the finished bread.

## Panning

Moulded dough units are put into bread pans which have been sufficiently but not excessively greased. The seam side of the dough piece should be placed down so that it will become the bottom side of the loaf and danger of seam opening during baking is avoided. The dough pieces are placed in the centre of the pan.

## Pan Proofing

The dough pieces are given final proof in a properly controlled room. The relative humidity and temperature of the room are maintained at 80-85% and 37oC respectively. This pan proofing step is necessary to allow the loaf to expand before final baking. the stresses and strains imposed upon the structure of the loaf during moulding, are eased during this step as expansion goes on, until the loaf is at its desired maximum, and the loaf is ready for the oven. If the room has low humidity the dough surface will dry resulting in a loss of bloom on the crust of the baked loaf. If air draughts are there then grey patches will form on a hard crust. During baking mishappen loaves may also result. Excessive humidity and high temperatures of the proofing room will result in tough leathery crusts, a srinkled surface and holes under the top crust of the loaf.

To determine whether the loaf is properly proofed, the load is pressed lightly with finger-tip; if the impression made by the tip of the finger remains or fills up very slowly then the loaf is considered to be proofed. If the imprint does not remain and fills out, the loaf is still too light and compact and should be further proofed. Usually, 60 to 70 minutes time is sufficient for proofing. In small plants proofing rooms with controlled conditions are not available.

## Baking

Baking is the final stage in the production of bread, it changes the dough to an appetising, digestible product. the dough units in the pans are put in an oven which has been heated to 225°C. This heats the dough mass very quickly. Yeast activity increases rapidly until it is destroyed at 60°C. Carbon dioxide produced during fermentation expands; this raises and alcohol does not allow the interior dough temperature to rise above 100oC. Sugar, starch and other ingredients of the exposed dough surface caramelise forming the crust and give it the required colour; this happens at about 135°C. Inside the loaf enzymes remain active even at about 75 to 80°C producing sugars that remain internally to sweeten the crumb; at this temperature proteins coagulate, the dough structure is set, and all activity within the loaf ceases.

The oven temperature and the time required to bake a loaf of bread will depend on the size and shape of loaf and total sugars in the dough at baking time. Too high oven temperature will form the crust too quickly resulting in a bread of loose shape, loose crust and unbaked interior. Oven humidity is also important; if humidity is too high then bread with tough leathery crust and a glazed unattractive shine shall be obtained; and if humidity is too low the bread obtained shall be similar to that obtained from too hot oven. Large units require a longer baking time than small breads. Loaves doughs require higher oven temperature and bake faster than rich doughs Hard type bread and rolls require a well baked crust.

## Final Stages

After baking the bread is cooled so that it does not dry excessively. the modern practice of slicing and wrapping makes this even more necessary, if it is not done then mould formation will take place. On cooling, due to the gelatinised starch and coagulated protein, the bread becomes stronger. Sliced bread is now-a-days in greater demand hence a bread slicer is used for the purpose. the sliced bread is wrapped in a waxed paper which is heat sealed.

## BREAD SPOILAGE

Staling of bread has been described elsewhere. 'Rope' and mould growth are the two most common types of bread spoilage. 'Rope' is a bacterial infection. Bacteria occur in flour yeast and sugar syrups and are not killed even during the baking process. When bread is held under warm conditions these bacteria produce an objectionable odor and sticky crumb. The name 'rope' is given to this kind of spoilage because when a bread of this kind of spoilage is pulled apart, threadlike strands form at the point of break. the second type of bread spoilage is due to mould or fungus. Mould spores come from air, machinery and the wax packaging paper.

To reduce the chances of bread spoilage the bakery premises should be kept clean. Good quality ingredients should be used and as far as possible contamination of dough with the dough or previous batch should be avoided. Everyday all the plant and equipment should be thoroughly cleaned. Spoilage can also be reduced by making the dough slightly acidic; this acidity may come from the lactic acid formed during fermentation of the dough or by additon of acetic acetic acid based on dough may be used for this purpose. If instead of acid vinegar is to be used then its quantity may be calculated according to its strength. 'Rope' and mould can also be inhibited by using 0.1% to 0.2% calcium propionate based on flour, for this purpose. Its effectiveness increases with increase in the acidity of the dough. Thus for greater effectiveness, longer fermentation may be carried out. In the sponge dough process calcium propionate should be added at the final mixing stage.

## PACKAGING OF BREAD

Sliced bread is usually packed in waxed paper. The main constituent of the waxed paper is paraffin wax, sometimes blended with suitable modifiers in order to improve the properties of the wrapper. The modifiers help provide better barrier against moisture, grease, oil etc. a more effective heat sealable bond, improved machineability, enhanced printability, increased gloss and scuff resistance. the base paper generally used for making wax paper is manufactured from the bleached sulphite titanium dioxide treated paper. The wax paper is usually muticoloured and printed paper bags, of special sulphite paper (32-40 gsm.), are used for wrapping bread; such bags are more economical than wax paper. Bread wrapped with wax paper is heat sealed.

## WHOLE WHEAT BREAD

Whole wheat flour has better dietary value than fine white flour. It is rich in natural vitamin and mineral etc. which are concentrated near the surface of the wheat grain. Bread made from whole wheat flour contains large bran flakes, coarse grain and more nutlike taste and flavour. Bread may be made from 100% whole wheat flour or it may be made with a blend of whole wheat flour and patent or fine wheat flour in requisite ratio.

*Following formulation may be used for this type of bread :-*

| | |
|---|---|
| Whole wheat flour | 2.55 kgs. |
| Bread flour, patent | 2.6 kgs. |
| Sugar | 0.4 kg. |
| Shortening | 0.2 kg. |
| Salt | 0.1 kg. |
| Yeast | 0.3 kg. |
| Milk powder | 0.2 kg. |
| Molasses | 0.15 kg. |
| Water | 3.2 kgs. |

The procedure of mixing is as follows. Sugar, salt, milk powder, molasses and water (2.4 litres) are mixed and dissolved carefully in right quantities. Yeast is dissolved in 800 cc. water separately. Flour is sifted without removing the bran flakes and is added to the previous mixture with stirring, to this yeast solution is added and the mixture is stirred until flour is absorbed and dough is formed. To this shortening is added and a smooth dough is developed. When dough works smoothly away from the kettle sides and balls up it may be considered to be properly developed. the dough is then fermented, during this fermentation it stiffens slightly as the bran absorbs additional moisture. the dough is punched once and allowed to rise again. the gluten in this dough is not as strong as that in white bread, thus over-fermentation should be avoided.

The dough is now divided as usual into 460 gms. round pieces (for 400 gms. loaf) and left to stand for 15 minutes. the mould and dusted pieces are put in clean, lightly greased pans. The units are proofed (3/4). The units are then baked in the oven at about 215°C. A small amount of steam may be allowed to enter the oven before loading the bread and during baking steaming may be continued until the crust starts to show signs of colour. Baking time for this type of

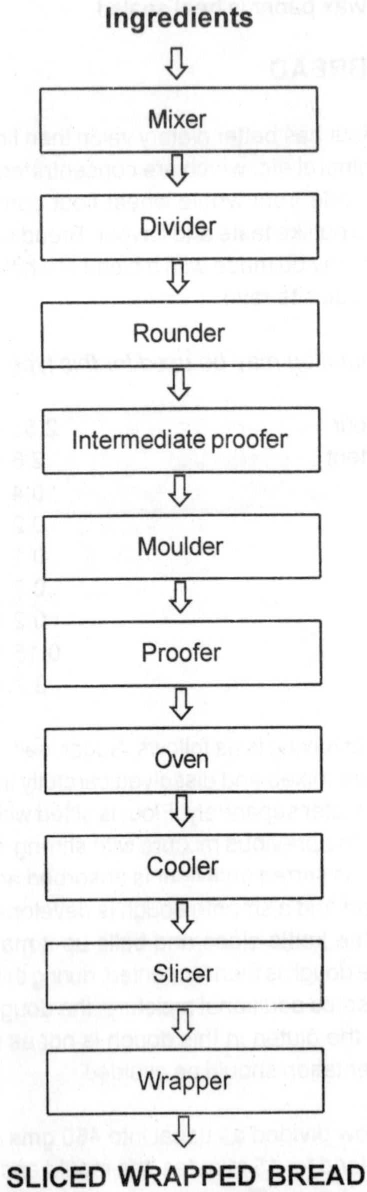


**Scheme for Bread Making**

bread is a bit longer than that for white bread. Usually a 400 gms. loaf requires about 40 minutes baking. Molasses keeps the loaf soft; dark molasses gives best colour and taste.

The formulation with the quantities of ingredients given above will yield about 19-20 loaves of 400 gms. each.

## RAISIN BREAD

Raisin bread is a specially bread containing raisin upto 50% of flour (by weight) and even more. Raisins are soaked in water before being mixed in the dough so as to bring them in equiolbrium with the moisture of the dough. Excess soaking should be avoided to prevent effusion of acid and sugar into the dough with consequent detremental effects and also not make them so soft as to make them more prone to breakage during mixing. Usually raisins are put in lukewarm water for 15-30 minutes to soften them to the desired level, and then draining the excess water.

The cost of bread depends upon the richness of the dough and raisin content. Being a sweeter and richer bread syrup and icings should be used in a correct manner. The formulation of the raisin dough will depend on the requirements; and two typical formulations are given below :-

| | *1* | *2* |
|---|---|---|
| Flour | 100 | 100 |
| Water (variable) | 65 | 58 |
| Salt | 2 | 1.8 |
| Sugar | 2 | 6 |
| Milk solids | 4 | 5 |
| Shortening | 5 | 6 |
| Yeast (compressed) | 3 | 4 |
| Eggs | — | 6 |
| Raisins (Moist) | 50 | 50 |

Sugar, salt, milk powder and shortening are mixed to a smooth paste. To this eggs if any are also blended well. Compressed yeast is dissolved in 3-4 times water and set aside. To the previous blend water is added with stirring, followed by sifting in of the flour and mixing. To this dough yeast solution is added and mixed until it is almost developed. At the final stage of mixing raisins are added and lightly mixed. Too much mixing at this stage will tear the raisins resulting in smearing or streaking of the dough. The dough is then allowed to ferment and punched once.

The dough is scaled (500 gms. for 400 gms. bread), divided, rounded, intermediate proofed. The bread top at 3/4 proof is given a light egg-wash. Bread is then baked at 200°C with some mild steam injection in the oven to avoid blistering of the egg-washed crust. A longer baking period than that for ordinary bread is required for this bread e.g. about 40-45 minutes. The bread is removed from the oven and its top is immediately given a hot, light syrup wash. The breads are cooled until slightly warm and their tops are given a warm simple icing. these breads may be made in round form or in the ordinary tread loaf form.

For better appearance and consumer acceptance diced mixed fruit may also be added to the dough. This makes the bread richer and colourful.

## EGG BREAD

Egg bread is also known as challah, it is quite tasty and attractive in appearance. It contains high quantity of eggs which gives it richness, volume and superior keeping qualities; also the dough gets dried out rapidly and due to this reason more fat is used in the recipe to prevent drying. As compared to the usual white bread the egg bread contains more sugar. The flour used for this bread should be stronger to prevent tearing during make up and to maintain shape during baking. increase and decrease in the quantity of egg yolks should be accompanied with reduction and increase in the salt content.

| *Recipes* | *1* | *2* | |
|---|---|---|---|
| Flour | 100 | 100 | parts |
| Water | 63 | 50 | |
| Salt | 2.1 | 1.7 | |
| Malt | 0.5 | — | |
| Mineral yeast food | 0.4 | — | |
| Shortening | 5 | 5.6 | |
| Sugar | 5 | 8 | |
| MSNF | 5 | — | |
| Egg yolks | 5 | 10 | |
| Compressed yeast | 2 | 3 | |

### Process

First compressed yeast is dissolved in some water. Ingredients other than flour are well mixed and to the flour is added and mixed; followed with yeast. the dough is stiff and develops quickly therefore care should be taken to prevent overdeveloping. The dough is scaled and allowed to ferment. The shapes given to the egg bread may be of different kinds. The egg bread is made by braiding 3, 4, 5 or 6 strands into one bread. The section bread is made by putting 6 pieces in a pan so that on baking a loaf is obtained having 6 sections on the top. The oval shaped egg bread is also made. Snail-shaped egg bread may be made by puttiong the dough strip in snail form.

The dough is scaled into the desired weight for the presses of dough. The presses of dough are allowed to relax for 10-15 minutes before pressing out. The pieces of dough are rolled to make fingerlike long strands which are thicker at the centre and thin at the ends. These strips are lined and dusted with flourand braided. The strands are kept snug but should not be pulled. The braided dough

**Section Egg Bread**

**Six-Twist Egg Bread**

**Oval-shaped Egg Bread with Thin Strip of Dough Across the Top**

is egg washed and put in dusted pans. They are proofed 3/4 and are again egg-washed. They are then baked at an oven temperature of about 175°C until brown and crisp. The oven should not be too hot.

One of the common faults of braided egg breads lies in the fact that the strands are not shaped properly. Each strands should be molded so that all large air pockets are removed to avoid holes in the baked bread. Strands should be of equal size. Stretching of some strands will result in poor shape of the baked bread. Strands should be dusted with flour (rye) before braiding so as to keep them separate during proofing and braiding; preventing the baking of strands into each other. Larger breads require lower oven temperature while smaller breads and rolls require highher oven temperature than 175°C. the bread is tapped at the bottom before from the oven; a hollow sound insures proper bake.

### Rolls

Egg rolls are made just in the way as egg bread. Even the recipe is same. A strip or strands opf the dough is prepared similarly. It is also thin at the ends and thick at the middle. It may be rolled to get snairoll. Two strands may be twisted to get a Braided-Roll. Other shapes may also be made simply by hand. These small units are put in pans and baked at lower oven temperature.

## CHEESE BREAD

Cheese bread loaf has a softer texture and closer grain, it has a typical taste in accordance with the nature of cheese. Hard cheddar cheese gives a stronger cheese flavour than the flavour given by grated softer cheese. The amount of cheese used in the formulati varies acordin to the requirements of bread characteristics e.. taste, texture, flavour and structure. It is not a popular bread but some customers have strong liking to it due to its flavour and nutritional value.

*Two formulas for cheese bread are being given below :-*

| | *1* | *2* | |
|---|---|---|---|
| Flour | 100 | 100 | parts |
| Water | 58 | 64 | |
| Salt | 2 | 2 | |
| Sugar | 2 | 6 | |
| Milk powder | 2 | 4 | |
| Shortening | 5 | 4 | |
| Malt | — | 2 | |
| Compressed yeast | 3 | 4 | |
| Dehydrated or grated Hard cheese | 10 | 10 | |

Yeast is dissolved in some water and set aside. Sugar salt, malt, milk powder are mixed and dissolved in water. To this mixture flour is added and stirred. Now shortening is added and the dough is developed. Cheese is added before the dough is fully developed, otherwise the cheese will be hard to incorparate and may get smeared resulting in excessive discoloration of the dough. The dough is allowed to rise well and is punched. It is allowed to rise again.

The dough should not be allowed to overferment; as overfermentation and even full fermentation will increase the acidity of the dough beyond the desired point. The cheese itself decreases the pH i.e. increases the acidity of the dough.

The loaf units are scaled as usual, made up and placed in greased bread pans. The dough pieces are 3/4 proofed and are baked with a mild amount of steam bread, to avoid a slight sogginess caused by melted cheese. A slight decrease in volume will be noticed in the baked bread due to the added weight of the cheese and adjustments should be made for a larger loaf.

## DATE-NUT BREAD

It is also a speciality bread having the nutritional value of dates and nuts; it has special flavour and appearance.

A typical recipe is given below :-

| | |
|---|---|
| Flour | 100 parts |
| Sugar | 12 |
| Salt | 2 |
| Milk powder | 6 |
| Shortening | 8 |
| Yeast | 8 |
| Water | 64 |
| Chopped dates | 20 |
| Toasted chopped nuts | 24 |

Eggs may also be added to the formulation. Addition of 5 parts of egg yolks will necessitate the addition of further 5 parts of flour. This will further improve the bread, increasing the cost. The amount of dates and nuts may also be increased; this will make the dough richer and costlier. Addition of dates and nuts increases the weight comparatively keeping the volume of the bread smaller

Sugar, salt, milk powder and shortening are blended to a smooth paste. To this about 50 parts of water are added with stirring. The yeast is dissolved in remaining water and set aside. In the previous paste flour is sifted in with slight stirring followed by the addition of yeasst solution. Dough is developed until almost smooth. Now datess and nuts are blended in. After this overmixing should be avoided otherwise, the dough will get smeared and disscoloured. Dough is allowed to rise well, punched and allowed to rise again.

Dough is scaled into piecpss. The pieces may be round in shape of 225 gms. (final weight 180 gms.) or may be in elongated form for usual loaf form, weighing 500 gms. (final loaf weight 400 gmss.) It should be remembered that dates and nuts add to the weight not to the volume. The molded units ar put in a clean, greased pan and are given 3/4 proof followed by an egg-wash. They are allowed to get almost full proof and are baked at 190 to 200°C for about 40 minutes for 400 gms. loaf. Some steam may be put in the oven during the first stage of baking to prevent splitting of the crust. the baked bread may be washed with syrup immediately after baking and iced with simple icing when they are somewhat warm.

## POTATO BREAD

Potato bread is made by incorporating potato flour and not potato starch in the recipe containing wheat flour. Potato flour increases the nutritional value of the bread and improves its softnesss, tenderness and shelflife.

*Following is a typical recipe :-*

| | |
|---|---|
| Wheat flour | 100 parts |
| Potato flour | 6 |
| Water | 68 |
| Sugar | 4 |
| Shortening | 4 |
| Milk Powder | 4 |
| Salt | 2.5 |
| Yeast (compressed) | 2 |
| Malt extract | 0.5 |

Yeast is first dissolved in 8 parts of water and set aside. Sugar, salt, malt, potato flour and milk powder are blended together and mixed at slow speed in water. Bread flour is added and mixed slightly followed by the yeast solution. To the resulting dough yeast is added followed by shortening. The dough is developed at slow or medium speed. Water temperature should be such that the dough comes out of the mixer at about 25° to 30°C.

The dough is allowed to rise fully scaled and rounded. The dough pieces are given 3/4 proof. The pieces are moulded in regular loaf form or in round form. The pieces may be washed and cut if desired. They are then dusted with flour and baked with moist steam at 190 to 200°C.

The rolls obtained from this recipe will also be soft, light and tender.

## FRUIT BREAD

Fruit bread is made in the same way as date-nut bread and instead of chopped dates and nuts pieces of candied pumpkin (petha) properly coloured yellow, green or red are used.

**Figure: Fruit Bread**

## GENERAL BREAD DEFECTS ITS CAUSES & REMEDY

The quality of a loaf should be assessed by taking into consideration all the desirable features, both external and internal.

1. **External features**
   a) Shape symmetry
   b) Volume of loaf
   c) Crust colour

2. **Internal features**
   a) Crumb colour
   b) Structure/texture
   c) Crumbling
   d) Holes in bread
   e) Aroma and taste

### EXTERNAL FEATURES

**(A) Causes of poor shape symmetry**

1. Over ripe dough
2. Skinning during proving
3. Incorrect twisting in the mould
4. Damaged & deshaped moulds
5. Weaker or stronger flour
6. Inadequate addition of Potassium bromate
7. High Maltose value of flour

**Remedial action**

1. Correct dough wiping fire
2. Develop more humidity in the final prover
3. Correct twisting and placing in the moulds
4. Use undamaged moulds/hammering
5. Standardised quality flour to be used
6. Correct the addition of Potassium bromate
7. Reduce maltose value

**(B) Causes of poor volume:**

1. Weak flour
2. Low Maltose value of flour
3. Excess addition of salt
4. Too tight or too slack dough
5. High dough temperature
6. Wrong proving time and temp.

**Remedial action**

1. If flour is weak, blend it with strong flour
2. Add malt extract
3. Increase yeast quality
4. Reduce salt
5. Correct dough consistency
6. Reduce dough temp.
7. Adjust proving time and temp.

**(C) Crust Colour Lacking Causes**

1. Low maltose value flour
2. Insufficient salt addition
3. Over ripe dough
4. Dough skinning during proving
5. Low over temp.
6. Over proving
7. Insufficient sugar

**Remedial action**

1. Add malt extract
2. Correct the salt quality
3. Correct dough temp. & adjust yeast quality
4. Increase humidity in final prover
5. Adjust ove temp.
6. Reduce proving time
7. Add sufficient amount of sugar

**INTERNAL FEATURES**

**(A) Causes of poor crumb colour**

1. Dull colour of flour
2. High maltose value of flour
3. Over proving
4. Inadequate addition of salt
5. High dough temp.
6. Under mix dough
7. Low over temp.
8. Improver twisting or without twisting

**Remedial action**

1. Better colour flour to be used
2. Do not add malt
3. Reduce proving time
4. Add sufficient quality of salt

5. Adjust dough temp.
6. Dough mixing to be adequately
7. Adjust baking time
8. Proper twisting essentially

**(B) Causes of poor texture**

1. Flour quality is not upto the mark
2. Slack dough
3. Over ripe dough
4. More proving
5. Untwisting
6. Low over temp.

**Remedial action**

1. Blend with patent flour
2. Add sufficient quantity of water
3. Adjust fermentation timing
4. Adjust proving time, temp. & humidity
5. Proper twisting is essential
6. Adjust oven temp.

**(C) Causes of crumbling**

1. Over proving
2. Improper fermentation
3. Slack dough
4. Less quantity of salt
5. Hot loaves slicing
6. Knives are not properly sharped

**Remedial action**

1. Adjust proving
2. Correct fermentation
3. Add sufficient water
4. Add sufficient salt
5. Avoid hot loaves slicing
6. Blades (Knives) to be properly sharpened

**(D) Causes of holes in bread**

1. Under ripe dough
2. Improper moulding
3. Overproving
4. Excesssive dusting on dough pieces

**Remedial action**

1. Increase ripening time
2. Craps of moulders to be adjusted
3. Adjust proving condition
4. Avoid skinning of dough pieces

**(E) Causes of odd aroma and taste**

1. If old wheat flour is used in bread manufacturing, than it will impart musty odours
2. Off odour may be due to the fat or water, which is being used
3. Unhygenic conditon of storage and equipments, may also lead to odd odours
4. Insufficient addition of salt
5. Inadequate fermentation

**Remedial action**

1. Avoid old wheat flour
2. Use good fat and chlorine treated water
3. Pay attention on hygienic conditions of store shop, flour and equipments
4. Add sufficient quality of salt
5. Proper fermentation

**(F) Moistness**

Moistness in bread is not determined by the water content alone, but by the capacity of loaf to remain fresh for many days. By eating a portion of crumb, when its apparent moistness can be assessed by the palate. If it is dry and harsh this is readily detected. If under-baked, and too moist, it will form into a ball in the mouth. The quality of moistness desired is only obtained when bread is made from fully developed dough.

# EFFECT OF STORAGE ON CHANGES IN FAT ACIDITY OF BREAD WHEAT, DURUM WHEAT AND TRITICALE WHOLEMEALS AND FLOURS

## INTRODUCTION

Cereal grains/flours on storage over longer periods show a considerable increase in titrable acidity of their lipid extracts. This results into the deterioration of their quality. During the translocation of wheat reserves by FCI, to its userss viz. millers, bakers and ordinary consumers, the wheat is likely to undergo deterioration in its quality. Each group amongst consumers has its own specific requirement for wheat. With three types of wheats/triticles available in the market, it becomes inevitable to study the changes in their quality during storage. Very little work has been reported regarding these changes in grains/flours of Indian wheat varities, during storage. The present study was therefore aimed to work out suitable storage period with ragard to the changes in fat acidity in wholemeals/ flours of these three classes of wheats, over a longer period of storage.

## MATERIALS AND METHODS

Two kg of each of six varieties of wheat viz HD 2329, WL 1562, PBW 34, DWL 5023, TL 419, and TL 1210 were procured from the Department of Plant Breeding, PAU, Ludhiana. One kg of each variety was ground in stone chakki to get wholemeal, while the other part was conditioned to 14% moisture level before ground in Quadrument Junior Mill to get the flour. A part of each of the wholemeals and flours was stored at room temperature, in dark, while the other part heated at 110 C for 2 hrs in an oven in the form of very thin layers. Fat acidity was measured according to the standard methods of AACC (1970). Samples were drawn from each lots of wholemeals/flours at a regular intervals of 1 month and fat acidity estimated. Grain hardness was measured using Barley pearler (Scott, 7810 Model). The results have been reported in this paper.

## RESULTS AND DISCUSSION

### Wholemeal

Moisture content of the grains, wholemeals and flours before and after heating at 110oC is reported in table. Mean values for moisture content for aestivum, during and Triticle wholemeans were 7.55%, 8.3% and 9.6 per cents respectively. On heating the wholemeals, the retained moisture was 3.0, 2.8, 1.5, 2.3, 2.9 and 3.1 per cent for HD 2329, WL 1562, PBW 34, DWL 5023, TL 419 and TL 1210 respectively. Durum wholemeals exhibited lowest moisture percent as compared to aestivum and triticales. Similar trend of moisture content was exhibited by flours. The moisture content of unheated flour ranged from 7.2

and 8.5%. On heating the flour, the moisture decreased (range 1.4-3.1%). The percent decrease in moisture content was maximum in durum wheats (76.5%), followed by Triticale (av 72.3%) and aestivum (64.8%).

Fat acidity values at the time of storage were 21.3, 15.9, 20.7, 19.9, 15.9 and 16.8 per cents for varietiess listed as above. After one month, storage period unheated durum wheat wholemeal exhibited increase in fat acidity (1.34 folds) followed by aestivum wheat (1.61 folds) and triticale (1.76 folds). Similar pattern was obtained in heated wholemeal. This shows that lipase activity was highest in Triticale flours than with aestivum and durum wheats and that even after 4 months of storage period, there was 4.44, 6.37 folds increase in acidity in aestivum wheats HD 2329 and WL 1562 in unheated wholemeals. In case of PBW 34 and DWL 5023 it was 3.8 and 3.72 folds and in TL 419 and TL 1210 it was 6.41 and 7.73 folds. At the end of storage period, the unheated wholemeals of TL 419 exhibited 12.51 and 13.3 foldss increase in fat acidity followed by HD 2329 (7.68 folds) WL 1562 (11.69 folds) and PBW 34 (6.71 folds) and DWL 5023 (6.40 foldss). Munzing et al 1988 studied lipid changes in milled wholemeal products over period of 30 months. Their results reported an increase in FFA content over a few months and then fall back to initial level. Heating of wholemeal resulted in decrease in fat acidity in all the classes of wheats and triticale. Percent decrease in fat acidity in heated wholemeals was highest in triticale (av. 68.01) followed by aestivum (av. 60.81) and durum (55.51). Thiss again confirm that on heating the active lipase in durumss was much easily destroyed than that of bread wheat or aestivums. This account for the stability of durum wholemeal over prolonged period if heated prior to storage. WL 1562, PBW 34 and TL 419 (atta) amongst all varieties seem to be most suitable for storage (if heated) without much of the deterioration in their quality.

## FLOUR

Reduction of grain into flour resulted into decrease in fat acidity at zero hour. This may be due to the removal in part of bran/embryo portion of the grain resulting into partial loss of bran/embryo lipids alongwith outer covering layer of grain. No. of Foldss increase in the acidity amongst flours was almost similar to that of wholemeal. At the end of the stoı age period (7 months), the fat acidity was found to be maximum in triticales TL 1210 (272.5%) and TL 419 (180%). The least in HD 2329 (144.3%) unheated flours over control at zero hours. The average folds increase in fat acidity in unheated flours wass least in durum (6.38 folds) followed by aestivum (9.97 folds) and triticales (14.64 folds). However on heating the flours, the corresponding mean fat acidities were 2.89, 4.37 and 4.86 folds respectively for all the three categories of flours. Percent change (decrease) in fat acidity in flours was maximum in Triticale (71.97%). For aestivum and durum flourss the figures were 53.44 and 54.8% respectively at the end of 7 months storage period.

## QUALITY CHARACTERISTICS OF BREAD WHEAT DURUM WHEAT AND TRITICALE :-

| VARIETIES | MOISTURE CONTENT | | | | | | | Grain protein (%) | Pearling index (%) | Grain hardliness (kg/grain)* |
|---|---|---|---|---|---|---|---|---|---|---|
| | WHOLE MEAL | | | | FLOUR | | | | | |
| | GRAIN | UH | H | %Decrease | UH | H | %Decrease | | | |
| **BREAD WHEAT** | | | | | | | | | | |
| HD 2329 | 6.8 | 7.5 | 3.0 | 66.6 | 7.3 | 3.0 | 58.9 | 11.6 | 29.5 | 12.08 |
| WL 1562 | 7.5 | 7.6 | 2.8 | 64.0 | 7.2 | 2.1 | 70.8 | 11.6 | 32.9 | 13.09 |
| | | | | (65.3) | | | (64.8) | | | |
| **DURUM** | | | | | | | | | | |
| PBW 34 | 8.0 | 8.2 | 1.5 | 83.7 | 7.7 | 1.4 | 81.8 | 13.6 | 24.5 | 14.47 |
| DWL 5023 | 8.5 | 8.4 | 2.3 | 72.6 | 7.3 | 2.1 | 71.2 | 14.4 | 26.5 | 12.98 |
| | | | | (78.1) | | | (76.5) | | | |
| **TRITICALE** | | | | | | | | | | |
| TL 419 | 9.2 | 9.5 | 2.9 | 68.4 | 8.8 | 2.5 | 71.6 | 13.2 | 47.3 | 10.59 |
| TL 1210 | 9.3 | 9.7 | 3.1 | 68.0 | 8.5 | 2.3 | 72.9 | 12.8 | 63.4 | 13.72 |
| | | | | (68.2) | | | (72.3) | | | |

UH : UnheatedH : Heated
*Mean of 10 grains.

**CHANGES IN FAT ACIDITIES OF WHOLEMEALS/FLOURS OF BREAD, DURUM WHEAT & TRITICALE :-**

| VARIETIES | GRAIN FLOUR | | FAT ACIDITY | | | | | | | |
|---|---|---|---|---|---|---|---|---|---|---|
| | | | WHOLE MEAL | | | | FLOUR | | | |
| | Zero day | | 1st Month | | 7th Month | | 1st Month | | 7th Month | |
| | | | H | UH | H | UH | H | UH | H | UH |
| **BREAD WHEAT** | | | | | | | | | | |
| HD 2329 | 21.3 | 19.2 | 27.8<br>(1.3) | 30.2<br>(1.41) | 66.1<br>(3.10) | 163.5<br>(7.68) | 21.1<br>(1.09) | 27.2<br>(1.41) | 83.3<br>(4.33) | 144.3<br>(7.51) |
| WL 1562 | 15.9 | 14.0 | 24.7<br>(1.55) | 28.8<br>(1.81) | 69.3<br>(4.36) | 189.9<br>(11.69) | 24.1<br>(1.72) | 29.1<br>(2.08) | 61.8<br>(4.41) | 174.1<br>(12.44) |
| **DURUM WHEAT** | | | | | | | | | | |
| PBW 34 | 20.7 | 18.3 | 24.2<br>(1.17) | 28.1<br>(1.35) | 61.2<br>(2.95) | 138.9<br>(6.71) | 19.7<br>(1.07) | 21.0<br>(1.14) | 7.8<br>(3.32) | 121.2<br>(6.62) |
| DWL 5023 | 19.9 | 19.1 | 23.2<br>(1.16) | 26.2<br>(1.32) | 57.3<br>(2.88) | 127.4<br>(6.41) | 21.3<br>(1.11) | 23.1<br>(1.20) | 47.3<br>(2.47) | 117.3<br>(6.14) |
| **TRITICALE** | | | | | | | | | | |
| TL 419 | 15.9 | 14.8 | 28.7<br>(1.80) | 28.2<br>(1.77) | 59.7<br>(3.75) | 198.9<br>(12.51) | 18.1<br>(1.22) | 23.1<br>(1.50) | 53.3<br>(3.60) | 180.0<br>(12.16) |
| TL 1210 | 16.8 | 15.9 | 26.3<br>(1.58) | 29.4<br>(1.75) | 77.3<br>(4.60) | 223.2<br>(13.3) | 19.1<br>(1.20) | 26.2<br>(1.64) | 72.1<br>(4.53) | 272.5<br>(17.13) |

UH : Unheated H : Heated **Figures in parenthesis represent no. of folds increase in fat acidity over control.**

*Mean of 10 grains.

**PERCENT DECREASE IN FAT ACIDITIES IN WHOLEMEALS/FLOURS OF BREAD WHEAT, DURUM WHEAT AND TRITICALE :-**

| VARIETIES | FAT ACIDITY AFTER PROLONGED STORAGE PERIOD OF 7 MONTHSS | | | | | | | |
|---|---|---|---|---|---|---|---|---|
| | WHOLE MEAL | | | | FLOUR | | | |
| | UH | H | % change | Mean | UH | H | % change | Mean |
| **BREAD WHEAT** | | | | | | | | |
| HD 2329 | 7.78 | 3.10 | 59.63 | 60.81 | 7.51 | 4.33 | 42.34 | 53.44 |
| WL 1562 | 11.69 | 4.36 | 62.00 | | 12.44 | 4.41 | 64.54 | |
| **DURUM WHEAT** | | | | | | | | |
| PBW 34 | 6.71 | 2.95 | 56.03 | 55.51 | 6.62 | 3.32 | 49.84 | 54.80 |
| DWL 5023 | 6.40 | 2.88 | 55.00 | | 6.14 | 2.47 | 59.77 | |
| **TRITICALE** | | | | | | | | |
| TL 419 | 12.51 | 3.75 | 70.02 | 68.01 | 12.16 | 3.60 | 70.39 | 71.97 |
| TL 1210 | 13.03 | 4.60 | 65.41 | | 17.13 | 4.53 | 73.55 | |

UH : Unheated H : Heated

## CONCLUSION

These findings ssuggest that reduction of grain into flours resulted into decrease in fat acidity and that effect of heat treatment in inactivating the active lipase was maximum in case of durums as compared to aestivum and triticales. Durum flour can more easily be stored over prolonged period over aestivum and triticale flours as compared to their wholemeals.

# Chapter - 11

## *Sweet Yeast Dough Products (Buns etc.)*

Sweet yeast leavened doughs may be classified into two major categories namely remix sweet dough and the straight sweet dough. Other doughs of this type are sponge dough (Babka) and roll-in (Danish) type. Sweet doughs are much richer, in shortening, milk and sugar, than the bread-type doughs and they usually contain whole eggs, egg yolks or whites. Commonly used flavoures include spices, vanilla, nuts etc. By varying the flavouring, filling, sshape and icing an almost infinite number of types of cakes and rolls can be made.

*A typical basic formula of straight sweet dough is given below :-*

| | |
|---|---|
| Bread flour | 80 parts |
| Cake flour | 20 |
| Sugar | 20 |
| Margarine | 20 |
| Whole eggs | 20 |
| Milk powder | 5 |
| Non-diastatic malt syrup | 2 |
| Salt | 1 |
| Compressed yeast | 8 |
| Water | 45 |

Sugar, margarine or emulsified shortening, ssalt, eggs, malt and milk powder are creamed together. To this flours are added slowly with good mixing.

Finally water in which yeast hass been dissolved is added and the dough is developed. The dough is usually fermented for about 1½ hours at 30°C. To prepare a remix sweet dough, after fermentation about 20-22 parts of a strong flour, 13-14 parts of sugar, 13-14 parts of butter, margarine or emulsified shortening and 13-14 parts of egg yolks are added and mixed at medium speed. No further fermentation is required, the dough is immediately scaled and made up.

The basic formula given above is quite rich. If a lean dough is desired, the enriching ingredients can be reduced even upto 50% or more. In that case yeast may also be decreased due to increase in its activity.

The enriching ingredients soften the texture of the product and make it flakier. They improve the taste and colour and increase the nutritional quality of the product. Liquid skim milk may be used in place of powdered milk and water may be correspondingly decreased. Various dough improvers and yeast foods may be added as in the case of breads.

We shall now describe all the four types of sweet yeast dough products mentioned above.

## BUNS

Buns are almost similar to bread. Their dough is comparatively leaver dough. Due to leaver dough, they can be proofed longer and baked at higher oven temperatures.

*A typical bun dough formulation is given below:-*

| | |
|---|---|
| Flour | 100 parts |
| Water | 67 |
| Salt | 2.5 |
| Sugar | 15 |
| Compressed yeast | 4 |
| Milk powder | 10 |
| Shortening | 9 |
| Malt syrup | 1 |

Richness of the dough can be varied, a richer dough gives better bun of better keeping quaites. A well balanced sweet yeast bun dough recipe is given below:-

| | |
|---|---|
| Cake flour | 16 parts |
| Bread flour | 48 |
| Water | 33 |
| Sugar | 12 |
| Milk powder | 4 |
| Salt | 1 |
| Shortening | 12 |
| Eggs | 8 |
| Yeast | 4 |

Sugar, milk powder, salt shortening and mace are blended to a smooth paste. Eggs are also blended in well folowed by 24 parts of water. Flours are added to it and stirred followed by solution of yeast in remaining water. The dough is developed until smooth. Temperature of water is controlled to control the dough temperature. Dough is allowed to rise well in warm and moist place. When ready, it is punched and allowed to relax for 20 minutes. The dough is scaled, divided and rounded. The slightly pressed bun doughs are put on pans. The tops are washed with water, milk or egg wash. For better appearance buns may be sprinkled with Struessel topping. Buns are given 3/4 proofs and baked at 200°C until the crust becomes golden brown. The buns ar cooled.

## Various Types of Buns

Apart from the basic and usual type of buns described above other buns are also made differing in shape, size, method of preparation and fillings used. Cinnamon buns are made by rolling the dough in sheet form, brushing it with oil or fat, cake crumbs and cinnamon sugar and then rolling it up tightly. The roll is cut into pieces which are proofed and baked at 190°-200°C. The butterfly buns ar also made similarly except that pieces ar pressed at the centre with a thin rolling pin to cause the layers of dough to flange or spread out in the form of wings. After egg-wash the units are baked and cooled followed by putting some icing. Some of the buns are pressed at the centre with a round object, in this depression cheese filling, fruit filling, jelly, orange or lemon filling may be put. These buns are accordingly called cheese-buns, fruit-buns are then washed carefully with simple syrup, cooled and iced with simple icing. Twist buns are made by rolling the dough into sheets. The sheets are covered with melted fat or jam or jelly. The dough is then folded in such a way as to give three layers of dough and two layers of fillings. The dough is rolled again and cut into strips. the individual strips are twisted and baked.

**Common Bun**

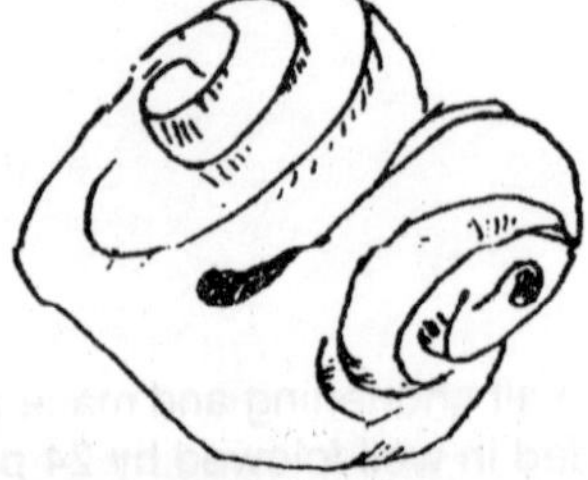

**Butterfly Bun**

Horseshoe-shaped buns may be made by washing the strips with egg wash and sprinkling with toppings. One side of the strips is given 5 slights cuts at one edge and then twisted and placed in a pan in horse-shoe shape, proofed and baked. Bow tie coconut buns are made by cutting the dough in the form of strips as in the case of twist-buns and then giving it one twist. the piece is egg washed, sprinkled with fine shread coconut, 3/4 proofed and then baked at 200°C. Overbaking is avoided so that coconut topping may not become brown. The buns are then lightly washed with syrup, cooled and then iced with simple icing.

## BABKA

Babka is a loaf-type cake made from a very rich sweet dough and is sometimes called 'Coffee cake loaf' or 'Grand-mother's loaf'. Because of the added richness, the dough is made by the sponge dough method. Comparatively more yeast is required due to high richness. In the straight dough method sugar, shortening, salt and eggs are creamed together. In sponge dough mixing the fat is melted and drawn into the final dough after the flour is added and the dough partially developed. Doughs made with the sponge method should be allowed to rise once and taken to the bench. Fillings should be put carefully. Toppings applied to Babka should be put on the pieces when almost 3/4 proofed.

The use of butter, eggs, yolks and other enriching ingredients determines the quality.

*A typical Babka recipe is given below:-*

| | |
|---|---|
| Bread flour | 80 parts |
| Water | 32 |
| Yeast | 8 |
| Sugar | 22 |
| Salt | 1.25 |
| Milk powder | 4 |
| Eggs | 24 |
| Melted butter | 16 |
| Shortening or margarine | 16 |

Yeast is dissolved in 32 parts of water and 2/3rd flour is mixed well. The mixture is allowed to rise well. Sugar, salt, milk powder, vanilla one part, cardamon 0.25 part, orange and lemon 1 part and eggs are added and mixed well. Remaining flour is then added and mixed. Melted fat is slowly added followed by fat. Dough is mixed until smooth. It is allowed to rise well. This method is sponge dough method and gives more rapid fermentation.

The dough is sealed into oblong shape and after relaxing, it is rolled ¼" thick. It is smeared with melted butter, or melted chocolate and chopped nuts, cake crumbs, cinnamon, sugar or raisins are sprinkled over it and rolled gently. The sheet may be rolled or cut into strips and twisted in the required form. The pieces are put on well greased or paperlined pans, washed with melted butter, and 3/4 proofed. Proofed units are sprinkled with Struessel topping and then baked at 175° to 180° C.

## DANISH PASTRY

Danish pastry has interleaving dough sheets and fat layers. The method of preparation is somewhat similar to that of puff pastry. In puff pastry the leavening action is that from the water vapors formed during baking while in the case of Danish pastry the leavening action is due to the yeast which gives it the required porous structure. The method of preparation results in separation of layers in the product. The fat layers are melted during baking and get absorbed into the dough layers, thus fat layers do not appear in the finished product. The amount and type of fat used is imoportant. Butter is expensive but gives the best product. Butter and margarine in equal proportions is also a good fat for this purpose; vegetable glue is also satisfactory.

The fat used should not be too hard or too soft. In the first case it will tear the dough layers during rolling resulting in large uneven pieces, and in the latter case the fat tends to run out of the sides of the doughs causing stickiness and other problems also crop up.

Since is important to maintain separation of the dough layers until the product is baked, Danish pastry dough is rolled while cold. The shortening is spread over a freshly thick piece of dough, it is folded over rolled again, folded again and repeated until a many layered structure has been developed. Refrigeration is desirable after each sheeting operation to dissipate the heat resulting from the rolling action; otherwise the fatty layers shall melt and dough layers sshall merge. Usually four times rolling is sufficient. To much rolling will make the layers of fat and dough so thin that they will blend together. Danish pastry doughs do not ordinarily receive much fermentation. An initial short period oif 20-30 minutes in the refrigerator before the fat is rolled in allows some gas and flavour to be developed. Dough is cooled between each series of sheetings and in each of these cases some fermentation will take place.

Danish pastry doughs are carefully proofed otherwise the units may tear during baking, or may become greasy, flat or lack volume. When toppings, such as coconut or fruit toppings, are to be applied they are sprinkled after ½ proof and then proofed upto 3/4 proofs. Baking is done as usual at the oven temperature of upto 200°C. Hot syrup wash is applied while the units are hot. Icing is applied when warm not hot, and icing should be warmed to 45°C before applying. This will avoid stickiness in the cool product.

### Method of Preparation

Sponge and dough method is employed for making Danish pastry. The first stage is called sponge and the second one is known as dough stage. The sponge usually contains ½ to 3/4 of the flour and all the yeast, yeast foods, and malt together with enough water to make a stiff dough. All or part of the shortening may be added here or later. ½ to 3/4 of the salt may be added to the sponge to control fermentation. The sponge is fermented until it begins to decline in volume i.e. starts dropping, this takes about 3-5 hrs. At the dough stage, the sponge is mixed with the remaining ingredients. The dough is developed to a peak and then proofed. The sponge and dough method is more cumbersome and time consuming then the straight dough method in which all the ingredients are mixed in the first mixing step. Some of the advantages of sponge method are about 20% saving in yeast; better volume, texture and grain; and greater flexibility.

## Formulations

*A typical formulation is given below:-*

| | |
|---|---|
| Flour | 64 parts |
| Sugar | 16 |
| Salt | 1 |
| Butter, margarine(Roll-in-fat) | 16 |
| Shortening | 24 |
| Yeast | 4 |
| Milk powder | 4 |
| Eggs | 16 |
| Water | 32 |
| Vanilla | 1 |

Sugar, salt, milk powder, 1/3rd shortening and cardamom or coffee cakes flavour (0.12 part) are blended to a smooth, soft paste. Eggs are added in two stages and blended well. Vanilla dissolved in 16 parts of water are added followed by flour which is stirred in slightly. Yeast dissolved in 16 parts of water is added and the mixture is developed to a smooth dough. Roll in fat and remaining shortening are mixed together and kept aside.

The dough is rolled in rectangular shape 1/2" thick. After relaxing for 5 to 10 minutes fat is spread over 2/3 of its surface and folded twice so that three

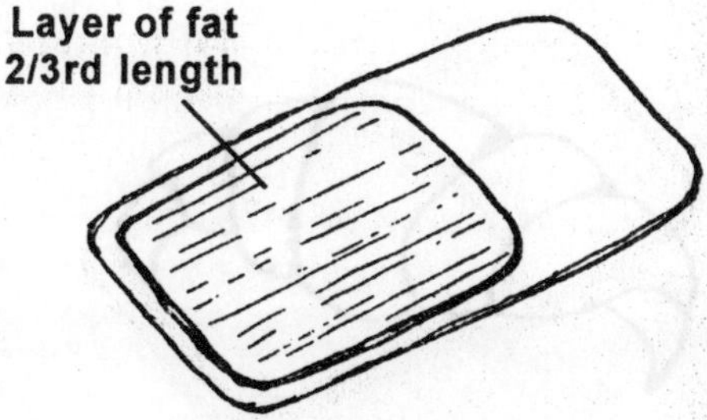


**Dough Before Folding**

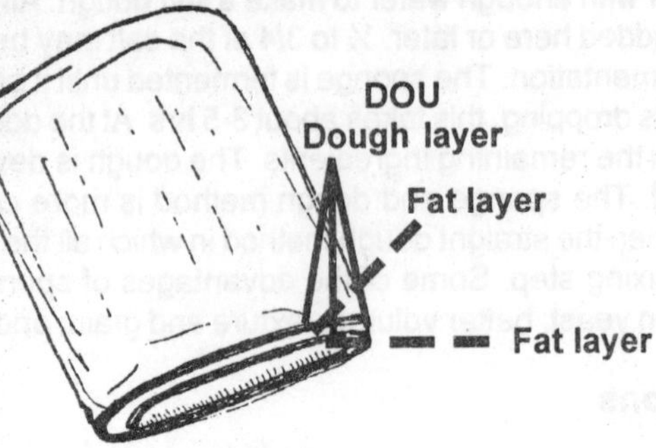


Dough Folded Twice

layers of dough have two layers of fat in between. After dusting with flour it is rolled again to 1/2" thickness and spread again with fat and folded again. This procedure is repeated 4 times. With relaxing time (under refrigeration) of 15 minutes between each two rollings. The dough is then cut into shape and baked at 200°C to get the required specific Danish pastry product.

The dough pieces ar finished with various sizes, shapes and designs to get specific Danish pastry products such as Danish Snacks, horns, twists, sticks, rings, miniatures, coconut rings etc.

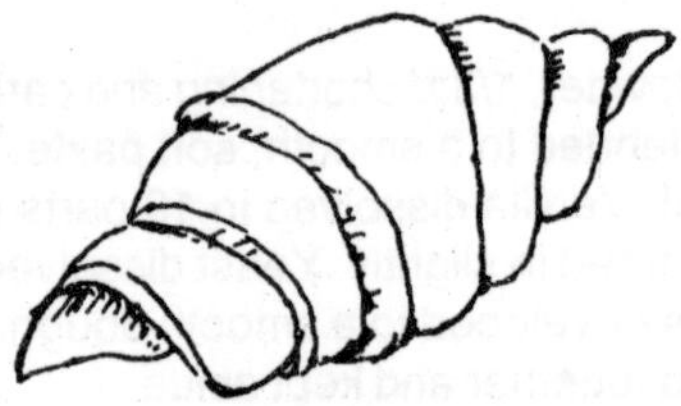

Danish Horn

Danish Crescent Horn

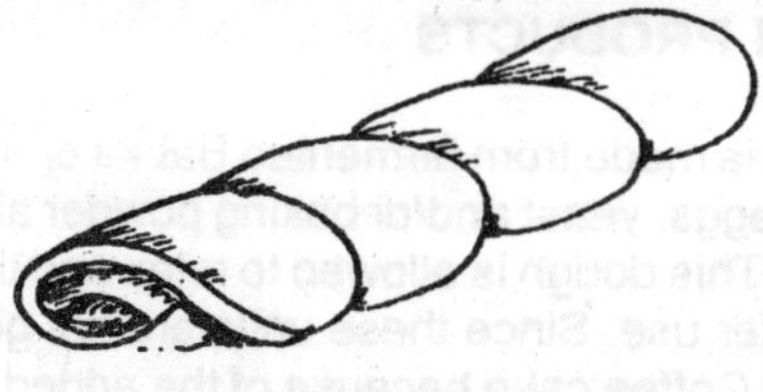

Danish Pastry Stick

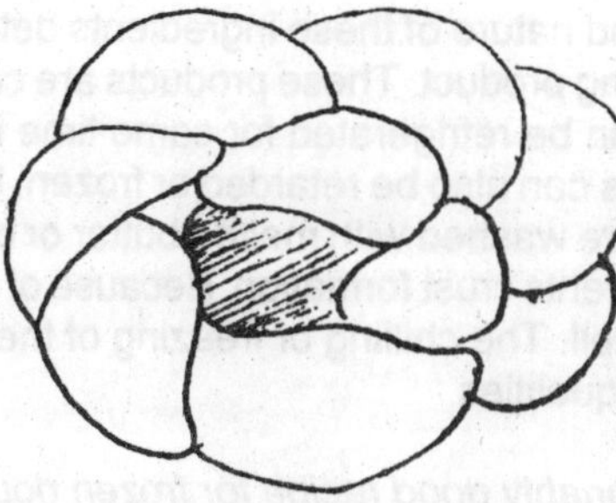

Snail-Shape Danish

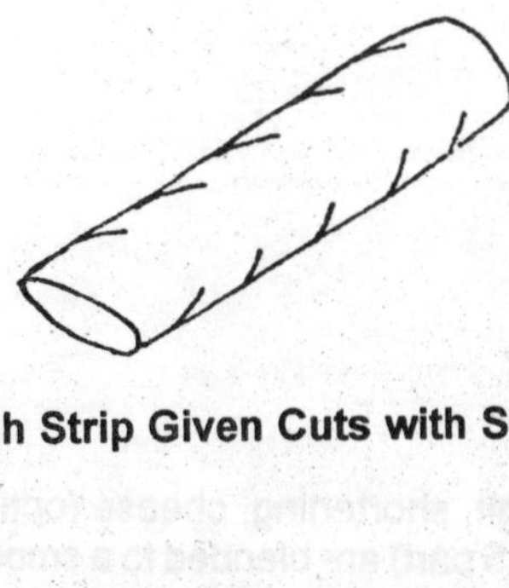

Dough Strip Given Cuts with Scissors

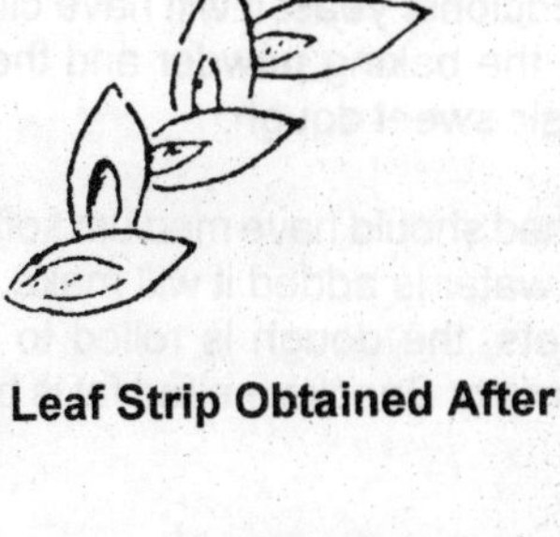

Palm Leaf Strip Obtained After Baking

## FROZEN DOUGH PRODUCTS

Frozen dough is made from fermented Babka or rich bun dough as base. Additional sugr, fat, eggs, yeast and/or baking powder are added with the additional flour required. This dough is allowed to relax and then made up or placed in the retarder for later use. Since these units are not given proof to the same degree as Danish or Coffee cake because of the added leavening of the yeast and baking powder, they are allowed to relax to soften the gluten and half proofed bafore baking.

The amount and nature of these ingredients determine the quality of the dough and the resulting product. These products are called frozen dough products as this dough can be refrigerated for some time before making into units and the made up units can also be retarded or frozen. When freezing or retarding these units they are washed with melted butter or other fat combination before freezing, this prevents crust formation. Because of it added richness, frozen dough retards very well. The chilling or freezing of the added fat and eggs assures better keeping qualities.

*A typical reasonably good recipe for frozen dough is given below:-*

| | |
|---|---|
| Fermented Babka or Bun Dough | 64 parts |
| Bread flour | 34 |
| Sugar | 24 |
| Salt | 0.5 |
| Shortening | 32 |
| Baker's cheese | 16 |
| Eggs | 20 |
| Yeast | 2 |
| Water | 4 |
| Baking powder | 1.5 |

Dough, sugar, salt, shortening, cheese (optional), vanilla (0.5 part) and mace or cardamom (0.25 part) are blended to a smooth paste. Eggs are blended in this paste in two stages. Yeast dissolved in water is also incorporated followed by flour and baking powder. The dough is mixed until smooth. The baker's cheese adds richness, taste and flavour to the dough. If cream cheese is used instead, then fat is reduced by 1 part for 2 parts of cream cheese. If frozen dough is made without any additional yeast it will have closer grain and for leavening depend primarily upon the baking powder and the leavening supplied by the yeast present in the basic sweet dough.

The dough obtained should have medium soft consistency, if it is stiff more eggs may be added, if water is added it will make the dough leaner to make it firm. For making pockets, the dough is rolled to 1/4" thickness and cut into squares. For Filled HOrns or Snecks melted fat is brushed on the dough before applying the filling, this will give added richness. Making up of units is done as usual. The dough is short hence units should be handled with care to prevent tearing the dough, particularly while making pockets. The made up units are washed with fat. They are topped with Strussel toppings, groundnut or sugar. After allowing the units to relax for 1 hour they are baked.

# Chapter - 12

# *Pies and Puff Pastries*

Pie crust and puff pastry come under the class of unleavened bakery products. This is due to the reason that no chemical leavening agent or yeast is included in the formula. Only rarely, a small amount of baking powder may be added to the pie crust recipe.

## PIE CRUST

Pie crust recipes have high fat and low moisture content. The ratio of various ingredients and method of preparation are such that there is no continuous gluten network and the baked product has a friable or flaky appearance. Leavening agents are not added so that the crust does not become porous, as it has to securely enclose high moisture content pie fillings. Depending upon the flakiness, pie crusts may be divided into three classess (i) Mealy (ii) Medium flaky, which is more popular, and (iii) the long flake type. Similar ingredients are used in all the three, but the amount of water, degree of mixing of shortening and flour differ. The mealy variety of the crust absorbs less water than either of the flaky varieties, it is due to the fact that the flour and shortening are blended to a degree where the flour is almost completely enveloped with shortening and less flour remains to absorb the water of the filling. When broken mealy type break in straight line like a biscuit while flaky varieties show a fracture along different lines at different levels.

### Ingredients

Flour for the pie crust should not be high or very low in gluten. High gluten flours give tough doughs while the very low gluten flours give pasty, sticky doughs. A blend of 60% cake flour and 40% bread flour or high-gluten flour with 20% starch is suitable for pie crust. Flour containing 7-8.5% gluten is the best. Lard is very good shortening for pie crust but imparts a flavour (sometimes unacceptable). Vegetable ghee is the usual material for this purpose and is used upto 60-70% based on the weight of flour. Cold water has to be used and particularly in warm weather ice-water should be used, this will prevent dispersions of the fat to a pasty, soft dough. 25 to 30% water based on flour is the usual quantity used.

Sugar, dextrose and corn-syrup are used to add colour and sweetness to the crust but impart the tendency to absorb moisture causing sogginess; if used they should not exceed 2%. Milk adds richness and gives a better colour to the crust, upto 2 to 3% dry milk may be used, in warm weather it imparts tendency to become soggy. Salt is added to accentuate the flavour of the crust and other ingredients. For thorough blending it should be dissolved in water first, 1.5 to 3% of salt based on flour is the usual range employed.

## Mixing Procedure

Pie crust ingredients are mixed in two steps. The sifted flour and shortening are mixed together for a period just sufficient to reduce the shortening to small lumps. If the fat particles are in small lump form the medium flake dough is obtained and if the blending is done to get a paste the result will be mealy crust. A cold solution of salt, milk and sugar are added, mixing lightly until the liquid is absorbed by the flour. Amount of water or liquid used is the critical factor in pie crust making and it should be very carefully measured. Dough is left at 10-15°C for several hours after mixing, this allows the water to distribute itself more thoroughly in the dough mass and hardens the shortening so that it is less likely to liquefy during handling and shaping. Chilling is particularly important for long-flake crusts. Mealy type crusts should be mixed at 15°C (using chilled water as the ingredient) and held covered at this temperature for 3-4 hours. The conditioning period helps in eliminating toughness, shrinkage and later soaking of the crust by the filling. Over-mixing should be avoided.

When shortening is mixed to a peas size only flaky crust is obtained while for mealy crusts, the shortening is completely dispersed in the dough. In the latter case the processing conditions are less critical and in this case refrigeration of ingredients and dough is not of much value.

## Pie Crust (for Apple Pie) Dough

| | |
|---|---|
| Cake flour | 48 parts |
| Bread flour | 32 |
| Shortening | 40 |
| Milk powder, optional | 2 |
| Salt | 1.5 |
| Sugar | 3 |
| Cold water | 40 |

Flour is sifted and to this shortening is added and rubbed together into small lumps avoiding the mixing to be carried upto pasty stage. Sugar and salt are dissolved in the water and added to the flour shortening mixture. It is folded over lightly until the flour is absorbed. The dough obtained should be lumpy and sticky.

## Long-flake Crust Dough

| | |
|---|---|
| Lard | 45 parts |
| Vegetable ghee | 15 |
| Flour | 100 |
| Skim Milk powder | 6 |
| Water | 38 |
| Salt | 4 |
| Sugar | 3 |

Both the fats are mixed, to this flour and milk powder are added and mixed until the fat is in pieces. Salt and sugar are dissolved in water and blended with the above mixture.

## Pie Making

The dough is placed on a floured pan and shaped into a rectangle. It is refrigerated before using, to prevent the fat from sticking and to make the rolling easier, in 1/8" thick and circular form. The dough is rolled slightly larger than the top of the pie tin so that the dough can cover the bottom and sloping sides of the tin. Pie is filled with the filling keeping it slightly below the pie rim. Pie rim or edge is washed with water. Egg wash may be used for better adhesion of the top and bottom crusts. Upper pie piece is also rolled and put over it and small hole is made in it. Rim of the pie tin is pressed to remove the excess crust. Pies are baked in an oven at 210 to 220°C. When the pie is shaken and the pie bottom moves freely in the tin, it is considered to be well baked.

The pies may be washed with milk, melted fat or butter or egg-wash. Washes of egg or milk or their combinations of these gives glossy and relatively dark crusts. Spray of skim milk to the top crust before baking, gives a golden brown colour and a drier and crisper texture. The crust may also be sprayed with melted shortening to give a flake on top of the product.

## PUFF PASTRY

Making of puff pastry cannon be mechanised. Layers of fat are interleaved between layers of dough; on baking layers separate out. Thus in puff pastry open network of crisp and flaky layers is obtained. Dough should be cold so that the shortening does not melt and thus does not get mixed up with the crumb.

## Ingredients

Cream of tartar, vinegar, or lemon juice may be added to the water in making of the dough. These acidic substances will not affect leavening or flakiness but will relax the gluten making the rolling easier and quicker. It may be emphasised here that addition of these substances is not a must. Addition of salt improves flavour. Puff pastry flour should be of the strong type with good quality gluten. Strong flour is necessary to support the large amount of fat used, (upto 100% of flour). Weak flour will yield a paste rather than the layers of fat and dough.

The puff pastry fat should be firm and plastic and stiffer than the dough. Harder fats containing an animal fat have higher melting points and blending of such a fat with vegetable shortening tends to mellow the hardness and eliminate the greasy taste or feeling when eating the product. Lecithin and monoglycerides may also be added. Sometimes instead of water skim milk is used.

## Making Up

In one method of making pastry dough a small amount of fat is rubbed with the flour, water is added and the dough is well developed. Pastry fat is distributed over 2/3rd of the dough and rolled. Dough is allowed to relax between rolls to allow gluten to relax. During the resting period the dough is placed in a fridge to keep the fat firm and prevent running out during rolling. Large number of fat and dough layers are thus formed. In a different method all the fat and dough layers are water is added to form a lumy moist dough. The dough is rolled. The previous method gives better distribution of the fat without excessive use of dusting flour while in the second process more dusting flour is required resulting in toughness of the dough.

Sharp knife is used to cut the rolled-out dough. Scrap pieces of puff pastry should be folded between layers of leftover dough and then rolled out. The puff pastry units should be allowed to relax 1/2 to 1 hr. before baking, this permits complete relaxation of the dough. The pieces should be egg washed twice. First wash is given as soon as made up and second before baking. This gives a desirable crust colour. Washing is very desirable as there is no sugar in the formulation to provide carmalisation for brown crust formation.

The units are baked in oven, the temperature is usually 200°C. During baking the steam released by the dough moisture pushes up the layers of the fat and dough, producing the laminated flakiness of the product. Cooler oven will give poor volume due to low rate of evaporation of moisture and a heavy product while a very hot oven will create an outside crust again resulting in poor volume, and the unit will crack due to pressure of the expanding steam of the layers.

## Formulations

| | | |
|---|---|---|
| (i) | Bread flour | 64 parts |
| | Cream of tartar | 1 |
| | Salt | 0.5 |
| | Shortening | 60 |
| | Eggs | 4 |
| | Water | 36 |

Flour, salt and cream of tartar are blended with some shortening. In place of cream of tartar lemon juice or vinegar may also be used. Water and eggs are stirred together and added to the above blend to get a smooth dough. The fat is put on 2/3rd of the rolled dough and given two folds to get three layers of dough and two layers of fat. After relaxing the dough it is rolled and folded again. This is repeated many tirnes. The sheet is given a wash and cooled. The pastry units are cut into the desired shapes and baked.

| | | |
|---|---|---|
| (ii) | Flour | 80 parts |
| | Salt | 2.5 |
| | Shortening | 40 |
| | Water | 16 |

Dough is made and rolled into rectangular shape and cooled. 40 parts of shortening is put over 2/3rd of the sheet and folded over as above. Thin sheet is formed and is folded again into 3 layers. After cooling it is repeated twice. The puff pastry pieces are then cut into shapes and baked at 200°C.

## Common Faults and their Removal

The product obtained shall be tough if the dough is over-worked or too much scrap is used. Shrinkage of the units indicates that the dough is tough and rolled too much without relaxation and the oven is too hot. If fat is not rolled in properly, or flour used is weak, or too hot or too cold oven, or if the dough is over-aged the fat runs out during baking. Poor volume is usually due to improper rolling in of fat, inadequate relaxation, improper fat, or too hot or too cool oven. If the edges of dough are not washed the product will show blisters and flaking.

# Chapter - 13

# *Cakes*

In cakes chemical leavening agents e.g. mixture of sodium bicarbonate and leavening acids are used for the expanding affect during baking. The mixing stage during cake manufacture, is the most important, if mixing is not done according to the set procedure the product obtained shall be poor even when the recipe is excellent.

## Functions of Various Ingredients

Various basic ingredients present in a cake mix perform some special function. Amounts of these ingredients are interlinked and when amount of any or more of the ingredients is varied the quantities of the remaining ingredients have to be balanced to get the best results. The following is a classification of various cake ingredients according to their functions :-

***Tougheners :*** Flour, milk solids, egg whites and other binding ingredients come under this category. They provide the structure and bind the cake.

***Tenderizers :*** Sugar, shortening, egg yolks, chocolate and other fat containing ingredients provide softness and shortness to the cake.

***Moisteners :*** Milk, water, eggs, syrups and other liquids provide moisture and impart keeping quality.

***Driers :*** Flour, milk solids and starches etc. Absorb and retain moisture and provide body to the cake.

***Flavorers :*** Cocoa, chocolate, butter, eggs and other natural flavour-bearing ingredients provide flavour to the cake.

*The functions of these ingredients have been elaborated as under :-*

The wheat flours used in cakes are weaker, i.e., they contain lower quantity of gluten and also as compared to bread the quantity of flour used is itself smaller in the recipe. Thus the cakes have denser structure than the breads. Apart from the sweetening effect sugars have a tenderizing effect and also imparts good colour to the cake crust. Invert sugar and glucose imparts better colour to the crust than cane sugar. Usual sugars help in retaining the moisture thereby reducing the staling of the crumb; glucose and invert sugar exert better effect than canesugar.

Increasing the concentration of sugars in the cake recipes makes the latter more fluid and thus less air is entrained during whipping.

Shortening apart from tenderizing the crumb and imparting it some flavour, helps in entrapping air during mixing of the latter. The entrapped air bubbles give the leavening effect and help control the grain size. It has to be confirmed that all the air bubbles are enclosed in the layers of fat; which is known as the creaming action of fat. Emulsified shortenings increase the amount of water which can be used, this improves tenderness and the resistance to staling. Addition of egg whites compensates the otherwise poor ability of the cake flours to support the formation of large cells. Angel food cake for instance the entire leavening effect is obtained from the air enclosed by the egg white during vigorous whipping. Egg white does not contribute to the texture. Eggs impart flavour and colour. Egg yolks have emulsifying and tendering effects. Thus eggs are the important ingredient to compensate or the excessively weak flours.

Addition of milk improves crust colour. Skim milk somewhat toughens the crumb but the whole milk has no such drawback due to the presence of milk fat which compensates it by imparting tenderness and lubrication. Milk also contributes to flavour and its lactose content helps in retardation of staling.

## MIXING OF CAME BATTERS

The mixing stage of cake making is very important and should be carried out according to the set procedures. Proper mixing helps in achieving a uniform mixture of the ingredients, incorporation of minute air-cells and in developing a desirable grain and texture in the baked product. Various techniques of mixing the cake batters are employed. Some of the more important are given below:

### Creaming Method

In this method sugar and shortening are beaten to get a light and fluffy or creamed mass. During this stage small air cells are formed and then incorporated into the mix; its volume increases and consistency becomes softer. The eggs are then added while creaming is continued at medium speed, and finally milk and flour are added alternately, in small portions. For best creaming fat or shortening should not be below 20°C and also their temperature should not exceed 45°C otherwise the fat will be too fluid to hold much air hence volume increase shall not be as high as desired. Speed of the mixer should be controlled properly. Sugar and shortening are best creamed at medium speed until soft and light.

Addition of eggs should be slow otherwise if eggs are added too quickly or if milk is added in one lot the mixture will curdle. Addition of the flour alternately with the liquid i.e. milk when the mix is creamed will eliminate the tendency to curdle.

## Blending Method

In this method flour and shortening are blended in the bowl until the flour particles are thoroughly coated by the fat. The remainder of the dry ingredients are then added and the batter mixed until homogeneous. Finally the remaining liquid is added in portions and mixed to get the desired result. Sometimes sugar and eggs are beaten together to form a foam before they are added to the flour and shortening mixture.

In this method also curdling has to be avoided. For high-ratio type mix a high-ratio shortening should be used. This emulsified fat enables the cells formed in mixing to hold the large percentage of moisture and sugar without curdling. As usual temperature of fat is important. When high percentage of sugar e.g. 140% or more is to be used it is best to dissolve it in the liquid before adding to the mix, so as to eliminate the possibility of incomplete blending of sugar; this modification will result in a more tender crust of the baked cake.

## Whipping Method

Generally most of the sugar is added to the eggs used in sponge cakes before begining whipping. Whipping introduces air cells which cause leavening without the need of baking powder. Eggs and sugar is the foam formation is improved. When large amounts of sugar are used compared to that of eggs, part of the sugar is dissolved in the liquid e.g. milk and then folded in after the eggs have been whipped e.g. if the sugar is above 100% part of it is added later. In the case of leaner sponge cakes, less amounts of eggs are used the liquid e.g. milk or water, is added after the eggs are almost completely whipped and the whipping is completed. In whipped type cakes, the flour should be sifted and folded in gently in stages, if added too much at a time, loss in aeration will take place resulting in poor volume of the baked cake.

In the case of Angel cake egg whites are whipped slightly to a foam and then slowly sugar is added. As amount of sugar used is high all of it is not added there. Otherwise maximum aeration will not be obtained. Part of the sugar is sifted with the flour and then folded in gently. Both over-whipping and under-whipping of the eggs should be avoided. Mixing machine speed is also important for best whipping. First machine is run at full speed and when whipping is almost complete the speed is reduced to second place to ensure maximum aeration. If high speed is maintained at final stages, there will be loss in volume as the air cells formed will rupture due to high speed.

## Creaming and Whipping Combination Method

As the name itself suggests this method is a combination of the whipping method and creaming method. In this method flour and shortening are creamed until soft and tight. The eggs and sugar are whipped as in the whipping method. The two mixtures are gently combined by folding the whipped eggs and sugar into the creamed flour and shortening. Leavening is mostly obtained by aeration and sometimes chemical leavening agents may also be added in small quantities. Care result in loss of volume, large holes and uneven grain of the cake. As usual over-mixing and under-mixing should be avoided.

## Choice of Mixing Method

Creaming method allows entrapment of a maximum number of air bubbles in the fat with the result that grains of the finished product are better; and also four gluten is not developed as much as in other methods, thus texture of the cake is somewhat better. The blending method of mixing is used primarily in the making of high ratio type cakes. The chief advantage of the blending method is that it permits a very thorough dispersion of the shortening thoroughout the batter. This results in a very fine and uniform grain in the product. The whipping method of mixing is mainly used in the preparation of sponge and angel cakes and also in the whipping of egg whites for meringues, marshmallow-type icing and whipped cream etc. The combination method of mixing is very often used in the making of pound-cake, and also for wonder cakes and cheese cakes.

# FORMULATION AND BLEACHING OF CAKE RECIPES

Various ingredients and their functions in cake recipes have already been given. They have effects on each other and also some of them have opposite effects hence in balancing a cake recipe, it is a must to have proper proportions of toughners and tenderisers, and the driers and moisteners, so that the cake obtained may be of the desired characteristics.

At first a type of pound cake was made by mixing equal parts of sugar, butter, eggs and flour. With the refinement in mixing methods and experience various types of cakes with excellent quality are now-a-days manufactured. In general following guidelines may be let in mind while formulating the cake recipe. Taking the weight of flour as 100 parts, the sugar may be kept at about 110-160 parts in yellow layer and white layer cakes, and at 110-180 parts in Devil's food and chocolate layers. Eggs as liquid eggs should be equal to or more than the shortening. The total liquid in the recipe should be more than the amount of sugar by 25-35%. Amount of shortening should be about 30-70 parts, sodium bicarbonate should be 1.2-2 parts and salt should be 3-4 parts. If in a formula the quantity of sugar is to be increased the egg content should also be equally increased. When quantity of eggs is to be increased shortening is also increased.

Rich formulas used less chemical leavening agent as during mixing more air gets incorporated. Rich formulas thus have low sp. gravity and are baked at lower oven temperature. Batters to be baked in large sizes require less water in the recipe and also less leavener than those baked in smaller sizes.

## Balancing of Pound Cakes and Creamed Cake Mixes

Usually the weight of sugar is equal to that of flour which in the leaner cake mixes the weight of sugar should be less than that of flour. The weight of shortening or fat should be equal to that of flour or sugar and the total weight of eggs and milk should be equal to the weight of sugar or flour. If the quantity of sugar and/or flour is more than eggs milk is required for moistening and baking powder has to be incorporated for supplementing the leavening power of eggs. In other words if the total of sugar and flour is more than double of eggs, that 2/3rd weight of the difference is added as milk, but milk is not a leavening agent as is eggs hence baking powder is required otherwise the cake will have poor volume and very dense grain.

In the case of wine cake the structure has to be more porous than that of the pound cake. Thus in creamed cake mixes for every 100 parts of liquid milk or water 6 to 9 parts of baking power should be added. The quality of lour used also affects the recipe balance. A strong flour necessitates the incorporation of extra baking powder in the recipe. If some acid-containing ingredient, such as cocoa, is present in the recipe then some baking soda has to be used for part of baking powder.

## Balancing of High-Ratio cakes

In the recipes of high-ratio cakes the quantity of sugar should be equal or more than that of flour and the amount of eggs should be more than that of fat or shortening. The weight of the liquid (eggs and milk) should equal or exceed that of sugar. As mentioned earlier special or emulsified high ratio type shortening should be used for these cakes, this will allow incorporation of these high quantities of sugar and milk. Blending method of mixing is usually employed for these cakes and fine cake flour should be used so that it may absorb and retain moisture and also provide structure. In high-ratio yellow cakes sugar may be as high as 1.5 times that of flour white in chocolate cakes it may be ass high as 1.65 times. Due to this higher quantity of sugar more liquid will be required to dissolve it and also to gelatinise the flour starch; thus more milk and eggs have to be used in the recipe.

Eggs supply moisture and also toughen the product due to the protein content. Apart from this they function as emulsifier also. To compensate for the toughness of the eggs the fat used should not be much less than the quantity of eggs. Egg yolks contain neutral emulsifier (lecithin); hence when yolks are used small amount of emulsified shortening will be required. Emulsified fat helps in carrying the added liquid without curdling. Any change in the quantity of sugar must be compensated by adjustment in the amount of flour and liquid. Excess of sugar and liquid will result in a cake of dense grain and poor volume. In high ratio cakes amount of leavening depends on the weight of flour; for 100 parts of flour depending upon the amount and types of eggs 4 to 6 parts of baking powder may be used.

Varieties of Cakes

## ANGEL FOOD CAKE

Angel food cakes are based on egg whites, sugar and flour, and do not contain any shortening; other ingredients present are salt, cream of tartar and flavour etc. The ranges of the main ingredients used are flour 20-40 parts, sugar 80-100 parts and egg whites 100 parts.

### Ingredients

Egg white is the critical ingredient of angel food cakes. Usual whites or dried albumen may be used. They affect the whiteness of the crumb, crust appearance, texture and flavour. Thinner whites can be whipped quickly but give less stable foam than the viscous whites. Sometimes water is added to the whites (upto 10%) to get additional moistness and closer grain in the finished cake but some reduction in volume may take place. Usual cane sugar may be used in the mix, but fine grain sugar is preferably due to case of dissolving in the egg whites. The flour used should be quite weak and for this reason weak soft wheat flour is used, replacement of part of flour with wheat starch shall give excellent cake. Egg whites and sugar act as tougheners by contributing to the strength or resilience to the foam structure. Due to the absence of shortening, the function of sugar as tenderiser is much more pronounced.

Whipping aids are necessary to improve the foam properties of the albumen, for this purpose cream of tartar, i.e. potassium hydrogen tartrate is very good imparting the cake a fine texture; it imparts a brighter colour to the crumb. Some acids like acetic acid, malic acid, citric acid and tartaric acid also improve the cake structure and colour but are inferior to cream of tartar, hence the latter is used upto 1-2% in the formulations. Emulsifiers like triacetin, sodium oleate, oleic acid and triethyl citrate are used for improving the whipping qualities of dried albumen. Flavours free from fatty materials are used in angel food cakes. Vanilla, almond extract and imitation rum extract are suitable for this purpose. Citrus fruit juices may also be used for this purpose but due to acidity the cream of tartar should be somewhat reduced to compensate. Spices may also be used but presence of oil will affect the cake volume. Cocoa is also sometimes added but it has some collapsing effect on the bubbles due to melting in the early stages of baking. Nut pieces may be used but they are not popular due to their unacceptable texture. The basic recipe remains almost the same but with variation in flavouring materials chocolate, fruit flavoured and marbled varieties of angel food cake may easily be produced.

## Method of Manufacture

Angel food cake is a product very sensitive to changes in preparation method. One method is the two-state one, in which case the egg whites containing the cream of tartar are whipped with or without a part of the sugar, followed by the mixing in one of the remaining sugar with continued beating. In the second stage flour is folded in with least disturbance while ensuring good distribution, this keeps the collapsing of the bubbles to the minimum. In a different procedure egg whites are whipped at medium speed until a soft structure is obtained and to this 50-60% sugar is slowly added with continued whipping, when wet peak is obtained, flavour, remaining sugar and flour are added with continued intermittent, and lowest speed of mixing, until uniform. Whipping is a critical step, underwhipping results in low volume and texture while over-whipping results in low volume and coarse crumb due to collapse of bubbles during baking. Best whipping temperature is 15-20°C and whipped sp. gr. is 0.15-0.17 with sugar.

Angel food cake pans should be free from grease and if they are slightly wetted before filling with batter, the crust colour will be lighter due to delay in the dehydration of the surface. Aluminium or thin steel pans are preferred. The best baking temperature range is 175-200°C, the higher temperature limit being used for smaller cakes.

## Formulation

*A typical formulation for Angel food cake is given below:-*

| | |
|---|---|
| Egg whites | 8 parts |
| Sugar | 8 |
| Cream of tartar | 0.006 |
| Salt | 0.06 |
| Cake flour | 3 |
| Vanilla | 0.12 |
| Almond flavour | 0.006 |

Egg whites are whipped to a froth. Half of sugar, cream of tartar and salt are sifted together and added as a steady stream during whipping of eggs, until a wet shiny peak is obtained. Flavours are folded in gently followed by gentle addition and folding in of the remaining sugar and flour. The batter is baked at 175°C in most ungreased, clean, pans. The cakes are trained upside down to cool them. They may be finished with a thin covering of fondant icing, before that the cakes may be filled or left plain. Icing may have the required colour and flavour.

It chocolate angel cake is to be prepared the quantity of the flour is reduced to 2.5 parts instead of 3 parts, and 1 part of natural cocoa is incorporated in the last stage with the flour.

## POUND CAKE

The name pound is due to the fact that these cakes were traditionally formulated using one pound each of flour, butter, whole eggs and sugar, but now-a-days better formulas are employed. As distinct from angel's food cake they contain shortening and whole eggs.

*An old fashioned pound cake formulation is given below :-*

| | |
|---|---|
| Shortening | 10 parts |
| Butter | 10 |
| Cake flour | 10 |
| Bread flour | 10 |
| Sugar | 20 |
| Salt | 0.3 |
| Eggs | 20 |
| Vanilla | 0.4 |

Flour is mixed carefully with fats and cream until soft and light. Sugar, salt and eggs are whipped until light. Vanilla is then added. Whipped sugar and eggs are added into the creamed fat and flour, taking care to avoid collapsing the bubbles. Baking is carried out at 175°C.

*A modern high ratio pound cake may have the typical formulation:-*

| | |
|---|---|
| Sugar | 20 parts |
| Salt | 0.4 |
| Milk powder | 1 |
| Cake flour | 20 |
| Emulsified shortening | 12 |
| Water | 7.5 |
| Eggs | 12 |
| Flavour | 0.4 |
| Baking powder | 2 |

Sugar, salt, milk powder, shortening and water are blended to get a soft, smooth paste, at medium speed for about 7 minutes. Eggs are added in 3 stages blending well after each addition, with this addition flavour and baking powder are also added. Rapid mixing should be avoided as it gives lumps and heavy, thin consistency. Blending method gives smaller air cells than those obtained with creaming. Baking is as usual carried out at 175°C.

As can be seen from above these pound cake formulations do not contain whipping improvers and acidifying agents (cream of tartar). Modern formulations contain some baking powder but the quantity is kept low to retain the dense, firm, tender and crumbly texture; quantity of eggs is lower but sugar is more to make it more sweet and tender. Replacement of butter by vegetable shortening reduces cost. Pound cake formulations may be used as the basis for tastes, petit fours, jelly rolls and trifles also but usually sponge cakes formulations are preferred for this purpose.

## Varieties of Pound Cakes

In above formulations a few percentages of invert sugar syrup or glycerine may be added to increase moistness of the crumb, more yolks or whites may be added for the desired textural improvement. In place of part of sugar corn syrup of high DE may be used, white pound cakes require only egg whites instead of whole eggs.

Good chocolate flavoured cakes can be made by replacing a few percentage of the shortening with chocolate liquor or by adding a good grade of cocoa. Marzipan cakes contain a few percentages of almond paste or combinations of almond paste and kernel paste. Fruit Pound cake is obtained by mixing some diced nuts, raising, glace fruit, or orange peel. Raisins and other fruits, but not nuts, are dusted with flour before adding to the mix. All these materials are added at the final stages of mixing to avoid smearing and discoloration of the cake.

## WHITE LAYER CAKE

White layer cakes contain egg whits while yellow layer cakes contain whole eggs. They usually contain a high percentage of sugar as compared to other types of high ratio cakes. In high ratio cakes i.e. in the cakes containing a high proportion of sugar to flour, high emulsifying shortening is used. In white layer cakes usual flavour is vanilla (extract or artificial) at about 0.5 to 1% level. Almond flavour may also be added.

*A typical universal white layer cake mix is given below :-*

| | |
|---|---|
| Cake flour | 37.5% |
| Sugar | 41 |
| Dried egg whites | 3 |
| Dried skim milk | 2.5 |
| Shortening, with emulsifiers | 13.7 |

| | |
|---|---|
| Sodium bicarbonate | 0.55 |
| Sodium acid pyrophosphate | 0.15 |
| Monocalcium monohydrate | 0.55 |
| Salt | 0.9 |
| Powdered vanilla | 0.15 |

To this dry mix is added 35 to 40% water depending upon the quality of the flour and emulsifier efficiency. This formulation is very versatile and is immune to failure even when other than usual mixing procured is used.

*A typical formulations of high ratio white layer is given below:-*

| | |
|---|---|
| Cake flour | 11 parts |
| Sugar | 12 |
| Skim milk powder | 1 |
| High ratio shortening | 5 |
| Salt | 0.2 |
| Water | 7 |
| Egg whites | 7.5 |
| Baking powder | 0.6 |
| Vanilla | 0.25 |

Sugar, salt, milk powder, flour and shortening are mixed together, to this 4 parts of water is added with mixing at medium speed for about 5 minutes. This is followed with the addition of remaining water and mixing until a smooth paste is obtained. Egg whites are added in three lots, in the last lot baking powder and flavour are also added. If desired about 0.1 part of almond flavour may also be added. Cakes are baked at 175-180oC. To reduce the alkaline effect of the egg whites, about 0.05 part of cream of tartar may also be added, this will impart a softer cake structure.

## YELLOW LAYER CAKE

Yellow layer cakes contain whole eggs as compared to white layer cakes which contain egg whites only. Due to the presence of egg yolks, yellow layer cakes are richer. Emulsified shortening is used in these formulations.

*A typical fomulation is give below :-*

| | |
|---|---|
| Sugar | 12 parts |
| Cake flour | 12 |
| Milk powder | 1 |
| Emulsified shortening | 5 |
| Water | 8 |
| Whole eggs | 6 |
| Salt | 0.25 |
| Baking powder | 0.6 |
| Vanilla | 0.25 |

Sugar, salt, milk powder, flour and shortening are blanded at medium speed for 5 to 6 minutes, with 6 parts of water, the remaining water is added and blended at medium speed. Eggs are also blended in stages, with the last lot baking powder and vanilla are also incorporated. Baking is done as usual.

Yellow cakes are particularly suitable for the addition of special flavours. In spice cakes mixture of cinnamon, nutmeg, ginger, and all-spice in the ratio of 8:6:1:1 are added. Further varieties of yellow cake can be made by adding pumpkin, applesauce, or mashed bananas.

## Filling and Icing

The cake is cut into layers of required thickness, with the help of a knife. Each layer is filled with butter-cream, jam, jelly or fudge etc; required number of layers are placed on each other and gently pressed to ensure sticking. Any icing which come out on the sides is used for giving, the sides of the cake, a thing covering. The cake is placed on cake liner and the top is covered with a layer of garnish, sometimes sides are also garnished with toasted cake crumbs, toasted nuts, sliced almonds or chocolate sprinkles etc.

## CHOCOLATE CAKES

Chocolate cakes contain cocoa or chocolate liquor. Devil's Food cake described later also contain cocoa but the difference between the two is that of pH which affects the texture, colour and flavour. Chocolate cakes are basic cakes to which cocoa or chocolate liquor has been added and their pH is almost same ass that of yellow cakes.

*A typical chocolate cake (High-ratio) formulation is give below:-*

| | |
|---|---|
| Flour | 12 parts |
| Sugar | 13.5 |
| Shortening | 5 |
| Milk powder | 1.5 |
| Cocoa | 2.2 |
| Baking powder | 0.6 |
| Salt | 0.25 |
| Water | 12 |
| Whole eggs | 6 |

Sugar, salt, milk powder, cocoa, flour, shortening and 2/3rd water are blended at medium speed until soft and smooth. Remaining water containing small amount of soda is also blended, followed by 3-stage blending of eggs containing the remaining soda in the last-stage. Vanilla is also added. The blend obtained should be soft and smooth and should pour like a thick gravy. The mix is baked as usual in the form of cupcakes, sheet cakes or loaf cakes. Marshmallow icing, whipped cream or cream tapping is also applied when desired. The cake may be finished in the form of layer cake as described earlier. It may be garnished with chocolate cake crumbs, malted chocolate, fudge icing or long-shred coconut.

## DEVIL'S FOOD CAKE

As mentioned above Devil's Food cake is also a cocoa containing cake. It contains extra soda and the pH is alkaline, thus the devil's food cake has a slightly reddish colour, more open grain and it is somewhat leaner in fat content. The reddish tone is imparted due to the reaction between cocoa and baking soda. Chocolate cake formulation may be used as a base.

*The following is typical formulation for high-ratio Devil's Food Cake:-*

| | |
|---|---|
| Cake flour | 12 parts |
| Sugar | 13.5 |
| Emulsified fat | 5 |
| Milk powder | 1.25 |
| Salt | 0.25 |
| Natural cocoa | 2.25 |
| Water | 12 |
| Baking soda | 0.2 |
| Eggs | 6 |
| Baking powder | 0.4 |

Mixing done as usual, baking powder and vanilla are added last.

## SPONGE CAKES

Sponge cakes are primarily leavened with eggs, using the whipping method. In the mix some baking powder is also added:

| | |
|---|---|
| Cake flour | 8.5 parts |
| Sugar | 8 |
| Glucose or corn syrup | 1 |
| Eggs | 9 |
| Salt | 0.06 |
| Water | 1.5 |
| Baking powder | 0.12 |
| Flavour | 0.3 |

Eggs are whipped and to this sugar, salt and glucose are added and whipped, 2/3rd of the water is added slowly and whipped. Remaining water and flavour are added and gently mixed. Slowly cake flour and baking powder are mixed in avoiding overmixing. Baking is done as usual. Lemon flavour may be used.

## CHIFFON CAKE

Chiffon cake is somewhat similar to Angel's food cake as egg whites are used instead of while eggs, due to the same reason it differs from sponge cake. The main difference between the chiffon cake and Angel's food cake is that the latter contains fat in the form of vegetable oil.

Baking powder is added to assist the oven spring. Additional egg yolks are also added. Two typical formulations are given below:-

| | *1* | *2* |
|---|---|---|
| Egg whites | 32 | 20 |
| Salt | 0.4 | 0.5 |
| Egg yolks | 10.7 | 16 |
| Vegetable oil | 10.7 | 10 |
| Sugar | 32 | 27 |
| Cake flour | 14 | 20 |
| Cream of tartar | 0.2 | 0.1 |
| Water | - | 6.9 |
| Baking powder | - | 1. |

Egg whites and salt are whipped to get a soft then the cream of tartar and sugar are added with continued heating until a soft peak is obtained. The yolks are whipped separately until thoroughly blended and aerated. Egg yolks and oil mixture is added, to the previous foam, gently, sugar and flour as gently added. Baking powder if used is added with flour. Baking is done as usual. Orange and lemon flavoured cakes are more popular while chocolate flavoured cakes are also made.

## FRENCH PASTRY

French pastries are square, triangular, rectangular or diamond-shaped pieces cut from cake sheets. The cake sheets are layered with fillings and creams. The cakes used may be of high ratio types e.g. yellow, chocolate etc., sponge or chiffon type. Two or more (usually 3) sheets are put one over other with filling e.g. cream filling and cut into pastries of above mentioned shapes.

The cake or pastry pieces then iced and finished. The cake is made in sheets about 1/2" thick. Light butter cream combination of butter cream and jelly or jam, or fudge kind are used in between the layers. The total height should not be more than 2". The sheets stick to each other. The layered cake is then chilled and cut with sharp knife dipped frequently in hot water, to get the pieces of required size and shape. The sides of the pieces may be iced with butter cream or fudge and topped with finely ground cake crumbs or ground nuts or chocolate strips.

The pastry tops are also decorated with neat design, proper colour blend and granish. The units may also be covered with warm fondant or dipped into the warm fondant.

The pastry pieces may also be cut from the layered cake sheets the top of which may already be decorated with butter cream before being cut into pastries.

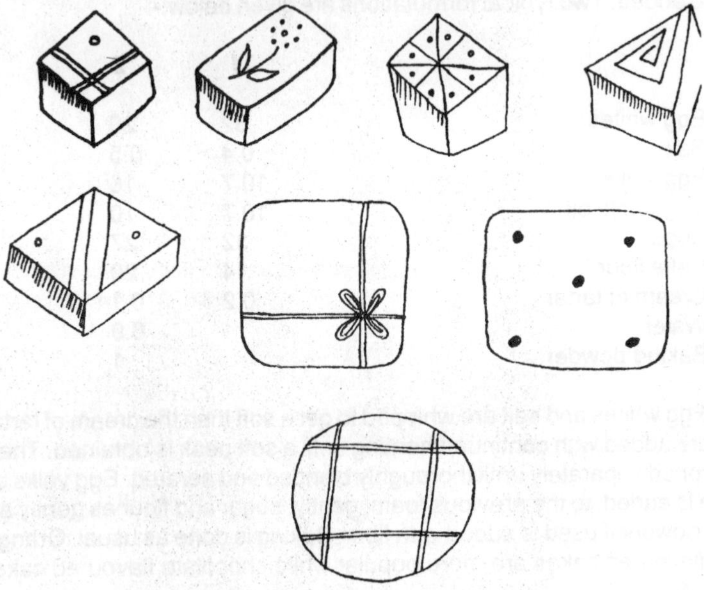

**Various Shapes of French Pastries**

# Chapter - 14

## *Biscuits, Cookies & Crackers*

Biscuit, cookies and crackers are important bakery item and are used all-day and are not restricted to any particular time of the day. They have very long shelf-life as they are not prone to destruction by fingers etc. They are quite popular in all countries especialley in india.

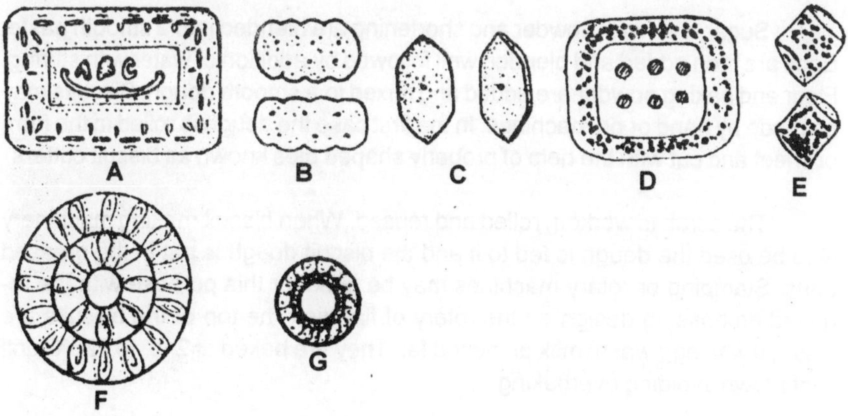


**Varieties of Biscuits**

## BISCUITS

Usual ingredients e.g. flour, sugar, salt, milk, shortening and leavening agents are used in making biscuits. Eggs, butter and other ingredients are also sometimes added for variety. They improve quality but raise the cost. Addition of eggs improves volume, taste and flavour of the biscuits; due to the natural leavening effect to eggs the chemical leavening agents are appropriately reduced. Biscuit doughs are mixed for complete development to get a soft, cake-like interior. The recipes which are richer in fat content are mixed like a pie crust. The fat and flour are rubbed together and the disolved sugar and salt are added with the liquid and folded in very gently.

This makes a flaky type of biscuit. These biscuits should be handled carefully because the dough becomes tough very quickly. These biscuits also tend to lose some of their shapes and bake somewhat flatter than others.

*A typical biscuit recipe is given below:-*

| | |
|---|---|
| Flour | 56 parts |
| Sugar | 8 |
| Salt | 0.5 |
| Shortening | 8 |
| Milk powder | 4 |
| Eggs | 4 |
| Baking powder | 3 |
| Water | 32 |

Sugar, salt, milk powder and shortening are blended into a smooth paste. Eggs are then added and blended well followed by addition of water with stirring. Flour and baking powder are added and mixed to a smooth dough. Biscuits may be made by hand or on machines. In the first case the dough is rolled in the form of sheet and cut with the help of properly shaped dies known as biscuit cutters.

The scrap is worked, rolled and reused. When biscuit making machinery is to be used the dough is fed to it and the biscuit dough is put in the greased pans. Stamping or rotary machines may be used for this purpose with the required embossing design on the rotary of flat die. The top of the biscuits are washed with egg wash, milk or melted fat. They are baked at 210° to 215°C unti light brown avoiding overbaking.

## Combination Biscuits

Combination biscuits are those biscuits which contain both yeast and chemical leavening agents e.g. baking powder. This combination results in a biscuit of lighter texture and grain with a variation in taste and appearance. The dough should be allowed to relax for 1/2 hr. before makeup thus permitting the yeast to condition the dough. The conditioning time is controlled by the temperature of water or milk.

*A typical recipe of combination biscuit is given below:-*

| | |
|---|---|
| Flour | 58 parts |
| Sugar | 10 |
| Salt | 1 |
| Milk powder | 4 |
| Shortening | 8 |
| Eggs | 4 |
| Yeast | 4 |
| Baking powder | 1 |
| Water | 32 |

Sugar, salt, milk powder and shortening are blended together to a smooth paste followed by the mixing of eggs and 16 parts water. Flour and baking powder are added with stirring. Yeast dissolved in 16 parts of warm water is added and the dough is developed until smooth. It is kept in a warm and moist place to rise keeping it covered to prevent crust formation. It is rolled and cut in suitable shape of biscuits with a hand cutter, reusing the scrap or moulded with the help of stamping or rotary biscuit machine. The biscuit pieces are placed in gresed pans, proofed, washed with egg-wash or melted fat and are baked at 200-210°C.

Cinnamon Biscuits are made by rolling the dough in sheet form 1/4" thick. The sheet is brushed with melted fat and sprinkled with cinnamon sugar. The filled dough is rolled up and brushed with melted fat; and cut into round slices 3/4' thick. The pieces are put in greased pans, half proofed, egg washed and baked at 200°C. After this the biscuits are washed with syrup and when mildly warm, iced with simple icing.

**Cutting of Brushed Rolls with Scraper**

**Cinnamon Biscuit**

## SODA CRACKERS

Soda crackers are cheaper items hence higher quantities of flour and salt are used in these formulations, keeping in view the cost and quality factors.

### Ingredients

Soda crackers contain upto 80% or more of flour, hence its quality is important particularly for texture. Specifications for cracker flours are narrower than those cookies flours. The sponge flour should be stronger, unbleached and with an ash content of 0.39-0.42% and protein content of 8.5-10%. The dough flour should be weaker with 0.4% ash and 8-9% protein content. Strong flour tend to increase oven spring and give tougher crackers while weak flours give lesser spring and tender cracker. Lard gives better flavour and tenderness while vegetable glue has the advantage of improved spring.

Sometimes emulsifiers are added, topping salt is also required apart from the salt in the dough. Salt with special particle size is used for this purpose and about 2.5% of salt based on dough weight is required for topping. Amounts of fines in the salt should be minimum. Rapidity of fermentation depends on dough temperature, absorption, quantity of salt, and sugars. Increase in the quantity of water increases the rate of fermentation while higher quantity of salt reduces it. Sugars in the form of corn syrup, sucrose or invert syrup serve as yeast food thus increasing the rate of fermentation.

*Soda cracker recipes are give below:-*

| *Sponge Ingredients* | *Range* | *Typical* |
|---|---|---|
| Flour | 60-80 | 70 parts |
| Yeast | 0.1-0.5 | 0.2 |
| Water | 28-34 | 30 |
| Shortening | 0.8 | 4 |
| Diastatic malt | 0-0.1 | 0.02 |
| ***Dough Ingredients*** | | |
| Flour | 40-20 | 30 |
| Shortening | 0-10 | 5.8 |
| Salt | 1.3-1.6 | 1.4 |
| Sodium bicarbonate | 0.5-0.7 | 0.6 |
| Malt syrup | 0-1.5 | 0.9 |
| Water | 0-2 | 0.8 |

Sponge time is about 16-20 hrs. and fermentation time about 3-5 hrs. at a temperature of about 25-30°C.

All the crackers are made from laminated doughs with the help of automatic laminators when required. At least 6 to 7 layers are preferably put. In contrast to puff pastry no interleaving ingredient is put between the layers; but in the case of cream crackers a mixture of flour and shortening may be put between the dough sheets. Shortening is usually added to the sponge, as this ensures adequate dispersion of the shortening and if any crust form on the sponge, it gets softer by the shortening. Even rancidity is also decreased, while fermentation is not appreciably affected by the fat. The amount of sodium bicarbonate in the dough is adjustable depending upon the pH required in the baked crackers.

## COOKIES

Cookies are one of the most important bakery items. Various types of cookies are made and the principle of their production are being given here:-

### Ingredients

As usual sugar, salt, flour, shortening, milk solids, eggs, leavening agents and cocoa and flavours are the basic ingredients for making cookies. Flour, water, milk solids, eggs and cocoa or chocolate products are binding materials and tougheners. Water assist in gluten formation; milk solids are not very effective due to low quantities used and egg whites are better binders or tougheners than whole eggs. Sugars are most important tenderising materials while shortening leavening agents and egg yolks are less important. Baking acids, oat flour, soy flour act as tougheners and ground raisins, ground dates etc. act as tenderisers, corn flour acts as tenderiser but only minor amounts are used otherwise an off-flavour is imported. Starch is a good and cheap tenderiser.

Flour supplies the continuous structure to the cookies. Strong flours require more shortening and sugar to obtain an acceptable texture. Strong flour gives hard texture and coarse grain and surface appearance. Soft cake flour results in too much spread and loss of design. Cake flour (weak flour) is used in recipes containing egg whites. Wafers are made with egg whites and when yolks are also added strong flour should be used. If the quantity of flour is reduced too much or when more enriching ingredients are added the cookies, will lack body and will become very fragile. Coarse or fine sugar or their blends may be used in cookies to adjust spread and machining properties. Coarse sugar requires longer mixing period and result in too much spread thereby making the cookies difficult to handle. It also results in more breakage during finishing and handling. Fine sugar produces close, dense grain, mixes quickly but may result in separation of fat from the mix, white bagging out, which will produce greasiness and toughness in the baked product. Sugars and especially syrups in large amounts tend to make the dough sticky and harder release from dies and wires. Invert syrup should be used with care, it makes wire-cuts, especially wafers, soft, light, and spongy with an open texture; the crust colour is often brighter and develops earlier in the baking.

Milk solids suppress harsh flavours and are used at 5% of the flour weight. It improves the crust colour and gloss. It binds water and makes the dough stiffer and stickier. The toughening effect is quite mild. Most cookies are rich in fat. The bagged out creamed cookies may contain upto 65 to 70% fat based on flour. Fat improves taste, tenderness and keeping qualities when used in increasing quantities. Vegetable glue is usually employed but a mixture with butter is the best. Too much shortening may lead to a greasy, smeary cookie which is susceptible to rancidity because the fat soaks into the package, this necessitates the use of cellophone overwraps. The natural flavour of butter will impart its flavour to the neutral flavour of the shortening. Ideal maounts of shortening and sugar vary with the kind of method used for cookies, e.g. for cutting machine 15% shortening and sugar variable, rotary machine 30% shortening and 30% sugar, wire-cut 50% sugar and 50% shortening based on flour weight. If amount of shortening is increased too much higher than the indicated amounts then problems arise in the case of rotary and cutting machines.

Use of egg yolks as part of whole eggs will give a tender cookie with excellent eating quality but the grain or internal structure of the cookie may not be as good as with whole eggs. Use of eggs imparts natural flavour, taste and keeping qualities. Egg whites are generally whipped to a wet peak rather than a dry peak when nuts, flour and other ingredients have to be folded into the beater whites.They blend in more easily and avoid overmixing without loss of volume. Salt is added in the formulation of biscuits upto 1% based on flour, in cracker doughs it is used upto 1.5% of flour weight. In the recipes containing nuts etc., or more fat, even higher quantities of salt may be used. Based on fat weight salt may be used upto 3%. Addition of lecithin increases the shortening effect of fats and the tendency for the fat to cover or spread amont sugar, flour etc. particles. Lecithin make rich sweet doughs seem drier thus improving their machineability. Particularly it ensures better die release from rotary cutters and improves impression and reduces cripples. Lecithin reduces mixing time thereby improving tenderness by minimixing gluten development particularly when strong flours are used.

## Formulation Aspects of Different Cookies

One of the most important formulation aspects of cookies is the 'spread'. The cookie should have the desired spread. Too much spread will result in cookie becoming too big for the package while too little spread will result in slack fill in breadth and excess height. Tougheners usually decrease spread while tenderisers increase it. Increased amounts of leaveners, use of finer sugar, increased amounts of shortening or water result in greater spread. Spread can be decreased by using stronger flour, increasing the mixing time and using cold water.

Too much salt can reduce spread while increase in trhe amount of sugar often increases it. When other method fail, 0.12% potassium carbonate may be added to increase spread. Increasing the temperature in the first oven zone tends to decrease spread while reducing the temperature spread increases.

The amounts of major ingredients in cookie doughs depend on the method of production employed. In the case of rotary molded cookie doughs 5-15% water, 10-40% shortening, 20-45% sugars and 0-20% syrups may be taken based on flour. In the case of stamping cookie doughs 10-25% water, 5-20% shortening, 15-50% sugars and 0-20% syrups are recommended. In the case of wire cut cookie doughs 20-40% water, 10-50% shortening, 40-85% sugars and 0-20% syrups are recommended. The average amounts of these ingredients are 22.2%, 33.7%, 43.7% and 16.9% respectively based on flour weight. The method of production used influeces the texture apart from the affects on formulation.

Deposit cookie are similar to the hand bagged cookies. They contain 35-40% sugar, 65-75% shortening and 15-25% whole eggs. In the dough should be quite cohesive, nonsticky and short enough to be separated cleanly after being cut by wire. The dough may contain upto 100% shortening and even more of sugar based on flour. The doughs may be as soft as cake batters or too stiff to be moulded by hand. Wire cut cookies have more open grain and softer texture than the deposited cookies and have more uniform shape; but have less potential for making surface design and less uniformity of size and shape than cookies made by rotary molded cookies.

For rotary molded cookies, the dough should have such a consistency that it feeds uniformly and readily fills all the crevices of the die cavity. The dough blank should be capable of being extracted from the cavity without distortion, but it must adhere to the die roll long enough to prevent the piece from falling out before it reaches the extraction roller. The blank should not break before or after baking and the finished cookies should have smooth surface. Spread and rise should be controlled so that design does not get distorted. Doughs formulated to meet these requirements are usually fairly high in sugar and shortening and low in water. Lecithin at about 0.4% level improves machineability. One stage mixing is quite satisfactory but a creaming operation with most of the minor ingredients added before the flour goes in ensures the freedom from lumps in the cookies. for ratory sandwich bases 20-30°C dough temperature is quite suitable.

## Making up of Cookies

The dough for making cookies should be properly mixed otherwise the cookie shall become tough. Proper mixing or creaming of the mix is essential before adding the flour. Short doughs do not require creaming but good blending before adding flour is essential. Flour is folded ion gently to avoid development of gluten, otherwise tough cookie will be obtained. In over mixed short doughs the dough pecomes tougher to roll and stretches and is not tender. In the case of doughs containing egg whites a dry peak will not permit easy absorption of flour and will result in toughness. Each cookie should be of the same size and evenly spaced on conveyor or greased pans. Pans should be greased evenly and with minimum of fat. Excessive greasing results in too much spread while lack of greasing results in sticking and little spread. Garnishing should be done just after being put on the pans otherwise crust formation will prevent the nuts or fruit pieces from sticking.

## Baking

Cookies being small in size require short baking period and lower oven temperature. Cookies containing 35% or less sugar, based on flour, require higher baking temperature than the cookies low in fat and high in sugar content. An oven temperature of 190 to 200°C is quite satisfactory. Special care should be taken in the baking of wafer type cookies and those which are to be rolled and filled after baking. Overbaking will cause them to crack and break while they are being rolled; they should be rolled while slightly warm. the cookies shall be taken out of the oven just before the desired stage of baking, as baking continues outside the oven due to the heat in the cookie and the pan.

## Decoration and Finishing

Addition of food colour is desirable in the cookie, to supplement the natural colour obtained due to baking and caramelisation of the sugar on the surface. Deep colours should be avoided as they affect the flavour and taste by dominating the natural colour and flavour. Combination colours and flavours should also be avoided. the cookies should be properly finished. They may be dipped in or decorated with chocolate of the fast drying type containing an emulsifier, and lesser quantity of natural cocoa butter. For sweetening purpose additional 20-25% sugar may be added. Due to the lesser amount of cocoa butter it will not have the defect of graying. It is not as good as natural fine-grade sweet chocolate. Chocolate should be dissolved in a double jacketed vessel taking care not to exceed the temperature of 40°C. Cookies should be given an even and equal dip. Dipping temperature should be carefully controlled as at lower temperature it gets thickened and the coating becomes thick.

When fudge icing is to be applied the fudge should be warm and should firm up when cool. Fat must be added to those fudge icings which dry quickly and crust too heavily, for this purpose emulsified fat is the best. If jam is not used for sandwiching the cookies, fudge should be used, it is tasty and prevents separation of cookies. A fine grade jam should be used instead of flavoured jelly otherwise the product will be ruined. Nut granish or fruit garnish may be applied on the top of dipped or bagged out cookie. A whole or half nut e.g. cashewnut may be put at the centre of the cookie. Variety in the types of nuts and fruit pieces will increase the variety of the cookies.

## Production Aspects of Different Cookies

In the case of short Dough Cookies the dough is chilled before rolling on a flour dusted canvas cloth. Excessive dusting flour is avoided and the scrap dough is folded into the fresh dough after each rolling of the dough to avoid toughness from excessive scrap dough. In the case of Bagged-out cookies, the cookies are bagged out evenly in size and shape; even and enough space is allowed for cookies to spread in baking.

Cookies are garnished before they dry or develop a crust and if jelly or jam is used they should be used in small amounts. For Ice Box cookies the dough is chilled before making various designs, too much colour should be avoided and should be evenly blended. the madeup units are frozen before slicing into even thickness with a sharp knife. Cookies are allowed to return to the room temperature before baking.

In the case of coconut Macroons the mix is heated in a double jacketted vessel to avoid scorching, mixing is carefully done to avoid scorching and creation of own or burned spots. The mix is bagged out while warm; if it cools, reheating is required. Macroon is garnished before drying. Macroons are allowed to dry and form a crust before baking on paperlined pans. For chocolate coconut macroons cocoa is blended with sugar before adding it to the egg whites. When making chocolate macroons additional egg whites are added to allow for the absorption of the cocoa. For almond Macroon cookies the paste is blended with a little egg white to remove lumps or dried pieces before adding the sugar.

Egg whites are added gradually to ensure proper blending. Canvas bag is moistened with cold water before filling with the mix. Parchment paperlined pans are used and cookies are garnished before they get dried. Cookies are allowed to dry and form a crust before baking. Plain macroons are allowed to dry overnight. Overbaking should be avoided. 3 to 5% of corn syrup based on weight of sugar may be added to the mix to keep the cookies fresh and soft for a longer period. The cookies are washed with a hot glaze just after the removal from the oven.

## Sugar Cookies

*Following formulation is quite suitable for these cookies :-*

| | |
|---|---|
| Weak flour | 64 parts |
| Sugar | 32 |
| Salt | 0.5 |
| Milk powder | 2 |
| Glucose or corn syrup | 2 |
| Eggs | 8 |
| Baking powder | 2 |
| Water | 12 |

Sugar, salt, milk powder, shortening and syrup are creamed together, followed by creaming in of eggs. Water is added with vanilla. Flour and baking powder are folded in, avoiding overmixing, otherwise the cookies will be tough. Dough is chilled before using. Dough is rolled to 1/4" thickness. Egg wash, water or milk wash is given to the dough. Granulated sugar is sprinkled over it and cookies are cut in the desired size and shape e.g. round, heat, diamond, square etc. Dough may be left unwashed and cut cookies may be dipped into a pan of sugar. They may be garnished with jam or nuts before baking at 200°C until golden brown. For chocolate sugar cookies 6 parts cocoa is added and flour is reduced by 5-6%. 0.25 part of baking soda is added and baking powder is reduced to 1.5 parts.

## Coconut Cookies

| | |
|---|---|
| Flour | 28 parts |
| Sugar | 28 |
| Salt | 0.5 |
| Milk powder | 1.5 |
| Shortening | 16 |
| Baking soda | 0.25 |
| Eggs | 6 |
| Water | 12 |
| Coconut powder | 26 |
| Baking powder | 0.25 |

Sugar, salt, milk powder, shortening and baking soda are creamed with eggs; water and vanilla are then added followed by coconut powder. Finally flour and baking powder are mixed until smooth. Cookies are bagged out on lightly greased pans and baked at 190°C until golden brown.

## Jumble Cookies

| | |
|---|---|
| Flour | 39 parts |
| Sugar | 24 |
| Salt | 0.5 |
| Milk powder | 2 |
| Glucose | 2 |
| Shortening | 21 |
| Macroon paste | 8 |
| Eggs | 19 |
| Water | 8 |
| Baking powder | 1.5 |

Macroon paste and 1/6th egg are blended until smooth and then rest of the method is as usual. For chocolate jumbles 5 parts of dark natural cocoa is added to the flour. Flour is reduced to 35 parts. 0.25 baking soda is also added, and baking powder is reduced to 1.25 parts.

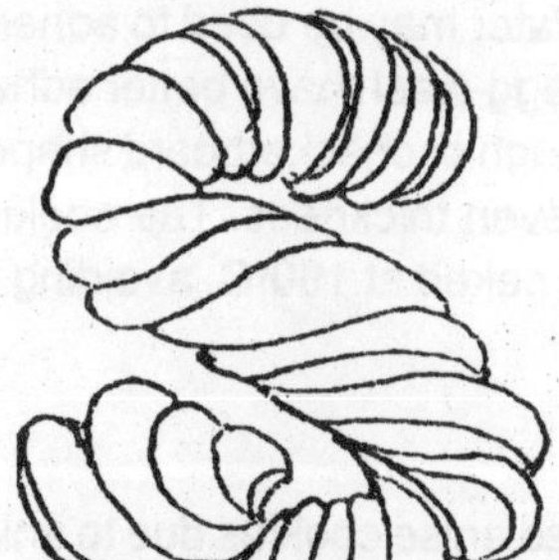

'S' Shaped Jumble

Ring Shaped Jumble

Thus with slight variation in the cookies formulation and method of making different types of cookies may be produced.

## Ice Box Cookies

| | |
|---|---|
| Flour | 56 parts |
| Confectionery sugar | 24 |
| Salt | 0.5 |
| Shortening | 36 |
| Glucose or corn syrup | 2 |
| Eggs | 10 |
| Vanilla | 1 |

Method of mixing is as usual. All or part of this dough may be coloured by blending colcur in the required amount of dough. melted chocolate or fudge base is best used for making the dough chocolate. The addition of cocoa causes toughness and craking when the dough is handled for makeup. Each coloured piece of dough is kept separate from the rest. The dough is refrigerated before making up the cookies. Water may be used to adhere different layers of dough but egg whites or regular egg-wash have better adhesive qualities. Before slicing the made up rolls of dough or checkerboard shapes it is chilled. Each layer is cut with a sharp knife to even thickness. The cookies are allowed to come to rook temperature and are caked at 190°C, avoiding overbaking.

## Anise Cookies

The cookies ar called anise cookies due to anise flavour. Ground anise is used for this purpose.

| | |
|---|---|
| Flour | 64 parts |
| Ground anise seed | 1 |
| Sugar | 64 |
| Salt | 0.5 |
| Eggs | 48 |

Eggs, sugar and salt are whipped and to this flour containing ground anise seed is gently folded in. overmixing is avoided. The bagged out cookies are left overnight to get dried, this also forms a crust which cracks during baking at 190oC. The cookies will have a white crustlike effect and will be slightly brown around the edges.

## Spices Drops

| | |
|---|---|
| Flour | 72 parts |
| Honey | 48 |
| Brown sugar | 8 |
| Eggs | 4 |
| Oil | 3 |
| Salt | 1 |
| Cinnamon | 1 |
| All spice, Ginger, cloves | 0.25 each |
| Water | 12 |
| Baking soda | 1.5 |
| Ammonium bicrbonate | 1.25 |

Honey, sugar, eggs, oils, salt, spices are mixed until, to this soda dissolved in ammonium bicarbonate is added with good stirring. Finally flour is added and the dough is mixed until smooth. Small amount of molasses may be used in place of some honey. Spices should be carefully weighed and excess should be avoided at all costs. To make the dough easier to handle it may be cooled. The dough is rolled to 1/4" thickness and cut into strips of 1" length. Each piece is rolled into a ball form and put on paper-lined pans about 1" apart. they are baked at 180°C avoiding overbaking. Otherwise they will become hard. The cookies are put in a bowl and hot syrup is poured over them, with gentle stirring, to coat them with syrup. The syrup is made by boiling 100 parts of sugar with 25 parts water at 115°C to a soft ball. Cookies are then place in a pan filled with confectionery sugar and rolled until coated with it. The sugar may be coloured pink or green for variety.

## Sugar Wafers

The sugar wafer base cake contains only small amounts of leavening agents e.g. ammonium bicarbonate or soda and the major leavening action is due to steam. Structurally sugar wafer mix is a dehydrated starch gel with a supporting gluten network. The batter is closely onfined so that the steam cannot readily escape, thus its leavening effect is much greater than it would be if the thin sheet were exposed to the atmosphere, sugar-shortening fillings are used with sugar wafers, as presence of excess moisture will ruin the texture of the base wafer. The wafer batter is a quite thin mixture of flour and water to which small amounts of other ingredients are added. Appropriate amounts of colour and flavour are also added. Vanilla is used upto 0.025 to 0.05% as flavour. Chocolate or dark coloured wafers sometimes do not contain any cocoa products and are coloured with caramel or food dyes. For chocolate flavour about 10% cocoa may be added together with additional 15% water.

Previously enriching agents like milk, sugar and eggs used to be added but they result in carbon deposit on the plates which causes the wafers to stick. Small amount of lecithin and some shortening, e.g. coconut oil, are added to facilitate release of the wafer. Addition of some starch makes the wafer tenderer and improves the texture. General formula for the sugar wafer batter is given below:

| | |
|---|---|
| Flour | 100 parts |
| Water | 125-150 |
| Sodium bicarbonate | 0.2-0.7 |
| Ammonium bicarbonate | 0-0.5 |
| Milk powder, skim | 0-5 |
| Whole milk powder | 0-3 |
| Starch | 0-5 |
| Dried egg yolks | 1.2-2.5 |
| Salt | 0-0.7 |
| Lecithin | 0-0.4 |
| Coconut oil | 0-2 |

*A typical formulation is given below:-*

| | |
|---|---|
| Flour | 100 parts |
| Water | 140 |
| Sodium bicarbonate | 0.5 |
| Salt | 0.5 |
| Lecithin (optional) | 0.1 |
| Coconut oil | 1 |

If the flour used is too weak the wafer iwll have a too dense or too close texture while a too strong flour will result in a hard and flinty wafer. The dry ingredients are first blended and then water is added gradually while mixing, shorteing if used, is blended in while the mixture is still of a doughy consistency. If eggs and milk solids are to be used, they are added to the mixer at the start with about half of the water, followed by other dry ingredients and finally he remaining water is added.

Special wafer ovens are used for baking sugar wafers. In these ovens pairs of plates or continuous bands travel with the batter confined between them. The baking time is about 2 minutes. When cream is applied the wafer should contain less than 2% moisture for best strength and crispnesss.

The basic principle used in making the flat, cream-layered sugar wafer are also used in making ice-cream cones or waffle cones and novelty cream filled shapes such as circles, hemispheres, half-cylinders and peanut shell etc. These may be filled with cheese-flavoured or other fat based fillings instead of usual sugar-shortening mixture.

# BISCUIT INDUSTRY SCENARIO IN INDIA

## Introduction

Biscuits are manufactured by both organised and unorganised Sectors. Biscuit industry has undergone lot of ups and down with time; e.g. it was reserved for small scale sector by the Government in 1978. Now as per the latest trends, the Government is thinking of dereserving this industry. This thinking is perhaps in line with the Government policy of liberalisation. This will create its own problems and opportunities with respect to industry and consumer. The net effect may be the enhanced capabilities of the industry to produce quality biscuits due to tough competition.

This change hopeful may take place in the next 2-3 years only subject to various other considerations. This article attempts to summarise :-

(a) The current status of the Biscuit industry

(b) Government related indirect control affecting cost of major raw materials.

(c) Consumer preferences and buying patterns

(d) Taxation

(e) Latest trends etc.

## Present Status:

It is estimated that 12 lac tons of Biscuits of various types were manufactured during 1995 in the Country, out of which 1/3rd was manufactured by organised sector.

The organised sector consists of large, medium and small biscuit manufacturers who produce packaged biscuits. The unorganised sector comprises of small bakery units, cottages and household type manufacturing plants. These units distribute their biscuits in the surrounding vicinity of their manufacturing locations of say 20 to 50 Km. The unorganised sector has it own problems like lack of appropriate technical know-how, equipments and managerial skills. On the other hand organised sector having small scale operations face the problems of advertising marketing and distribution logistics.

The trend is emerging towards medium to large scale manufacturing plants in the organised sector. Most of the medium scale plants have a manufacturing capacity of 3 to 5 tons per shift whereas the large scale units may have a capacity of 15 to 35 tons per shift.

**Zonewise Breakup of Market Share of Biscuits of Organised Sector**

| Zone | Volume (Tons) | Value (Rs. Crore) | % Contribution |
|---|---|---|---|
| North | 78109 | 354 | 20% |
| East | 75449 | 342 | 19% |
| West | 132067 | 599 | 34% |
| South | 104396 | 475 | 27% |
| All India | 390020 | 1770 | 100% |

**Consumer Preferences for Biscuit Varieties in Different Regions - %**

| Variety | West Zone | North Zone | East Zone | South Zone | All India |
|---|---|---|---|---|---|
| Glucose | 64 | 64 | 3 | 26 | 41 |
| Milk | 1 | 8 | 24 | 33 | 16 |
| Marie | 11 | 3 | 24 | 13 | 12 |
| Arrowroot | 1 | 1 | 23 | 4 | 6 |
| Salt Crackers | 5 | 2 | 5 | 0.50 | 3 |
| Non Salt Crackers | 7 | 5 | 6 | 15 | 8 |
| Sweet Cookies | 3 | 1 | 4 | 1 | 3 |
| Creak Biscuits, Wafers & Others | 8 | 16 | 11 | 7.5 | 11 |

**Buying Pattern of Biscuits by Different types of Households - %**

| Types of Household | West Zone | North Zone | East Zone | South Zone | All India |
|---|---|---|---|---|---|
| Nuclear Family | 57 | 83 | 66 | 69 | 67 |
| Joint Family | 38 | 16 | 31 | 27 | 29 |
| Singles | 4.5 | 0.5 | 2 | 3 | 3 |
| Others | 0.5 | 0.5 | 1 | 1 | 1 |

## Biscuit Brands:

The major biscuit brands and different pack sizes introduced by the organised sector of Biscuit industry in the last decade is summarised in table. It can be seen that some of the brands like Little Hearts, 50/50 and Snax of Britannia Industries Limited have been good success. Similarly the smaller packs of 50 gm. and 75 gm. of Parle-G and Consumer Packaged forms of Jeffs and Cheeslings have been successful of Parle Products Limited.

It is heartening to note that the pace of introduction of new packs sizes and product varieties are on increase. It has been observed that 200 g. transparent packs are more successful than 100 g. packs of marie type of biscuits. Thus, this will make more variety available to the consumer besides convenience by way of availability of smaller packs.

**Eating Habits of Biscuits**

| Description | West Zone | North Zone | East Zone | South Zone | All India |
|---|---|---|---|---|---|
| Vegetarian | 56 | 26 | 13 | 17 | 30 |
| Egg-Vegetarian | 23 | 13 | 8 | 31 | 21 |
| Non-Vegetarian | 18 | 59 | 76 | 50 | 47 |
| Others | 3 | 2 | 3 | 2 | 2 |

## Taxation

33% of the cost of ex-factory prices of biscuit is composed of Goverr ment levies in the form of Excise Duty, Sales Tax, Octroi and TOT etc. Durin 1993, the custom duty on general machinery including baking machinery wa reduced from 85% to 65%. Further, in 1994, the Government allowed the impo of second hand capital goods by actual users at a normal duty subject to a min mum residual life of 5 years. However, there is a need to consider the followin aspects of taxations by the State and Central Governments.

(a) In 1993, the excise duty on biscuit was reduced from 11.5% to 7.5% b this was again increased to 10% in 1994. There is a need to reduce th excise duty to 5%.

(b) Sales tax on biscuit varies from 5% in U.P. to 15% in A.P. There is a urgent need to rationalise this tax structure to uniform level of say 5

(c) There is an under utilized capacity of the order of 35% in small scale sector which perhaps can be utilized if excise component is reduced.

## Dereservation

In keeping with the policy of liberalization of Trade and Industries, the Central Government is planning to dereserve 8 Food Processing Industries which include Biscuits, Ice Creams, Pickles, Sugar Confectionery, Bread, Rice Milling oleoresins and essential Oils. The limit of investment is proposed to be raised from Rs. 75 lakhs to Rs. 3 crores. Dereservation of biscuit industry will result into the entry of many big international names like United Biscuits, Nebisco etc. in the market very soon. The range and variety of biscuit available to the consumers in the market will be more than the present range by both small scale and big industrial houses. However, the stiff competition will have to be faced by the industry for survival and ultimate success. As Mr. Gurucharan Das, the Ezx-CEO of Procter & Gamble India, only 2/3rd of Indian business is going to survive the onslaught of reforms. Time will tell happens to the biscuit industry.

The consumer is becoming more and more demanding and is having a more teeth due to the legitimate fight achieved through Standards of Weighs & Measures Act, 1976, Consumer Protection Act, 1986 and such other legislations. This means that the industry has to be well prepared to ensure not only a complaint free product but aim should be to satisfy the consumers so that they feel delighted. There has to be a focus on achieving excellene in product and services, otherwise survival may become difficult.

## ISO 9000

In recent years many industries in the country are going for ISO 9000 for achieving excellence in quality of products manufactured by them. It is estimated that as on December, 1995 there would be about 1300-1400 certified manufacturers in the country holding ISO 9000 Certification. It is a matter of great pleasure to learn that one of the small scale biscuit manufacturing company i.e. Ajmer Food products Pvt. Ltd. Ajmer has also got the ISO 9000 Certification on October 17, 1995 for biscuits. This is the First certification in the country ever given to biscuit industry. This is a good trend in the country for marching towards production of quality biscuits to satisfy the ever increasing expectations of consumers. It proves that quality biscuits can be produced equally by big and small houses provided the company takes the path of quality excellence with changes mind set.

ISO 9000 basically allows the implementation of an appropriate system and processes, this is one step towards total quality management of TQM. Biscuit industry should aim for achieving TQM which means continuous improvement in quality of (a) people (b) products (c) processes and systems and (d) customer satisfaction.

## Technical Developments:

There are lot of technological changes which have taken place in country for manufacturing biscuits. Some of these are summarized as under:

**Fuel:** Earlier, electric oven was a common baking medium used universally, as this was available cheap and the maintenance of such an oven was relatively simple. This trend has changed over to the use of Light Diesel Oil (LDO) fired oven. These ovens can be of direct or indirect heating types. In view of this, future trend will be to explore the use of alternative fuel such as furnace oil, low stock high sulphur (LSHS) etc. Thus, a lot of engineering work is required before such fueld can be used successfully for baking biscuits. These fuelds contain high sulphur and could adversely affect the quality of Biscuits if used in direct fired baking oven. LPG is a good alternate fuel for baking of biscuits, but its easy availability is difficult in various parts of the country.

There is a good scope for saving of the fuel the extent of 10% by improving the quality of insulation of baking oven, efficient combustion of burners by controlling air and fuel ratio and control of heat wastage through exhaust chimneys.

**Microwave Oven:** Recent trend has been to use microwave oven in conjunction with conventional type of baking ovens. This helps to increase the output of certain varieties of biscuits by about 25-30%. The initial cost of equipment is however, very high.

Vanaspati System: The conventional method of handling Vanaspati in the tin is being replaced by a bulk handling system wherein Vanaspati/Hydrogenated is purchased in bulk in road tankers. Under this system, the storage silos and pipe lines require adequate heating when this system is used particularly in the colder regions of the country, like North. Use of this bulk handling of Vanaspati leads to not only saving of the cost of the tins, but also eliminates the need for manual cutting of the tins. During manual cutting of tins, at times, there are stray chances of metallic chips falling into Vanaspati, ultimately leading to metallic contamination of biscuits, if proper care and control are not exercised.

The other alternate way is to substitute costly tins with bag in box type of corrugated box for packaging of Vanaspati. This leads to current saving of Rs. 20-25 on purchased of 15 kg. tin of Vanaspati.

## Conclusion:

The cost of advertising is becoming enormous due to the use of effective T.V. media of modern changed time. The reach of T.V. is very wide and even penetrating into the rural market. The ever increasing cost of advertising and marketing of biscuits is likely to affect smaller section of Biscuit Industry in the organised sector. The market share of organised and unorganised sector may shift from existing 35:65 to 50:50 by the year 2000 when the expected production is likely to be 19.3 lac tons per year. The chances of higher mortality rate for both new brands and new companies due to increased competitiveness will be the changed scenario.

The biscuit industry need to concentrate on quality improvement techniques alongwith innovative ways of cost controls and improvement of managerial skills of the supervisory staff. Thus training and development will play great role for achieving this objective. Government need to take appropriate measures by way of reducing the Excise Duty from 10% to 5%. Further, the Government should ponder over to stabilise the prices of the major inputs like Wheat Flour, Vanaspati, Sugar etc. so as to ensure normal growth of 10% per year of biscuit industry, major portion of which is consumed by common man as a wholesome and nutritious food.

# Chapter - 15

## *Quality Control*

As in other industries quality control of the products in Bakery Industry is very important, particularly because it is a food industry. In addition to satisfying the consumer, the bakery product from a factory must meet the requirements of governmental regulations. Thus the product apart from having good looks, good taste and flavour and good texture for consumer acceptance, should also satisfy legal requirements and standards. It should also conform to labelling and packaging requirements. Even if it is not contaminated it has to be prepared and stored under hygienic conditions.

For good quality control of the final product following steps are necessary :

(i) Thorough check of quality of raw materials, and packaging materials

(ii) Accurate weighing and measuring of ingredients according to the given formulation

(iii) Preparation of the product according to the set methods

(iv) Manufacture under sanitary and hygienic conditions

(v) Storage of raw materials and finished products carefully depending on the item

(vi) Regular batch-wise quality checking of the finished product

(vii) Careful & serious follow-up of complaints from the retailers & customers regarding quality of the product, etc. It must be emphasised here that some of the standards such as texture or flavour of the product are subject to interpretation, and opinions of two persons may differ regarding the same product. We shall now discuss some of the more important points of quality control in bakery factory, while leaving the quality considerations of the production aspects.

# RAW MATERIALS QUALITY CONTROL

In a cottage scale bakery no facility for testing the quality of various ingredients are available; only inspection by look, taste, touch and smell is done and also it is seen that changes in quality of different batches is not due to any change in quality of any of the ingredients. In mechanised bakeries and other bakeries of larger capacity a quality control unit is always there which checks the quality of raw materials according to the specifications of supplier, or that of the bakery or that of any other standard, e.g. ISI etc. Quality control tests may be physical or/ and of chemical nature and should be easy to carry out. Many a time functional qualities of some ingredients cannot be evaluated except by performance tests, conducted under conditions as much as possible resembling those of actual production in the factory. For reliable test results an average sample representing a particular batch of the raw material should be taken according to set and consistent procedure. Following is a summary of the quality control test methods for some of the more important bakery raw materials.

## Flour

Flour is the most important ingredient of the bakery industry and thus for quality control of the product, the flour should be tested to the set specifications.

A small scale baker, not having sophisticated laboratory testing equipment, can check the quality of flour as follows. The flour should be tested (organoleptic test) for its taste and flavour, for example if the flour has come in contact with kerosene or similar non edible item, it can be easily detected by taste and smell. Baker's colour test may also be conducted easily be placing some flour on a glass plate to form a 1/2 cm. Thick layer and pressing it compactly; this is placed in a trough of water to detect visibly the excess percentage of bran and for the creamish yellow colour of the flour. 10 to 12.5% of gluten of medium strength is suitable for bread making and this can also be tested easily as follows. 100 gms of flour is made into a dough with 50 to 44 cc. of water; perfect gluten formation is ensured by thorough kneading. This dough ball is completely immersed in water and carefully and gently starch is removed from it, with fingers, changing the water frequently, until washed gluten is obtained and water is clear. The gluten thus obtained is stretched to see whether it is strong, medium-strong or weak. This gluten is stretched on a preseighed paper board and this is kept in the oven for 30 minutes at 150°C. The weight of dry gluten determined, thus, gives the percentage of protein in the flour.

***Physical Dough Testing*** **:** Various mechanical and electro chemical machines are available which evaluate the baking quality of flour; the basic principle is the measurement of resistance to mixing or to extrusion of a dough of standard composition under carefully controlled conditions, indicating roughly the strength of the sample. Mixograph is a device for measuring resistance of doughs to mixing; it consists of a special mixer equipped with special levers, instruments and charts. The Farinograph is also a more complicated and popular apparatus for measuring the resistance to mixing stress of a standard dough. Extrnsograph is used to measure the resistance to stretching offered by a cylinder of dough. All these apparatus give an indication of protein content, strength and loaf volume.

***Chemical Testing*** : Standard specifications for flour specify moisture, ash, protein fat and pH etc. These are determined by chemical tests. Moisture is determined by calculating the loss in weight of flour by drying the sample in an oven. Ash content of the flour is an indicator of its grade. As the ash content of the bran is about 20 times that of endosperm, the flour with lower ash content will be of superior quality. Ash content is determined by usual methods. Colour tests may be conducted as per Pekar Test and other methods on flour or its acetone extract. Protein content of the flour can be estimated by Kjeldahl Test, which is based on the titration of ammonia released by an acid digest of the flour when excess alkali is added, this indicates the baking quality of the flour. This test is very cumbersome and costly. Other tests for this purpose are based on biuret reaction and binding capacity of protein for some dyes. Protein content can be determined by washing test also, described earlier. Baking quality of flour can also be determined by measuring the rate at which the flour particles sediments in acid solutions; these tests are rapid and accurate (Aeleny sedimentation test) and also give a measure of a combination of protein quality and quantity.

The best test that can be carried out by a small baker as well as in bigger plants for checking the quality of a flour is 'Test Baking' or 'Performance Test'. For this purpose 1 kg. of flour sample is taken and dough is prepared according to the formulation and baking is carried out as far as possible in similar conditions as those existing in normal manufacture, the finished product is tested to a set of standards.

In the case of Rye Flour the principal criterion of the quality is colour. Dress or granulation and flavour are also important quality factors. Protein and ash content are associated with colour but are secondary in importance as they do not affect the baking properties to an appreciable extent. Rye flour is cheaper than wheat flour hence fine rye flour can be used in lieu of part of the wheat flour in a biscuit etc. (where gluten is not important). Slightly off flavour will be covered up by other ingredients.

## Yeast

The best and easiest way to test the quality of yeast is to check its Dough raising capacity, which is determined as follows: 100 gms. of A.R. quality wheat flour (maida) is taken. 1.5 gms. of sucrose is dissolved in 60 cc. of water; this solution is heated to 40°C and to this 4 gms. of dried baker's yeast or 8 gms. of compressed yeast is added and mixture is left standing for 10 minutes. The contents are stirred till the yeast disperse completely. Dough is prepared using yeast suspension and wheat flour, and is well kneaded. It is put in wide mouth 500 ml. graduated cylinder and is pressed with a circular flat plate with handle to expel all the entrapped air in the dough. The initial volume, which should be about 100 cc., if properly pressed, is noted. The cylinder is kept at 27°C in a thermostatic bath for a hour. If bath is not available the cylinder may just be kept at room temperature. At the end of one hour the final dough volume is noted and the rise in volume is expressed ass percentage of original volume.

The yeast is considered to be of good quality if the rise is 80%, on the original volume, or more. If the yeast has less than 80%, than more yeast than the quantity indicated in the formulation will have to used and if it is more than 100% then it has to be reduced, proportionately.

## Shortenings

In small scale units the quality of fats could be roughly checked by physical examination and organoleptic tests i.e. by flavour and taste. Bakery fat is supposed to be plastic without any granular formation, and should be semi-solid at room temperature and should be free from any extraneous matter. Some of the tests, applied for checking the quality of shortening in larger plants, are being given here.

***Analytical Tests*** **:** Determination of melting point, stability, solid, fraction, plasticity, flavour, iodine value etc. are some of the important analytical tests applied for quality control of shortening. Fats do not have sharp melting points, capillary melting point is the temperature at which a sample of fat in a capillary becomes completely clear; another method is Wiley melting point test in which a moulded fat tablet is floated at the interface of a water and alcohol bath, the bath temperature at which batlet assumes a spherical form is the melting point. Thus there are various methods for determining the melting point of fat and according to the standard method is chosen. Iodine value is found out to determine the unsaturation in the fat, which is a rough measure of its storage stability. Hydrogenated fat has low iodine value. Except for butter and lard the shortening should have a bland flavour. Various viscometers are available to determine the apparent viscosity or plasticity of shortening. Viscosity or plasticity depends on the temperature and affect the mixing of the dough and its final consistency.

Stability of the shortening or their resistance to rancidity is an important factor. Free fatty acid content and peroxide value are the indicators of deterioration in the fat. Peroxide value is determined by reacting a sample of the fat with potassium iodine and titrating the excess iodine with potassium thiosulphate. It is expressed as milliequivalents of oxygen/kg. of fat. It is an indication of the extent to which the fat has already reacted with oxygen and thus indicates approximately how much storage life remains. Free fatty acid is determined by titration with a standard solution of alkali. The proportion of solid to liquid fat in a shortening at a give temperature is determined by dilatometry and is known as Solids Fraction Index or SFI. This has important relationship with the performance of the shortening at that temperature. Smoke point, fire point and flash point are the valuable tests for frying fats and are determined by noting the temperature at which the fat emits smoke or catches fire when gradually heated in standard equipment under rigidly specified conditions.

***Performance Tests*** : The analytical tests do not give direct correlation of the results with the behaviour of the fat in a bakery product. Thus as usual, the best way will be to use the material in a test batch under standard conditions. For general purpose shortening, a lean pound cake formula, not containing any chemical leavening agent, may be used for test baking. For high absorption shortenings, 140% sugar white cake may be chosen. Every step is conducted at standard conditions and the only variable is the shortening under test. Specific gravity measurements may be made on the batter during mixing. In the case of cakes, after baking volume is measured, together with other characteristics. Shortening intended for use in icings may be tested for icing volume. The shortening is considered satisfactory if the volume of the icing exceeds a certain minimum value and is satisfactory in other respects. Creaming quality of a fat may be tested by somewhat simplified procedure rather than a complete cake test. A dry creaming volume determination in which only sugar and fat are creamed together may be run. Fats which cream equally well at this stage may behave differently after the addition of liquids, therefore a wet creaming volume including water is somewhat more meaningful.

Fats to be used for frying should have higher smoke point and low free fatty acid and peroxide value, than the ones used for shortenings or as coatings.

## Sugars

Quality of sugar can be judged by look, clear colour sugar being of the best quality. It's flavour and smell will indicate the presence of impurities if any. Particle size of the sugar is also important. Sugar should be stored under dry conditions otherwise caking will take place. The quality of invert syrups is determined by determining their solids content. Quality of molasses is determined by its sucrose and invert sugar percentages, ash content, colour and flavour. In the case of corn syrups, two important specifications are the Dextrose Equivalent (DE) and the Degree Baume' (°Be'). The former is a measure of sweetness, viscosity and preservative quality of the material while the latter is a measure of its solids content. Dextrose equivalent (DE) is based on an analysis for total reducing sugars and is expressed as glucose calculated us a percentage of the total dry substance. DE range of various syrups is as under

| | |
|---|---|
| Low conversion corn syrup | 28 to 38 DE |
| Regular conversion corn syrup | 38 to 48 DE |
| Intermediate conversion corn syrup | 48 to 58 DE |
| High conversion corn syrup | 58 to 68 DE |
| Extra high conversion corn syrup | 68 or higher DE |
| Crude corn sugar '70' | 80 to 89 DE |
| Crude corn sugar '80' | 90 to 94 DE |

Measurements of refractive index or density gives a quick indication of solids content. Density or specific gravity can be found out quickly by special hydrometers indicating the results in °**Be'**.

Honey can be evaluated by colour, flavour and test etc.

## Milk

Standard specification for various different types of milk and milk products are available. Butterfat content of milk can be determined by Babcock Test involving a volumetric measurement of the fat present in a measured portion of milk after the digestion of milk proteins by sulphuric acid. This method is employed by dairies etc. and is very popular and simple. Acidity of the milk indicates the extent of bacterial decomposition and is measured by determining the quantity of standard alkali required to neutralise the acidity in a given quantity of milk sample; it is expressed ass percentage of titrable acidity calculated as lactic acid. The flavour and odour of all sweet milk products should be blend, slightly sweet and free from acid and other foreign flavours; flavour and odour of dried milk products are usually determined on a reconstituted basis. In dried milk powers scorched milk particles are present and their quantity is determined by Scorched Particles Test or Sediment Test. In this test specific quantity of milk is reconstituted and filtered through a 1¼" diameter cotton pad.

Moisture content of milk products can be determined by vacuum oven drying to constant weight. Sp. gravity of liquid milk can be determined with the help of lectometer and from that water content can be calculated. Infra-red moisture meters and tool distillation methods may be used to estimate moisture content of dried milk samples. Bacteriological quality of milk products can be estimates by reduction tests, microscopic clump counts or standard plate count methods. The Solubility Index, measures the relative quantity of destabilised milk protein in dried milk powders, and is found out by reconstituting a known quantity of milk and centrifuging it to separate the insoluble portion. Spray type dry powders have lower Solubility Index than roller dried milks.

Dried milk powders used for baking purposes should posses certain special qualities apart from those given above. Harland Ashworth whey Protein Test is used for evaluating the baking quality of MSNF (Milk Solids Not Fat). Hoffman

Dalby Farinograph Test is also used for the evolution of baking qualities of milk powder. Brookfield Viscosity Test may also be performed. Baking performance test can also be performed by using a standard milk powder in the formulation and also the test powder in same formulation under similar condition, and comparing the results. A good quality milk powder will produce a dough which remains easy to handle throughout the baking process and which produces a good loaf volume and quality score.

## Eggs

Tests for protein, fat, total solids and inorganic matter are the common tests applied to egg products. At least odour, taste and colour must be checked. If of good quality, egg whites should cause little change in flavour although they apparently can act to blend off or ameliorate harsh odours and tastes. In elaborate tests, testing for total solids, fat by acid hydrolysis, yolk colour, salt content, sugar content, whip test for liquid egg white and for dried albumen, surface film method for percentage of yolk in whites, Stuart Solubility Index, insolubles of dried albumen plate count, coliform count, yeast and mould count and direct microscopic count etc., are included. All these tests are cumbersome and a small scale baker can gauge the quality of eggs by the following method.

The eggs may be graded in terms of the depth of thickness of air pocket, movement of the yolk, its position from centre, firmness of the whites, clarity of yolks and whites, and condition of the shell. Quality of the egg may be determined by 'candling'. In this test the egg is held up to a light to see its contents, if the yolk is in the centre, the air pocket is small, the yolk is held firmly by the white when the egg is turned, and the shell is unbroken and clean, then the egg is considered to be of good quality. Musty-smelling or hay egg should not be used. Smell does not becomes evident until the egg is broken, bad odours are caused by bacteria or mould. Mixes that contain a musty egg should be throws away. Spots in eggs are generally due to blood vessel fragments and are found, as spots on the yolks or suspended in the whites; such eggs are edible and may be used. Eggs are fine medium for the development of bacteria and molds and should be stored under refrigeration when not used in a day.

## Water

Water exerts some influence on the quality of bakery products; the dissolved minerals and organic substances present in water affect the flavour, colour and other physical properties of the product. Usually tap drinking water is used in food industries, and suitable for bakery also; but, for specialised products it should conform to certain standards. Certain products e.g. marshmallow, jellies etc., are quite sensitive to the quality of water. Standard methods are available for estimating the acidity, almalinity, aluminium, arsenic, boron, calcium, carbon dioxide, chloride, chlorine, chromium, colour, sp. conductance, copper, cyanide, fluoride, grease, hardness, iodine, iron, lead, magnesium, manganese, nitrate, nitrite, oxygen, pH, phenol, phosphate, potassium, selemium, silica, sodium, sulphate, sulphite, taste, odour, turbidity and zinc, present in water. Bacteria content of water is also checked.

## Other Ingredients

Other ingredients are also tested for quality and general appearance etc., as per set procedures and specifications.

In a bakery unit ingredients should be properly stored and sanitation should be satisfactory. As mentioned earlier the product should also be subject to various checks for quality. It should be emphasised again that samples from market should also be collected and tested for quality; and also all the complaints from the consumers and retailers should be seriously and carefully followed up.

# Chapter - 16

## *Fruit Juices, Squashes and Cordials*

In India, cold drinks are in demand practically throughout the year. Among these, fruit juices have an important place. Being rich in essential minerals, vitamins and other nutritive factors, they are quite popular. Besides, they are delicious and have universal appeal unlike other beverages.

The nutritive value of real fruit beverages is far greater than that of synthetic products which are at present being bottled and sold in large quantities throughout the country. The annual production of carbonated beverages like lemonade, orangeade, strawberry, lime juice, etc. ass well as various kinds of *sherbat* and other artificially flavoured beverages runs into several million bottles. If real fruit juices could be substituted for these synthetic preparations, it would be a boon to the consumer as well ass to the fruit grower. There is, therefore, great scope in the country for the production of fruit juices and other fruit-based beverages.

With the rapid progress in fruit farming that has taken place during the last two decades, fresh fruit juices are being increasingly sold by vendors in some of the larger towns. The demand for fresh fruit juices is on the increase, but these cannot be had easily, when the fruits are out of season. Fruit juices have, therefore, to be preserved in a form in which they can be made available to the public during the off-season.

Preparation of fruit beverages on a commercial scale was practically unknown in the country till about 1930. New products such as squashes and cordials are, however, now being packed to the extent of more than three million bottles annually. If aerated water factories begin to use pure fruit juices instead of synthetic colours and flavours, that alone will create a steady demand for utilization of several thousand tons of fruit every year.

In the U.S.A., the annual production of juices is more than a hundred million gallons. Till about 20 years ago, only grape and apple juices were produced there in any considerable quantity. In those days, these juices were used almost exclusively for medicinal purposes and were generally recommended by doctors for infants and invalids. Now-a-days, however, on account of the common use of fruits juices as breakfast foods a large variety of them is produced on a big scale from fruits such as orange, pineapple, grapefruit, apple, and grape. Small quantities of juices are also produced from sour lime, lemon, tangerine, loganberry, cherry, blackberry, apricot, peach, plum, prune, pomegranate, papaya, currants, pear, etc., Several of these tart juices are largely used for preparing mixed drinks and in bakery products. They are now becoming more popular than the carbonated beverages from apples and grapes.

In this country, the pure fruit juice industry is still in its infancy. Preparation of these juices is limited to small scale productions only, because rather sophisticated and costly. Quite recently, however, a few units have come into existence to pack fairly large quantities of pure fruit juices from citrus fruits, pineapple, grape, apple etc. Fruits such as apple grape, pomegranate, mulberry, jamun (Eugeniz jambolana), phalsa (Grewia asiatica), mango, pineapple, etc., are generally utilized for the preparation of juices. The scope for large scale production of fruit juices is, however, limited at present, as these are not yet included to any considerable extent in the normal dietary of the people. Tomato juice, however, which is in fair demand already, has considerable scope for large scale production.

**Sherbat**. It consists of sugar syrups flavoured with artificial essences of fruits or herbs, and have been produced in India from times immemorial and are, therefore, well known practically throughout the country.

Of late, large scale manufacture of orange squash, lemon squash, lime juice cordial, pineapple squash and mango squash has made considerable progress in different parts of the country. Methods for the preparation of other fruit beverages like passion fruit squash, pomegranate syrup, mulberry syrup, plum squash, peach nectar, etc., were standardised in the Fruit Preservation Laboratories at Lyallpur and Quetta. There appears to be scope for these beverages also. Proper education and publicity of the dietetic value of fruit beverages is necessary to stimulate a general demand for them.

Fruit juices, especially orange, apple and grape juice, are concentrated using modern equipment so that there is practically very little loss in their nutritional properties and flavour characteristics. Sometimes, the recovered flavour is added back to the concentrate to get full fruit taste and flavour on dilution for serving. These concentrate are used as basis for soft drinks, pharmaceutical preparations, baby foods, tonic foods, etc. The frozen orange juice concentrate (four to one) is an excellent example in this case. Concentration is effected by freezing or by application of heat employing high vacuum. Conventional equipments such as climbing and falling film evaporators and more employed. Fruit juices and concentrates are further converted into free-flowing fruit juice powders by adopting methods such as puff-drying, foam mat drying, freeze drying etc. Sometimes, sealed-in flavours are blended with the powders so as to get natural fruit juices on reconstitution for serving as beverages etc. A considerable amount of work has already been done in recent years at the Central Food Technological Research Institute, Mysore, on several aspects of these products and such work is still continuing. The results promise to be of great scientific as well as industrial importance.

## Equipment for Fruit Juices

Until recently, the equipment used for the extraction of fruit juices was similar to that used in the manufacture of wine, vinegar, etc. There has, however, been a rapid advance in the fruit juice industry in the U.S.A., the U.K., and several other countries. Consequently, one can now get equipment ranging from the simple household juice extractor or press, to the fully automatic juice lines capable of handling several thousand bottles daily. Particularly, the development of the citrus juice industry, has been the most important factor in revolutioning the entire fruit juice industry. It is essential that suitable equipment is employed for the successful operations of this industry.

## Washing Equipment

For washing apples, citrus fruit, tomatoes berries, etc., different kinds of equipment are available. Tender fruits like berries, tomatoes, etc., are usually washed with fine overhead sprays of water, whereas the fruits travel on a continuous woven wire belt. A rotating rod-cylinder with a helical screw inside to push the fruit along, and fitted with jets of water, forced by a centrifugal pump, has been found highly useful for washing loose jacket mandarin oranges. On a small scale, cement or galvanised iron tanks for holding water are quite useful. A battery of these will be adequate even for a factory of moderate size.

## Sorting Equipment

In large factories, a continuous broad belt, made of woven metal, is generally employed for sorting the fruits. In smaller factories, however, batch sorting will suffice.

## Extraction Equipment

There are two types of extractions. In one case, the fruits are crushed and pressed continuously in one operation, whereas in the other, the fruits are crushed or cut into small pieces or comminuted in a mill, and these are subsequently pressed in a suitable press.

In citrus fruits, the juice is enclosed in small natural sacs. Besides, there are other adhering tissues also in the fruit. The peel consist of an inner white spongy portion called the albedo, and an outer yellow coloured portion called the flavado. The oil glands are embedded in the flavado and are easily ruptured even with a gentle pressure. Substances which are responsible for the bitterness of the juice are located chiefly in (i) the fruit tissues in which the juice sacs are embedded, (ii) the inner portion of the flavedo, (iii) the albedo, and (iv) the seeds. The presence of these (containing bitter substances) makes it rather difficult to extract the juice free from bitterness. An ideal equipment would be the one in which the juice is extracted from the juice sacs only without its coming into contact with the other tissues of the fruit. No perfect mechanical devices has so far been developed for this. With the existing equipment, the bitter substances also are extracted to varying extents and get incorporated with the juice.

Extraction of juice from peeled segments as such, or from segments dipped in lye solution for removing most of the adhering tissues helps to minimise the incorporation of bitter substances into the juice, especially in the case of the loose jacket mandarin type oranges such as Coorn and Nagpur oranges. In the Taglith type of press, developed by the Central Food Technological Research Institute, Mysore, the unpeeled orange is cut into halves held against cups in two stainless steel drums revolving towards each other, employing synchronised plungers with conical fluted heads having holes for carrying away the pressed juice down their steam. In this arrangement, as in the case of the small super-juicer employing the same principle, the inner and outer juices from the cut half of the oranges are collected into two separate channels. The inner juice is practically free from the peel emulsion, whereas the outer juice contains oil-rich peel emulsion. The juice is fairly thin in body, unlike the juice got from the screw type extractor. As such, it is better suited for subsequent concentration. Juice with 'thicker body' is generally preferred for canning and for making squash. Broadly, there are four type of equipment employed for the extraction of fruit juices.

## Halving and Burring Machines

Malta orange or Sathgudi or mosambi oranges (*Citrus sinensis* Osbeck), grape-fruit (*Citrus paradisi* var *maximum*), lemon (*Citrus medica* var. *Limonum*) and *galgal* (*Citrus limonia* osbeck) are cut by a special machine in which the fruit is placed in a conical cup in a wheel which brings the fruit against a stationery or revolving knife. The fruit is cut into two halves, which drop into a receptacle placed below. The burrs (or roses) are generally made of stainless steel, monel metal, aluminium, nickel, or non-odorous hard wood. They are conical in shape and are ribbed. They are driven by a motor. The cut half of the fruit is held against the revolving burr and the reamed juice is collected in a vessel kept below. There are generally two burrs, one each on either side of the shaft. Several single burrs can also be fitted in series. By regulating the speed of the burr and the pressure on the fruit held against it, any excessive tearing of the tissues can be avoided. In the U.S.A., and other large citrus juice processing countries, several types of automatic burring or rosing machines and pressing machines are in use.

## Continuous screw expeller press

These presses are similar in principle to the familiar household meat mincer. The segments of the fruit are fed through a hopper at one end of a feeding screw, revolving inside a conical jacket, which is perforated in sections or throughout. The diameter of the perforations depends upon the type of fruit. The juice flows out through the perforations and the pomade comes out at the end of the conical jacket. The flow of pomace, and hence the pressing pressure of the screw, can be adjusted to some extent by means of a movable disc at the conical end of the perforated jacket. Small power driven screw type extractors (1/2 to 1 HP) have now been introduced in several factories in the country. Very large units are not, however, in general use at present. The juice extracted is generally thick and cloudy and contains a considerable amount of macerated pulp. The juice should be passed through sieves to remove the pulp to the desired extent. Screw-type juice extraction are useful in the case of a tomatoes, grapes, etc. In the case of pineapple, however, the pieces of fruit are first crushed in a screw type crusher and then from the crushed material, the juice is separated effectively in a centrifuge widely employed in the sugar and chemical industries. This technique has recently been found highly effective in pineapple juice production.

## Plunger-type press

The halved citrus fruit is held on an inverted cup in which it is pressed by an automatic adjustment against a metallic cone fitting into the cup. The clearance between the cup and the cone is slightly greater than the usual thickness of the peel of the fruit so that very little of the peel oil or emulsion is pressed out. This type of press i being used in one or two factories only in the country.

## Roller-type press

Roller presses made or hard granite or wood, are specially designed to extract juice from sour limes (*Citrus medica* var. *acida*) which are popularly known as *kagzi* or *kagdi nimboo* or *limboo*. The whole lime i fed through the rollers. These presses are in extensive use in West Indies and Jamaica. They have been introduced in some of the Indian factories also.

## Double operations

Fruits like apples, grapes, berries, etc., are first crushed in a greater or crusher or comminuting mill, and the juice then extracted from the crushed material by means of a hydraullic press. In large scale production ass in the case of apple juice, the crushing device forms an integral part of the press itself.

**Apple greater**. The skin and other tissues of apples do not have any undesirable constituents, which adversely affect the taste and flavour of the juice, as in the case of citrus fruits. The entire fruit is, therefore, crushed and pressed. A battery of such graters can be employed for large-scale production. The grated consists of a heavy steel cylinder fitted on its surface with short knives which are spring-loaded and work against a corrugated plate, attached to the frame of the press by the side of the steel cylinder. The springs give a certain amount of flexibility to the mechanism so that the grater is not damaged in case pieces of wood or stone, etc., get into the press along with the fruit. Gear arrangement is provided for running the rollers at higher speeds. Apples are fed whole into the hopper. They are crushed and grated between the cylinder and the corrugated plate, and the crushed material falls into a receptacle below. The grater can be set to crush the fruit to the desired degree of fineness. Pieces of 0.3 to 1.2 cm thickness are the best for extraction of juice. In recent years, a different type of crusher known as 'Hammer type pulper' has come into use in the U.S.A. and elsewhere.

## Crusher for grapes, berries.

A grape crusher consists of two fluted or grooved rollers made of wood or metal. These are arranged hortizontally and revolve towards each other. The clearance between the two is adjustable. The fruit which is fed to the hopper at the top falls between the rollers and gets crushed. Strawberries and some other berry fruits which contain gums, are first heated and then crushed. Tomatoes can also be crushed in these crushers.

## Pressing

**Basket-press**. In the industry two types of presses are used for pressing the juice from the crushed fruit. They are : (i) the basket press, and (ii) the rack and cloth press. Basket presses which are of various designs and capacities, are worked manually by hydraulic pressure. The manually operated press consists of a strong cylindrical basket made of wooden slats. It rests on a wooden or matallic base. There i a strong screw at the top of the frame. The crushed fruit is folded in a piece of strong cloth and placed inside the basket. By turning the screw by hand or with a hydraulic pump, the juice is pressed out. It flows out through the slates in the basket into the bottom tray from which it is channelled into a collecting vessel. The basket press has been found useful in the case of apple, grape, pomegranate, phalsa, etc.

**Rack and cloth press**. In this type of press, the crushed fruit is spread as a layer in a coarse woven cloth of cotton or nylon and folded into a square suited to the size of the platform of the press. Several such layers are arranged alternately between racks built of wooden slats. The built-up layers are subjected to hydraulic pressure by means of a pump. The juice is pressed out gradually due to increasing pressure in the pile. The released juice is collected at the base of the pile. Various types of these presses, which are in use in several countries, are claimed to give higher yields of clear juice than the basket type presses. In California, however, basket presses are preferred for extraction of juice from grapes. Rack and cloth presses are in use in a few factories in India specialising in the production of apple juice.

**Other types of extractors**. Special devices for extracting juice have been designed in the U.S.A., Australia, etc., for fruits like pomegranate, passion fruit, etc. Chace et al., have described a press for pomegranate in which the whole fruit as such is pressed. At the Quetta Fruit Preservation Laboratory, a manually worked basket press has been successfully employed for the extraction of juice from whole pomegranates. Poore has described a special pulper for passion fruit in which the juice is extracted by reaming the halved fruit. A continuously operating device has been employed in Australia to extract the pulpy juice along with the seeds from passion fruit.

**Pulping equipment.** Fruit juices extracted or pressed by any of the methods described contain suspended matter like coarse fruit tissues, pieces of skin seeds, and finally divided fruit pulp. These are separated from the juice in various ways, depending upon the nature of the product required, e.g., cloudy, sparking, clear, etc. Three important methods in common use are : (i) straining or screening, (ii) settling or sedimentation, and (iii) filtration .

**Straining or screening equipment.** Several types of equipment, varying indesign and capacity, are in use for straining juices. A pulper made of stainless steel with power-drived wooden, metallic or brush paddles, which revolve inside, has been highly useful in the case of citrus, tomato and mango juices. The fruit, which is fed through a hopper, is crushed and pressed by the paddles against the sieve. The juice flows out through the sieve into the jacket and is collected at the outlet below, while the coarse residue passes out at the lower end of the sieve.

**Equipment for settling and sedimentation.** For sedimentation and settling of the juices only a few wooden barrels are required.

**Filtration equipment.** Finally suspended particles in the juice are removed with a special equipment known as 'Filter press'. Filter presses are of various designs and capacities. The filtering media may be finely woven cloth, canvas, fibre, asbestos pads, cotton or wood pulp discs, porous porcelain wares etc. The frame and filter press, which is similar to that used in sugar factories, but made of wood, has been highly effective for the clarification of lime juice required for the preparation of lime juice cordial. Seitz filter of various designs and sizes are widely employed for filtering wines, spirits, sugar syrups, cordials, apple and other fruit juices, etc.

A simple filtering device, however, is a large conical bag of heavy drill cloth or felt, similar to the ordinary jelly bag. The juice is heated with filter aid and placed inside the bag. Filtration is rather slow, but the output can be increased by having a battery of such filter bags.

**Deaerator and flash pasteuriser.** Freshly extracted and screened juices contain appreciable quantity of oxygen which should be removed before packing. The special equipment used for the purpose is called a deaerator. The deaerated juice i subsequently heated in a flash-pasteurisation equipment.

Commercial deaerators and flash pasteurisers they greatly in design, construction and capacity. Deaeration and flash-pasteurisation units have been greatly developed in the U.S.A. Special mention may be made of Sterovac Process developed by Ayers in 1937. This process is a combination of deaeration and flash-pasteurization and has been successfully employed in the case of citrus, pineapple and tomato juice. Such advanced processes and equipments are not yet in common use in India. They are, however, recommended for improving the quality of the natural fruit juice products.

## FRUIT BEVERAGES

Fruit juices are preserved in different forms such as pure juices, squashes cordials, fermented juices, etc.

*These are broadly defined as follows :*

**Unfermented juice or pure fruit juice**. This is the natural juice pressed out of the fruit, and remains practically unaltered in its composition during preparation and preservation.

**Fruit juice beverage.** This is a fruit juice which is considerably altered in composition before consumption. It may be diluted before it is served as a drink.

**Fermented fruit beverage.** This is a fruit which has undergone alcoholic fermentation by yeast. The product contains raying amounts of alcohol. Grape wines, apple ciders, berry wines etc., are typical examples of this kind of beverage.

**Fruit juice squash.** This consists essentially of strained juice containing moderate quantities of fruit pulp to which cane sugar is added for sweetening, e.g. orange squash, lemon squash, pineapple squash, mango squash.

**Fruit juice cordial.** This is a sparkling, clear sweetened fruit juice from which all the pulp and other suspended materials have been completely eliminated, e.g., lime juice cordial.

**Sherbet or syrup.** This a clear sugar syrup which has been artificially flavoured, e.g., *sherbets* of sandal, *sangtra*, almond rose, *khuskhus, sarasparilla, kewra*, etc.

**Fruit juice concentrate**. This is a fruit juice which has been concentrated by the removal of water either by heat or by freezing. Carbonated beverages and other products are made from this.

**Fruit juice powder.** This is fruit juice which has been converted into a free-flowing, highly hygroscopic powder to which natural fruit flavour in powder form is incorporated to compensate for any loss of flavour in concentration, dehydration, etc. Freeze-dried fruit juice powders form the last word among sophisticated fruit juice products. They are reconstituted readily to yield full-strength, full-fruit, fruit juice drinks.

## Preparation and preservation

Fruit juices have their best taste, aroma and colour when they are freshly extracted or expressed. All subsequent efforts to preserve them adversely affect their quality to varying degrees, depending upon the method of preservation employed. The most important problem, therefore, is to adopt only such methods as would help retain their quality to the maximum extent possible.

The most important steps in processing fruits juices are : (i) selection and preparation of fruit, (ii) extraction of juice, (iii) deaeration, (iv) straining, filtration and clarification, and (v) preservation. The quality of the juice will depend on the manner in which these several processes are carried out.

**Selection and preparation of fruit.** All fruits are not suitable for making fruit juice, either because of difficulties in the extraction of juice, or because the juice got is of poor quality. Even some of the jelly fruits are not quite suited as they do not yield juice of good beverage quality. The variety of fruit, its maturity, and the locality in which it is grown, have a marked effect on its flavour as well as keeping quality. The best juice is, therefore, extracted from freshly picked, sound and suitable varieties, when they are at the optimum stage of maturity. Fully-ripe, mid-season fruits, particularly citrus fruits, generally yield juice superior to that of fruits picked early or late in the season. Decayed or damaged fruits do not yield good juice. Small cull fruits, i.e., undersized, over-sized, malformed or blemished fruits, which do not fetch a good price in the fresh fruit market, but which are otherwise of good quality, can be profitability for the production of fruit juices.

The fruits should be washed thoroughly with water, and in some cases scrubbed also, while washing to remove any adhering dust and other extraneous matter. Residues of sprays of arsenic and lead should be removed with dilute HCl. Twenty-three litres of HCl in 455 litres of water is adequate for this purpose. All mouldy and decayed parts should be removed as in the case of fruits prepared for canning.

**Juice extraction**. The method of juice extraction willdiffer with the structure and composition of the fruit. Generally, juice from fresh fruits is extracted by crushing and pressing them. In the case of fruits in which the juices is in sacs of in cells, during the extraction of the juice, the other tissues of the fruit, in which these sacs or cells are embedded, are also broken or crushed, resulting in the incorporation of some undesirable constituents in the juice. The admixture of these extraneous constituents with the juice should be avoided as far as possible by adopting a suitable method of extraction. Further, during extraction, the juice should not be unduly exposed to air, as oxygen of the air will adversely affect the colour, taste and aroma and also reduce the vitamin content of the juice. Citrus juices, tomato juice, and even the more stable juices such is those of apples and grapes, deteriorate rapidly in quality, when they are extracted by adopting methods which expose them to air for unduly long periods. For products like tomato juice, special extraction equipment has been designed recently to reduce incorporation of air to the minimum. The entire process of manufacture of tomato juice should be conducted in an atmosphere of steam to protect the juice from oxidation by air.

**Deaeration.** In spite of all improvements made so fat in the extraction equipment, fruit juices do retain some air. This is due to the difficulty of extracting the juice without some aeration, and also the presence of air in the intercellular spaced of the fruit. Most of the air is present on the surface of the fruit particles, while some is found dissolved in the juice. In the case of citrus juices, particularly orange juice, which is highly susceptible to the adverse action of the residual air, immediately after extraction the juice is subjected to a high vacuum where by most of the air as well as, others gases are removed. This process is known as deaeration. The equipment employed is fairly expensive. It is, however, necessary for large-scale production of orange and other pure fruit juices. A simple laboratory deaeration units is therefore desirable.

**Streining, filtration and clarification.** Fruit juices, after extraction, always contain varying amounts of suspended matter, which consists of broken fruit tissue, seed and skin, and also various gums, pectic substances and proteins in colloidal suspension. Usually, coarse particles of pulp, seeds and pieces of skin are removed by means of screens in the case of almost all juices. The presence of these generally causes deterioration in the quality of the final product. In the early years of the fruit juice industry, it was a common practice to remove completely all the suspended matters, including colloidal suspension, before packing the juice in containers. This, no doubt, improved the appearance of the product, but quite often resulted in lack of fruit character and flavour. The present trend is to let fruit juices and fruit beverages remain reasonably cloudy or pulpy in appearance. The recent comminuted fruit beverages, employing the whole fruit for extraction, are based on this concept and they are claimed to be more nutritive than the clear juices. Some juices and juice beverages like grape juice, apple juice, lime juice cordial are, however, still packed brilliantly clear, employing enzymes clarifying agents, fine filtration etc., to make them remain perfectly clear during storage and distribution.

Coarse particles of suspension in the juice are removed either by straining through sieves of non-corrodible metal, or by sedimentation. For sedimentation, the juice is stored in carboys or barrels, adding a chemical preservative to ensure that the juice does not undergo fermentation during storage. The supernatent juice, which contains mostly fine suspended particles and colloidal suspensions, is syphoned off for subsequent treatment. The type of equipment used for straining the juice depends upon the kind of juice. It is fitted with screens having holes of varying dimensions. The juice is passed through the sieve soon after extraction. Coarse particles of tissues, skins and seeds are separated by vibratory action, and the juice still retaining the desired amount of fine pulp and juice sacs is collected in a vessel. Recently a high speed centrifuge, similar to Sharpless centrifuge, and having an automatic sediment discharge device, has been employed for removal of pulp from orange juice prior to its concentration.

When prefectly clear juices are required, complete removal of all suspensions is effected either by filtration or by clarification. For this, enzymes and fining agents are employed. The methods of clarification, and sugar manufacturers, are now being increasingly adopted in the fruit juice industry also.

Filtration is necessary for removing completely all the fine and colloidal suspensions. In this process, which is physical in nature, the juice, which has been strained, and from which the coarse particles have already been removed, is forced through a filtering medium. The filtering medium usually consists of woven fibre cloth, asbestos pads, cotton pulp, porous porcelain or wood pulp. The colloidal suspension tends to clog the filters in the press. In order to minimise this, filter aids such as diatomaceous or infusorial earth, also known as Kieselghur, Kaolin, Spanish clay, etc., are added to the juice so that the filtering medium is coated with these, without blocking the fine pores, and thereby facilitating filtration. The use of these filter-aids, however, tends to impart to the juice a slight amount of earthy taste, which may be unacceptable to some persons. These aids should, therefore, be used with caution and in small persons. These aids should, therefore, be used with caution and in small quantities only. Further, they should be kept in uniform suspension by constant agitation when the juice is being forced through the press by means of a pump. They can be ignited and reused a few times before they are finally discarded.

Boiling of the filter-aid with one per cent of citric or tartaric acid, before use, in order to minimise the adverse effect on the taste and aroma of the juice, For clarification of unfermented apple juice, the use of ignited Kaolin as filter-aid at the rate of 1 kg of it to 100 kg of juice. The resulting juice will be clear and sparkling. A variety of equipment like multiple disc filters, frame and plate filters, etc., employing different kinds of filter-aids, is available now-a-days.

# Chapter - 17

## *Jams, Jellies and Marmalades*

Among preserved fruits, jams jellies and marmalades form an important class of products. During World War II, fairly quantities of these were imported into India from the U.S.A., the U.K., and Australia. Now-a-days, such products are being manufactured extensively in several factories in this country, as by-products or joint products in fruit canning units. They are also made in many of the homes all over the country. Their production and demand can be increased manifold by making better use of cull fruit that is being wasted at present.

Jam is prepared by boiling the fruit pulp with a sufficient quantity of sugar to a reasonably thick consistency, firm enough to hold fruit tissues in position. In its preparation, about 20.4 kg of fruit should be used for every 24.9 kg of sugar. It should contain not less than 68.5 per cent soluble solids as determined by refractometer, when cold, and uncorrected for insoluble solids.

Jelly is prepared by boiling the fruit, with or without addition of water, straining the extract, and mixing the clear extract with sugar, and boiling the mixture to a stage at which it will set to a clear gel. A perfect jelly should be transparent, well-set, but not too stiff, and should have the original flavour of the fruit. It should be of attractive colour and should keep its shape and show a clean-cut surface. It should be tender enough to quiver but not flow.

Marmalade is a fruit jelly in which the slices of the fruit or of the peel are suspended. The term 'marmalade' is generally associated with the product made from citrus fruits like oranges and lemons, in which shredded peel is included as the suspended material.

The term fruit jelly covers, in a general sense, jams and marmalades also which posses the consistency of jelly (whether made from clear juice or from pulp).

## JAMS

The method of preparing jams is similar to that used for jelly-making except that pulp and pieces of fruit, instead of clear extract, are used. Jams may be made from a single fruit, or from a combination of two or more fruits.

A jam differs from a preserve in that it does not contain pieces of the whole fruit as in the case with a preserve. In preparing the jam, the fruit is crushed, or otherwise finely cut, so that when cooked, the mass is fairly uniform throughout. A jam is more or less a concentrated fruit possessing a fairly thick consistency and body. It is also rich in flavour, because ripe fruit, which have developed full flavour, are used in its preparation. Pectin present in the fruit gives it a good set. high concentration of sugar facilitates preservation. A great advantage in its preparation is that it can be made completely in a single operation, unlike the preserve which has to pass through several stages over a number of days, before it is complete.

*Analytical data for some of the jams from other countries as well as of those made in India are given in the following table :*

**Analysis of Different kinds of Jams**

| Description of Jam | Total soluble solids by refractometer | Acidity as citric acid | Degree of inversion | Remarks |
|---|---|---|---|---|
| | % | % | % | |
| Gooseberry jam (Indian) | 71.5 | 0.48 | 50.0 | |
| | 78.0 | 0.70 | 55.2 | |
| | 72.0 | 0.74 | 80.0 | |
| Apricot jam (Indian) | 72.0 | 0.74 | 80.0 | |
| Peach jam (Indian) | 75.5 | 0.50 | 54.0 | |
| Mixed fruit jam (Indian) | 67.5 | 0.52 | 64.0 | |
| Mixed fruit jam (Foreign) | 69.5 | 0.68 | 72.7 | |
| Gooseberry jam (Foreign) | 73.4 | 0.53 | 81.0 | |
| | 71.5 | 0.67 | 85.1 | |
| Raspberry jam (Foreign) | 73.8 | 0.57 | 59.0 | |
| | 72.5 | 0.81 | 71.6 | |
| Strawberry jam (Foreign) | 72.7 | 0.52 | 48.6 | |
| Greengage jam (Foreign) | 74.0 | 0.50 | 76.8 | Stone included |
| | 73.0 | 0.62 | 79.8 | Stone excluded |
| Plum jam, stoneless (Foreign) | 79.6 | 0.71 | 78.6 | Data on stone free basis |
| Plum jam (Foreign) | 78.3 | 0.99 | 75.3 | Stoneless jam |

*A jam manufacture can choose fruit from the following five classes :*

1. Fresh fruit
2. Frozen, chilled or cold-stored fruit
3. Fruit or fruit pulp preserved by heat
4. Sulphited fruit or fruit pulp, i.e., fruit preserved with sulphur dioxide
5. Dried fruit

## Fresh Fruits

Fresh fruits generally give the best jams. There are, however, certain difficulties in using fresh fruits. Firstly, the supply of the fruit has to be regular so that it can be used in fresh and sound condition. Otherwise it is likely to spoil, especially in hot weather. Use of fresh fruit for day-to-day manufacture of jams is possible only when the factory has its own orchards in its neighbourhood or it is located in an area where the particular fruit required is grown on a large-scale. If the fruit has to be transported over long distances, there will be the problem of spoilage during transit. Secondly, due to the short duration of the fruit season, large stocks of the fruit will have to be held in cold storage or frozen or chilled, or preserved with chemicals, or by heat treatment.

As pectin is the main ingredient in the fruit which gives a set to the jam, it is preferable to use some green fruit which is rich in pectin along with the ripe fruit to secure the desirable jellying effect in the jam. Over-ripe fruits should not be used as it produces pasty product. In some cases, where the fruit is deficient in pectin, pectin from other fruits or commercial liquid or solid pectin may be added to supplement it.

## Frozen Fruits

In a modern fruit preservation factory, a cold store is considered a necessary adjunct. During the season when the fruits are in glut, they are stored to ensure regular supplies to the factory over a period during the off-season. It has been found that the flavour and aroma of the cold-stored fruits remain practically unimpaired, and jams prepared from the cold-stored fruit are as good as those made from fresh fruit. Fruits which cannot be kept in cold storage for long periods, are kept in the frozen condition. Some fruits such as cherries and plums, discolour badly on freezing and turn brown. Such fruits are frozen after adding sugar or sugar syrup to prevent browning. In this country, fresh fruits are generally employed for the manufacture of jams. During World War II, dried fruits, especially apricots, were used, to some extent, to meet the demand for special kinds of jams.

## Fruits Preserved by Heat Treatment

The fruit is prepared in the same way as for canning, and heated to a sterilizing temperature in hermetically sealed containers. Some-times a small quantity of sugar is also added to preserve the aroma, colour and texture of the fruit. Plums, apricots, pineapples, and peaches are stored without addition of sugar whereas strawberries and raspberries are stored after adding sugar. The added sugar is taken into account at the time of making the jam. This method is not, however, generally used largely for the following reasons :

1. Difficulty of storing the fruit in barrels;
2. Loss of colour in fruits such as strawberries and raspberries during the treatment and subsequent storage;
3. A certain amount of loss of pectin while the fruit remains hot for a long period in bulk packing.

## Sulphitation for Storing

For preserving fruits in bulk, sulphur dioxide is universally employed in the form of sodium or potassium meta-bisulphite, sulphurous acid or calcium sulphite. Calcium sulphite provides an additional advantage in that it hardens the tissues of soft fruit and thereby prevents their disintegration.

The preservative fluid in the fruit should be an aqueous solution containing 0.08 to 0.1 per cent of sulphur dioxide. In general practice, the total quantity of sulphur dioxide in the fruit and liquor is kept at 1,500 to 2,000 p.p.m. as a safeguard against any possible leakage of sulphur dioxide.

Sulphur dioxide temporarily bleaches the red colour of fruits like red plums, strawberries and raspberries. The colour is, however, restored when sulphur dioxide is driven off at the cooking stage of making the jam.

Sulphur dioxide causes complete stoppage of enzymic activities of the fruit, its presence in soft fruit causes the pectic enzymes to convert pectin into pectic acid, and thereby practically destroys all the jellying power of the pectin of the fruit.

Sulphur dioxide toughens the skin of some fruits such as gooseberries and red currants. These fruits should, therefore, be heated to boiling temperature and then cooled before adding $SO_2$. This preliminary heating will destroy the enzyme in the fruit that would, otherwise, destroy the jellying power of the pectin present in the fruit.

## Preparing the Fruit for Jam-making

The fruit is washed thoroughly to remove any adhering dust and dirt. Leaves, stalks and other undesirable portions are removed. The fruit is then subjected to preliminary treatment which varies with the type of fruit. For example, strawberries are crushed between rollers. Raspberries are steamed, crushed and passed through sieves to remove the hard cores. Plums are heated with a small quantity of water until they become soft, and are then passed through a wide mesh sieve to separate the stones. Sometimes, the stones are not removed while making whole fruit plums jam. Cherries are treated in a similar way. Gooseberries are whirled in a rotary vertical cylinder lined with carborundum to rub off the tops and tails. They are then passed through sieves to separate the stalks. Pears are pooled, cored and cut into small pieces. Peaches are lye peeled, and the stones removed. They are then cut into small pieces. Apricots are cut and the stones removed, unless the jam to be made with the stones in also included. Mangoes are peeled; stones separated, and then sliced.

The slices are passed through a pulper. Pine apples are peeled, sliced and the cores punched. The slices are then cut into smaller pieces and passed through a screw-type crusher to get a fairly coarse pulp suitable for making the jam. In the case of loose jacket oranges like Coorg and Nagpur oranges, the segments are separated and lye dipped to remove the outer covering, and then passed through a screw type extractor to get a fairly coarse pulpy juice, fir for making oranges jam. Bananas are peeled and crushed in a screw extractor fitted with a coarse sieve. Grapes are heated and passed through a screw type juice extractor for getting a coarse juicy pulp. Other fruits are suitably treated to get a fairly coarse pulp suitable for making the jam. The pulp should contain recognisable pieces of fruit. In the case of mixed fruit jam, two or more fruits or fruit pulps are taken in the proportion found suitable for the purpose.

## Addition of Sugar

Generally, cane sugar (sucrose) of good quality is used in the preparation of jams. The proportion in which it is added depends not only on the fruit, but also on its acidity and degree of ripeness. Sweet fruits require less sugar than tart fruits do. The quantity added should be adequate to give the maximum strength to the pectin-sugar-acid gel. To ensure a minimum of 68.5 per cent sugar in the jam, generally 24.9 kg of sugar is required for every 20.4 kg of fruit taken. The finished jam should contain 30 to 50 per cent invert sugar, or of glucose, to avoid crystallization of cane sugar in the jam during storage. If the percentage of invert sugar (reducing sugar) is less than 30 cane sugar may crystalize out; if it is more than 50 per cent, the jam will develop into a honey-like mass due to the formation of small crystals of glucose. Alternatively, corn syrup or commercial glucose may be used along with cane sugar to avoid crystallization.

Sugar in excess of the requisite quantity should not be added because, if the percentage of total soluble solids becomes very high, the jam becomes gummy and sticky. In case excess of sugar has been added, the remedy lies in adding pectin or acid or both, to counteract the effect of excess sugar. If, on the other hand, the percentage of soluble solids is low and there is premature setting of the jam, indicating thereby that the material contains excess of pectin, it is advisable to add more sugar. Under exceptional circumstances where more sugar is not added, it would be desirable to and a small quantity of sodium bicarbonate to reduce the acidity and thus prevent pre-coagulation.

## Addition of Acid, Colour and Flavour

**Acid**. Generally, citric, tartaric or malic acid, which are natural fruit acids, are used to supplement the acidity of the fruit for jam-making. Addition of acids to fruits, deficient in it, is a necessity because appropriate combination of pectin, sugar and acid is essential to give a 'set' to the jam.

Tarr is of the view that the pH of the mixture of fruit juice and pectin should be 3.1 before sugar is added. However, purified pectin gives the best 'set' at pH 2.0. As fruits contain natural buffering salts and other associated materials, the best results are obtained when the pH of the mixture is about 3.0.

**Colour.** Only permitted edible food colours should be used, if necessary, and these should be added towards the end of the boiling process.

**Flavour**. Ordinarily, jams do not require the addition of flavours. If aluminium, stainless steel or copper heavily lines with tin or silver, is generally used for boiling jams. They are of the stationery or of the tilting type. They are highly convenient for rapid boiling of jams. The fruit sugar-acid-pectin mixture is boiled in these pans, heated by steam at 60 to 80 psig (4.20 to 5.60 kg/cm$^2$). Each batch of mix is in small lots of 45.3 to 54.4 kg. Sugar and fruit are first weighed separately.

The fruit is placed in the boiling can and, if necessary, a small quantity of water is added to facilitate pulping. It is then cooked sufficiently to liberate the pectin. Sugar is added next.

The fruit-sugar mixture is then boiled rapidly to concentrate the soluble solids to about 68.5 per cent and also to effect the necessary degree of inversion of the sugar. To avoid excessive frothing during boiling, a small quantity of butter or some other brand of edible oil may be added to the boiling mixture. If the fruit does not contain sufficient pectin, commercial pectin may be added to make good the deficiency.

## Boiling under Vacuum

Sometimes, jam is boiled in a vacuum pan under reduced pressure at a lower temperature of 65° to 76°C. The advantage of vacuum boiling or cooking is that it minimises the undesirable changes in colour and prevents loss of vitamin C. The disadvantage, however, is that the jam mixture has to be boiled for a longer for a time to soften the fruit pieces with the result that there is some loss of flavour. This drawback can, however, be over-come by recovering the volatile esters and putting them back into the jam.

Proper control of boiling is necessary to avoid over-concentration of soluble solids, over-inversion of sugar, and hydrolysis of pectin.

## JELLIES

In jelly making, pectin is the most essential constituent. Although there is difference of opinion about the exact nature of pectin, it is generally accepted that pectins from jellies, when mixed and boiled with the proper amounts of sugar, acid and water. All these constituents must be present in a particular proportion for making a good jelly.

### Classification of Fruits for Jelly-Making

| Fruits rich in pectin & acid | Fruits containing less pectin and acid | Fruits rich in pectin, but low in acid | Fruits containing acid, but low in pectin | Fruits low in pectin and acid |
|---|---|---|---|---|
| Apples, sour and crab | Apples, ripe | Apples, kinds low in acid | Apricots, sour | Apricots, ripe |
| Blackberries, sour | Blackberries | – | – | Elder berries |
| Cranberries | Cherries, sour varieties | Bananas, unripe | Cherries, sweet varieties | Peaches, ripe pomegranates |
| Currants | Fejoias | Cherries, sour | Peaches, sour | Prunes |
| Gooseberries | Grapes, California | Figs, unripe | Pineapples | Raspberries |
| Guavas, sour | Loquats | – | Rhubarb | Strawberries |
| Grapes, eastern | Plums | Pears | Strawberries | Overripe fruits |
| Kumquats | Grapefruits, peel | | | |
| Logan-berries | Guavas, ripe | | | |
| Lemons | Orange, peel | | | |
| Oranges, sour | Quince, ripe | | | |
| Plums, sour | | | | |

## Fruits for Jelly

Pectin is present in the cell walls of fruits. Its quantity, however, varies with the kind of fruit and even with the variety of the same fruit. Many fruits are rich in pectin as well as acid, and are thus well suited for jelly-making. There are other fruits, however, which are either rich in pectin or in acid, or deficient in both. In order to get a jelly from fruits rich in pectin, but deficient in acid, it is necessary to add either fruits rich in acid, or an acid like citric, tartaric or malic.

In the case of fruits deficient in pectin but rich in acid, either fruits rich in pectin or commercial pectin should be added. Both these methods have their own merits. Combining of fruits rich in acids with those rich in pectin is less expensive than using acid or commercial pectin to supplement the deficiency, but the drawback is that the flavour of the jelly is affected. Special care is, therefore, necessary to ensure that the fruits are mixed in proper and juicious proportion. On the other hand, commercial pectin does not have any deleterious effect on the final flavour of the jelly made from any particular fruit.

## Selection of Fruits

The fruits should be sufficiently ripe, but not over-ripe, and they should have good flavour. Slightly under-ripe fruit yields more pectin than over-ripe fruit does because as the fruit ripens, the pectin present in it decomposes into pectic acid, which does not form a jelly with acid and sugar. The amount of pectin extracted from a fruit depends on the degree of disintegration of protopectin during the heating process. In practice, a mixture of under-ripe and ripe fruits is used; under-ripe fruits for their pectin content and ripe ones for their flavour.

## Preparation of Fruits

Fruits are washed thoroughly with water to remove any adhering dirt. If the fruit has been sprayed with lead or arsenical sprays, it should be washed in a warm solution one per cent hydrochloric acid and then rinsed in water.

As jellies are made from aqueous extracts, ordinarily it is not necessary to peel the fruit. For example, fruits like guavas and apples do not require peeling. Plugs from berries not be removed. In the case of oranges and lemons, it is necessary to remove the outer yellow portion of the peel, i.e., the flavedo, to get jellies free from excessive bitterness. Fruits are cut into thin slices so that the acid pectin in them can be extracted easily.

## Extraction of Pectin

Only a minimum quantity of water should be added to the fruit for a simple extraction of pectin. If necessary, a second and even a third exrtraction may be taken and these extracts combined with the first extract. Addition of large quantities of water for extraction should be avoided, because excessive dilution of pectin would necessitate prolonged boiling, which in turn would reduce the jellying strength. If, on the other hand, water is added in too small a quantity, the pectin extract will be viscous and cloudy, and difficult to clarity. Further, there is also the danger of scalding the fruit during boiling.

The quantity of water to be added would depend on the fruit used. Usually it is added at the rate of 1.25 kg to 1 kg of apples and 2.5 kg to 1 kg of oranges or guavas. In the case of grapes, water is not added, the fruit being heated in its own juice. Highly juicy fruits, such as berries, are merely crushed and boiled.

*The proportion of water, sugar and fruit, which would give a good jelly in the table.*

## Proportion of Water, Fruit and Sugar for Jelly-Making

| Kind of Fruit | Quantity of water to each pound (.45 kg) of prepared fruit | Time of boiling fruits to extract juice | Quantity of sugar to each cup of fruit juice |
|---|---|---|---|
| | cup (s) | minutes | cup (s) |
| Apple | 1 | 20-25 | 3/4 |
| Crab apples | 1 | 20-25 | 1 |
| Black-berries, firm | 1/4 | 5-10 | 3/4-1 |
| Black-berries, soft | nil | 5-10 | 3/4-1 |
| Black raspberries | nil | 5-10 | 1 |
| Cran-berries | 3 | 5-10 | 3/4 |
| Currants | 1/4 or more | 5-10 | 1 |
| Gooseberries | 1/4 | 5-10 | 1 |
| Grapes such as Concord | 1/4 or more | 5-10 | 1 |
| Grape, wild | 1 | 5-10 | 3/4-1 |
| Plums, wild goose type | 1/2 | 15-20 | 3/4 |
| Quinces | 2 | 20-25 | 3/4 |
| Red raspberries | nil | 5-10 | 1 |

Successful preparation of a jelly depends largely on the extent to which pectin is separated from the cells of the fruit. Fruit juices, when extracted in the cold condition, without heating, do not contain the required amount of pectin and hence, do not form a satisfactory jelly. To get the desired pectin requirements, the fruit should be cooked (boiled), because protopectin, the precursor of pectin, is insoluble in the cold juice and this remains in the pomace or pulp when juice is extracted in the cold. It is, however, readily converted into pectin on heating. Further, heat treatment also destroys the enzymes responsible for the destruction of pectin.

The quantity of pectin extracted from a fruit depends on the degree of disintegration of protopectin on heating. To get satisfactory results, heating should be limited to a comparatively short period only, if heating is prolonged, the fruit becomes pulpy, making it difficult to get a clear pectin extract. Further, the jelly prepared becomes cloudy. If the heating is just sufficient to extract the pectin, there will hardly be any loss of flavour.

## Time Requirement for Extraction of Pectin

| Name of fruit | Time of boiling of fruit to extract pectin (minutes) |
|---|---|
| Apples | 20-25 |
| Crab apples | 20-25 |
| Black berries, firm | 5-10 |
| Cranberries | 5-10 |
| Gooseberries | 5-10 |
| Currants | 5-10 |
| Crape, wild | 5-10 |
| Grapes such as Concord | 5-10 |
| Plums, wild goose type | 15-50 |
| Quinces | 20-25 |
| Red raspberries | 5-10 |
| Black raspberries | 5-10 |
| (*) oranges | 45-60 |
| * Jamun (Eugenia jambolana) | 20-25 |
| * Guava (Psidium guava) | 30-35 |
| * Grape fruit (Citrus paradisi) | 20-25 |
| * Roselle (Hibiscus sabdariffa) | 20-25 |

* Authors' data.

**Effect of Heat on Pectin.** Although it is well known that high temperatures decrease the jellying power of pectin, the minimum temperature at which degradation of pectin may occur is not well defined. The pectin when extracted by heating under pressure, losses its jelly forming properties. If pectin is heated at 100°C for 30 minutes, it loses half of its jellying strength. The loss of jellying power is independent of the pH in the range of 2.5 to 3.0. There is, however, no loss of jellying power when pectin is heated at 80°C.

Addition of sugar helps in retarding the hydrolysis of pectin. Pectin and acid should not therefore, be boiled without addition of sugar.

In commercial pectin as well as in crude pectin extract, there is practically no loss of jellying power, When they are heated to 100°C for 30 minutes. Even heating for 60 minutes at 100°C does not seriously injure the jellying strength of pectin. Degradation of pectin however, occurs if it is heated to 105°C and above.

Demethylation in pectin can be controlled at low temperatures of about 50°C, and at a pH of 1.5. By this means, pectin of practically any methoxyl content can be obtained. The methoxyl content of pectin is normally about 11 per cent.

To prepare jellies from vegetables which contain pectin and calcium phosphate. Tomato juice belongs to this category.

**Effect of different metals.** For boiling, copper and iron kettles should not be used as these are acted upon by the acids and salts of the fruits, resulting in the discoloration of the extract. Aluminium equipment is satisfactory, if the fruit is not highly acidic. The best equipment is the one made from stainless steel or monel metal or glass lined or enamelled materials.

## Straining and Clarification

The pectin extract can be clarified by passing it through bags of linen, flannel, felt or cheese cloth, folded several times. Cheese cloth and linen cloth are more durable than the other materials. The bags should be scalded in boiling water, squeezed and used while still hot and wet. The bags containing the fruit extract should not be squeezed, because otherwise the pectin extract will not be clear due to particles passing through the pores in the bag. For large-scale production, a basket type press o~ hydraulic press may be used, and the pectin solution clarified by passing it through a filter press. For production on a small scale, the pectin extract is allowed to settle overnight and the supernatent liquid drained off.

## Pectin Requirement

Usually, 0.5 to 1.0 per cent pectin of suitable quality in the extract is sufficient to produce a good jelly. If the pectin content is in excess of this a firm and tough jelly is formed and if it is less, the jelly may fail to set. Pectin, sugar, acid and water, which are the four essential constituents of a jelly, must be present approximately in the following proportions.

| | |
|---|---|
| Pectin | 1.0 per cent |
| Sugar | 60 to 65 per cent |
| Fruit acid | 1.0 per cent |
| Water | 33 to 38 per cent. |

## JAM MARMALADE

The method of preparation of the jam-type marmalade is practically the same as that for making jelly marmalade. No attempt is, however, specially made to clarify the pectin extract of the fruit. The whole of the pulp mass is used.

The fruits are taken in the same proportion as recommended for jelly marmalade. The orange peel is removed along with the inner, white albedo portion, and the peeled fruit is sliced into pieces 0.3 to 0.45 cm thick. The peel is shredded and treated as in the case of the jelly marmalade. In the case of *khatta* (*Citurs aurantium*) or lemon, the outer yellow portion of the peel is peeled off thinly and discarded.

The sliced fruit (orange, lemon, *khatta*) mixture is boiled with a little added water, till the slices become soft, and sufficient quantity of pectin has been extracted. The boiled fruit mixture is passed though a coarse sieve or through a pulper to remove the seeds and coarser material. To the sieved pulp, the prepared shreds are added, and the mixture containing the requisite amount of added sugar, is boiled to get a jam marmalade.

In the preparation of jam marmalade, the pectin test is not quite essential, because it will not give any indication of the amount of sugar needed. The pulp will make the marmalade thicker in consistency. Sugar is, therefore, added on the basis of the weight of the fruit taken, generally in the proportion of 1 : 1.

The pulp-sugar mixture is cooked till the marmalade contains 65 per cent sugar.

After cooking, a small quantity of orange oil is added to enhance the flavour of the marmalade, as is done in the case of the jelly marmalade.

When the marmalade is ready, it is filled into cans, scalding hot. The cans are sealed hermetically and inverted for 5 to 10 minutes to sterilize the lids also. No further sterilization of the cans is necessary. In large-scale production, however, it is necessary to heat-process the product at 82° to 88°C for about 30 minutes in the case of A 2½ size cans. The time of processing will vary slightly for cans of other sizes.

**General**. To prepare perfectly clear and sparkling marmalades in glass jars, which are popular in this country, it is absolutely necessary to employ filter aids and a good filter press for clarification of the pectin extract of the fruit. Orange as well as lemon marmalades, with their golden and silver grey colours and sparkling appearance, are preferred by consumers.

# Chapter - 18

## *Tomato Products*

Fresh tomatoes are highly refreshing and appetizing. They are a good source of vitamins, particularly vitamin C. In this country, tomatoes are grown both in summer and winter, but those grown in winter are superior because they contain more solids.

Two types of tomatoes more commonly grown in India are the large and the round ones and the small and oval ones. In other countries well-known varieties like Marglobe, Sanjose etc., are grown for their better suitability for preserving and processing. Tomato processing industry packing large quantities of canned tomatoes, tomato paste and puree, tomato juice, sauce and ketchup, etc, is a major food processing industry in some parts of the world like the U.S.A., Canada, Mediterranean countries, Australia, etc.

In this country, fairly large being manufactured on an increasing scale, mostly in small units. Large tomato processing units employing fully automatic equipment, have not yet come into being, although proposal to set a few such units are being actively considered.

The tomato changes in colour during different stages of its maturity and ripening i.e., from green to pale-white, yellow and finally red. The yellow colour is owing to the presence of carotene. The red colour appears when the lycopene is formed in the fibres.

As tomatoes are available practically throughout the year in this country there is scope for setting up a large-scale processing industry. Equipment for the purpose is standard and can be obtained without much difficulty. Tomato products are judges by their colour, which in turn, depends on the degree of redness of tomatoes. The red pigment, lycopene, being a highly characteristic and rather unique pigment in tomatoes, can be used as an index of the amount of the real tomato used in a product. In fact some of the analytical methods are based on this concept.

*The following rules should be kept in mind to secure a product of high quality:*

1. Use only plant-ripened red tomatoes as far as possible. The yellow and greenish portions not only mask the red colour of the fully ripe tomatoes, but also turn brown owing to oxidation.

2. Never use iron equipment at any stage of processing. Lycopene, which is a self-oxidizing isomer of carotene, and to which tomatoes owe their red colour, turns brown when it comes into contact with iron. Iron also forms black compounds with the tannin of the tomatoes or of the spices used. Equipment should be glass-lined, or made of monel metal or preferably stainless steel. Copper equipment also adversely affects the colour of tomato products. Further, there is a severe legal limitation on the amount of copper in tomato products.

3. Avoid prolonged heating, and cool the product quickly after preparation. Tomato juice, cocktail, ketchup, sauce and soup, and chilli sauce are some of the more important products made from tomatoes. The method of preparing these is described briefly in the following sections.

## TOMATO JUICE

For this product, only plant-ripened and fully red tomatoes should be used. All green, blemished and over-ripe fruits should be rejected as they adversely affect the quality of the product. Juice got from over-ripe tomatoes is usually thin and not quite pleasant in its taste and aroma.

The yield, colour and flavour of the juice depend on the degree of ripeness of the tomatoes, the variety and the place where grown. The following points should be kept in view to ensure good quality of the juice :

1. The juice should be of deep red colour. As the red colour is contained in the fibres, and not in the serum of the juice, the fibrous portion as much as possible should be incorporated in the juice in finely divided condition.

2. The juice should posses the characteristic taste and flavour of tomato.

3. The acidity of the juice as citric acid, should be about 0.4 per cent.

4. The vitamins present in fresh tomatoes should go into the juice during its preparation. Their retention in the juice depends on the methods of extraction used. It has been found that while carotene (ß-carotene) is fairly resistant to heat and oxidation in various processes of preparation; vitamin C (ascorbic acid) is lost appreciably, particularly during the screening of the juice, on account of oxidation.

5. For uniformity in quality, either the tomatoes used should be from one stock and place or the juice should be suitably blended.

## Washing and Trimming

Mere rinsing of tomatoes in water is not enough, because mould filaments and other micro-organisms found in the cracks, wrinkles, folds and stem cavities, are not easily dislodged by gentle washing alone. For thorough cleaning, tomatoes should be washed in plenty of running water. For commercial production, rotary washers, or trough washers fitted with moving conveyor belt and soft roller brushes, are generally employed.

Great care should be taken in trimming the washed tomatoes. The loss on account of trimming green and yellowish portions, stalk end, and cracked portions etc., varies from 4.0 to 17.0 per cent with an average of about 8.0 per cent, according to data collected over a period under Indian processing conditions. The heavy wastage is mostly owing to absence of standard varieties for defects in picking, packing, and transport and marketing. The loss can be cut down to a bare minimum by adopting gradually improved methods of handling. Recently, considerable work has been done on several of these aspects with the result that tomato products manufactured in the country are of high quality and stand comparison with similar products produced elsewhere. The methods currently practised in the Mediterranean countries, Australia etc., for producing and manufacturing tomato products are well suited for maintaining high standards of quality in the products. Large-scale commercial production is, however, necessary for attaining this objective.

## Crushing

After trimming, tomatoes are cut into 4 to 6 pieces for boiling to soften the tissues. Alternatively, they may be crushed by means of fluted wooden roller-crushers.

## Pulping

*Tomatoes can be pulped by the 'hot' process or by the 'cold' process described below :*

**Hot Pulping**: The crushed tomatoes are boiled in their own juice in steam-jacketed stainless steel pans or in aluminium pans for 3 to 5 minutes to facilitate pulping. This method has the following advantages:

1. The tendency of the juice to separate into liquid and pulp can be overcome if the pectin naturally present in the seed and in the skin can be incorporated into the juice. During the preliminary boiling, this pectin is released and it thickens the pulp. The pectase enzymes which would otherwise hydrolyse the natural pectin present in tomatoes and thereby make the juice thin, are also destroyed during boiling.

2. Boiling sterilizes the juice partly, thereby checking to some extent the growth of micro-organisms which cause fermentation etc., in the juice. It also inactivates

the oxidative enzymes which are responsible for the destruction of vitamin C in the juice.

3. A light cooking releases the red colour present in the skin.

4. The yield of juice is higher than in cold pulping of the tomatoes.

**Cold Pulping**: The tomatoes are crushed in the cold and as such passed through a pulper. This method has the following defects :

1. As compared to the hot process, the extraction of juice is somewhat difficult and the yield is less.

2. Air gets incorporated into the juice in the process of extraction and this oxidizes vitamin C in the juice. There are, however, suitable equipments available now-a-days which minimise considerably the mixing up of air with the juice.

3. The juice extracted by this method is somewhat lighter in colour, since it is necessary to heat the skin to release the colour from the fibrous tissues.

4. The whole process of crushing, pressing, etc, has to be completed quickly to avoid microbial spoilage, especially during the initial stages of preparation.

Recently, Penfold has pointed out that cold pulping yields a juice whose flavour and consistency are different from those of the hot-break juice. The manufacturers have, therefore, to decide about the type of juice most likely to satisfy the market demand. The flavour of the coldbreak juice is much sharper and more acidic than that of the hot-pulped juice. This is due to the extra pressure applied in the cold pulpin and extraction process, whereby the juice surrounding the seeds, which is richer in acid and poorer in sugars than the other portions of the tomato, is extracted first. On account of this, the cold-break juice is also of lighter consistency than that got from hot-break method. It has, however, a better fresh flavour.

## Extraction of Juice

There are two types of juice extraction in use, namely the Continuous spiral press and the Cyclone.

**Continuous Spiral Press.** This consists of a long spiral screw which presses the tomatoes against a tapered screen of fine mesh having 25 holes per linear inch, each hole being of a diameter of 20/1,000 of 2.5 cm. The juice passes through the screen, but the skin and seeds are expelled at the lower end of the sieve. When this type of extractor is operated at a speed of about 250 revolutions per minute (RPM), there is practically very little or no incorporation of air into the juice. The crushed tomatoes which are fed to the screw from a hopper at the upper end, should be subjected to a jet of steam to prevent oxidation and destruction of vitamins in the juice.

**Cyclone or Pulper**. Juice can also be extracted by passing the crushed tomatoes through a Cyclone or Pulper. The main defect in this type of machine is that a considerable amount of air is incorporated into the juice. With special attachments to the Cyclone, this defect can be minimised now-a-days. In these machines, the insoluble solids in the juice are very finely divided and stay in suspension in the juice for longer periods.

In small-scale production, the tomatoes can be strained through monel metal, nickel or stainless steel sieves having one milimeter diameter holes. Not more than about 60 per cent of the fruit should be recovered as juice, because with higher yields, the juice becomes unduly thick and harsh in flavour.

## Total Solids

On an average, juice should have a total solids content of 5.66 per cent (sp. gr. 1.0240) at 20°C. The amount of total solids present in the juice can be determined in a number of ways, such as by weighing the dried sample, by noting the refractive index and by using a specific gravity hydrometer. For routine work, the specific gravity method gives fairly satisfactory results. The juice is strained through a piece of thick cloth, and the specific gravity of the strained juice determined with a hydrometer at 20°C. If the specific gravity is measured at a temperature higher than 20°C, a temperature correction is applied to the reading.

The percentage of total soluble solids is deduced from standard tables showing the relationship between specific gravity and the percentage of solids present in the juice.

## Common Salt and Sugar

On an average, 4 to 6 kg of common salt is added to every 1000 kg of the juice to counteract the astringent taste of the juice.

Sometimes, sugar also is added to improve the taste. About one per cent cane sugar to the juice improves the flavour.

## Packing

The juice can be packed in glass bottles or cans. Canned juice has, however, better taste, aroma, colour and keeping quality than the bottled juice. Further, the public has got accustomed to the slight metallic tang in the taste of the canned juice, and likes it. This is another typical instance of a product which becomes popular with public through long usage, in spite of the drawback owing to the presence of traces of metal in it. The processing temperature and time for canned tomato juice are given in the table on the next page.

The juice is generally homogenized to retard separation of liquid from the pulp to give it a thick consistency and uniform appearance. It is heated to about 66°C and forced through a small orifice under a high pressure of about 70 kg per square cm. This shears the particles and tends to reduce all of them practically to the same size. The juice is afterwards heated 82° to 88°C and filled into hot sterilized bottles of 316 to 454 g capacity. The bottles are then hermetically closed by means of crown corks and sterilized for about 30 minutes in boiling water (100°C).

| Size of can | Sterilization time when the juice is filled into can at 82° to 88°C | Sterilization temp. |
|---|---|---|
| | Minutes | 0°C |
| No. 1 | 15 | 100 |
| No. A 2 | 25 | 100 |
| No. A 2¼ | 30 | 100 |
| No. 10 | 40 | 100 |

For canning, plain cans are the best, although enamelled or lacquered cans also may be used. In this case also, the juice is filled hot into the cans at 82° to 88°C leaving practically very little head-space, to avoid marked loss in colour, flavour and vitamin C content, which would occur when the head-space is considerable. The cans are then sealed and processed, according to size, as shown in the accompanying table (above). After processing, the cans are cooled in running cold water.

In the case of the large No. 10 cans, owing to the longer processing time, the juice has generally a slightly cooked taste and flavour.

Tomato juice may be presterilized by heating in a continuous heat exchanger to temperatures much above the boiling point of water. The following temperature-time relation-ships are considered to be approximately equivalent in sterilizing value :

| Temperature of juice (°C) | Holding time (minutes) |
|---|---|
| 116 | 3.3 |
| 118 | 1.5 |
| 121 | 0.7 standard process |
| 124 | 0.32 |
| 127 | 0.15 |
| 129 | 0.07 |

This procedure is effective for destroying the flat-sour organism, B. *thermacidurans*, which often causes trouble in the case of canned tomato juice. Before filling into cans, the juice should be cooled slightly below the boiling point, but should still be sufficiently hot to sterilize the containers also.

## Analysis of Juice

A comparative analysis of four Foreign & two Indian brands of tomato juice, and their data is give in the following table.

***Analysis of Various Brands of Tomato Juice Obtainable in Indian Market***

| S. No. | Brand of Juice | Sp. gr. of juice at 20oC | Sp. gr. of filtrate at 20oC | Per cent solids in juice | Salt, as sodium chloride in 100 c.c. of juice | Total acid as malic acid in 100 c.c. of juice |
|---|---|---|---|---|---|---|
| 1. | Foreign I | 1.0240 | 1.022 | 5.66 | 0.89 | 0.38 |
| 2. | Foreign II | 1.0240 | 1.022 | 5.66 | 0.79 | 0.36 |
| 3. | Foreign III | 1.0334 | 1.031 | 7.99 | 0.84 | 0.49 |
| 4. | Foreign IV | 1.0250 | 1.023 | 5.91 | 0.82 | 0.38 |
| 5. | Indian I | 1.0387 | 1.036 | 9.27 | 1.74 | 0.59 |
| 6. | Indian II | 1.0292 | 1.027 | 6.95 | 1.11 | 0.56 |

## Tomato Puree

Commercial tomato pulp without skin or seeds, with or without added salt, and containing not less than 8.37 per cent of salt-free tomato solids, is 'medium tomato *puree*'. It is further concentrated to 'heavy tomato *puree*' which contains not less than 12 per cent solids.

## Preparation

The first step in the preparation of tomato *puree* is the preparation of tomato pulp. This pulp is prepared from plant-ripened tomatoes in the same manner as tomato juice.

## Pulp concentration

Concentration of the pulp is carried out in two types of vessels, namely, (i) open cooker, and (ii) vacuum pan.

**Open Cooker**. When dealing with small quantities of the pulp, an aluminium *patila* (vessel) will do. For large-scale or commercial production, glass-lined tanks or tanks made of stainless steel, monel metal or nickel, and fitted with flash-coils, are used. The open pan method, although employed generally, has obvious disadvantages. During boiling, the juice is exposed to the oxygen in the air, which not only destroys vitamins in it, but also makes the juice brown. It is pointed out that unless special equipment is used to prevent the incorporation of air during the entire manufacturing process, a considerable loss of vitamin C occurs. Butter or an edible oil is added to the juice during boiling to prevent it from foaming, boiling over sticking or burning, Incidentally, it also helps in lessening oxidation. This method has, however, now been superseded by the vacuum pan method, which gives a product of superior quality.

**Vacuum Pan.** The installation of a vacuum pan is rather expensive for a small factory. Its main advantage is that the juice can be boiled at a much lower temperature under reduced pressure, i.e., at about 71°C, thereby facilitating the retention of the original red colour and flavour of the tomato to a marked degree. As air also is removed during boiling, there is very little likelihood of oxidation or loss of vitamin C. In order to sterilize the product, the vacuum is broken towards the end and the temperature raised to 100°C and maintained at that level for about 10 minutes.

## Pulp Consistency

*The two method used for the concentration of pulp are as follows :*

**Method I**. Sufficient pulp is transferred to the boiling pan till the heating coils are fully covered. Heating is then commenced. More juice is added and the heating continued till the pan is practically full of pulp. Heating is then stopped and the total solids content of the pulp determined. If the total solids content is higher than the required percentage, more juice is added to lower it; if it is lower, concentration is continued till the desired concentration is reached. Manufacturer generally finds it easy and convenient to follow this method.

**Method II**. In this method, a known volume of the juice is concentrated to a known volume of the finished pulp. The juice is let into the boiling tank and when the heating coils have been fully covered, heating is commenced and the tank is filled to capacity. Heating is continued till the pulp begins to boil vigorously. Steam is then shut off momentarily and the volume of the hot pulp is measured with a measuring stick. Then a small sample of the pulp is drawn for the determination of tomato solids by the specific gravity method. When the determination of the solids is being 'carried out, boiling of the pulp in the tank is continued. By making use of Standard Tables (appendix I) the pulp is boiled down to the desired specific gravity. As both the original and the final measurements of volume are taken at the boiling point, temperature correction for the readings is not necessary.

## The End Point

The total solids in the juice, in the beginning, during boiling and at the finishing point can be determined either with a specific gravity hydrometer or with an Abbe' or pocket refractometer, or by drying the juice in vacuum at 70°C. In practice, the first two methods are employed as they are fairly simple.

## Packing

Tomato puree can be packed in plain as well as lacquered cans. The puree is filled into the cans, scalding hot, at 82° to 88°C., and the cans closed without exhausting them first. In the case of 453 g cans, they are processed for 20 minutes at 100°C. Larger cans are not generally processed, the temperature of the puree itself being sufficient to sterilize the cans also.

## TOMATO PASTE

A concentrated tomato juice or pulp without skin and seeds, and containing not less than 25 per cent of tomato solids, is known as tomato paste. If the pulp is further concentrated so as to contain 33 per cent and more of tomato solids, it is called concentrated tomato paste. Common salt, basil leaf also may be added. Part of its acidity may be neutralized with sodium carbonate or bicarbonate. Ordinarily, tomato juice can be concentrated to 14 to 15 per cent times solids in open pans, but for higher concentrations, vacuum pans are required. The initial concentration is generally carried out in open pans and the product is then finished in vacuum pans.

As the product is very thick, the total solids in it are determined with an Abbe' refractometer.

## TOMATO COCKTAIL

Tomato cocktail is gaining popularity in many of the high class hotels and restaurants. It is prepared just before serving and sometimes is also served from stock. In the latter case, the cocktail is preserved by pasteurization in bottles. Although the recipes vary, the main constituent is tomato juice to which common salt, vinegar, Worcestershire sauce, lemon or lime juice, Tabasco sauce etc., are added in different proportions to suit the palate. Two typical formula are given here.

### FORMULA I

| *Ingredient* | *Quantity* |
|---|---|
| Tomato juice (sp. gr. 1020) | 4.53 kg |
| Cloves (headless), whole | 1.5 g |
| Cumin, black pepper & cardamon, in equal quantities | 4.5 g |
| Cinnamon, broken | 1.5 g |
| Coriander seeds | 1.5 g |
| Red chilli, finely ground (Kashmiri) | 0.25 g |
| Vinegar (10 per cent acetic acid) | 283 g |
| Common salt | 45 g |

Simmer the tomato juice, with the spices loosely tied in a cloth bag for about 20 minutes in a covered vessel. Then add the lime juice, vinegar and common salt.

### FORMULA II

| *Ingredient* | *Quantity* |
|---|---|
| Tomato juice (sp. gr. 1020) | 4.53 kg |
| Cloves, (headless) whole | 1.5 g |
| Cumin | 1 g |
| Black pepper | 1 g |
| Cardamom | 1 g |
| Red chilli, finely ground (Kashmiri) | 0.25 g |
| Ginger, dried | 1.5 g |
| Lime juice | 42 g |
| Vinegar (10 per cent acetic acid) | 212 g |
| Common salt | 45 g |

### Quality of Ingredients

**Tomato juice**. If possible, use fresh juice, otherwise, use cannot juice.

**Vinegar**. Use only malt or cider vinegar of good quality and not acetic acid.

**Lime juice**. Only crystal clear lime juice should be used, because any sediment in it will impart an undesirable flavour. Moreover, it gives a 'foreign' taste to the cocktail when it is pasteurized in containers. Citric acid is not a good substitute, as it does not produce as good a taste as natural lime juice does.

**Sugar**. This should be of good quality.

### Pasteurization

When all the ingredients have been mixed and the cocktail is ready for bottling, heat it to 82° to 88°C and fill it into 340 g bottles, which have been sterilized and kept hot for filling. Close the bottles and keep them immersed in boiling water (100°C) for 30 minutes and then cool them.

## TOMATO KETCHUP

Tomato ketchup is a fairly common and popular tomato product in this country. It is made by concentrating tomato juice or pulp without seeds and pieces of skin. Spices, salt, sugar, vinegar, onion, garlic, etc., are added to the extent that the ketchup contains not less than 12 per cent tomato solids and 28 per cent total solids.

### Raw Material

Select sound ripe tomatoes having deep red colour. Remove all green and yellow portions. Green fruit makes the ketchup inferior in colour and flavour.

## Juice Extraction

The juice is extracted in the same manner as in the case of tomato juice or *puree*.

## Juice Standardisation

The raw juice is a thin, watery fluid and its specific gravity varies with the kind of tomato and the duration of boiling. It follows, therefore, that spices to be added each time vary in proportion. This would not, therefore, yield a standard product. Standardisation can be achieved by using a recipe based on tomato juice of 1.0220 specific gravity, an equivalent quantity of juice of any other specific gravity can be conveniently added.

## Recipes

*There are several recipes which give ketchup of good quality:*

### RECIPE I

| | | |
|---|---|---|
| Tomato juice (sp. gr. 1.022-1.027) | 27.27 | litres |
| Onion (chopped) | 375 | g |
| Garlic (chopped) | 25 | g |
| Cloves (whole) headless | 10 | g |
| Cardamon | 4 | g |
| Black pepper | 4 | g |
| Zira | 4 | g |
| Mace (jalvatri), not ground | 2.5 | g |
| Cinnamon (broken) | 17.5 | g |
| Vinegar, 6% acetic acid | 0.68 | kg |
| Sugar | 0.9 | kg |
| Salt | 312 | g |
| Red chilli (powder) | 12.5 | g |

### RECIPE II

| | | |
|---|---|---|
| Tomato pulp (sp. gr. 1020) | 1498 | litres |
| Sugar | 54.4 | kg |
| Salt | 12.2 | kg |
| Vinegar, 100 grain, white, distilled | 31.8 | litres |
| Cloves (headless) | 425.2 | g |
| Cinnamon, broken and sifted | 425.2 | g |
| Mace | 28.3 | g |
| Cayenne pepper | 141.7 | g |
| Garlic (freshly ground) | 708.7 | g |
| (or onions 708 g and garlic 142 g) | | |

Cook to a finish of 568.2 litres. This makes a mildly spiced product.

## RECIPE III

| | |
|---|---|
| Tomato pulp (sp. gr. 1.022) | 2727.6 litres (about 2700 litres) |
| Sugar | 136.1 kg |
| Salt | 22.6 kg |
| Paprika | 3.6 kg |
| Onions (chopped and ground) | 4.5 kg |
| Garlic | 0.9 kg |
| Mace | 340 g |
| Cinnamon (broken and sifted) | 283 g |
| Cloves, headless | 340 g |
| Cayenne pepper | 368.5 g |
| Vinegar, 100 grain | 54.5 litres |

Cook to a finish of 200 gallons or about 900 litres. This makes a spiced ketchup with a good colour, which is partly due to the paprika.

## RECIPE IV

| | |
|---|---|
| Heavy tomato puree (sp. gr. 1.06) | 454.6 litres |
| Salt | 793 g |
| Sugar | 3542 g |
| Chopped onions | 708 g |
| Cinnamon (broken bark) | 708 g |
| Mace | 100 g |
| Clove (whole, headless) | 425 g |
| All spice | 425 g |
| Cayenne pepper | 100 g |
| Chopped garlic (optional) | 113 g |
| Vinegar (distilled, 10% acetic acid) | 54.5 litres |
| Paprika, ground (optional) | 0.9 kg |

Place all the spices except paprika, onion and garlic in vinegar in a covered kettle and simmer the mass for about 2 hours. Add sugar and salt to the vinegar and stir. Add the vinegar extract of spices thus got, after removing the spice residues to the ketchup towards the end of the boiling process. If desired, add the paprika powder directly to the ketchup. This recipe yields slightly more than 454.6 litres of ketchup.

Recently, using 227.3 litres steam jacketed pans and freshly extracted juice, the following recipe has been found to yield ketchup of good quality in every respect.

The spices are added by the bag method. Oleoresins and essential oils of some of the spices used may also be employed in the preparation of the ketchup.

## RECIPE FOR TOMATO KETCHUP

*(using fresh tomato juice)*

| | |
|---|---|
| Tomato juice | 120 kg |
| Sugar | 8 kg |
| Salt | 1 kg |
| Acetic acid (glacial) | 400 ml |
| Red chilli powder | 60 g |
| Ginger (green) | 160 g |
| Onion, (fresh chopped) | 1 kg |
| Clove (headless) | 40 g |
| Cinnamon (broken) | 40 g |
| Cardamom | 40 g |
| *Zira* | 40 g |
| Black pepper | 40 g |
| Colour (blended, 6% solution) | 100 ml |
| Sodium benzoate at 750 ppm. of ketchup (as preservative) | 30 g |

Yield : approximately 120 x 370 g ketchup bottles.

***Note :***

1. Chilli powder, spices, onion, ginger should be tied loosely in a muslin cloth bag.
2. Acetic acid and colour may be added towards the end of boiling.
3. One-third of the sugar may be added in the beginning to preserve the red colour of the pulp.
4. Instead of clove, cinnamon and cardamon, essences of these spices may be added more conveniently.

The table gives the approximate relation the whole spices and the equivalent essential oils of the spices.

| Spices (100 kg) | (Equivalent weight of essential oil (kg) |
|---|---|
| Cinnamon | 0.5 |
| Clove | 1.5 |
| Mace | 3.5 |
| Pepper | 1.0 |
| Cardamom | 3.0 |

It is advisable to standardize the amount of spice, essential oil or oleoresin required as the equivalents vary with the brand of the essential oil available in the market.

5. Instead of tomato juice, tomato *puree* of 15 per cent total soluble solids, which has been canned for use during the off-season, may be used for the preparation of the ketchup on an equivalent basis, *vis-a-vis* the fresh juice.

6. Garlic may or may not be added alongwith the spices, depending upon consumer acceptance.

7. As the most suitable component for tomato ketchup colour blend, namely, Acid Magents II now been deleted from the list of permitted food colours, one has to choose other red and orange colours such as Erythrosine, Carmoisine, Sunset Yellow etc. Addition of a yellow component in the form of tartrazine will be useful.

A suitable combination of Carmoisine, Greengage and Ponceau 4 R has also been suggested.

It is, however, advisable to use the best tomatoes to avoid the necessity for reinforcing the colour of the ketchup. Ketchup without the addition of any colour would be the ideal product, one should attempt to achieve. This is not impossible. Recently the government has banned the use of any coalter colour in tomato ketchup. Some varieties of tomatoes have been found to yield ketchup of excellent red colour.

## Addition of Ingredients

**Spices.** The spices should be of good quality and they should be added in the proper proportion to give an agreeable taste and flavour to the product. The blend should be such that no single spice dominates the natural flavour of tomato. The spices may be used in the following way.

**Bag Method**. The spices are tied loosely in a muslin cloth bag, and the bag placed in the tomato juice during boiling. The bag is taken out, and the ketchup in it pressed and then removed before bottling the ketchup. The spice bag can be used for a second batch of juice also. The bag method of adding spices has, however, the following drawbacks :

1. The bag may give way during boiling and spoil the whole product. In that case, even if the pulp is again forced through a fine sieve, particles of the spices will still pass through and darken the ketchup prepared.

2. The taste and flavour of the ketchup may vary from time to time depending upon the variation in the composition of the spices used and the duration of boiling on different occasions.

3. All the flavour of the spice is not extracted in the first boiling itself. Moreover, some of the volatile flavouring substances may be lost during boiling. To counteract these, a quantity of spices greater than what is actually required, will have to be used. This will add to the cost, although the once-used spices can be utilized in the preparation of pickles.

In spice of these drawbacks, the bag method gives a ketchup of superior quality.

**Use of essential oils**. The essential oils of the spices do not contain tannings and do not, therefore, adversely affect the colour of the ketchup, in the way the whole spices contain in tannins do. Essential oils of spices may be easily blended. They do not, however, give exactly the same true and characteristic aroma of the whole spice. The equivalent of the essential oil *vis-a-vis* the whole spice has also been mentioned earlier under the recipe for the ketchup.

**Use of Oleoresins**. There are true aromas of the spices and can be used with advantages in commercial production. They are added to the ketchup for a few minutes before the boiling is complete.

**Use of Extracts**. Spice extracts can be prepared on a large scale by prolonged steeping or boiling of the spices in vinegar. The use of these extracts helps to standardise the proportion of spices and to maintain the same taste and aroma in the ketchup. This process is now being adopted by some of the ketchup manufacturers in this country also. Spiced vinegar exrtract is widely employed in several other leading tomato ketchup and sauce manufacturing countries.

**Sugar.** About one-third of the sugar required should be added initially at the time of commencing the boiling. This helps to intensify and fix the red tomato colour. The rest of the sugar is added a little before the ketchup is ready. If the whole of the sugar is added in the beginning itself, the pulp will have to be boiled for a longer time and at a higher temperature with the result that the colour of the ketchup will be adversely affected. In a kethcup manufactured on a commercial scale, the proportion of sugar varies widely from 10 to 26 per cent.

**Common salt.** Salt bleaches the tomato colour and also dissolves to some extent copper from the kettle or the coil, when the equipment is made of copper and tinned. it is, therefore, desirable to add it towards the end of boiling. Finely powdered salt is evenly sprinkled on the surface of the ketchup in the boiling pan and stirred well. In commercial ketchups, the proportion of salt ranges from 1.3 to 3.4 per cent.

**Vinegar**. Well-matured salt vinegar is essential for the preparation of ketchup of high quality. Spirit vinegar does not produce a good flavour in the product. Cider vinegar although highly pleasant, has rather a mild flavour. Good vinegar should have 5.0 to 5.5 per cent acidity in the form of acetic acid, It is necessary to use vinegar of the same strength and quality to obtain a ketchup of standard quality. Vinegar should be added when the ketchup has thickened sufficiently, so that the acid does not volatilize away, leaving the ketchup deficient in acid and flavour.

Tomato ketchup generally contains 1.25 to 1.50 per cent acid, expressed as acetic acid. Glacial acetic acid is sometimes used, as it has the following advantages :

1. It is cheaper than vinegar.
2. Being clear and colourless like water, it does not impart any colour of its own to the product.
3. It is 100 per cent acetic acid and can be added practically at the end of boiling without causing any loss of flavour or acidity.

When spiced vinegar or acetic acid is used, the acidity of the vinegar already present in it should be taken into account at the time of adding the vinegar according to the recipe.

## Thickening Agents

The tendency of tomato ketchup to separate into pulp and clear juice depends largely on the amount of pectin present in it. In order to increase the viscosity of the ketchup and prevent the separation of the pulp, pectin is usually added to the extent of 0.1 to 0.2 per cent by weight of the finished product.

## Cooking and Concentration

To get a product of uniform taste and flavour and also of the texture and thickness or body, the total solids in the finished product should be maintained constant at the same level. In commercial ketchups, the percentage of total solids varies from 20 to 37. A ketchup with 28 to 30 per cent total solids has a better flavour than a ketchup having more than 30 per cent solids. A higher proportion of the total solids dilutes the concentration of tomato solids, because it contains more of sugar and vinegar. As a ketchup with 28 to 30 per cent solids does not generally keep for a long time after once opening the bottle, the general tendency is to increase the total solids from 32 to 37 per cent. This increases its keeping quality on account of its higher sugar, salt and vinegar content.

Some well-known brands of ketchup have been found to contain 31.5 to 32.6 per cent of total solids.

Total solids in the ketchup can be determined by means of a specific gravity hydrometer. This method is, however, tedious. The refractometer method is more convenient, although it does not give highly accurate results due to the presence of salt, acetic acid, etc. There is also a slight deviation in the relationship between total solids and refract meter solids. In commercial practice, the juice (sp. gr. 1.0220) is concentrated to one-third of its original volume as determined with a gauge-stick.

## Bottling

When the ketchup is ready at the end of boiling, it is passed through a finishing machine fitted with a very fine sieve, to remove any tomato fibre, small pieces of paper, wood, etc., that might have got in through sugar or spices.

The ketchup should be bottled hot at about 88oC to prevent darkening of its colour and loss of vitamin content during subsequent storage and distribution. On cooling, the ketchup shrinks in volume producing thereby a high degree of vacuum in the bottle. Sometimes, a black ring is formed on the surface of the ketchup in the neck of the bottle. This is known as 'black neck'. It is stated to be due to the oxidation of iron compounds which get into the ketchup from the boiling equipment, and from the metal of the cap through the action of acetic acid. When the iron comes in contact with the spice tannins, it forms ferrous tannate which, on oxidation, forms the black ferric tannate. To overcome this defect, the ketchup should be deaerated and a tin foil-faced linear should be inserted under the caps.

## Pasteurization

Even under the most favourable conditions, pasteurization of tomato ketchup in bottles in essential. Some manufacturers are of the view that the hot ketchup may come in contact with the cap and thus sterilize it. This is not always safe on account of the wide variation in temperature at different points in the container. The temperature at the centre approaches the filling temperature, whereas that at the bottom, sides and the neck of the bottle is considerably less. Thus, it is not possible to know quite definitely whether the cap also will get sterilized by mere contact with the ketchup.

It, is, therefore, necessary to pasteurize the product in the bottle. Ketchup is filled into bottles at about 88°C, and the bottles sealed with crown corks and pasteurized for 30 to 35 minutes in hot water at 85° to 88°C.

With a modern filling machine, the bottles are filled at 88°C, sealed and washed with warm water to remove any adhering ketchup. The filled and closed bottles are not sterilized, the filling temperature being considered adequate for their sterilization. During filling, the temperature of the ketchup should not be allowed to fall below 88°C at any stage.

A ketchup made from tomatoes of good quality, using sugar, salt, vinegar and spices in the correct proportions, does not generally spoil for a fairly long time even after opening the sealed bottle, if it is kept in a cool and clean place. It, is however, preferable to add 0.025 per cent sodium benzoate to the product before bottling and then pasteurize the bottles as a safeguard against spoilage during 3 to 4 weeks when the ketchup in the opened bottle will be used in small proportions at a time. The sodium benzoate in the ketchup can be determined by the method given in A.O.A.C. The interference of vanillin in the estimation of benzoic acid has recently been studies by Sowbhagya et al. (1963). the Fruit Products Order lays down limits for benzoic acid in ketchup and other products.

## CHILLI SAUCE

Chilli sauce is a highly spiced product which is prepared from plant ripened and peeled tomatoes. It is mostly used as a flavouring material in cooking, and also as a table relish to some extent.

### Preparation

The tomatoes are washed thoroughly, rejecting any blemished or rotton portions. They are then blanched in hot water or in steam till the skin is losened. They are then dipped in cold water to stop further cooking and softening. They are then peeled by lifting the peel easily by means of pointed end of a knife and chopped. The seeds are not removed. During cooking of the chopped material, spices are added, tied loosely in a muslin cloth bag, just as in the case of tomato ketchup.

The following method of preparation has been recommended.

To 45.3 kg of peeled tomatoes add 1.0 kg of sugar, 10 g of red chillies (Kashmiri), 0.9 kg of peeled and finely chopped onions and the following spices tied loosely in a muslin cloth bag :

| | |
|---|---|
| Mace, (not ground) | 7 g |
| Cinnamon, (broken) | 18 g |
| Cumin, cardamom & black pepper, in equal quantities | 22.5 g |
| Ground white pepper | 10 g |
| Ground ginger | 10 g |

Cook the whole mass in a steam-jacketed kettle down to about 25.4 kg, crushing the tomatoes with a ladle, if necessary, during the process. Add 2.2 kg of sugar, 0.67 kg of common salt and finally 1.6 kg (10 per cent) vinegar. Continue the cooking of the mass for 5 to 10 minutes and then pack the finished sauce immediately in plain A 2 1/2 size cans. Close the cans and sterilize them for half an hour in boiling water.

*The following recipe gives a sauce of good quality :*

| | |
|---|---|
| Tomato, (peeled) | 22.6 kg |
| Sugar | 2.4 kg |
| Common salt | 255 g |

| | |
|---|---|
| Chillies, (ground) | 42 g |
| Garlic, (chopped) | 255 g |
| Onions, (chopped) | 100 g |
| Vinegar (5% acetic acid) | 8.6 kg |

To the tomatoes add all the ingredients except vinegar, and cook to a thick consistency. Next, add the vinegar and boil for a few more minutes. Then pack the product hot into wide-mouthed jars, close and sterilize them for 30 minutes in boiling water.

## TOMATO SAUCE

The standard method for the preparation of tomato sauce, This sauce has been found satisfactory also for canning of baked beans in tomato sauce. The composition of tomato sauce is similar in many respect to that of the thicker ketchup.

### RECIPE

| | |
|---|---|
| Tomato pulp (6% soluble solids) | 29.4 kg |
| Cardamom, pepper, cumin (zira) in equal quantities | 8.5 g |
| Cloves (headless) | 8.5 g |
| Cinnamon (broken) | 10 g |
| Mace (not ground) | 5.7 kg |
| Common salt | 0.67 kg |
| Onions, (chopped) | 155 g |
| Garlic, (ground) | 18 g |
| Sugar | 2.2 kg |
| White vinegar, 100 grain | (58 cc of 100% acetic acid) |
| Red chilli powder | 15 g |

Cook to about half the volume of the pulp taken, i.e., 26 to 28 per cent refractometer solids, taking necessary precautions as in the case of tomato ketchup. Fill into plain A 2 1/2 cans, close and process for 45 minutes in boiling water.

## TOMATO SOUP

Tomato soup is a fairly popular product now-a-days. In its preparation, the first step is the preparation of tomato pulp just as in the case of tomato juice. The main constituents of the soup are :

Tomato juice, butter or cream, spices, arrow root starch (for thickening), etc. These are added in different proportions to suit the customer.

*The following typical formula yields a good soup :*

| | |
|---|---|
| Tomatojuice (sp. gr. 1.0220) | 31.8 litres |
| Onion, finely chopped | 368 g |
| Cinnamon, broken | 5 g |
| Cloves, whole, headless | 5 g |
| White pepper, ground | 7 g |
| Red chillies, ground (Kashmiri) | 0.7 g |
| Cumin (zira), cardamom and black pepper, in equal quantities | 5.3 g |
| Ginger, dried, ground | 4.2 g |
| Cream (30 per cent), | 0.55 kg |
| or butter | or 191 g |
| Sugar | 481 g |
| Common salt | 318 g |
| Arrow root starch | 120 g |

## Preparation

Neutralize about 1/6 of the acidity of the juice by adding a thin paste of sodium bicarbonate in water. Place 27.2 litres of the juice in a boiling pan and boil to concentrate it. While it is being concentrated, add the spices in a cloth bag as in the case of tomato ketchup. In the meantime, mix arrow root and butter (or cream) with the remaining 4.6 litres of the juice to form a smooth paste. When the juice in the pan has been sufficiently concentrated, add this paste. Continue boiling to the desired consistency, stirring it continuously to prevent clotting of the starch. At the end, add sugar and salt and boil the mixture for about two minutes to dissolve them Then fill the soap into cans and close them.

## Sterilization

Sterilize the cans at 115°C 10.7 kg/cm2 for 45 minutes in the case of A2 cans and for 40 minutes in the case of 0.45 kg milk cans or 0.45 kg jam size cans. Cool the cans quickly after processing.

# MICROBIOLOGY

When tomatoes of poor quality are used in the preparation of tomato products, excessive amounts of moulds, yeasts, bacteria and fragments of insects lower the quality of the product. The U.S. Department of Agriculture has prescribed limits up to which moulds, yeasts and bacteria may be permitted in tomato products. Of these, the mould count is the most important, as it is a sure and positive indication of the condition of the tomatoes used. The insect fragment count also is highly indicative of gross contamination of the fruit and unhygienic conditions during handling and preparation of the raw materials and finished products.

The control of fermentation in vegetable sauces, which are substitutes for tomato sauce. The main ingredient is pumpkin (Cucurbita moscheta). The sauce is slightly thinner in consistency than the normal tomato sauce, but comparable with it in taste and other characteristics. Sodium benzoate is the preservative employed. In the case of Lactobacilli lycopersici even 0.2 per cent sodium benzoate has very little inhibitive effect in neutral tomato broth. Yeast is more tolerant than L. lycopersici to sodium benzoate and could be inhibited at 0.17 per cent level. A minimum of 10 minutes heating of the sauce with 0.5 per cent acetic acid could ensure the destruction of spore formers and addition of 750 ppm of sodium benzoate to the sauce would prevent spoilage during storage. The present practical of adding sodium benzoate to tomato ketchup and sauce which contain acetic acid, and then heating them in boiling water for 15 to 20 minutes, is in line with the above findings. Under such conditions, the sauces rarely undergo any microbial spoilage.

# Chapter - 19

## *Chutney, Sauces and Pickles*

Chutneys, sauces and pickles of various kinds are prepared in Indian homes and also on a commercial scale. They find a ready market in many countries. Standard recipes have been modified to suit local taste in the country and consumer acceptability in other parts of the world. Fruits such as apple, peach, plum, apricot and mango and vegetables like turnip, cauliflower, carrot, etc. are the basic raw materials. Onion, garlic, spices, herbs, etc., are added for flavour. Vinegar, common salt and sugar are also used to make the products more palatable. Vinegar serves as a preservative also to some extent.

### CHUTNEYS

A chutney of good quality should be palatable and appetising. the method of preparation is similar to that adopted in the case of jams except that spices and vinegar are added. Mango chutney is one of the better known products of its kind in several countries. Apricot chutney is another popular product and so also is apple chutney.

The fruit or vegetable is cut into slices or pieces of suitable size and softened by boiling in water. Slow cooking at a temperature below the boiling point yields a better product than brisk heating at a comparatively higher temperature. Onion and garlic are added at the start to mellow their strong flavours. Spices are coarsely powdered before they are added to the product. Sometimes a vinegar extract of spices is used instead of whole spices.

Spices as well as vinegar extract should be added just a little before the final stage of boiling, because during prolonged boiling, some of the essential oils of the spices as also of the vinegar, are likely to be lost by volatilization.

## Cooking Process

Sweet chutneys such as mango and apricot chutneys are generally cooked to consistency of jam to avoid fermentation of the product during storage. Where vinegar is used in fairly large quantities, the amount of sugar may be reduced correspondingly, because vinegar itself serves partly as a preservative.

## Bottling

Only clean and dry bottles and jars earlier sterilized in boiling water should be used and they should be warm at the time of filling. If the bottles and the jars are not properly cleaned, fermentation is likely to set in through fermentation organisms adhering to the walls of the containers. It is safer to pasteurize the filled bottles are sealing them at 82°C for about 30 minutes in 0.45 kg size jars.

## Equipment

Equipment made of iron and copper not be used as they are acted upon by vinegar. Further, small amounts of these metals, dissolved in oil act as catalytic agents for development of rancidity in the product. These metals also form black compounds with the tannins of fruits and spices, and thereby adversely affect the colour, taste and flavour of the product.

The vessels used should be glass-lined, or they should be made of nickel or stainless steel. Copper utensils freshly tinned adequately can also be used without risk.

## Recipes

There are a large number of recipes for chutneys. Apricot, mango, and apple chutneys are, however, of particular interest in this country. A considerable amount of research and development work has been carried on to standardize these products for indigenous as well as export purposes. Recipes for peach, plum, date, tomato chutneys and some mixed chutneys will be found in some books and bulletins on pickle-making and preservation.

The recipes recommended in these publications should, however, be tried on a small-scale in the first instance, and wherever found necessary they should be modified before taking up large-scale production.

Some chutney recipes, which have been tried with some degree of success, are given in the following section :

## Apple Chutney

*Poultney gives the following two recipes for apple chutney :*

### RECIPE I

| | |
|---|---|
| Apple | 18.1 kg |
| Sultanans | 9.0 kg |
| Onion powder | 226.7 g |
| Sugar | 13.6 kg |
| Salt | 28.3 g |
| Cassia, ground | 28.3 g |
| Pimento, ground | 28.3 g |
| Nutmeg, ground | 14.1 g |
| Caramel | 283.4 g |
| Acetic acid | 0.9 kg |
| Malt vinegar | 13.6 litres |

Peel, core and slice the apples. Cook the slices alongwith the other ingredients, till they become tender. Bottle the product hot. The final acidity of the chutney should not be less than 2.4 per cent.

### RECIPE II

| | |
|---|---|
| Apple | 2.7 kg |
| Onion powder | to taste |
| Brown Sugar | 2.27 litres |
| Preserving sugar | 2 heads |
| Cayenne (red chilli powder) | 1/4 tea spoonful |
| Garlic | 1/2 tea spoonful |
| Salt | 3 tea spoonful |
| Vinegar | 2 tea spoonful |

Peel, core and cut the apples into small pieces. Core and cut the onions very. finely. Mix all the ingredients withe the vinegar and boil gently till the chutney 'becomes thick. Pick while hot and seal the bottles air-tight. Use wide-mouthed bottles or jars for packing the chutney.

*A typical recipe for the preparation of apple chutney to suit Indian taste is as follows:*

| | |
|---|---|
| Apple slices | 35 kg |
| Apple pulp | 15 kg |
| Sugar | 55 kg |
| Salt | 1.2 kg |
| Cardamom | 70 g |
| Cinnamon | 70 g |
| Clove | 70 g |
| Red chilli powder | 200 g |
| Black pepper | 70 g |
| Ginger, dried | 70 g |
| Apple essence | 5 ml |
| Sodium benzoate (as preservative) | 50 g |

## Apricot Chutney

*The following process for the preparation of apricot chutney :*

Take firm, but fully ripe apricots of the whole or the yellow variety. Cut them into slices about 0.3 cm thick. Cover the slices with sugar and allow the mixture to stand for 1 to 2 hours so that sugar partially dissolves in the juice liberated and the mixture becomes fairly thin in consistency. Fill the spices loosely in a muslin cloth bag, tie it up and place it in the mixture in a boiling pan. Boil the mixture to about 105°C (at sea level). Add salt and vinegar to the boiling mixture and continue boiling for another 5 minutes. The chutney will be ready now to be filled hot into sterile hot bottles. Fill it into the bottles and close them tight.

### RECIPE

| | |
|---|---|
| Apricot slices | 1.3 kg |
| Sugar | 1.3 kg |
| Salt | 56.6 g |
| Cardamom, roughly ground | 2 g |
| Black pepper, broken grains | 2 g |
| Cumin (zira), whole | 2 g |
| Cinnamon, whole | 2 g |
| Red chilli powder (according to taste) | 7 g |
| Cloves, headless | 1 g |
| Mace, broken | 0.5 g |
| Unions, sliced and gently crushed | 28.3 g |
| Vinegar, 4 to 5% strength | 226.7 g |

This recipe will yield about 2.2 kg of apricot chutney. It cah be sealed up for large-scale production.

## Bamboo Chutney

Tender bamboo shoots made a good sweet bamboo chutney. Select, young tender bamboo shoots and remove the outer sheaths. Cut the tender portion into small pieces. Boil the pieces in water twice or thrice, each time for about half an hour to remove the bitter poisonous principle, hydrocyanic acid. Discard the water used for boiling each time. Mince the boiled pieces finely.

### RECIPE

| | |
|---|---|
| Minced bamboo shoots | 1.8 kg |
| Sugar | 1.8 kg |
| Salt | 85.0 g |
| Caldamom, cinnamon and cumin mixed in equal proportion | 56.6 g |
| Red chilli powder | 28.3 g |
| Onions, chopped | 28.3 g |
| Garlic, chopped | 28.3 g |
| Vinegar | 85.0 g |

Add the sugar, salt and a little water to the minced bamboo pieces and warm the mass to dissolve the sugar and salt. Place the spices loosely in a muslin cloth bag, tie it up, and place the bag in the mixture in a vessel. Cook slowly unti the mass attains the consistency of jam. Remove the spice bag from the pan, and add vinegar to the hot mixture in the pan.

Boil again for a short period to ensure that the product is of the desired consistency. Cool the product, fill it into clean-mouthed glass bottles or jars and seal them tight. Bamboo chutney is an exotic product of the East.

## Mango Chutney

This is a typical product of India. For its preparation, slightly under rupe fruits of seedling varieties are preferable. Fresh as well as brined and peeled mango slices can be used in its preparation. Both types of raw material are employed by the industry. The latter is used to extend manufacture of chutney beyond the mango season. In this case, the slices are preserved in a brine of 15 per cent strength, the percentage of salt being maintained by adding salt from time to time. Some of the manufacturers prefer to add dry salt to the slices. The main drawback in this simple method is that the slices shrivel due to osmosis and do not regain their original size and shape in the final product. Further, the slices also become hard. Usually, 1 kg of finely powdered salt is added to every 4 kg of slices. The amounts of sugar, spices, vinegar, etc., added depend largely on the local taste.

*Some typical recipes for mango chutney are given here.*

## Sweet Mango Chutney

### RECIPE

|  |  |
|---|---|
| Peeled mango slices | 0.9 kg |
| Sugar | 0.9 kg |
| Salt | 56.6 g |
| Mixed spices (cardamon, cinnamon, cumin etc., in equal quantities) | 28.3 g |
| Garlic, chopped | 6.0 g |
| Red chilli powder, finely ground | 14.0 g |
| Vinegar | 113.4 g |
| Onions, chopped | 28.3 g |
| Ginger, green | 113.4 g |

Take slightly under-ripe mangoes, peel and cut into thin slices. Heat the slices in a small amount of water to make them soft. Add sugar and salt. Tie the other ingredients loosely in a cloth bag; place the bag in the slices in a boiling pan and cook the mass to the consistency of jam. Then add vinegar and boil for about 5 minutes. Remove the spice bag. Fill the hot product into hot and dry bottles that have been previously sterilized.

Seal them air-tight. The product is generally of high quality and keeps well in storage.

## Sliced Mango Chutney

The following recipes are typical ones for sliced mango chutney. Some of the spices, garlic and other ingredients can be varied or omitted.

### RECIPE

| | I | II | III |
|---|---|---|---|
| Sliced mangoes | 3.6 kg | 2.2 kg | 2.2 kg |
| Sugar | 2.7 kg | 2.2 kg | 1.92 kg |
| Almonds (blanched & peeled) | 0.45 kg | - | - |
| Raisins (stemmed) | 0.45 kg | - | - |
| Salt, finely ground | 170 kg | 141 g | 114 g |
| Ginger, finely ground | 227 g | - | - |
| Vinegar | 0.78 kg | 0.78 kg | 0.67 kg |
| Red chillies, finely ground | 56 g | 56 g | 28 g |

| | | | |
|---|---|---|---|
| Cinnamon, broken | 14 g | - | - |
| Cumin, black | 28 g | 14 g | - |
| Mustard, finely ground | - | - | 56 g |
| Garlic, chopped | - | - | 56 g |

The method of preparation of the chutney is the same as that for the sweet mango chutney.

*A typical recipe for commercial production of mango chutney as follows :*

| | |
|---|---|
| Mango slices | 25 kg |
| Sugar | 25 kg |
| Salt | 1 kg |
| Ginger, dried | 125 g |
| Clove, headless | 25 g |
| Cardamom | 125 g |
| Red chilli | 200 g |
| Acetic acid, glacial | 250 ml |
| Sodium benzoate | 25 g |

## Peach Chutney

*Sarson gives the following recipe for peach chutney:*

### RECIPE

| | |
|---|---|
| Dried peaches (equal to 4.5 kg of peeled peaches) | 0.9 kg |
| Onion | 0.45 kg |
| Raisin | 0.45 kg |
| Sultanas | 0.22 kg |
| Cinnamon, powder | 14 g |
| Ginger, ground | 14 g |
| Vinegar | 1.1 litre |

Cut the dried peaches into quarters. Place them in a shallow pan and cover with vinegar. Set aside for 24 hours to allow the fruit to swell. Chop the onions finely and cut the raisins into halves. Then add them along with the spices to the rest of the vinegar. Bring the mass to a boil and let it simmer for about 15 minutes. Transfer the peacher and vinegar into the pan and continue to cook toll the product becomes sufficiently thick. Bottle hot.

In the case of fresh peaches, the peeled slices can be cooked directly with the vinegar till they bacome soft. The rest of the process is the same as for as dried peaches.

## Plum Chutney

*The following recipe for a good plum chutney:*

### RECIPE

| | |
|---|---|
| Plums, fully ripe | 1.8 kg |
| Sugar | 1.8 kg |
| Vinegar | 0.45 kg |
| Mace (jalvatri) not ground | 1 blade |
| Cloves (headless) | 6 in number |
| Pepper, black, ground | 10 in number |
| Chillies, Kashmiri, finely ground | 7.0 g |
| Salt, finely powdered | 14.1 g |

Wash the plums and place them in a large cooking pan alongwith the other ingredients except sugar and vinegar. Heat the mixture with a small quantity of water till the plums become soft. Pass the whole mass through a coarse sieve of aluminium or monel metal or stainless steel to remove the stones and skin. Add sugar and boil till the pulp becomes thick. Then add vinegar. Stir well all the time and continue boiling till the chutney is ready. Fill into sterilized bottles and seal them air-tight.

## Tomato Chutney

*The following recipe gives a good tomato chutney:*

### RECIPE

| | |
|---|---|
| Tomato | 13.6 kg |
| Onions, chopped | 9.5 kg |
| Sugar | 18.1 kg |
| Salt | 0.9 kg |
| Ginger | 56.0 g |
| Chillies | 14.1 g |
| Vinegar | 20.4 litres |
| Garlic vinegar | 9.0 litres |

Peel the tomatoes by blanching. Place all the ingredients except vinegar in a pan and cook to a thick consistency. Add the vinegar, cook for another five minutes and pack the finished chutney in wide-mouthed and sterilized dry bottles and seal them air-tight.

Chutneys can also be made from fruits like pear, greengage, date, banana, papaya etc., by adopting with slight modifications, the above mentioned recipes and following a similar procedure.

## Thin Sauce

Sauces are generally of two kinds, and they are the thin and the thick sauces. Thin sauces mainly consist of vinegar extract of various flavouring materials like spices and herbs. Their quality depends mostly on the piquancy of the material used.

Some sauces are matured by storing them in wooden barrels or casks. During storage, they develop flavour and aroma. Freshly prepared products have often a raw and harsh taste and they should, therefore, be matured by storage. For the preparation of sauces of high quality, the spices herbs, fruits and vegetables are macerated in cold vinegar. Sometimes, they are also prepared by boiling them in vinegar. The sauce is filtered through a fine or coarse mesh sieve of non-corrodible metal, according to the quality desired. The skin, seeds and stalks of fruits, vegetable and spices used, should not be allowed to pass through the sieve as they spoil the appearance of the sauce. The usual commercial practice is to prepare vinegar extracts of each kind of spice and fruit separately, either by maceration or by boiling in vinegar and then blending these extracts suitably before filling the sauce into barrels for subsequent maturation.

*A few typical recipes for thin sauces are given here:*

## Soya Sauce

Soya sauce is made from soya beans. The sauce has usually a predominant saltish taste and has a dark brown colour. It is made by cooking soya beans and wheat, and then allowing the mass to undergo mould fermentation for 3 to 4 days. The mouldy mass is then mixed with strong brine (15 to 20 per cent) to form a mash which is filled into wooden barrels to bring about bacteriological and chemical changes in the presence of a high concentration of salt. In due course, a thick brown liquid is formed. It is boiled and filtered. To the filtered liquid, molasses are added to improve the flavour. The finished product, which is known as soya suace, is bottled in the usual way.

The high concentration of salt in the medium prevents any harmful microbial changes taking place in the sauce. Soya sauce is a highly popular product of China, Japan and the Far East and it is considered to be not only a relish, but also a nutritious product on account of the protein hydrolysate of the soya bean, which is rich in protein as well as fat. Soya sauce is becoming popular in a limited way in this country also. There is scope for developing similar products from indigenous materials like horsegram, groundnut, etc., by adopting improved local methods and by introducing the techniques employed in Japan and elsewhere for commercial production. The Cftri, has developed a method for the preparation of soya sauce and a similar sauce from peanuts.

## Worcestershire Sauce

This is another sauce which is well known in the U.K. and elsewhere in Europe. Tamarind, which is a typical acidic material employed widely in South Indian cooking, is an important constituent of this sauce. This sauce is utilized in the preparation of cocktails also.

*The following recipe for the preparation of the sauce:*

### RECIPE

| | |
|---|---|
| Malt Vinegar | 5.6 litres |
| Tamarind | 226 g |
| Garlic | 56 g |
| Onion | 56 g |
| Essence of lemon | 28 g |
| Essence of vanilla | 28 g |
| Dried ginger | 56 g |
| Common salt | 28 g |
| Cumin | 7 g |
| Cardamom | 7 g |
| Clove, headless | 7 g |
| Sugar | 113 g |
| Lemon juice, filtered | 0.45 kg |
| Ethyl acetate | 0.5 ml |

Macerate tamarind in a small quantity of vinegar and filter the extract through muslin cloth. Prepare an extract in vinegar of garlic, onion, dried ginger, cumin, cardamom, cinnamon and clove, and mix it with the tamarind extract. Then add essence of lemon and vanilla and also sugar, salt, lemon juice and ethyl acetate. Place the blended mixture in a wooden barrel for maturing over a period of about two months. After maturation, filter the mixture again through a coarse sieve to get the sauce. Bottle it properly. If desired, a small quantity of caramel may be added to the sauce to give it an attractive colour. There are various popular brands of Worcestershire sauces in the market.

The following recipe for Worcestershire sauce. The figures are conveniently expressed as percentages.

**RECIPE**

| | *Percentage* |
|---|---|
| Malt vinegar (6% acetic acid) | 70.0 |
| Sugar | 4.0 |
| Molasses | 9.5 |
| Caramel | 0.5 |
| Salt | 2.5 |
| Mixed spices | 3.5 |
| Onion, brined | 7.0 |
| Tamarind | 2.5 |
| Protex (or meat extract) | 0.5 |

The mixed spices are prepared by mixing the following ground spices.

| | *Percentage* |
|---|---|
| Capsicum | 20 |
| Hungarian paprika | 15 |
| Black pepper | 25 |
| Clove | 10 |
| All spices | 15 |
| Ginger | 10 |
| Mustard | 5 |

Prepare tamarind extract by simmering it in a portion of the vinegar. Prepare an infusion of the spices and crushed onions, preferably in the cold. Mix all the extracts, place the mixture in a clean barrel and allow to stand for about six months for maturing. At the time of bottling strain the sauce. Meat extract may be avoided if it is not desired in the sauce.

Mushroom and walnut ketchup sauces popularly known as ketchups are also produced commercially. ketchup is generally the name given to tomato sauce of thick consistency. Thick sauces made from other fruits or vegetables are not generally called ketchups or catshups. This is a widely accepted definition and classification.

## Mushroom Ketchup (Sauce)

The following method for the preparation of this product.

Select dry fully grown and unbruised mushrooms of edible harmless variety. Break them into pieces and place them in layers with salt in a deep bowl.

Sprinkle salt at the rate of 1 kg for every 8 kg of mushroom. Allow the mushroom to stand in the brine formed for 4 days, stirring the mixture twice a day. Cook the mass gently for about 45 minutes and strain the liquor. To every quart of the liquid, add the following ingredients :

| | |
|---|---|
| *All apices | 1 teaspoonful |
| Pepper | 1 - do - |
| Ginger | ½ - do - |
| Mace | ½ - do- |
| Clove | A pinch |
| Cinnamon | - do - |

* A mixture of equal quantities of cumin, cinnamon and cardamom may be used instead of all spices.

Simmer the ketchup in a pan until it is reduced to about a third of its original volume Bottle hot.

## Walnut Ketchup (Sauce)

*The following recipe prepared for Walnut Sauce :*

### RECIPE

| | |
|---|---|
| Tender, green walnuts | 100 numbers |
| Vinegar | 2.2 litres |
| Chopped onions | 0.45 kg |
| Salt | 0.22 kg |
| Pepper corns | 28 g |
| *All spices | 14 g |
| Clove | ½ teaspoonful |
| Nutmeg | ½ - do - |

* Instead of all spices, cumin, cinnamon and cardamom mixed in equal proportion may be added.

Cut the walnuts into halves. Crush them and place them in a deep jar. Place the rest of the ingredients in the vinegar; bring the mass to a boil and pour it over the crushed walnuts. Allow the mixture to stand for 2 weeks, stirring it daily. Draw off the separated liquid, simmer it for about half an hour and fill it into bottles.

## Thick Sauces

A sauce which does not flow freely and which is highly viscous is called a thick sauce. On the other hand, thin sauces, described earlier are less viscous in consistency. They also contain more of sugar and less of acid. Generally spices and colouring added are practically similar to those in the case of the thick ketch-ups and sauces. It should contain at least 3 per cent acetic acid to ensure its keeping quality. The acidity should not however, exceed 3.4 per cent as otherwise the sauce would taste sharp. The sugar content may usually vary from 15 to 30 per cent according to the kind of sauce made. Usually malr vinegar is used. In addition to contributing to acidity of the sauce, it also improves its flavour. The sweetness is derived partly from fruits like date, raisin, sultanas, apple and tomato, and partly from the sugar added. The colour of the sauces varies with the raw material used. Sometimes, a little caramel is added.

The manufacturing process is the same as for chutneys. Thickening agents also are added to prevent or retard sekimentation of solid particles in suspension in the sauce. In this country, apple pulp is often used for this purpose, Sometimes, the fruit which is used in the preparation of the sauce, is boiled to soften it, then pulped and added as a filler. The starches of maize, potato, arrow root (cassava starch), sago and rye also are used as thickening agents. The use of Indian gum, locust kernel gum, tagacanth, karaya gum, gelatin, Irish moss, pectin and other similar substances have been advised. These are not, however as good as the cereal and root starches. When using these thickening agents, it is advisable to consult the food laws of the country such as the Prevention of Food Adulteration Act (P.F.A.A.) of the Govt. of India etc., because some of them ar not allowed as adjunct in food by some of the importing countries.

There is considerable scope for developing a variety of thin as well as thick sauces, making use of indigenous material and effecting suitable changes in the spices and other ingredients added.

Apple sauce and tomato sauce are quire popular in this country. The following tentative recipes may be adopted in their preparation.

## Apple Sauce

### RECIPE

| | |
|---|---|
| Apple pulp | 100 kg |
| Sugar | 28 kg |
| Salt | 750 g |
| Red chilli powder | 150 g |
| *Dried ginger, onion, garlic each | 250 g |
| Clove oil | 30 ml |
| Cinnamon oil | 10 ml |
| Cardamom oil | 10 ml |
| Acetic acid | 1200 ml |
| Malt vinegar | 1200 ml |

| | |
|---|---|
| Apple essence | 40 ml |
| Citric acid | 200 g |
| Sodium benzoate | to the desired extent |
| Red colour (6 per cent solution preservative) (within permitted limit) | 50 g |

*Fresh ginger, onion and garlic may be used in equivalent quantities instead of the dried materials. The proportion of other ingredients may be varied to suit consumer taste. The sauce is prepared as usual by boiling and is bottled hot.

## Tomato Sauce

### RECIPE

| | |
|---|---|
| Tomato juice | 120 kg |
| Sugar | 9 kg |
| Salt | 1.35 kg |
| Acetic acid, glacial | 230 ml |
| Chilli powder (to suit taste) | 60 g |
| Ginger, green (optional) | - |
| Onion, fresh, chopped | 680 g |
| Clove, headless | 35 g |
| Garlic dried (optional) | - |
| Cinnamon | 4 g |
| Cardamom | 12 g |
| Cumin (zira) | 12 g |
| Black pepper | 12 g |
| Colour, red, (6% solution) | as required |

Prepare the sauce by boiling as usual 26 to 27 per cent total soluble solids and can it hot. Process A 2½ cans for 45 minutes in boiling water. The sauce can also be bottled by adding sodium benzoate as chemical preservative within the limits prescribed by P.F A.A.

The spices added in the case of tomato sauce ar considerably less than in the case of tomato ketchup.

## Fruit Sauce

Besides tomato and apple sauces, mixtures of various other fruits and starchy vegetables like pumpkin, papaya, ash-gourd etc., are sometimes employed in the preparation of fruit sauce to which quite often the characteristic red colour of the tomato is added with the result that the cheaper product passes off as the more expensive tomato product. Legislation is under way to protect the genuine tomato product by insisting that fruit sauces other than genuine tomato sauce, do not have a red colour. They should contain some other colour. Experimental work is needed to recommend a suitable colour for this purpose. Recently addition of colour has been banned in the case of tomato ketchup in this country.

## SOUPS AND SOUP MIXES

Ready-to-serve soups such as tomato soup, mushroom soup, mixed vegetable soups, especially dried vegetable mixtures for quick preparation of supos at home, are gaining popularity now-a-days. Liquid soups ar generally canned. They are warmed at the time of serving. In the case of typical soup, namely tomato soup, the following two recipes; one for home-scale preparation and the other for commercial production will be useful as guidelines.

### TOMATO SOUPS (home-scale)

| | |
|---|---|
| Tomato pulp (6% soluble solids) | 5 kg |
| Water | 1.75 kg |
| Onion, chopped | 75 g |
| Salt, powdered | 90 g |
| Butter | 90 g |
| Sugar | 100 g |
| Flour | 50 g |
| Garlic, chopped (optional) | 5 g |
| Pepper, ground | 5 g |
| Cinnamon, cardamom and other spices, as desired | 2.5 g each |

Make the flour into a thick paste, boil and strain it. Place the spices in a muslin cloth as in the case of tomato ketchup. Add the starch paste to the tomato juice in a boiling pan. Add sugar, salt and butter. Place the spice bag in the juice. Heat the juice till it becomes fairly thick. Remove the spice bag and can the soupn in plain cans. Process A 1 tall (453 g) cans for 45 minutes at 115°C (10 psig) or 0.7 kg/cm$^2$ in a pressure cooker. Cool the cans after processing.

### TOMATO SOUP (large-scale)

| | |
|---|---|
| Tomato juice (5% T.S.S.) | 50 kg |
| Water | 16 kg |
| Sugar | 1 kg |
| Salt | 800 g |

| | |
|---|---|
| Butter | 800 g |
| Onion, chopped | 800 g |
| Flour (wheat, rice or barley) | 450 g |
| Garlic (optional) | 35 g |
| Pepper, ground | 30 g |
| Cinnamon, cardamom & other spices, as desired | 15 g each |

After the preparation of the soup as in the case of the home-scale method, fill into cans at 74°C, close and process at 115°C (10 psig) or 0.7 kg/cm$^2$ for 45 minutes in the case of No. 1 tall cans (453 g).

## PICKLES

The process of preservation of food in common salt or in vinegar is called pickling. Spices and edible oil also may be added to the product.

Pickles of various kinds are known throughout India and many parts of the world. Some of the typical Indian pickles made from mango, lime, turnip, cabbage, cauliflower, etc., have become popular in several countries. There is a wide and growing export market for these products which are associated with the well known Indian condiments.

Pickles are good appetizers and add to the palatability of a meal. They aid digestion by stimulation the flow of gastric juice. Very little scientific data is, however, available regarding their nutritive value. Different kinds of pickles contain varying amounts of nutrients depending upon the raw material taken and the method of preparation followed. the food value of cucumber pickle exceeds that of eggs, rice, fresh onions and fresh tomatoes.

Different kinds of pickles are made in several Indian homes in fairly large quantities. Pickles are also manufactured on a large scale and exported to other countries. In Indian pickles in oil, mustard, rape seed and sesamum oils are generally used. Some pickles are made in lime juice. Pickles made to resemble imported pickles are made in vinegar. Onion pickle in clear spiced vinegar belongs to the latter category.

## Problems in Pickling

The changes that the place during pickling on account of the activity of micro-organisms depend largely on the composition of the fruit or vegetable. Yeast and mould can grow in the presence of acid. Thus, fruits and acidic vegetables spoil either by yeast fermentation or by moulding. As acidity is not favourable for the growth of putrefactive bacteria, fruits and vegetables are not generally spoiled by them. On the other hand, the decay of vegetables which have little or no acid in them, is always mainly owing to the action of bacterial. In the preparation of pickles, however, the desired fermentation is brought about by the action of lactic-acid forming bacteria, which are capable of growing in an acid medium. In this respect, they differ from the putrefactive bacteria, which cause decay of fruits and vegetables.

There are mainly two methods of preserving fruits and vegetables, namely (i) by killing all the micro-organisms responsible for spoilage, by heat or other means, and then checking the entry of fresh organisms into the preserved product, and (ii) by making the conditions most unfavourable for the growth and multiplication of micro-organisms. The first method is generally employed in the preservation of fruits and vegetables, and the second method in the preparation of pickles.

## Action of Preservatives

Salt, vinegar and acetic acid are the three important ingredients used in pickling. These substances when used in sufficient quantities, act as preservatives either singly or in combination.

**Salt**. - Vegetables do not ferment when they are covered with a strong brine, or packed with a fairly large quantity of salt. Spoilage is prevented by adding sufficient common salt, bringing its final concentration in the material from 15 to 20 per cent. At this high salt concentration, mould and even lactic acid-forming bacteria do not grow. This method of preservation is applicable only to vegetables which contain very little sugar because sufficient lactic acid cannot be formed by fermentation to act as preservative.

**Vinegar**. - In vinegar pickles, vinegar acts as a preservative. In order to ensure satisfactory results, the final concentration of acid as acetic acid, in the finished pickle should not be less than 2 per cent. To avoid dilution of the vinegar by the water liverated from the tissues, the vegetables are generally placed in strong vinegar of about 10 per cent acidity for several days before final packing. This treatment helps to expel the gases present in the intercallular spaces of the vegetable tissue and also prevents subsequent dilution of the vinegar in the pickle.

**Lactic acid**. - Bacteria prefer for their growth material with little or no acid. The lactic acid bacteria, however, can grow in acid media and can also produce acid through their action on the substrate. They can grow in the presence of 8 to 10 per cent salt. Advantage is taken of these two factors in pickling. The growth of undesirable organisms is inhibited by adding salt, while allowing the lactic fermentation to proceed.

When vegetables are placed in brine, the soluble material present in them diffuses into the salt water owing to osmosis and the liquid penetrated into the tissues. The soluble material, besides containing mineral matter, contains fermentable sugars also. The sugars serve as food for lactic acid bacteria, which convert them into lactic and other volatile acids. In practice, usually 2 to 3 kg of salt is mixed with every 100 kg of the material and the mixture allowed to stand for 12-24 hours, when sufficient juice comes out from the material to form the brine. If the vegetable does not contain sufficient juice, it is covered with brine containing 5 per cent salt.

The soluble material extracted is fermented by lactic acid forming bacteria, which are generally present in large numbers on the surface of fresh vegetables.

When lactic acid is formed in sufficient quantity, the lactic acid bacteria cease to function, and any further change in the composition of the material is prevented. Although the pickle is ready for consumption, precautions should be taken to save it form spoilage by aerobic micro-organisms.

The presence of salt and the lactic acid formed preserved the pickle by preventing the growth of putrefactive bacteria provided air is excluded. In the presence of air, however, 'pickle scum' is formed and it destroys the lactic acid and brings about putrefaction. The acid brine formed during pickling acts upon the vegetable tissues and produces the characteristic taste and aroma of pickle.

Temperature is the most important factor for successful lactic fermentation. Lactic acid bacteria are most active at a temperature of about 30°C. It is, therefore, essential that the temperature of the product undergoing lactic acid fermentation should be kept as close to 30°C as possible, especially in the beginning.

## Raw Materials

Raw materials used in pickling should possess certain definite characteristics.

**Salt.** For pickling any variety of common salt is suitable, provided it is pure. At any rate, it should not contain more than one per cent of impurities, nor should it contain chemicals like tricalcium phosphate or magnesium phosphate, which are generally added to salt to reduce its tendency to cake. Salt should be free from lime (CaO), as it reduces the acidity of the vinegar in which brined vegetables are pickled, and also sometimes causes lime deposits on the bottom of the container. Salt should also be free from iron, which in contact with the tanin of the fruit, vegetable and spice, produces blackening of the pickle. It should not also contain magnesium salts which impart a bitter taste to the pickle. Carbonates, being alkaline, lower the acidity of the pickle and also make the pickle soft in texture.

**Vinegar**. Vinegar of good quality should contain at least 4 per cent acetic acid. Vinegars of low acid content or imitation or ssunthetic vinegars, are not suitable for pickling. For pickles of high standard and quality, the vinegar used should be of good quality and should be of 40 to 60 grain strength, that is, it should contain 4 to 6 per cent of acetic acid. Usually, malt or cider vinegar is used.

Some manufacturerss prefer to use acetic acid, becuase it is highly concentrated and practically free from colour and sediment. If a fruit vinegar is used, it should be filtered first to remove any sediment. Vinegar should not come in contact with iron as it leads to the blackening of the pickle.

In order to ensure good keeping quality, the final concentration of acetic acid in the pickle should not be less than 2 per cent in addition to the other organic acids naturally present in the raw material.

**Sugar**.Sugar used in the preparation of sweet pickles should be of high quality.

**Spices**. Spices are added practically to all pickles, the quantity added depending upon the kind of fruit or vegetable taken and the kind of flavour desired. The spices generally used are bay leaves, cardamom, chillies, cinnamon, clove, coriander, dill herb, ginger, mace, mustard, black pepper, cumin, turmeric, garlic, mint, sage, parsley, thyme, fennel, aniseed etc. These should be of good quality and should be stored in friction-top tins in a cool and dry place.

**Water**. Only potable water should be used for the preparation of brine. Hard water contains salts of calcium, sodium, magnesium etc, which interfere with the normal salt-curing of the vegetable. If hard water is to be used, a small quantity of vinegar should also be added to the brine to neutralize its alkalinity. Iron should not be present in the water in any appreciable quantity as it causes the blackening of the pickle.

## Colouring and Hardening Agents

Once it was the practice to heat the vinegar pickle in a copper vessel so that the pickle might acquire a green colour. It has now been shown that the green colour is owing to copper acetate, which is a poisonous compound. The use of copper vessels for making pickles has, therefore, been prohibited in many countries.

Colours are not generally added to pickles, although they are used, to some extent, in sauces. Some manufacturers use alum for firmness in pickles. It is, however, a doubtful expedient, because the same results can be obtained by employing proper pickling methodss. The use of alum in pickle-making is not therefore, recommended as a normal practice.

## Equipment

Wide-mouthed stone jars with straight sides are highly suited for making small quantities of pickles. The advantages of such containers are that they can be easily cleaned and they absorb any undesirable flavours and odours to a less extent than wooden containers. For large scale production, 227 litres capacity water-tight kegs or barrels are sutable. Before use, the barrels must be washed thoroughly with a strong lye solution to remove any undesirable flavours and odours. To remove traces of lye, they should then be cleaned thoroughly with hot water. The covers for the kegs should be thick and they should be made of a material that would not impart any colour, taste and flavour of its own to the pickle. They should be 2.5 to 5 cm less in diameter than the inside of the container so that they can be easily placed inside the keg on the top of the vegetable and can be removed, when desired. They should be coated with paraffin wax to fill up any pores in them and thereby facilitate their cleaning.

## Weighing Scales

For small-scale production, an ordinary country balance would do. A platform balance is, however, essential for large-scale work.

## Measures for Liquids

Water, brine and other liquids can be measured conveniently and need not, therefore, be weighed. Half litre, one litre, two litres and flour litres measures are most suitable.

## Cooking Utensils

Metallic vessels should be non-corrodible. Vessels made of iron or copper are not suitable. Glass-lined vessels, those made of stainless stee, monel metal, incone, and aluminium are preferable. The ladies, spoons and measuring vessels should also be made of non-corrodible materials.

# PICKLING PROCESS

Pickling is done is two stages : (i) by curing or fermentation with dry salting or fermentation in brine, or salting without fermentation; and (ii) by finishing and packing.

## Dry Salting

In this method, the vegetable is treated dry salt. The salt extracts the juice from vegetable and forms the brine, which is fermented by lactic acid-forming bacteria. The method of dry-salting in general, is as follows.

The vegetable is prepared, washed thoroughly in running cold water, drained and weighed. For every 100 kg of the prepared vegetable, 3 kg of salt is used. The vegetable is placed about 2.5 cm deep in the keg or barrel and is sprinkled with a small quantity of salt from the weighed amount. Another layer of the vegetable is added and again sprinkled with salt. The salt is added, layer by layer, in this manner till the keg is three-quarters full. Then one or two-folds of cheese cloth are spread over the ssalted vegetable, tucking in the cloth at the sides, and then placing a wooden board on the top of it. A clean stone, which is not acted upon by salt and organic acids, is placed on the board to press the vegetable so as to form a brine. Generally, a stone weighing about 4.54 kg will ve sufficient in the case brine does not form after the material has stood for sometime. Generally, brine is formed in about 24 hours.

After packing the vegetable, the keg is placed in a warm and dry place and fermentation is allowed to proceed. In a short time, due to osmosis, juice from the vegetable forms the vegetable submerged in the brine.

As soon as the brine to rise from the liquid. Fermentation is usually carbon dioxide begin to rise from the liquid. Fermentation is usually completed in 8 to 10 days under favourable conditions which are attained in the temperature range of 27° to 32°C. In cold weather, however, it may take 2 to 4 weeks for the fermentation to be completeWhen the fermentation iss over,gas bubbles cease to form and rise.This may be confirmed by tapping the keg gently.

The product may now be preserved and kept by excluding air.If this is not done, 'pickle scum' a kind of wild yeast, appears on the surface. It soon destroys the lactic acid formed by fermentation with the result that the pickle is ultimately spoilt.

**Method I**:- An air-seal on the surface of the brine can be made by pouring on top of it an edible oil-like rape seed oil or cotton seed oil.The oil, being lighter than the brine, flats on the surface and thereby prevents the access of air to the pickle below.A layer of oil about a 0.6 cm thick is generally sufficient to keep the pickle indefinitely.The only drawback in this otherwise simpel method iss that the vegetable cannot be taken out from the container without getting covered with the oil. To overcome this, the oil may be removed from the surface by decanting, syphoning or skimming, or by making it overflow by adding more brine to the keg.

**Method II**:- After dry-salting and fermentation, the barrel or keg is filled with the vegetable ot its maximum capacity, and the cover replaced. A 1.25 cm hole is bored in the head. Then the barrel is filled to the brim with the brine so that very little air is left inside. It is allowed to stand for about 48 hours, or till such time that bubbles of gas cease to rise. If necessary, more brine is added at intervals to keep the barrel full. When the bubbling has stopped, the vent-hole is closed tightly and the barrel kept in a cool and dry place. The product packed in this manner will keep indefinitely.

**Method III**:- Hot molten paraffin wax is used to cover the surface of the brine. The barrel is kept in a place where it will not be disturbed until the material is ready for use. Sufficient paraffin wax is melted and poured over the surface of the brine. If it is not enough to warm up the surface of the brine, a smooth and even layer of it will be formed before it cools and hardens. This will give an air-tight seal.

There are two advantages in using paraffin wax. They are : (i) it can be easily separated from the fermented brine before removing the vegetable from the barrel, and (ii) it can be remelted, refined and used again. The only disadvantage, however, is that in case any gas is produced in the brine after sealing it, it will rise up and break the seal, and resealing will be necessary. The wax seal should not, therefore, be applied before fermentation is complete and gas formation has ceased.

## Fermentation in Brine

Steeping of the vegetable in a salt solution of pre-determined concentration for a certain length of time is called brining. This type of treatment is adopted in the case of cucumbers and similar vegetables, which do not contain sufficient juice to form brine with dry salt.

## Brine Preparation

Brine can be prepared by dissolving common salt in water and filtering it through jelly bags to remove insoluble impurities. the amount of brine necessary to cover the vegetable is usually equal to about half the volume of the material to be fermented. To be more precise, if a keg of 45.4 litres capacity is to be packed, the amount of brine required would be 22.7 litres. It is preferable to make the whole quantity of brine needed for the day in one lot.

Brining is the most important step in pickling. Although no set of conditions, ordinary practicable in pickle-making will destroy or retard the growth of every kind of bacteria, yet the growth of a majority of them is checked in a brine containing 15 per cent salt. Lactic acid bacteria, which are salt-tolerant, can flourish in a brine of 8 to 10 per cent strength only.

Fermentation takes place fairly well in a brine containing approximately 5 per cent salt (20°Salometer). In a brine containing approximately 10 per cent salt, fermentation proceeds somewhat slowly. To some extent fermentation takes place up to 15 per cent also, but at 20 per cent strength, all fermentation stops. It s, therefore, customary to place the vegetables in 10 per cent salt solution to allow lactic acid fermentation to take place and then to increase the proportion of salt gradually, so that by the time the pickle is ready, salt concentration would have reached 15 per cent level. It is to be borne in mind that vegetables contain a certain amount of moisture, which exudes from them in the presence of salt and lowers the strength of the brineThe brine strength can, however, be maintained by adding dry salt. The time required for proper fermentation is determined by experience.

## Keeping Quality

Properly brined vegetables will keep well in vinegar for a long time. The duration of brining is of importance. If the vegetables are soaked for a short time of about 12 hours only, the curing of the vegetable tissues will be incomplete with the result that the pickle will not have proper texture and taste. Brining has, therefore, to be controlled properly. On curing, the vegetables become semi-translucent, and their colour changes from green to dark olive green or yellowish green. This is an indication of correct curing. This usually takes 4 to 5 weeks. By this method, the vegetables can be kept more or less for an indefinite period, provided the right storage conditions are maintained. if the vegetable is to ve kept in brine of 10 per cent or less, all air should be excluded from the containers. During curing, the vegetables lose their 'raw' flavour and become firm and crisp.

**With salt**:- In this method, vegetables are packed with a large quantity of salt to inhibit fermentation. In practice, generally 25 kg of salt is mixed with every 10 kg of the prepared vegetables.

The cured vegetables are drained, and excess salt is removed by soaking them in cold or warm water, as may be necessary. After removing the salt, the vegetables are stored for several weeks in plain vinegar of 10 per cent (10 grain) strength. This treatment reduces the tendency of the vegetable to shrivel when packed in sweetened and spiced vinegar and also helps absorption of vinegar by the vegetable tissues.

**Spiced vinegar**:- Spiced vinegar should always be kept ready so that it available at the time of pickling. It is made as follows:

**Method I**:- The ground spices are soaked in vinegar and set aside for 2 to months, stirring accasionally. The spices are then squeezed out, and the vineg allowed to stand. When it has become clear, it is decanted or syphoned from th sediment.

**Method II**:- The spices are boiled with the vinegar till the flavours are extract fully. The extract is then filtered.

**Method III:-** Essential oils of spices are used. This, however, does not alwa impart to the product the original aroma of the spices.

The kind and quantity of spices required depend upon the piquancy desired in the pickle. There are numerous recipes, each having its own adherants. A few of these are given here to serve as guidelines.

*Sweet spiced vinegar is made as :*

## RECIPE

| | |
|---|---|
| Sugar | 213.1 kg |
| Clove, hole | 4.9 kg |
| Coriander seed | 5.8 kg |
| Mustard seed | 7.2 kg |
| Cardamom seed | 0.67 kg |
| Celery seed | 0.56 kg |
| Ginger, whole | 1.69 kg |
| Caraway seed | 0.22 kg |
| Vinegar | 227.3 litres |

The sugar is dissolved in vinegar by heating. The spices placed in linen bags, are suspended in the vinegar. The batch is simmered gently for 6 hours and is then allowed to cool.

The bags are removed and the vinegar filled into casks for storage. Spiced vinegar with essential oils is made as follows:

## RECIPE

| | |
|---|---|
| Oil of ginger | 42 g |
| Oil of cloves | 39 g |
| Oil of mace | 8 g |
| Oil of coriander | 85 g |
| Oil of mustard | 49 g |
| Oil of cardamom | 226 g |
| Oil of bay | 28 g |
| Vinegar | 908 litres |

The essential oils are stirred with the vinegar. For proper emulsification a little gum may be added. The oils may also be mixed with sugar and then dissolved in the vinegar.

*The following recipe gives a good spiced vinegar:*

RECIPE

| | |
|---|---|
| White vinegar (100 grains) | 90.9 litres |
| Water | 77.2 litres |
| Garlic | 311 g |
| Cayenne, finely ground | 680 g |
| Cloves, headless, finely ground | 1360 g |
| Mace, finely ground | 226 g |
| Coriander, finely ground | 1360 g |
| Mustard, finely ground | 1360 g |
| Cardamom, finely ground | 226 g |
| Bay leaves, finely ground | 680 g |
| Caraway, finely ground | 92 g |
| Ginger, finely ground | 907 g |

The spices should be leached in the vinegar for about a week.

## Packing Methods

Pickled onions and mixed pickles should be packed finally into bottles o jars loosely so as not to damage the shape and appearance of the pieces. Fresh vinegar is then added to fill up the spaces between the pieces. The bottles o jars are then allowed to stand for a while, with the lids loosely on, covered agai with more vinegar, if necessary and then closed air-tight. They are stored for a few days, the storage period depending upon the vegetables used for pickling the size of the pieces, condition of the cured vegetable, etc., so as to ensure thorough absorption of the vinegar vbefore the pickles are sent to the market.

# Chapter - 20

## Drying/Dehydration of Fruits & Vegetables

Dehydration or drying by means of mechanical equipment is a process quite distinct from sun-drying. The prepared fruit or vegetable is placed on trays stacked inside a chamber called a 'dehydrater' in which the temperature, humidity and rate of air-flow can be controlled. Dehydraters vary considerably from the simple home set to the large commercial units provided with trolleys, fans, temperature and humidity regulators etc.

### Home Made Drier

A small cabinet drier has been found highly useful for small-scale dehydration of fruits and vegetables for experimental work. It consists essentially of a box of galvanised iron sheet, 90 x 60 x 90 cm, with a perforated iron sheet at the bottom. The sides and the top of the box are fixed in a wooden frame, and the whole thing supported on an angle iron stand about 38 cm high. In order to let off the moisture, there are two slits 5 cm x 3.7 cm, along the top end of the two long sides and about 10 cm below the top. These slita can be closed or opened as desired, by means of metallic shutters. Inside the box, seven trays (87 cm x 60 cm) can be stacked on supports in staggering positions. The perforated iron plate at the bottom of the cabinet can be heated by means of a charcoal oven or an oil stove.

### Commercial Dehydraters

Commercial dehydraters are fairly large in size and are of various types. They are based either on natural or forced draught circulation of air. The kiln and stack driers and the Oregon tunnel driers work on natural draught. The modern dehydrater is generally based on forced draught. For drying at comparatively low temperature, vacuum driers are necessary. They are not, however, in general use on account of their high cost. In the forced draught drier, the temperature and humidity can be carefully controlled to get a good dehydrated product.

**Kiln drier.** The kiln drier is of the old type and is used for drying apples, hops etc. It consists of two floors, the upper one for spreading the fruit and the lower one for housing the furnace. The heat for drying is conveyed through the ventilator at the top.

**Tower or stack type drier.** This type of drier consists of a furnace room containing the furnace and the heating pipes and of a cabinet in which trays of fruits are kept for drying. The heated air from the furnace rises through the trays, which are interchanged from top to bottom shelves, as drying progresses. The cabinet drier is similar to the stack drier. Heating is through steam coils placed between the trays.

**Oregon tunnel unit.** An Oregon tunnel drier consists essentially of several parallel, sloping and narrow chambers above a furnace room. The trays are placed on these sloping floors. Each tunnel is about 6.0 metres long, 1.5 metres high and 0.9 metre wide, with a slope of about 5 cm per 30 cm. The trays of fruit enter at the cooler upper end on runways and move towards the warmer lower end. The dried fruit is removed from the lower end.

**Forced draught tunnel.** This type normally consists of a long chamber through which the trays of fruit move on trolleys. The heated air is let in at one end and drawn at the other end. The loaded trolleys are pushed into the tunnel through an air-lock door. When one trolley of the dried fruit is taken out at the exist end, another trolleys of fresh fruit is pushed in at the entrance. The air for drying the fruit is recirculated by a fan. Humidity inside the tunnel is controlled by letting in occasionally fresh air from outside by means of damper devices.

## Heating System

Heating is direct or by radiation. In direct heating, the products of combustion are mixed with hot air and passed over the drying material. Although this is highly efficient, there is the risk of overheating and deposition of soot and other harmful substances on the material.

In the radiation method, the air is heated over pipes carrying hot gases from the furnace. Alternatively, the air is drawn through pipes heated from outside. This system also is as efficient as direct heating. In another system, the air is heated by means of steam pipes. Although, in this case, heating can be controlled accurately, it is costly and also less efficient than the other two methods.

## Circulation of Air

Several types of fans are used to force the air through the tunnel by suction or by blowing. The axial-flow fan is preferable to other types of fans such as propeller type fan, multivane fan etc. To prevent case-hardening of the drying material and also to increase the thermal efficiency of drying, a portion of the air is recirculated after heating. In general the temperature of the in going air should not exceed 71° to 77°C, and the humidity at the exist end should be about 65 per cent. The rate of drying increases with the velocity of the air passing through the tunnel. An air velocity of 183 to 244 metres per minute gives satisfactory results in tunnel driers. Lower velocities will be adequate in compartment driers.

## Counter-current and Parallel Current (Concurrent Systems)

When the airflow is in the direction opposite to that of the drying material, the system is known as counter-current system. In the parallel, system both the flows are in the same direction. In the first case, the material is drawn out from the hottest end. There is therefore, a likelihood of some scorching of the material. There is also much loss of heat. In the second case, the process starts with dry and hot air and is completed at a moderate temperature in moist air. Moreover, there is less loss of heat. The parallel system is better for small fruits like grapes, apple slices, etc., to prevent scorching and case-hardening. Sometimes, both systems are combined in twin tunnel dehydraters.

## General Concentration

On an average, about 1.5 kg of fresh fruit can be spread on each 1000 square cm of the tray. On this basis, the capacity of the tunnel can be calculated. The trays are arranged, leaving about five cm space between them. The rate of evaporation is deduced from the initial and the final moisture contents, the initial weight of the material taken and the drying time. In designing a dehydrater, allowance should be made for loss of heat owing to radiation and leakage, and during the removal of the trolleys from the tunnel.

A small tunnel dehydrater of circulating-air-blast type is described here for experimental work in connection with dehydration of vegetables. It is a three-trolley unit with the following parts :

(i) **Drying chamber :** Tunnel measures 3.9 metres long, 1.5 metres wide and 1.9 metres high.

(ii) **Heating chamber :** 3.1 metres long, 1.5 metres wide, and 0.9 metre high.

(iii) **Fan chamber** : 0.9 metre long 1.5 metres wide and 0.9 metre high.

Hot air draft inlet slit in the drying chamber at the hot end is 1.5 metres by 0.3 metre (hot air from the heating chamber passes through this slit into the drying chamber).

1. **Fresh air arrangement**. Fresh air damper at the cold end measures 1.0 metre by 0.45 metres. This has an adjustable cover for controlling the flow of air.

2. **Side damper**. This measure 45 cm by 22 cm. There are two dampers on both sides of the tunnel near the cold end. These have metallic flaps to regulate the flow of the outgoing air in accordance with the humidity in the drying chamber.

3. **Heating system**. Heating is by means of steam pipes. Two sets of coil, one 48.7 metres long and of 2.5 cm diameter and the other 33.5 metres long and 1.2 cm diameter are placed in the heating chamber just in front of the blower fan. This can be replaced by a coal furnace with flue inside the heating chamber to reduce the cost without any loss in efficiency.

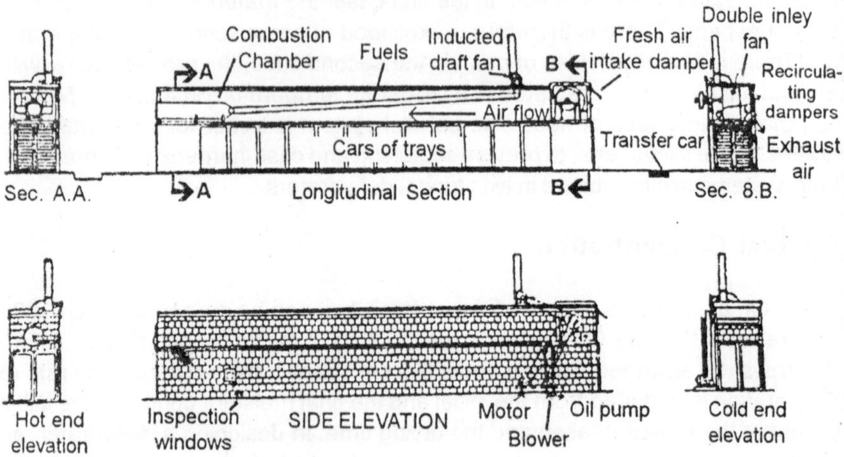


**Circulating-air-blast type funnel dehydrater**

**Airflows system.** One multi-vane fan, 50 cm in diameter, and with 12 blades is placed in the fan chamber. For a 3.9 metres tunnel, the speed of air flow in the chamber works out to be only about 60 linear metres per minute. The space around the first trolley near the hot end is totally closed to stop the escape of air through the empty spaces without passing over the trolleys.

**Trays and Trolleys** (i) Trays : 0.75 metre x 0.6 metre with wire gauze of 0.3 cm mesh, fixed in the bottom frame; (ii) Trolleys, 0.75 metre long, 1.40 metres wide and 1.7 metres high. There are four trolleys, each accommodating 40 trays in two rows, the distance between the trays in a stack being 5 cm. The tunnel is worked as a three-trolley unit, one trolley being extra for loading

**Trolley track and turn-table.** To facilitate pushing in and taking out of the trolleys, a track 0.70 metre wide and 30.4 metre long is built and provided with three turn-tables.

## Working Instructions

The prepared material (potato slices in the case) is placed on trays at the rate of 4.88 kg to 6.10 kg per sq metre of tray surface, and the trays are loaded on one trolley.

The trolley is pushed into the tunnel from the cold end and the doors are closed. The temperature is maintained at 60° to 63°C at the cold end and at 80° to 82°C at the hot end. After about 2½ hours, a second loaded tray is pushed in, and the tunnel is closed air-tight. The process is repeated for the third trolley. The first trolley with the dried potato slices is taken out 2½ hours after the third trolley is pushed in. The process is made continuous in this manner. The temperature and humidity are controlled as follows :

| | Temperature | Humidity |
|---|---|---|
| Cold end (damper end) | 60°-63°C | 40-45 per cent |
| Hot end | 71°-74°C | 20-25 per cent |

The humidity is determined at intervals of 30 minutes with the help of a dry and wet bulb thermometer. The drying time varies from 7 to 8 hours per trolley. The capacity of the dehydrater is about 145 kg of dried potatoes per 24 hours working continuously. For commercial working, the tunnel length of 3.9 metres is rather small, and it should at least be doubled.

## PROCESS VARIATIONS

Particulars regarding the preparation, preliminary treatment such as sulphuring etc., temperature and humidity for the dehydration of various fruits are given briefly in the following paragraphs :

**Apple**:- Apples are peeled, cored and cut into cubes or slices. These are then sulphured for 15 to 30 minutes and dried at 60° to 71°C for 6 to 10 hours. The yield varies from 10 to 15 per cent.

**Apricot**:- Both white and yellow apricots can be dried whole or as halves. They are sulphured for 15 to 25 minutes and dried at 57° to 68°C for 10 to 12 hours. The yield varies from 15 to 19 per cent.

**Banana**:- Greens as well as ripe banana can be dehydrated. The fruit is peeled, cut into slices and the slices sulphured for 15 to 30 minutes and then dried at 55° to 91°C for 18 to 20 hours. Several of the well-known South Indian bananas have been found quite suitable for drying into banana figs or for the preparation of banana flour. The yield varies from 14 to 20 per cent.

**Grape**:- The grape are lye-dipped, sulphured for about 30 minutes and dried at 66° to 82°C for 20 to 30 hours. The yield varies from 21 to 27 per cent.

**Mango, Guava and Jack Fruit**:- Methods for drying these have been worked out at the Central Food Technological Research Institute, Mysore. A method for the preparation of sheets or slabs of fruit pulps has also been standardized and patented.

**Peach**:- The ripe fruit is cut into halves, and the halves sulphured for 15 to 20 minutes and dried at 60° to 63°C for 15 to 24 hours. The yield varies from 14 to 19 per cent.

**Other Fruits**:- Berry fruits, prunes, cherries, etc., can also be dehydrated to get satisfactory products.

## Sulphur Dioxide Content

*The following are the permitted limits of sulphur dioxide in different countries.*

| Country or State | P P M of Sulphur dioxide |
|---|---|
| Great Britain | 2,000 (750 for raisins) |
| Canada | 2,500 |
| Switzerland | 2,000 |
| Germany, Austria | 1,250 |
| Caechoslovakia | 1,250 (raisins only) |
| France | 1,000 |
| Japan | 1,000 (apricot only. None allowed in other fruits) |
| U.S.A. (New York) | 2,000 |
| U.S.A. (New Hampshire) | None |

## PROCESSES FOR VEGETABLES

Although in this country, considerable quantities of different vegetables like cauliflower, cabbage, bitter-gourd, carrot, turnip, *okra*, banana, etc., are dried in the sun, the quality of the dried products is rather poor. The vegetables are not generally given any preliminary treatment such as blanching, which is necessary to destroy enzymes that cause discoloration. Even after blanching, the sun-dried vegetables were found unsatisfactory at the end of one year's storage. They were poor in colour and remained tough even after prolonged cooking Earthen jars, although suitable for sweating of the dried vegetables, are not suitable for storage, as they are highly porous and abrosb moisture, which spoils the product

For large-scale production of dried vegetables, dehydration is the proper method. To meet the demand of the armed forced during World War II, a series of investigations were carried out to standardize methods for the dehydration of potatoes, onions, garlic, cauliflower, etc. The experimental dehydrater described earlier was used. Details regarding the dehydration of some of the important vegetables are give here. Recent improvement in technique are also referred to briefly in the case of some of the products.

**Beans**:- Tender string beans, known as French beans, are used. They are cut into small lengths, blanched in steam for 3 to 6 minutes and dried until both the pods and the beans inside them become brittle. The drying ratio is about 7:1.

**Bitter-gourd (*Karela*)**:- The gourds are scraped and cut into slices about 0.6 cm thick. The slices are blanched in a boiling water for 7 to 8 minutes and dried at 66° to 71°C for 7 to 9 hours. The drying ratio is about 16:1.

**Brinjal**:- The brinjals are cut lengthwise into slices about 0.6 cm thick, and the slices immersed in a 0.5 per cent solution of $SO_2$ for 1½ hours. They are then taken out and blanched in boiling water for 4 to 5 minutes and dried at 49° to 54°C for 9 to 11 hours. The drying ratio is about 33:1. Contact with iron should be avoided during handling of the slices as otherwise they become brown.

**Cabbage**:- Outer leaves and the core are removed and shreds of 0.5 cm thickness are cut. The shreds are either blanched in steam for 5 to 10 minutes or in boiling 2.0 per cent sodium bicarbonate solution for 2 to 3 minutes.

Blanching in water, containing ½ per cent of sulphite and bisulphite gives a product with a better colour. The shreds are dried at 60° to 66°C for 12 to 14 hours. The drying ratio is approximately 18 : 1.

**Carrot**:- Yellow carrots are better suited for drying. They are scraped and the stalks and tips removed. They are then cut into slices, 0.5 cm thick, and the slices blanched in a boiling common salt solution of 2 to 4 per cent strength for 2 to 4 minutes and then dried at 68° to 74°C. Drying time is 14 to 16 hours and the drying ratio approximately 18 : 1.

The starch coating probably helps in preventing oxidative changes which result in discoloration and development of off-flavour resembling hay-flavour in the dried product.

**Cauliflower**:- The flowers are separated and cut into smaller pieces. The pieces are blanched for 4 to 5 minutes in boiling water, steeped in a 0.5 per cent $SO_2$ solution for about an hour and then drained and washed. They are then dried at 60° to 66°C for 10 to 12 hours. The drying ratio is about 35 : 1.

**Garlic**:- Garlic powder has considerable export potentiality. The individual cloves or buttons are separated manually and dried at 57° to 60°C as such, without any preliminary blanching etc. Central Food Technological Research Institute, Mysore, have carried out a systematic investigation on the dehydration of garlic with a view to prepare garlic powder which finds extensive use in the manufacture of soup powders and medicinal preparations with bacteriostatic properties. The method of preparation of garlic powder has been patented and released to the industry. The powder is hygroscopic and requires stringent packaging conditions. Browing was maximum at 37°C and minimum at 0-2°C. At 37°C, browing was minimum in polythend bags (optical density 0.31). This has been attributed to the lowering of moisture of the powder from 7.3 to 5.0 per cent during storage.

**Knol-Khol**:- These are peeled and cut into slices 0.5 cm thick. The slices can be dried as such, or after steeping for 30 to 40 minutes in a 1/4 per cent $SO_2$ solution. The drying temperature is 54° to 60°C and the drying time 11 to 13 hours. The drying ratio is about 19 : 1.

**Okra (Lady's Finger)**:- Tender Okra is a popular vegetable in this country. It may be dried whole, or in the form of discs or halves cut lengthwise. The discs should be 0.6 cm thick. They are blanched for 4 to 8 minutes in boiling water or for 2 to 5 minutes in steam, and then rinsed in cold water to remove the gelatinous coating. They are then dried at 63° to 68°C for 6 to 8 hours. The drying ratio is approximately 12 : 1.

**Onion**:- The outer leaves are removed and the peeled onions are cut into 0.25 cm thick slices. The slices are immersed in 1 5 per cent solution of common salt for about 10 minutes and then drained. They are dried at 60° to 65°C for 11 to 13 hours. It is, however, preferable to keep the drying temperature below 57°C. The drying ratio is about 10 : 1. The dried product can be powdered and packed for use in several ways.

Dried kibbled onion and onion powder are in extensive demand in several parts of the world for the preparation of condiments, relishes, soup mixes, etc. There is scope for setting up onion dehydration industry in this country as the product has an export potential. Onions grown in the Nasik district and preferably white and pungent onions are preferred for drying. For free flowing with minimum colour and flavour changes onion powder should have a moisture content not more than the optimum of 4 per cent.

**Peas**:- Only tender green peas, known as garden peas, are dehydrated. They are blanched for 1 to 2 minutes in boiling water and dried at a temperature not exceeding 63°C. Peas are dehydrated extensively in Australia and some other countries. In this country also, peas of special varieties, grown round about Delhi, are dehydrated by adopting an improved method, which consists of puncturing the skin mechanically to facilitate uniform and quicker drying of the peas. The dehydrated peas packed in aluminium and polythene pouches, have recently become highly popular. They reconstitute well and cook well. There is scope for organising the dehydration industry on a much larger scale in India. Preliminary blanching of the peas in water containing Na $HCO_3$-Mgo-K.M.S. mixture for a short period softens the skin of the peas sufficiently for 'checking' during the subsequent blanching in steam at 0.5 kg/cm2 for about 3 minutes improves the texture of the reconstituted dehydrated peas. Dehydration should be programmed using initially a fairly high bulb temperature.

**Potato**:- The potatoes should be large, free from disease and should be fully matured. They should have the minimum number of eyes to cut down the loss by trimming. They are washed thoroughly in water and peeled manually with a stainless steel knife or by means of an abrasive potato peeling machine. The peelings are washed away with sprays of water.

They are then trimmed and placed in water to prevent browning. They are cut into slices, 0.4 to 0.6 cm thick in a slicing machine, and the slices again placed in cold water. Whenever there is considerable delay in the subsequent operations of blanching etc., the slices may be kept in water containing 0.05 per cent potassium meta-bisulphite to prevent spoilage. The slices are blanched for 3 to 5 minutes in boiling water and spread on trays at the rate of 4.88 kg to 7.30 kg per square metre of tray surface. The trays are then loaded on the trolleys which are pushed into the dehydrater tunnel. The drying temperature range is 60° to 66°C (i.e. 60°C at the cold end and 66°C at the hot end). The drying time is 7 to 8 hours and the drying ratio about 7 : 1 in the case of unprepared potatoes. Dried potatoes reconstitute well in 4 to 5 times their weight of water. It is preferable to pack the dried slices in an inert gas like nitrogen to minimize oxidative changes in colour and flavour. The dried material has a tendency to turn pinkish and to pick up a hay-like flavour which is not liked.

Dried potato was extensively packed and distributed among the armed forces. On account of an undesirable taste and flavour and poor reconstitution property especially in the early stages when improved techniques of drying and packaging were not adopted, the dried product was not quite popular. The method have since been improved greatly resulting in a product of superior quality in every respect.

Various techniques of dehydration have now come into vogue. Mashed potato powder produced by the foam-mat drying technique, vacuum puff dried potato powder, potato cubes dried by expansion through sudden release of pressure, etc., are being produced and accepted freely by the consumers. The freeze-dried potato powder produced by adopting the technique employed in the case of fruit powders, is a product of exceptionally superior quality. Investigations are continuing in several research laboratories to further improve the quality of the dried material by adopting advanced techniques at every stage of production.

**Pumpkin**:- Ripe pumpkin is taken and cut into strips to facilitate removal of the thick and hard peel. The peeled strips are cut into slices about 0.6 cm thick. The slices are placed in a 2 per cent common salt solution for about 10 minutes. They are then blanched for 3 to 4 minutes in 2.0 per cent boiling common salt solution and then dried at 65° to 71°C for 9 to 11 hours. The drying ratios is about 22 : 1.

Pumpkin pulp can be dried as flakes on a drum dryer in a manner similar to fruited cereal such as mango flakes guava flakes etc. The dried flashes are highly hygroscopic and should, therefore, be packed in airtight containers.

**Spinach**:- The leaves are washed thoroughly and dried as such or after steaming them for 4 to 5 minutes. The drying temperature is 63° to 68°C and the drying time 7 to 8 hours. The drying ratio is approximately 22 : 1.

**Tomato**:- The ripe tomatoes are scalded in boiling water for 30 to 60 seconds to facilitate the removal of the skin manually by means of a pointed knife. The peeled tomatoes are cut into slices, 0.6 to 0.9 cm thick, which are then dried at 60° to 65°C for 9 to 10 hours. The drying ratio is 27 : 1.

Tomatoes need not be peeled if the dried material is to be made into tomato powder has indicated the possibility of preparing tomato flakes similar to fruited cereals by drying the material on a drum dryer. The flakes can be spiced and flavoured also prior to dehydration. They have good consumer acceptability.

**Turnip**:- The turnips are peeled and cut into 0.47 cm thick slices. The slices are immersed in a 0.5 per cent SO2 solution for 1 to 2 hours and then blanched for 2 to 4 minutes in boiling water. They are then dried at 52° to 57°C for 11 to 13 hours. The drying ratio is approximately 28 : 1.

**General**:- A variety of other vegetables such as curry leaves, green chillies, radish, etc., are also dehydrated to some extent to form components in mixed packs of dehydrated vegetables and in the preparation of ready-to-serve soup powders, which are becoming popular in this country also as convenient foods. There is considerable scope for developing dried vegetable mixes and soup mixes adopting suitable flavourings.

# OTHER METHODS OF DEHYDRATION

A number of other methods of dehydration have been investigated at the C.F.T.R.I. Mysore. Some of these are described here and a number of references cited elsewhere.

## Drum Drying

One of the noval products developed from mangoes is fruited cereal namely, mango cereal flakes, which is prepared from mango pulp by drum drying. The method of drying and studies its storage behaviour etc. The finished product is of excellent quality. Mango pulp is blended with a small quantity of edible starch, and the blend adjusted for acidity and pH, and then fed on to the heated revolving stainless steel double drums of a roller drier is a slow stream. It dries in the form of a countinuous parchment-like sheet, which can be drawn continuously, broken to smaller pieces and collected in a tin container with a clinch-on lid. Being hygroscopic, the flakes have to be kept away from moisture. Hermetically sealed tin containers are the best for packing. Moisture proof plastic film of heavy gauge also can be used to some extent. In that case also, it in preferable to place the heat-sealed packets inside a large tin container which can be closed tightly.

Other products like tomato have been conducted at the C.F.T.R.I. etc. also can be dried by the above technique. The dried flakes have considerable market potential.

## Vacuum Puffing and Dehydration

The vacuum puffing and dehydration technique has been utilized fore the preparation of orange juice powder as already mentioned. Potato pieces prepared in the conventional manner, are cooked and subjected while hot, to a high vacuum for a short period. The instant flashing of water vapour from within the pieces creates a porous structure, which facilitates quick drying. The dehydrated pieces can be reconstituted quickly in about 5 minutes in boiling water.

The puffing unit consists essentially of a shallow receptacle with a close-fitting air-tight lid, connected through a quick opening valve to a vacuum reservoir maintained at 62 cm Hg vacuum. The lid of the receptacle can be closed and opened instantly by a pneumatic cylinder, which operates by the suction from the reservoir. The entire operation of transferring the trays to the receptacle, closing the lid, applying and releasing the vacuum, and opening the lid, can be completed within a short period of 15 to 20 seconds. The puffed porous pieces can then be dried in a tunnel (or shelf-drier) at about 66°C with an air velocity of 300 metres per min. The dried product has excellent consumer acceptance.

## Foam-Mat Drying

The foam-mat drying process consists essentially in incorporating small amounts of suitable foaming agents into the fluid food materials so that they could be whipped to a low density foam and then dried as a mat on trays, at relatively low temperatures, in an ordinary forced air circulation drier. The material can be dried in a relatively short period, and the dried product reconstitutes readily. The method is considerably cheaper than puff drying spray drying, drum drying, etc. The method for the preparation of powders from orange, tomato, pineapple and lemon juice, apple sauce, and various baby foods. Glyceryl-mono-stearate, egg albumin, groundnut protein isolate, guar gum, carboxymethyl cellulose, etc, are some of the useful foaming agents. The drying of fruit juices and pulps by the foaming technique in the case of banana juice concentrate, guava juice concentrate, Coorg mandarin orange juice concentrate, banana pulp and guava pulp. The foaming agent, dissolved or dispersed in a small quantity of water, was added to the fruit juice concentrate or pulp, mixed in a Waring blendor and then foamed in a Hobart mixer fitted with a wire whip. The foamed material was extruded into strips, 3-4 mm in diameter, and the strips spread on stainless steel trays. The trays were arranged inside a cabinet drier maintained at 65° to 70°C in such a manner that the strips were parallel to the flow of air. The material dried in 30 to 60 minutes, depending upon its nature. The dried strips were scraped from the trays and filled into air-tight containers as they were hygroscopic.

In a typical case, using banana concentrate and egg albumin, a foam density of 0.23 g/ml could be obtained in about 15 minutes. To stabilise the foams, it was necessary to incorporate with the concentrate 1/3 to 1/2 of its weight of cane sugar. The optimum amount of the foaming agent was 0.3 to 1.5 per cent of the material to be dried. The shreds could be dried crisp in 30 to 45 minutes to a moisture content of 1.5 to 2.0 per cent. The foam-mat drying technique could be successfully employed in the case of a variety of fruit pulps, concentrates and similar products by standardizing the conditions in each case.

## Freeze Drying

In this method, the material such as fruit juice concentrate, is first frozen on trays in the lower chamber of a freeze drier and the frozen material dried in the upper chamber under high vacuum. The material dries directly by sublimation of ice without passing through the intermediate liquid stage. The dried products is highly hygroscopic. It reconstitutes readily. Mango pulp, orange juice concentrate and guava pulp have been found to give freeze-dried powders of excellent quality in regard to taste, flavour, reconstitution property, etc. At present, the equipment needed for large-scale production is rather costly.

The experimental results regarding freeze-drying of passion fruit juice which was completed in three stages, namely.

**Preliminary freezing of the product.** It is on a stainless steel tray in 230 g lots in a room at - 18°C.

**Primary drying in a freeze drier.** With electrically heated shelves at 0.1 mm Hg pressure at 30°C for 24 hours, only the heat of sublimation by external radiation was supplied. With this temperature and heat input, the surface layers of the product were carefully dried. The greater part of water was then removal by the combined effect of radiation from the chamber walls and electrical heating. The temperature was maintained at -8°C. The condenser temperature and vacuum during the sublimation were fairly constant at -62°C and 0.1 mm Hg respectively.

**Secondary heating** (ordinary vacuum dehydration). Residual moisture was removed by electrical heating at 20°C. At the end of the evaporation the trays were quickly unloaded and transferred to a low humidity room (6% RH).

The porous product was scraped off, powdered quickly and promptly packed in 202 x 214 G.P. Lacquered cans, and the cans closed using in package desiccant of 5 to 10g of reactivated and powdered Desiccate No. 25 (a patented product with about 33 per cent w/w moisture absorption capacity), sealed in small Vitafilm (cellulose acetate film) bags.

The freeze dried powder had excellent taste, flavour and reconstitution properties. It has 168 mg/100 g of ascorbic acid.

## Accelerated Freeze Drying (A.F.D.)

This method which is an adaptation of the freeze drying technique, has been developed to a commercial process by the Aberdeen workers for drying fish, meat, etc, to meet Defence Services demands. On account of the low temperature employed for drying and the technique of drying the solid pieces of the product without unduly disturbing their shape and texture, the dried material has good reconstitution properties and possesses excellent taste and flavour, and as such, has been well accepted by consumers. The dried products are highly useful in the preparation of emergency food packs and rations for use by the Defence Services under difficult and adverse conditions of climate and terrain such as at high altitudes, mountain regions, etc. In this method, the pieces of material to be dried are kept pressed between two perforated or wire mesh trays, inside a cabinet freeze drier. As the material dries, the bulk of the pieces is gradually reduced by decreasing the dried material retains its normal shape and regains it when rehydrated.

This is a highly important consideration in the drying of meat, fish and other solid pieces of food. The equipment needed for large-scale accelerated freeze drying of foods is highly costly at present. In view of the decisive advantages, however, the Government of India have set up a 5 tonne capacity unit for meeting the needs of the Defence Forces stationed at high altitudes and on difficult terrains.

A.F.D. Products are of excellent quality in every respect. There is much scope for developing the process into large-scale commercial use and reduce the cost to a considerable extent so that the dried products could be brought within the reach of the common man.

### Dehydro-freezing

In this method, the product is first dried partially and then frozen, and it is thus slightly different from the usual freeze drying technique.

## PACKING AND STORAGE

Dried fruits and vegetables are subject to insect attack even when they have been properly dried and stored. Insects not only consume the material, but also leave much debris, which spoils the appearance of the product. To avoid insect infestation, great care is necessary in the construction of packing sheds and godowns. Bettles and moths are the most troublesome pests. The best way to avoid infestation is to adopt preventive rather than curative methods. The two important curative methods are heat treatment and fumigation.

### Heat Treatment

Dried fruits such as raisins, figs, peaches, etc., are dipped in boiling water or in a dilute solution of sodium chloride or sodium bicarbonate, and then re-dried at 54° to 65°C to destroy all insects including their formative stages. Dried vegetables may be heated as such directly without any preliminary dipping treatment. The heat-sterilized materials should be packed in clean and sterile containers, which are insect-proof and which have been properly treated against insect attack. Packing should be done expeditiously without any undue delay to avoid change of any reinfestation.

### Fumigation

There are several fumigants available in the market, but all of them are not equally useful in the case of dried fruits and vegetables. Fumifation kills insects including their eggs. Great care is necessary in using fumigation as some of the substances like carbon disulphide and hydrocyanic acid gas, are either highly inflammable or highly poisonous. It is also possible that the fruit may absorb a small amount of hydrocyanic acid rendering the product poisonous. The two fumigants are not, however, in general use now. Methyl bromide is becoming popular, as it is highly effective. This gas, which is heavier than air, is poured on the stored material from the top. The normal dosage is prescribed by the supplier. It is non-explossive, but is toxic to human beings also. Mixtures of ethylene dichloride and carbon tetrachloride, ethylene oxide and ethylene dichloride, have also been used for fumigation.

The individual components having specific fumigation characteristics, the mixture has additive insect-destroying properties, just as in the case of mixed chemical preservatives. Based on this principle, the Central Food Technological Research Institute, Mysore, has developed a highly efficient fumigation mixture and the process is known as Durofume process. Ethylene oxide, although highly explosive and inflammable, is by the large, an ideal fumigant for foodstuffs as it does not leave any residues likely to result as health hazards. This oxide is supplied in cylinders. It is vaporized inside the store, which is made air-tight by sealing all the leaks in the doors, windows, ceiling, etc. In the case of materials like walnuts and almonds, rather than in the case of dried fruits, fumigation can be carried out very effectively in a vacuum.

In Australia and some other countries, fumigants based on formalin or formaldehyde are sometimes used in the case of raisins packed in wooden boxes.

Packing is perhaps the most vital step for the success the dehydration industry. Dried fruits and vegetables should be quite dry and should be packed in moisture-proof containers such ass tin containers. If care is not taken to guard against entry of excessive moisture, the contents inside the package become mouldy. Wooden boxes or cardboard cartons are not generally moisture-proof and insect-proof, unless special methods are adopted to line them with waxed paper and seal them properly. Dried vegetables can be packed in large tin containers such as 18 litre tins in an inert atmosphere containing a gas-like nitrogen, to prolong the keeping quality of the product in regard to colour, taste and flavour. High density polythene package and multiple aluminium foil pouches etc. Are being utilized for packing dried vegetable like peas, vegetable mixes, soup mixes, etc, for retail distribution. Newer and better packaging materials are being developed during recent years.

## Examination of Dried Fruits and Vegetables

Moisture content, extent of browning, total and reducing sugars, reconstitution characteristic, freedom from insect and rodent damage, insect fragments, free and bound sulphur dioxide etc, are the more important analyrica determination. These are carried out by standard methods of analysis recominations in A.O.A.C., etc. Taste and flavour are evaluated with the help of a trained taste panel.

## Packaging Using Flexible Films

Proper packing of dehydrated fruits and vegetables and similar food products to prevent deterioration and spoilage during storage under ordinary conditions as well as under extraordinary adverse conditions, as in the case of Defence Services requirements, is a highly important problem. With the recent introduction of a variety of plastic packaging materials and films, a great deal o research work has been carried out in many parts of the world to develop suitable packages. In the case of highly hygroscopic dehydrated foods such as fruits juice powders, some spice powders and accelerated-freeze-dried products such as meat mince, etc, their packaging becomes highly critical and decisive. Packages based on cheap indigenous materials such as brown casing paper (6 gauge) aluminium foil (0.04 mm) polythene (150 gauge pouch with a 2 ply corrugated liner) waxed carton, etc., have been developed to ensure a minimum shelf life of one year under field conditions. Resistance to water vapour permeability and freedom from undesirable flavours are important considerations in the choic of suitable packaging materials.

A number of different kinds of plastic materials with varying densities an resistance to water vapour, etc. Such as high density polythene of varying gaug thickness, laminated foils based on paper, aluminium foil, etc., as cheaper substitutes for the rigid tin and aluminium containers, are rapidly being develope The recent technological developments in the packaging field have been amaz ing. A number of uses of which have been found in recent years.

# Chapter - 21

# *Manufacture of Pectin*

Pectin, which is one of the important constituents in the preparation of jellies and jams, is found present chiefly in fruit and vegetable pulps. Some of the important sources which are available fairly cheap are : (i) apple pomace from cider presses, (ii) apple skin and cores from canning and dehydration plants and also cull apples, and (iii) citrus residues such as inner rind and rag from citrus products factories.

Jack fruit residues, passion fruit rind and unripe papaya left after tapping for papain, have also been found to be fairly good sources of pectin. Papaya pectin in liquid as well as in powder form has recently been produced and used in the processing industry.

Pea hulls, grape marce and beets can also be used as raw materials for pectin.

*The following data regarding the percentage of pectin in some of the raw materials.*

| Material | Per cent pectin in fresh material | Per cent pectin on dry weight basis |
|---|---|---|
| Apple pomace | 1.5 - 2.5 | 15 - 18 |
| Lemon pulp | 2.5 - 4.0 | 30 - 55 |
| Orange pulp | 3.5 - 5.5 | 30 - 40 |
| Beet pulp | 1.0 | 25 - 30 |
| Carrot | 0.62 | 7 - 14 |

## PECTIN FROM APPLES

*The different stages in the manufacture of pectin are as follows :*

1. Washing, crushing and pressing the apples for extraction of juice
2. Drying of the pomace
3. Leaching
4. Extraction of pectin
5. Pressing of treated mass to obtain pectin solution
6. Removing the sediment from the pectin solution by settling or by centri fuging
7. Treating the pectin solution with proper enzymes
8. Treating the pectin solution with decolourising carbon to get a pure product
9. Filtration of the pectin solution to the required degree of brilliance
10. Concentration of the pectin solution
11. Standardization of the pectin solution for jelly strength
12. Bottling or canning of the standard solution
13. Preparation of powdered pectin.

Apples are washed with dilute hydrochloric acid to remove any spray residues. They are then crushed or grated and then pressed. The pomace is dried quickly to avoid fermentation. It is dried at 66° to 82°C in revolving drums or rotary driers to 6 to 8 per cent moisture content. About 45.3 kg of dry pomace are got from a tonne of apples. The dried pomace is leached with cold water to remove colouring and flavouring materials, and also sugars, if any. The leaching can be carried out conveniently in a tank fitted with a perforated false bottom and an outlet.

## Composition

Pectin does not have any definite composition. Its components differ in their jellying strength. Pectin with a high jellying power are intermediate bodies and are easily converted into less useful components like pectic acid and methyl alcohol. The time, temperature and the pH of the medium are important factors in the extraction of pectin. The pomace is heated at a pH of 3.5 for 1 to 1½ hours at about 88°C or for 30 to 40 minutes at 100°C. Addition of 0.2 per cent citric tartaric or lactic acid gives better results. After boiling, the pomace is pressed, and the solution clarified by settling or by contrifuging. The starch and proteins present are removed by adding specific enzymes, and the treated liquid is heated to kill the enzymes and then decolourized with activated carbon. It is then filtered in a filter press. It contains 0.7 to 1.0 per cent pectin. It is concentrated under reduced pressure to 4.5 per cent strength. The concentrate is standardized by carrying out jelly tests. It is then packed in cans of 4.5 tor 22.7 litres capacity, made from extra charcoal-tin plate or it is packed in dark-brown bottles. No. 10 cans are processed for 30 minutes at 77°C, whereas 22.7 litter cans are filled hot at 71° to 77°C, inverted and allowed to cool in air for 35 minutes. They are then cooled quickly in water down to 49° to 54°C. Five hundred ml capacity bottles are filled at 46° to 49°C, pasteurized for 30 minutes at 77°C and then cooled.

## Pectin Powder

Pectin in powder form can be prepared from the extract by spray drying or by precipitation with acetone or alcohol. The pectin extract is concentrated to a thick paste of 25 to 30 per cent solids and then treated with 2 to 3 volumes of 95 per cent alcohol to precipitate the pectin. The precipitated pectin is washed with alcohol, dried and powdered. Aluminium sulphate and ammonia also have been used for precipitating pectin. These methods have, however, been covered by patents. The aluminium precipitation method which has been fully investigated on a pilot plant scale at the Central Food Technological Research Institute, Mysore, has been produce purer pectin of high jelly grade with the minimum amount of alcohol for washing the precipitate, especially in the case of papaya and citrus pectins. The principle of the method is that pectin particles are negatively charged and can, therefore, be precipitated by adding a positive charge carried on colloidal particles. The aluminium in the precipitated pectin is removed by treating the mass with alcoholic hydrochloric acid and then washing it with alcohol of increasing strength and finally with absolute alcohol.

# PECTIN FROM CITRUS FRUITS

Citrus peels and residues contain 2.5 to 5.5 per cent of pectin. After the extraction of essential oil from the peel and juice from the fruit, the residue is dried. The peel should be sliced and ground. The residue is washed with cold water on a sieve, and the washed material boiled with 0.015 to 0.02 normal hydrochloric or sulphuric acid, or with 0.025 molar citric acid for 40 to 45 minutes. The liquid is pressed and filtered. The subsequent processes are practically similar to those employed in the case of apple pectin.

# FROM OTHER MATERIAL

Pectin of good quality can also be prepared from green papaya, jack fruit rind, guava, wood apple, etc. Useful research work on these materials has been conducted at the Central Food Technological Research Institute, Mysore. The preparation of pectin of good quality from green and tender jack fruit, and also from wood-apple. The reported that pectin of good quality can be prepared from tamarind pulp, the yield being 2.31 to 3.70 per cent on dry weight basis.

## Testing Jelly Grade

Pectin is standardized for jelly grade either by chemical methods or by actual jelly-boiling trials. The Care and Haynes method is widely employed for this purpose. In the chemical method, pectin is estimated as calcium pectate. This alone does not always give a true value for the jelly strength of pectin, as purified pectins may vary greatly in composition. Actual jelly-making tests are, therefore, more reliable.

Grade evaluation of high ester pectins, which are used for making jellies containing 65 per cent soluble solids, is carried out by standard methods. Besides these pectins, some more have been developed low ester pectins (low methoxyl content pectin) which can form good jellies with considerably less sugar. These are of considerable interest in connection with the preparation of dietetic jams containing only small quantities of sugar. These are prepared by graded demethylation of the pectin.

## Grading Methods

In these methods, attempts have been to establish a relation between viscosity of the pectin solution and the strength of jelly prepared from it. These tests are generally useful in the case of series of preparations of similar history. By means of calibration curves, the jelly grade of the pectin can be deduced fairly accurately. There are various devices for measuring the viscosity. Of these, mention may be made of the falling ball viscometer of Ogg and the simple capillary pipette of Baker, generally known as a jelmeter. The latter has already been described in an earlier chapter. In this device, viscosity measurements are made with 0.5 and 1.0 per cent pectin solutions and a curve drawn showing the relation between the grade and the corresponding viscosity of the pectin solution. From the standard curve, the approximate grade of any sample of pectin can be derived.

## Actual Tests

*The following problems arise in carrying out actual jelly-boiling tests :*

1. Variation in the method of preparation of the jelly
2. Variation in the property measured & use of the method of measurement
3. Desirable characteristics of the jelly

The method of preparation also has considerable influence on the properties of the jelly. In the method evolved by the U.S. Department of Agriculture, standard 100 grade pectin is used for the preparation of standard jelly. Jellies are made using the pectin to be tested and compared with the standard jelly made under the same conditions.

*The following method of testing jelly grade. General conditions for making compositions are :*

(i) 56 per cent sugar in jelly,
(ii) pH of jelly 3.00 ± 0.05, and
(iii) Jelly strength to be measured 18 hours after preparation.

A glass vessel with a glass rod is weighed, and 320 ml of the co[illegible]tilled water, 500 g of sugar and the requisite quantity of commercial pectin preparation (C.P.P.F.) as shown in table are added. The pectin is mixed with a portion of the sugar (about five times its weight). About 0.5 ml of citric acid solution, (50 g of citric acid in 100 ml of solution and 1 ml of sodium citrate (25 g of sodium citrate in 100 ml of solution) are added to the water. Three 225 ml jelly-glasses are taken and to each are added 2 ml of the citric acid solution and 0.5 ml of the sodium citrate solution. The pectin-sugar mixture is then added to the water and stirred. The mixture is heated rapidly to a boil, stirring it constantly. It is boiled for 30 seconds, after which the rest of the sugar is added. The solution is again heated to a boil & brought down to a net weight of 770 g. The vessel is removed

**Amount of Pectin Used in Jelly Tests to Determine Pectin Grade by C.P.P.F. Method**

| Grade | Weight (g) | Grade | Weight (g) |
|---|---|---|---|
| 10 | 50.00 | 120 | 4.17 |
| 20 | 25.00 | 130 | 3.85 |
| 30 | 16.66 | 140 | 3.57 |
| 40 | 15.50 | 150 | 3.33 |
| 50 | 10.00 | 160 | 3.12 |
| 60 | 8.33 | 170 | 2.94 |
| 70 | 7.14 | 180 | 2.78 |
| 80 | 6.25 | 190 | 2.63 |
| 90 | 5.55 | 200 | 2.50 |
| 100 | 5.00 | 210 | 2.38 |
| 110 | 4.55 | 220 | 2.27 |

from the fire occasionally to check the weight. When the correct weight is reached, boiling is stopped. The jelly is allowed to cool for about 30 seconds and any scum that may be formed is removed. It is then poured into the jelly glasses and stirred with a glass rod. The jelly is allowed to set for 18 hours at -3°C. The jelly i then taken out of the glass on to a flat surface and its firmness compared with that of a standard jelly made at the same time under similar condition. Generally, a piece of the jelly is sliced off and squeezed between the thumb and the fore-finger until the jelly breaks. Difference of about 5 per cent in jelly strength can be detected in this way after some experience.

The standardized method for the preparation of pectin from green papaya, wood apple and jack fruit wastes. The reported a pectin content of 2 per cent in ripe jack-fruit wastes. They have shown that a good jelly can be made from this waste material. In the case of green papaya, there is practically no loss of pectin owing to the extraction of papain from the fruit. They have also pointed out that it might be a workable proposition to collect the tapped fruits, dehydrate them and store the dried material for extraction of pectin.

This intefrated approach has since been developed subsequently by workers at the Central Food Technological Research Institute, Mysore, as pointed out already.

The methods that have been standardised for the preparation of pectin from indigenous sources are described briefly in the following section.

## PECTIN PREPARATION

### Processing of Raw Material

After washing, the green papaya fruit is grated or minced in a mincing machine. Wood apple pulp is removed with a sharp spoon-shaped tainless steel knife and broken into smaller pieces. The rind and core of jack fruit, including the perigones, which are left over in the canning of the fruit bulbs, are minced into small pieces or cut into thin slices.

### Washing and Leaching

Papaya and wood apple pulp are washed thoroughly in water to remove sugars, and other soluble materials. Jack fruit is washed and treated with a solution containing 0.1 per cent potassium metabisulphite and 0.05 per cent HCl. Washing is continued till the Brix of the wash water is practically zero. In the case of wood-apple, an extract suitable for the preparation of wood-apple syrup can be obtained by carefully controlling the washing process. In the case of jack-fruit rind also, much of the 5 to 7 per cent of the sugars present can be recovered by controlled washing.

### Extraction

After washing and leaching, the material is extracted with N/60-N/50 HCl in the case of papaya and jack fruit, and 0.5 per cent potassium metabisulphite in the case of wood-apple pulp. Three extractions are taken at 97° to 100°C by heating the material for half an hour each time and separating the extract by straining it through a sieve of suitable mesh. The extract should be cooled quickly to minimise depolymerisation of the pectin. The amount of water to be added for extraction in each case is 1½ to 2 times the weight of the fresh material for the first extraction and 1 to 1¼ times for the second and third extractions. For each extraction, the a boil and then the material is added. The boiled mass is strained through 8 to 10 mesh sieves to separate the extract from the residue. The residue is gently pressed in basked press and a second extract is taken without much delay. The extract is finally passed through a sieve of 80 to 90 mesh or through a piece of muslin cloth to separate the coarse pulp.

### Clarification and Demineralisation

The sieved extract is passed through a Sharples super-centrifuge for further clarification. There is no need to use any clarifying agent. In case a super-centrifuge is not available, the extract may be allowed to settle and then filtered through a piece of drill cloth using a filter press for the purpose. Sedimentation and filtration are particularly important in the case of jack-fruit and wood-apple extracts. Decolourisation of the extract is not essential in the case of the jack-fruit and papaya extracts. In the case of wood-apple pulp extract, it should, however, be decolourised with about 1.0 per cent activated carbon. Subsequent filtration of the extract, however, presents difficulties. A Sharples super-centrifuge is useful for clarification. Both the treatments, namely clarification and decolourisation, can be conveniently combined into one process.

## Concentration and Precipitation

The clarified and decolourised pectin extract is concentrated to 30° to 40o Brix at about 10°C and 26 to 28 inches (650-700 mm) vacuum. For the precipitation of pectin from this concentrated extract, two volumes of 95 per cent alcohol are used. A calculated amount of HCl is added to the alcohol before mixing so that its concentration in the final mixture is 0.1 N. Addition of 0.5 per cent potassium metabisulphite to the concentrated extract, prior to addition of alcohol, improves the colour of the precipitated pectin. The precipitated pectin is allowed to remain overnight in contact with HCl and $SO_2$ and is separated next morning by centrifuging or by squeezing the material in a piece of thick cloth. It is then washed twice with 80 per cent alcohol and finally with 95 per cent alcohol.

## Drying and Powdering

The pectin precipitate is dried preferably in a vacuum drier at about 40°C. It can also be dried at room temperature or in an ordinary oven or in the sun. The dried product i powdered and passed through a 100 to 120 mesh sieve to get commercial pectin powder.

## Standardisation

As series of jellies are prepared using varying amounts such as 20.00 22.5, 25.0, 27.5, 30.0 ml of 1.0 per cent pectin solution, (50-x) g of sugar and a sufficient amount of a 10 per cent citric acid solution to obtain a pH of 2.9 to 3.1 in the mixture. The value of 'x' is equal to the amount of pectin and citric acid solids collectively added to each individual sample. The ingredients are placed in clean dry glass beakers, with a glass rod placed in each of the beakers. The total weight of all the ingredients in each beaker is made up to 90 g by adding distilled water. The mixture is heated on an electric hot plate to a weight of 77.0 g and the jelly poured into clean, dry, 4 oz (114 ml) jelly glasses. The final weight of the jelly for 65 per cent soluble solids should be 76.9 g. Cooking is, however, finished at 77.0 g to allow any evaporation that might occur after pouring the jelly into the glass. The strength of the different jellies formed is compared after 20 hours' standing, with that of a standard jelly prepared under similar conditions, using a sample of standard pectin such as the 150 grade citrus pectin powder of the California Citrus Growers Exchange.

From the above tests, quantities of the pectin solution giving jellies, which are just weaker or just stronger than the standard jelly, are determined. A second series of jellies is then prepared using quantities of pectin solution ranging between these two quantities and with increments of 0.3 ml only. The quantity of pectin solution and the amount of pectin required to yield a jelly comparable with the standard jelly is determined and the jelly grade calculated.

If the pectin sample has a grade of over 250, a 0.5 per cent solution may be used instead of a 1.0 per cent solution. If the grade is less than 150, it is preferable to use a 2.0 per cent solution instead of using larger quantities of the weaker solution.

## USES OF PECTIN

Pectin is used as a thickening agent in the preparation of ketchups, sauces, jams, etc. It is also used as an emulsifying agent in the preparation of products like cod liver oil, ice cream, mayonnaise, etc. It can be used to increase the foaming power of gases in water and also to glace candied fruit. It is also used in the manufacture of explosives, lacquers, sizing for textiles, lotions, and as an agglutinant in blood thereby.

Powder pectin does not go into solution easily. It has a tendency to form lumps. In jam-making, it is, therefore, mixed with 5 to 6 times its weight of sugar, stirred in water at 60° to 70°C for a short time and then brought to a boil. It can also be mixed with sugar and sprinkled over the boiling jam mixture in the pan. This is generally practised in commercial manufacture of jams.

Apple pectin in liquid form and citrus pectin in powder form are important commercial products in the U.K. and in the U.S.A. Some of the well-known brands available at present in this country are the Obi and Marwel powder pectins from Switzerland, Genu pectin from Denmark, Pectina pectin from Italy, etc. Most of the pectin used in the country is being imported. There is, however, apple scope for manufacturing similar products from indigenous materials. Papaya pectin in liquid and in powder form is an important development in this direction. The powder pectin has a high jelly grade. Its production is, however, limited at present, With the growth of the citrus processing industry in the country, the re is good prospect for the development of pectin as a by-product from peel and pomace. For commercial success, the production of pectin should, however, be on a sufficiently large scale as the processes involved require costly equipment.

# Chapter - 22

# *Chocolate Candy*

## CHOCOLATE-COATED CONFECTIONS

### With Improved Moisture Barrier

The moisture loss of certain confectionery products during storage is a matter of common experience. Chocolate coated candies, cookies, cakes, doughnuts and other bakery products with high moisture centres and fillings tend to change in appearance under certain conditions of storage. While the phenomenon of bloom is observed with many such confectionery and bakery products, the related phenomenon of loss of moisture candy centres such as cream fondant, marshmallow, and coconut covered with chocolate or imitation chocolate coatings may rapidly lose moisture in storage.

F.P. Colten and M. Kaplan; U.S. Patent 3,784713; January 8, 1974; assigned to General Foods Corporations have found that by the incorporation of minor amounts of an alkali or alkaline earth metal derivative or isolated soy protein within a chocolate product the tendency of moisture loss from edible confectionery or bakery products coated with such chocolate product is greatly reduced. Thus, it has been found that decreases in moisture transmission of about 30 to 60% or higher as compared with regular chocolate have been obtained.

The additive of this process may be prepared by the conventional prior art processes for isolating soy protein. Dehulled soy beans are subjected to oil extraction to remove a preponderance of the nonprotein components. The protein, principally a mixture of amino acids commonly known as glycinin, is then rendered water-dispersible by treatment with an aqueous solution of an alkali or alkaline earth metal hydroxide, carbonate, phosphate or the like.

The alkali or alkaline earth metal derivative of the isolated soy protein is subsequently recovered by evaporation or spray drying. The preferred additive is sodium proteinate derived from isolated soy protein. This material is commercially available under the tredename Promine-D, and generally contains at least 90% protein on a moisture-free basis. The preferred level of addition of the sodium proteinate in the coating composition ranges from 0.25 to 4.0% by weight.

Example 1: Milk Chocolate with Promine D (Sodium proteinate) - A mixture is formulated as below and mixed in the melanger for 15 minutes.

| | | |
|---|---|---|
| Chocolate liquor | 3 lb | |
| Roller whole milk powder | 4 lb | 4 oz |
| Mil-lait* | | 4 oz |
| Promine D (sodium proteinate) | | 8 oz |
| Granulated sugar | 12 lb | 15 oz |
| Cocoa butter | 2 lb | |
| Total | 22 lb | 15 oz |

*Enzymatically treated whole milk powder.

Flavours are added at the beginning of the mix cycle: 7.10 g salt and 7.10 g vanillin. The melanger mix was then refined on the 5-roll refiners to give a fineness of 0.0011 inch. The refined dry mix was then added to a mixing kettle (Dopp pot) with 2 oz. lecithin and 1 lb. 15 oz. cocoa butter. Mixing time was 2 hours at 140°F. The coating was standardized to a final viscosity of 140° McMichael by the addition of 1 lb. 8 oz. cocoa butter. The final formula is as follows.

| | ***Percent*** |
|---|---|
| Chocolate liquor | 11.65 |
| Roller whole milk powder | 16.50 |
| Mil-lait | 0.97 |
| Granulated sugar | 50.25 |
| Cocoa butter | 18.20 |
| Promine D | 1.94 |
| Lecithin | 0.49 |
| Total | 100.00 |

Flavours/100 lb.: 28.40 g salt and 28.40 g vanillin.

Example 2: Milk Chocolate Without Promine D - A second batch of milk chocolate was formulated as in Example 1, but the Promine D was omitted. Final formula is as follows on next page.

| | Percent |
|---|---|
| Chocolate liquor | 11.97 |
| Roller whole milk powder | 16.96 |
| Mil-lait | 1.00 |
| Granulated sugar | 53.62 |
| Cocoa butter | 15.95 |
| Lecithin | 0.50 |
| Total | 100.00 |

Flavours/100 lb.: 28.40 g salt and 28.40 g vanillin.

The formulations of Example 1 and 2 were prepared for the hand dipping of cream fondant and coconut centres, doughnuts and sponge cake as follows. Four pounds of the chocolate was melted at 120°F in an aluminium pan. Melted material was stirred continuously by hand in a 70°F room down to 79°F (about 15 minutes).

Pre-weighed cream fondant and coconut centres, doughnuts and sponge cake were each hand dipped in the tempered formulations of Examples 1 and 2. The hand dipped items were than placed on a cellophane covered tray and let stand overnight at 65°F, 50% relative humidity. The moisture barrier properties of the coating containing the sodium proteinate (Example 1) and the control (Example 2) were evaluated according to the following procedure. Weighed samples of the coconut and cream fondant centres, doughnuts and sponge cake were placed in Petri dishes and sealed in a screw cap jar containing a suitable desiccant such as calcium chloride or calcium sulfate.

These sealed jars were then stored at 75°F. Each sample was weighed on a weekly basis and the weight loss recorded. Having recorded the weight of each item before and after coating, and the percent moisture of each centre immediately prior to the coating operation, the moisture transmitted from each centre through the chocolate shell was calculated as the percent of the total available moisture lost from the centre.

Results showed that the coating of Example 1 containing the sodium proteinate transmitted on the average from about 30 to 60% less moisture than the control coating of Example 2. Consequently, the fondant and coconut centres coated with the control coating of Example 2 exhibited a definite change in texture after 16 weeks of storage under test conditions, while the centres coated with the coating containing the sodium proteinate were still soft, moist and quite palatable.

The same condition was found to exist with regard to the coated bakery products after 4 weeks of storage. These results indicate that the shelf life of confectionery and bakery products having a chocolate coating containing the sodium proteinate is approximately doubled as compared with such items having a regular chocolate coating.

In similar work done by J.L. McReynolds and H.H. Topalian; U.S. Patent 3,784,714; January 8, 1974; assigned to General Foods Corporation, it was found that by the incorporation of minor amounts of calcium stearate within a chocolate product the tendency of moisture loss from edible confectionery or bakery products coated with such chocolate product is greatly reduced. Decreases in moisture transmission of about 25% or higher as compared with regular chocolate have been obtained. The preferred level of calcium stearate ranges from 0.1 to 5.0% by weight of the chocolate coating.

In further work by F.P. Colten and M.Kaplan; U.S. Patent 3,895,105; July 15, 1975; assigned to General Foods Corporation, it was found that the incorporation of minor amounts of hydroxylated lecithin (e.g., Centrolene S) in the chocolate coating reduced moisture loss from confectionery and bakery products coated with the chocolate. Decreases in moisture transmission of up to 60% or higher as compared with regular chocolate were obtained. The preferred level of hydroxylated lecithin ranges from 0.25 to 2.5% by weight of the chocolate coating.

## With Foamed Filling

The process developed by J.M. Abalo; U.S. Patent 3,798,337; March 19, 1974; assigned to Noel y Compania Limitada Sociedad Anoniam Argentina de Dulces y Conservas, Argentina is one for the continuous manufacture of sweets having a substantially cell-free chocolate shell and a filler made of a cell-containing foamed chocolate, or of an alveolar mass formed of fatty materials and ground fruits and the softening point of which alveolar mass is similar to that of the foamed chocolate and capable of softening and fusing at mouth temperature.

The process comprises the following steps of pouring into a mold, at atmospheric pressure, a flowable, plastic, warm mass containing bubbles which solidifies by cooling; locating the loaded mold into an isolated inclosure, the volume of which is only slightly larger than of the mold; moving the inclosure towards a low vacuum zone, and during the movement towards the low vacuum zone allowing the heat of the warm mass to act on the bubbles to slightly increase their volume and thereby to also slightly increase the volume of the mass in the mold; introducing the mold with the inclosure into a low vacuum zone to produce an additional increase in volume of the bubbles and mass.

This is followed by introducing the mold into a high vacuum zone to substantially increase the volume of the bubbles and thereby the volume of the mass, at the same time as, at least, the free face of the mass is subject to an intense cooling to rapidly solidify a layer of the mass including the free face and forming a rigid dome including cells produced by the bubbles in the mass; decreasing thereafter the degree of cooling and allowing the mass to progressively solidify towards its core under the high vacuum; thereafter discharging the mold from the high vacuum zone with the foamed, substantially solidified mass which has been allowed to solidify to a point only slightly above its softening point and which conveys to the mass a self-supporting characteristic; and thereafter discharging the resulting mass of sweet from the mold.

Upon manufacturing for instance a chocolate tablet according to the foregoing definition, the outer surface thereof will have recesses which decrease the aesthetic aspect of the product. According to a more sophisticated process, the possibility is conceived to produce, by means of a continuous process, a chocolate tablet having an outer chocolate shell which is not foamed and which contains within the space defined by the shell a filler of foamed chocolate. In this event it is also possible to use as filler an alveolar mass which instead of being made of chocolate, is made of other products, as well be described later on.

Upon manufacturing a chocolate tablet having a chocolate shell, the process becomes more complicated in order that the tablets may be produced by a continuous process. In this event it is important that the thickness of the shell be reduced to its minimum, so that the weight of the resulting tablet is not excessively increased, at the same time as special care has to be paid to the fact that both chocolate masses are well bonded to one another, without completely fusing the mass defining the shell during the bonding step, because this would destroy the smooth outer face of the resulting product.

This process comprises the steps of forming, at atmospheric pressure, in a mold which moves substantially continuously, a substantially bubble-free chocolate shell, solidifying and hardening by cooling the shell and then softening its inner face, pouring into the space defined by the shell a flowable filler mass including bubbles, the filler mass being at a temperature similar to that of the softened inner face of the shell, subjecting the mold with its mass first to a low vacuum to start the expansion of the bubbles in said filler mass and then to a high vacuum to increase the volume of the bubbles to form cells at the same time as, at least, the free face of the filler mass is subject to an intense cooling to rapidly solidify a layer including the free face of the filler and producing a rigid dome in the filler mass, thereafter decreasing the cooling, progressively solidifying the rest of the filler mass in a direction towards its core, thereafter cancelling the vacuum and thereafter discharging the resulting sweet from the mold.

Within this process, additional steps may be added both with regard to the manufacture of the chocolate shell in the mold prior to pouring the filler mass to from the foamed chocolate, as well as in connection with steps to follow after the mold has been discharged from the high vacuum chamber.

Equipment for this process comprises shaping molds, a mold conveyer which includes in succession a first shell forming chocolate loading station, a first scraper station adapted to scrape and clean said filler inlet and to level the shell forming chocolate mass housed in the mold with regard to the filler inlet, a first vibrating station adapted to vibrate the mold to substantially remove the bubbles contained in the shell-forming chocolate mass, a fluid chocolate discharge station for discharging fluid chocolate from the mold, a first chocolate discharge station for discharging fluid chocolate from the mold, a first cooling station for the mold for hardening the remaining chocolate mass which remains attached to the side wall portions and base portion of the mold and which defines the shell, a first hot gas blower station directed towards the inside of the mold and adapted to soften the inner faces of the shell.

This is followed by a second chocolate loading station for pouring warm filler chocolate adapted to form foamed chocolate at approximately the temperature of the inner temperature than the outer faces of the shell. The second loading station includes dosifying means capable of dispensing a predetermined volume of filler chocolate which is smaller than the volume defined by the inner faces of the shell, a high vacuum chamber having in inlet nozzle member and an outlet nozzle member. The conveyer means passes through the inlet nozzle member, high vacuum chamber and outlet nozzle member.

The conveyer means includes in the portions corresponding to said nozzle members spaced apart sealing means allowing the housing of molds between them, the lengths of the nozzle members being larger than the distance existing between two sealing means, the inlet nozzle member, at the zone adjacent to said chamber being connected to a low vacuum source and the zone of said chamber adjacent said inlet nozzle member including cooling sections arranged immediately above said conveyer means at a distance which substantially only enables the passing of said molds, and unloading means for discharging said molds from said discharge nozzle member.

With regard to said unloading means just cited, these consist actually of a series of devices which ensure that the final steps in the manufacture of the tablet or another product can be carried out with a minimum of products being discharged, prior to leading the resulting product to the packing station. More particularly, upon the mold having been subject to the high vacuum, the filler mass forms a dome-shaped top which conveniently should be removed and flattened so as to form in the mold an upper free zone which may be filled with a layer of chocolate to thus obtain a lid which is welded to the rest of the sweet already manufactured, so that upon discharging the resulting sweet already manufactured, so that upon discharging the resulting sweet with the lid from the mold, the resulting end product will have a complete outer smooth appearance. The equipment is illustrated and described in detail in the patent.

## Having a Lacy, Openwork Core

Confections, particularly candy bars, are typically manufactured by forming a solid central core of a confectionery substance, such as nuts, coconut or some other granular, edible material embedded in a matrix of a second edible material, and then coating the central core with a thin layer of chocolate. The chocolate coating operation can be conveniently accomplished by placing the core of the confection on a moving endless belt and pouring molten chocolate over the core as it passes underneath a suitable dispenser.

The solid central core of a typical chocolate coated confection can be inexpensively made with automated equipment long known in the confection field. Confections having a more intricate shape, however, such as an openwork or lace-like pattern, are rare and are conventionally made by hand in relatively small quantities. Moreover, manually produced openwork matrices cannot be satisfactory coated with chocolate using conventional machinery since the process would tend to fill in the interstices of the openwork structure and thereby diminish the aesthetically pleasing openwork appearance desired for the finished confection.

However, E.Tay; U.S. Patent 3,958,08; May 18, 1976; assigned to Magic Chocolate, Inc. has developed a process and apparatus for manufacturing a coated confection that has a core formed in a lacy, openwork pattern and is coated without permanently filling the interstices of the core. The apparatus includes a movable surface, such as is defined by an endless moving belt, and a reservoir containing a hardenable liquid material, such as molten sugar, that is to be distributed onto the moving belt. A dispending device communicates with the reservoir and has a plurality of distinct distribution openings. The dispending device can be maintained in a fixed transverse position relative to the moving belt so that the molten sugar from the reservoir is dispensed onto the belt from the distribution openings in a plurality of fine strands extending longitudinally of the belt.

A second dispending device also communicates with the reservoir and has a plurality of distinct distribution openings. The second dispensing device is movable transversely of the moving belt so that molten sugar is dispensed onto the belt in a plurality of fine strands extending transversely of the belt. Together, the longitudinal and transverse strands of the distributed molten sugar cool to define a self-supporting confectionery core having a lacy, openwork pattern.

The core of sugar distributed onto the moving belt is cut into convenient size segments and then transferred, by an intermediate transfer belt, for example, to a movable mesh surface such as a moving, endless mesh belt, that transports the sugar core under a device for distributing a second hardenable, liquid material, such as molten chocolate, over the core. The coated core of sugar is then carried by the moving mesh belt underneath an apparatus that directs a flow of air downwardly over the sugar core and the molen chocolate covering the core. The flow of air removes excess molten chocolate from the core generally and more specifically removes chocolate that has bridged the interstices of the sugar core to maintain the openwork patterns of the core in the finished product. Thereafter, the coated confection is allowed to cool and harden on another belt.

In a preferred embodiment of the apparatus, both devices for dispensing the molten sugar include a hopper having a plurality of distribution openings formed in its bottom and a conduit coupled to the reservoir and extending to the top of the hopper for delivering molten sugar from the reservoir to the hopper. Both dispensing devices also include heating elements to maintain the sugar in the hoppers molten while it is being dispensed onto the moving belt. A drive system automatically moves the hopper of the transversely movable dispensing device across the surface of the moving endless belt.

Disposed between the second diepensing device and the apparatus for applying the coating of molten chocolate to the sugar core is a mechanism for cutting the core material into distinct pieces. The cutting mechanism includes blades disposed transversely of the moving belt that sever distinct pieces of the core from the continuous openwork ribbon of sugar distributed by the two dispensing devices. The cutting mechanism also includes a blade or blades disposed parallel to the moving belt and intermediate its side edges for splitting the sugar core lengthwise.

The coating apparatus includes a reservoir containing the molten chocolate and positioned underneath the moving mesh belt. The reservoir has an open top so that is communicates with the underside of the mesh belt to catch any molten chocolate dripping from the belt. Positioned alongside the mesh belt and disposed so that its lower portion is in the reservoir and its upper portion is above the mesh belt is at least one rotatable member. The rotatable member defines a surface to which the molten chocolate can adhere as the surface passes through the reservoir. The chocolate covered surface can then move upwardly from the reservoir above the mesh surface toward a flexible scraper that scrapes the molten chocolate from the surface and directs the chocolate into at least one trough member.

The trough member extends transversely of the mesh belt and is disposed above the belt. A distribution slot in the bottom of the trough member also extends transversely of the mesh belt. Accordingly, the molten chocolate directed into the trough member by the flexible scraper passes through the distribution slot and is distributed over the pieces of sugar core moving underneath the trough member on the mesh belt.

Downstream, in the direction of movement of the sugar core, from the trough member is the apparatus for directing the flow of air over the coated pieces of sugar core. The air flow directing apparatus includes a blower for producing the flow of air and a plenum chamber coupled to the exhaust of the blower. The plenum chamber extends transversely of and above the mesh belt and includes at least 1 opening to direct the air flow from the blower downward over the coated sugar core. Molten chocolate that would normally bridge or fill the interstices of the core is thereby blown out of the interstices and through the mesh belt so as to reopen a substantial proportion of them. The molten chocolate may also be blown, at least to some extent, around the undersides of the strands of the sugar core to effect a more uniform coating of the strands and excess chocolate, generally, is returned to the reservoir. After passing under the plenum chamber, the pieces of coated core are transferred onto an endless moving belt that transports the coated pieces through a cooling station. The cooling station comprises a hood over the endless belt, through which air is forced from a cooling unit to cool and harden both the chocolate coating and the sugar core. At the end of the cooling station, the pieces of coated core are removed from the endless belt and packed for shipment and sale. The patent contains a number of figures illustrating the apparatus and a detailed description of the process.

## Chocolate-Covered Nut Clusters

Confections such as nut clusters generally are handmade by mixing the solid filler with molten chocolate and hand depositing the cluster in free forms on wax paper or similar release surfaces for cooling. The nut cluster, which is the most common of this type of confection, consists of about 1/3 to 2/3 by weight of whole or broken nuts, usually peanuts. Other solid fillers used in such candies are pecans, almonds, raising, coconut shreds and the like. Such clusters are characterized by their highly irregular surface where the nuts or solids protrude under the chocolate covering with slightly varying shapes about the perimeter.

Since it has been necessary to handmake these cluster type confections in order to achieve the free form or irregular shape, their manufacture has been laborious and relatively expensive. Various attempts have been made to develop machines for automatically manufacturing such confections, but these prior machines have had various drawbacks. In some current machines which produce nut clusters by depositing the solid filler and molten chocolate into molds for cooling, the resulting confection has a smooth outer shape. While some machines have utilized molds having a relatively irregular molding surface, nevertheless the formed confection is easily recognizes as a molded product, rather than a free-formed product.

The free form or home-made appearance of this type of confection has been found to be significantly more desirable from a merchandising standpoint than the molded form. Moreover, molding machines also have incurred problems in adequately mixing the solids with the chocolate and in properly tempering the chocolate during the process.

L. Bellew; U.S. Patent 4,010,284; march 1, 1977; assigned to W.C. Smith & Sons, Inc. has provided a method and apparatus for automatically and continuously making solid filled confections, such as chocolate nut clusters, which have an irregular home-made appearance.

The machine, which is illustrated and described in detail in the patent, includes a plurality of extrusion tubes each having a screw type auger, a supply for separate streams of nuts and hot fluid chocolate into each extrusion tube, elements for rotating and oscillating the augar to thoroughly mix the fluid chocolate and nuts that are introduced into the tube and to transfer the mixture to an extrusion orifice, and reciprocatable cutting blades located adjacent the extrusion orifice of each extrusion tube for successively cutting the extruded mixture into discrete pieces of predetermined size which thereupon drop onto a moving conveyer surface below.

# HOLLOW CHOCOLATES

## Base Chocolate Cone Which Can Be Varied in Shape

It is usual, in the confectionery business, to manufacture in certain periods of the year hollow articles of chocolate adapted to those periods, such as Santa Claus shapes for the Christmas season, chicken shapes for the Easter season, etc. All these articles are made by hollow molds. The process is expensive the chocolate articles suffer much breakage, large storerooms must be available to store the chocolate figures, etc.

E.J.M. Jamin; U.S. Patent 3,821,423; June 28, 1974; assigned to C. Jamin NV, Netherlands has, then, based a process of a method of manufacture which uses a basically-shaped hollow cone, cube, etc. of chocolate as a first body, on which there may be placed a second, removable chocolate body in the shape of Saint Nicholas, Santa Claus, a chicken figure, etc. Such a figured second body can easily removed from the basic article, whereupon a second body which is entirely differently figured can be disposed on the basic article.

The desired figured second body can be made in a simple way from a blank by punching or cutting. This is advantageous as the second body can always be modified when this is necessary for special seasons. The process will be clarified with reference to Figure 1.1a which represents a hollow basic article made of chocolate; Figure 1.1b and 1.1c, which are hollow articles comprising the same hollow basic article with differently figured bodies; and Figure 1.1d which represents a blank used as a second figured body in Figures 1.1b and 1.1c.

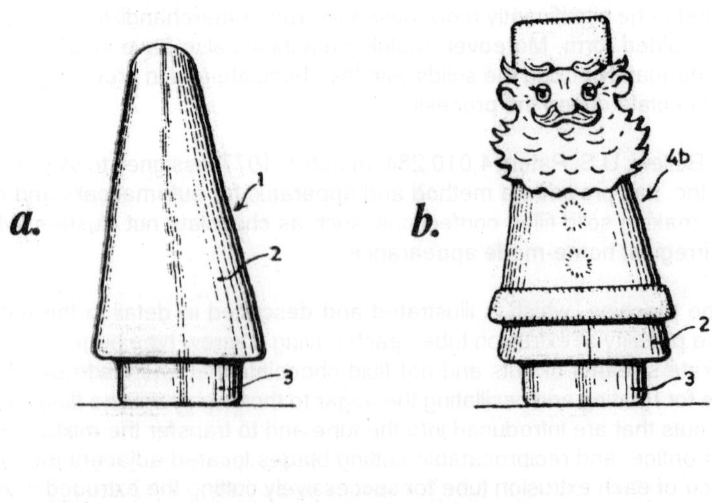


**Figure 1.1: Method of making Hollow Chocolate Figures**

**FIGURE 1.1: (continued)**

*c.*

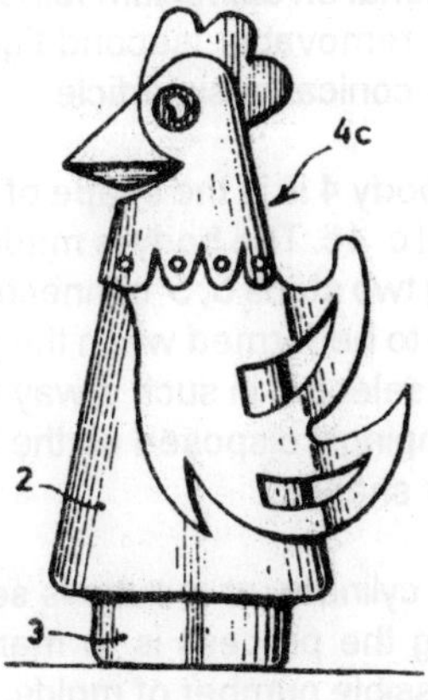


*d.*

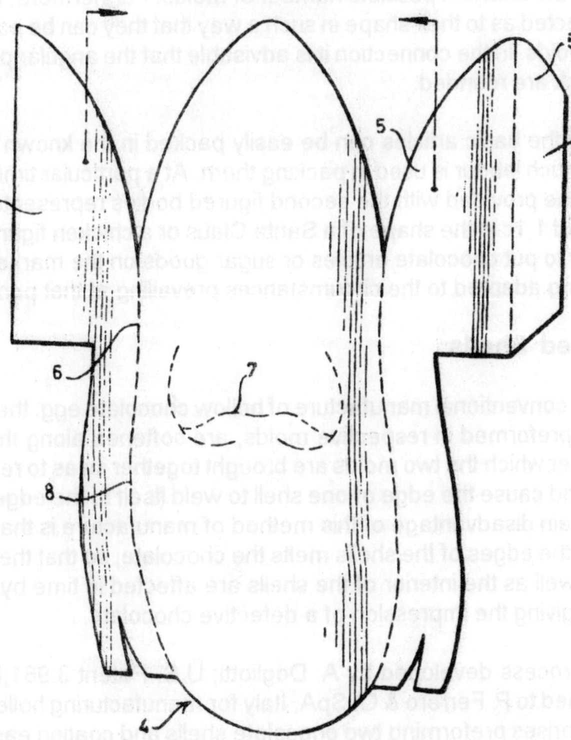


(a) **Hollow basis mold**
(b) **Santa Claus**
(c) **Chicken**
(d) **Blank for figures**

The hollow neutral chocolate basic article 1 consists in this case of a hollow rounded cone 2 which at the lower end rests on a cylinder 3 which is integral therewith. As a packing material an aluminium foil is wrapped around the whole. At the upper end a conical, removable, second figured article 4 is fittingly and clampingly disposed on the conical basic article.

This second figured body 4 is in the shape of a Santa Claus, Figure 1.1b, 4b, or a chicken in Figure 1.1c, 4c. The body is made from a blank by cutting out the finished figure comrising two strips 5, 5' connected with the side edges 6, the circumference of the space to be formed when the strips are interconnected by means of the part 5a being selected in such a way that the second deformable body can be fittingly or clampingly disposed on the basic article. Perforations 7 and 8 contribute to a proper shaping.

Preferably a cone, a cylinder, or a cube is selected for the basic article. One of the ideas underlying the process is to manufacture the desired basic articles with the smallest possible number of molds. Furthermore, the basic articles are selected as to their shape in such a way that they can be easily removed from their molds. In the connection it is advisable that the angular portions of the cube or block are rounded.

Since the basic articles can be easily packed in the known packing machines not much labour is used in packing them. At a particular time these basic articles can be provided with the second figured bodies represented in the Figures 1.1b and 1.1c in the shape of a Santa Claus or a chicken figure. In this way it is possible to put chocolate articles or sugar goods on the market any time of the year being adapted to the circumstances prevailing at that period.

## Egg-Shaped Shells

In the conventional manufacture of hollow chocolate egg, the two component shells, preformed in respective molds, are softened along their edges by warming, after which the two molds are brought together so as to reconstruct the entire egg and cause the edge of one shell to weld itself to the edge of the other shell. The main disadvantage of this method of manufacture is that the thermal softening of the edges of the shells melts the chocolate, so that the whole welding area as well as the interior of the shells are affected in time by a change of colour, thus giving the impression of a defective chocolate.

The process developed by A. Dogliotti; U.S. Patent 3,961,089; June 1, 1976; assigned to P. Ferrero & C. SpA, Italy for manufacturing hollow chocolate articles comprises preforming two chocolate shells and coating each of the two shells on the inside with a molten layer of edible material and joining together the two shells by welding of the two inner layers together whilst at least one of the layers is still in a sufficiently fluid condition for welding to the other inner layer.

In a preferred method one of the two inner layers is caused to set by cooling and the shell thus coated is kept with its hollow side turned upwards, while the other shell, with its inner coating layer still in a fluid state, is inverted upon the first shell and retained in this position so as to cause the material of the inverted fluid layer to flow over and adhere to the peripheral surface of the inner layer which has set. The two inner layers thus stuck together therefore, form upon the peripheral surface a welded seam, invisible from the outside but instantly recognizable if one cuts open the article transversely in the transverse meridian of the two shells. Hollow articles made by this method also have the advantage that they exhibit no change of colour at the internal welded seam. Preferably, in order to assist the flow of the material of the inverted fluid layer over the peripheral surface of the set layer, the two superimposed shells are subjected to vibration.

Figures 1.2a and 1.2b are cross sections, each taken upon the same plane, of a pair of molds in different stages of carrying out this process for the manufacture of an Easter egg. In the figures, reference numerals 10 and 10' indicate two metal molds which are hinged together like a book by means of ahinge 12. The molds are formed with mold cavities 14 and 14' disposed symmetrically with respect to the hinge 12. The mold cavities are identical to each other and are shaped to reproduce the two shells forming the halves of an Easter egg, which the latter can have, for example, a diameter of about 5 cm and a length of about 7 cm. In the closed position of the molds, the two cavities are disposed in exact register with each other and therefore, define the shape of a whole egg.

*a.*

*b.*

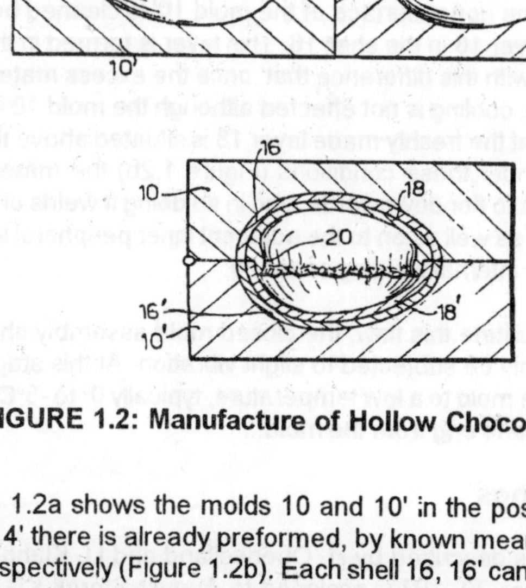


**FIGURE 1.2: Manufacture of Hollow Chocolate Egg**

Figure 1.2a shows the molds 10 and 10' in the position. In each of the cavities 14, 14' there is already preformed, by known means, a chocolate shell 16 and 16' respectively (Figure 1.2b). Each shell 16, 16' can be made, for example, of milk chocolate, which melts generally at 28° to 30°C. To form the two shells the cavities are filled with molten chocolate while the molds are at a temperature lower than the melting temperature, for example 25°C where the shells are of milk chocolate. Thus as the molten chocolate is poured into each cavity, a layer solidifies upon contact with each mold to form the shells, the surplus melted chocolate being poured from the molds. The thickness of each shell depends upon the time elapsing between the casting of the shell and the pouring off of the surplus chocolate. In the specific case considered here the thickness of each shell is typically 1.5 to 2 mm. The molds with the shells thus formed are cooled to a temperature such as to allow adhesion to the shells of the layers which subsequently form the inner coating without any danger of degradation of the shells due to the heat transferred thereto by the molten coating material, for example, 20° to 22°C. In these circumstances, molten material is poured into the shell 16', but not into other shell 16, and forms an inner layer 18 in the shell 16'.

The material which forms the inner layer 18' can also consist of chocolate, for example identical chocolate to that of the two shells 16, 16'. One can, however, use (for dietetic reasons, as well) a material poorer in cocoa and richer in milk, for example consisting essentially of powdered whole milk, cocoa butter and sugar, while being free of chocolate paste.

Such material possesses the colour of milk rather than the typical colour of chocolate. The melting temperature of this material is 30° to 31°C. In this case, also, after having poured the molten material into the shell 16', the material in contact with the shell sets to form the inner layer 18' and the excess material is poured off after a predetermined time when the layer has been formed with the desired thickness, for example about 2 mm. The layer 18' after formation is immediately cooled so as to cause it to harden before the material flows by gravity to the bottom of the shell 16'.

If necessary the upper surface of the mold 10' is cleaned before the formation of an inner layer 18 in the shell 16. This layer is formed in the same way as the layer 18', but with this difference that once the excess material is poured out from the shell 16, cooling is not effected although the mold 10 is inverted on to the mold 10' so that the freshly made layer 18 is situated above the previously formed layer 18'. Under these conditions (Figure 1.2b) the material of the inverted layer 18 tends to flor downwards, and in so doing it welds on to the upper edge of the layer 18' as well as on to the adjacent inner peripheral surface of the layer 18', forming an internal welding seam 20.

In order to facilitate this flow, the closed mold assembly shown in figure 1.2b should preferably be subjected to slight vibration. At this stage it is simply necessary to cool the mold to a low temperature, typically 0° to -5°C, as to permit removal of the complete egg from the mold.

## With Centre Fillings

The apparatus described by H. Oberwelland and U. Klahn; U.S. Patent 4,063,864; December 20, 1977; assigned to August Storck KG, Germany is one for the production of hollow confections with centre fillings which are produced by centrifugal casting in an open top mold charged with a flowable confectionery mass, the mold being temporarily rotated about a vertical axis by drive means and then cooled and discharged.

The centrifugal molds are mounted in transverse and longitudinal rows on conveyor means which carry them underneath a metering feed means for pouring the flowable confectionery mass, rotation being imparted to the molds by a main drive means through clutches controlled by a time switch.

In operation, apparatus of such a kind has proved to have certain defects. Due to wear of its components or to stretching of the chain conveyer which carries the molds trouble tends to arise when the cooperating clutch members move into engagement, particularly if the conveyors are of major length and carry a large number of molds. Clutch trouble may result in considerable dislocation in the entire production line.

Furthermore, the upper edge of the spinning confectionery case tends to be of unequal height if rotation of the mold is started during or immediately after the pouring of the confectionery mass into the mold. This apparatus was developed to remedy these defects and to ensure that by precise cooperation of the many parts and assemblies the entire apparatus will work trouble-free, irrespective of any possible wear of fatigue, so that accurately molded confections will be cleanly discharged from the molds.

This is achieved in that the two clutch members associated with the molds and/or with the drive means are displaceable in conveying direction in relation to their associated parts and adapted to pull themselves into axial alignment when they engage. Moreover, the spinning station follows the charging station in the direction of travel of the conveyer at a distance which corresponds to at least one step of the intermittent drive of the conveyer, so that rotation of the molds cannot begin until the confectionery mass which has been poured into the molds has formed a substantially horizontal surface. According to the process the distance of the spinning station from the charging station is variable and adjustable.

In order to ensure the desired correct cooperation of the two clutch members one of the two clutch members is connected to its associated shaft by a transmission, a Carbon shaft, or the like, permitting axial misalignment of the two shafts to be bridged. Conveniently the required compensation of axial misalignment may be achieved by the employment of a conventional double parallel crank coupling.

Owing to the displaceability of the clutch members, particularly in the direction of travel of the molds, engagement of the clutch members between the molds and the drive means is always assured, even should the molds that are to be rotated and their clutch members fail to move into precise axial alignment with the corresponding clutch members associated with the drive means or should faults in the pitch of the chain links and wear of the links or chain sheels and so forth after prolonged use cause the relative positioning of the clutch members to change. According to the process the cooperating clutch members are geometrically suitably designed or provided with projections, recesses and the like to pull the cooperating clutch members automatically into axial alignment when they engage.

With particular advantage several clutch members, particularly several driving clutch members, are mounted on a common clutch holder which is movable for engaging and disengaging the clutches and all the clutch members are geared to a common drive through intermediate gearing. The clutch members are preferably mounted severally or in groups on slides which are slidably displaceable in the common clutch holder in the direction of travel of the centrifugal molds, and the transmission means which permit compensation of axial misalignment may be interposed between the driving clutch members and the intermediate gearing. At the same time the intermediate gearing may also be accommodated in the clutch holder and connected to a fixed driving motor by a Carbon shaft. The complete clutch holder and all the parts and assemblies mounted therein can be advanced and retracted in clutch engaging and disengaging direction by means of a lifting gear besides being adjustably movable in the direction of travel of the molds in relation to the metering feed means for charging the molds, thereby to enable rotation to be briefly imparted to the centrifugal molds at points which are sufficiently far removed from the metering feed means at the charging station to allow for the consistency of the mass and existing operating conditions.

Preferably the arrangement is such that several centrifugal molds, each together with its associated clutch member attached to its spinning spindle, are freely rotatably mounted on a common transverse holder on the conveyer chain in one or more transverse rows and that the drive means for the molds are located at the spinning station below the conveyer chain. There is a plurality of driving clutch members corresponding in number to the number of molds that are to be simultaneously driven and having a self-aligning action upon engagement with the cooperating clutch members of the molds, each together with a transmission means which compensates axial misalignment.

The driving clutch members are mounted in a common clutch holder in a manner permitting displacement in the direction of travel of the molds and driven by a main drive means through intermediate gearing. In order to permit confections of different shapes to be produced the centrifugal molds in their holders or the transverse holders together with the molds and associated clutch members are exchangeably mounted so that they can be replaced on the conveyer chain. The patent contains a number of drawings of preferred apparatus for practicing this process, together with detailed description of the parts and how they operate.

# SPECIALLY CHOCOLATES

## Dietetic Chocolate

The process described by A. Riesen; U.S. Patent 4,011,349; March 8, 1977 provides dietetic chocolate compositions which in the form of finished chocolate candy products, have excellent smoothness and extremely appealing taste. These compositions include ground cocoa beans, added cocoa butter, whole powdered milk, skim powdered milk, and sorbitol as the major constituents and as minor constituents, a flavouring agent, especially vanilla, lecithin and a cyclamate or saccharin which provides a milk chocolate composition.

For dark chocolate, the compositions include ground cocoa beans, added cocoa butter, soy flour and sorbitol as major constituents with a synthetic sweetener and lecithin as minor constituents. The amounts of each major constituent must be maintained at approximately the specified levels to attain the desirable properties of the compositions whereas the minor constituents can vary to a slightly higher degree although their presence, in too, should not exceed about 1% of the total weight of the major constituents.

The milk chocolate composition is shown below all percentages being approximately as follows.

| *Ingredients* | *Percent* |
|---|---|
| Cocoa beans | 9 |
| Whole milk powder | 15 |
| Skim milk powder | 7 |
| Sorbitol | 31 |
| Cocoa butter (added) | 38 |
| Saccharin | 0.01 |
| Lecithin | 0.6 |
| Vanilla | 0.01 |

The dark chocolate composition is as follows.

| *Ingredients* | *Percent* |
|---|---|
| Cocoa beans | 36 |
| Sorbitol | 39 |
| Soy flour | 4 |
| Cocoa butter (added) | 21 |
| Saccharin | 0.01 |
| Lecithin | 0.6 |

## Hypoallergenic Chocolate

Many allergists have recognized that chocolate contains proteins which are allergens. The allergens in chocolate frequently cause the formation of reagins in many persons. Thus, many persons are allergic to chocolate, and chocolate allergy is common in both adults and children. The symptoms may include mild to severe allergic skin eruptions, respiratory tract allergy (allergic rhinitis and asthma), severe gastro-intestinal reactions, migraine, and allergic anaphylaxis. L.S. Girsh; U.S. Patent 4,078,093; March 7, 1978 prepares a hypoallergenic chocolate to be used in chocolate bars or for use as a flavouring ingredients in various food products.

The chocolate is prepared by treating cocoa powder so as to denature substantially all of the protein allergens which cause chocolate allergies. The cocoa powder with its denatured protein alergen is then mixed with sugar, cocoa butter, and other flavouring additives and further heat treated (and denatured) to produce the hypoallergenic chocolate.

Chocolate is manufactured from beans of the Theobroma cocoa tree. The beans are received by the chocolate manufacturer who processes the beans by cleaning, roasting, hulling, blending, and grinding them. As the shells are removed, the beans are broken into fragements called nibs. The nibs are then finely ground and chocolate liquor is produced. The mixture of cocoa butter, a tasteless fat, and cocoa in the finely ground nibs forms a free-flowing substance called chocolate liquor.

It is this chocolate liquor which is used in most chocolate flavoured food products. This chocolate liquor also contains the protein allergens which cause chocolate allergy. The chocolate liquor comprises cocoa butter and cocoa powder. When chocolate liquor is heated and placed under pressure, the cocoa butter is squeezed out of the chocolate liquor and separated from the remaining mass of material. This remaining mass is then finely ground to produce cocoa powder. Since the cocoa butter is simply a tasteless fat, it is the cocoa powder which contains all of the protein allergens.

The hypoallergenic chocolate of this process is prepared by treating the cocoa powder to denature the protein allergens contained therein. In the first step, cocoa powder is prepared by heating the ground nibs of roasted cocoa beans at a temperature of from 215° to 300°F in a hydraulic press at a pressure from 5,500 to 8,000 pounds per square inch, for 15 to 90 minutes.

Beans used for cocoa production are usually roasted at temperatures about 15° to 20°F higher (about 240°F) than beans used for production of chocolate liquor (about 220°F). Because of the exceedingly high pressure concurrent with high temperatures, the mass from which cocoa is produced may be considered super-heated. The majority of the protein allergens are denatuired by this first step.

In the second step, the cocoa powder prepared in the first step is mixed as a separate ingredient along with cocoa butter and sugar and is further treated at a temperature of 180° to 190°F for at least 48 hours, and preferably from 48 to 96 hours. The cocoa powder and cocoa butter may not be mixed in the form of chocolate liquor since, as described below, the prolonged heating required to denature the protein allergens has an adverse effect on the taste of the chocolate liquor.

Moreover, although it is not certain, the presence of the cocoa butter in the chocolate liquor may in some way interfere with the denaturation of the protein allergens; also, removing the fat from the lipoprotein in cocoa production may additionally disrupt the chocolate protein allergen.

**Example**: Cocoa powder was formed by being heated at temperature of 235° to 245°F at extreme pressure of about 6,000 pounds per square inch for about 30 minutes. A hypoallergenic chocolate composition was prepared by mixing 14% by weight of this cocoa powder, 33% by weight cocoa butter and 53% by weight sugar (sucrose). The mixture was then heated for 48 hours at 180°F.

The hypoallergenic chocolate was then centrifuged at 6,000 g and analyzed. 95 to 100% of the chocolate protein was found to be insoluble in 10 mm phosphate buffer, pH 7.2. This almost complete insolubility of the chocolate protein contained in the hypoallergenic chocolate produced in accordance with this process is an objective indicate that the chocolate protein has been denatured to the point where substantially all of the protein allergens have been denatured.

In contrast, only 73% of the chocolate protein was found to be insoluble upon centrifuging at 6,000 g a composition prepared using chocolate liquor heated for two additional hours at 180°F in place of the cocoa powder treated in accordance with the process. The step of heating to 245°F with 6,000 pounds per square inch pressure was omitted since chocolate liquor would no longer remain intact but would be converted to cocoa powder. The taste of this hypoallergenic chocolate was substantially identical to the taste of the monohypoallergenic chocolate.

When 89 patients known to have a chocolate allergy were fed hypoallergenic chocolate bars made with the chocolate prepared as in the example, 78 of them were symptom-free, or showed only mild allergic symptoms.

# Chapter - 23

## *Other Candies including Hard Candies*

### SOFT CANDIES

### Incorporating Beta-1,3-Pyranoglucose in Jellied Candy

The process developed by H. Kimura, K. Kusakabe, S. Sato and H. Nakatani; U.S. Patent 3,908,027; September 23, 1975; assigned to Takeds Chemical Industries, Ltd., Japan related to jelly-like foods with an elastic skin accounting for 55 to 88% of the total weight with a pasty or liquid core which contains 1.5 to 6% (w/v) of a polysacchride which is thermally gelable in a concentration not lower than 1% (weight/volume) suspension, and mainly consists of ß-1,3-pyranoglucose units and which have a bulk accommodated in the space of a cube 5 to 30 mm on edge.

The thermally gelable polysaccharides mentioned above can be obtained, for instance, by cultivating a microorganism belonging to the genus Alcaligenes or Agrobacterium in a medium containing glucose as a carbon source, and are recovered therefrom as a white or off-white powder in a dehydrated and dried form. Glucose in the main constituent sugar of the polysaccharide, and, in infrared analysis, the powders exhibit properties characteristic of polysaccharide and have an absorption characteristics of ß-linkage at 890 $cm^{-1}$. In addition, the polysaccharides exhibit very unique behaviours.

Thus, they swell and gel when poured in water and heated. For example, when suspended in water to a concentration of about 1% and heated, these polysaccharides form a gel which is thermally irreversible and not suspended upon the addition of water.

Although the preferred cultural conditions vary with different microorganisms employed, cultivation of the main culture for the production of the polysaccharides is generally effected at pH about 5 to 8 at a temperature of 20° to 35°C for 2 to 4 days, using such cultivation means as shake culture or submerged culture. An example of polysaccharide production is conducted as follows: Alcaligenes faecalis var. mysogenes Strain NTK-u (ATCC 21680) is inoculated in 30 ml of a seed culture medium charged in a 200 ml Erlenmeyer flask, the medium being composed of glucose (1%), $(NH_4)_2HPO_4$ (0.15%), $KH_2PO_4$ (0.1%), $MgSO_4.7H_2O$ (0.05%), $FeSO_4.7H_2O$ (0.005%), $MnSO_4.7H_2O$ (0.002%), $ZnCl_2$ (0.001%), $CoCl_2$ (0.001%), yeast extract (0.1%), $CaCO_3$ (0.3%), uracil (0.01%) and water and being adjusted to pH 7.0. Cultivation is effected under shaking at 32°C for 24 hours. A 2 ml portions of the resultant seed culture broth is inoculated in 20 ml of a main culture medium charged in a 200 ml creased Erlenmeyer flask, the medium being composed of glucose (10.0%), $(NH_4)_2HPO_4$ (0.23%), $KH_2PO_4$ (0.1%), $MgSO_4.7H_2O$ (0.05%), $FeSO_4.7H_2O$ (0.005%), $MnSO_4.7H_2O$ (0.002%), $ZnCl_2$ (0.001%), $CoCl_2$ (0.001%), $CaCO_3$ (0.3%), uracil (0.01%) and water and being adjusted to pH 7.0. Cultivation is carried out under shaking at 32°C for 90 hours.

The broths thus obtained in several such flasks are pooled. To 80 ml of the broth is added 240 ml of an aqueous 0.5 N NaOH solution, followed by thorough stirring until the produced polysaccharide is dissolved. To the mixture is added 160 ml of water. The diluted solution is centrifuged at 12,000 rpm for 10 minutes to remove the solids matters including the cells. The supernatent liquid is neutralized with 3 N HCl, whereupon gel sediments separate. The sediments are collected by centrifugation and washed with water until the salts contained therein are removed. Then, the sediments are again centrifuged to collect the desired polysaccharide PS-B. Dehydration with acetone and drying under reduced pressure yield 4.4 g of PS-B. The yield relative to the substrate glucose is 55%.

| | |
|---|---|
| Specific rotation : | -16±3° (c=0.5, dimethylsulfoxide) |
| | +31±6° (c=1.0, 0.1 N NaOH) |
| Elementary analysis (%) : | Calculated for $C_6H_{10}O_5$: C=44.44;H=6.17 |
| | Found: C=43.58±1; H=6.46±0.5; |
| Gel strength : | 650 x $10^3$ to 1,300 x $10^3$ dynes/$cm^2$ |

These polysaccharides are diluted or dispersed and suspended to a convenient, for there is no need to pay much attention to pH. Thus, since the gelling property of the polysaccharides is available over an unusually wide pH range, i.e. between pH about 2.0 and pH about 9.5, they can be utilized with little trouble for ordinary food processing purposes. In this method, it is generally convenient to dilute or disperse and suspend the polysaccharides with water.

It is also possible to cause the polysaccharides to gel after adding thereto additives as, for example, natural sweeteners such as sucrose, glucose, fructose, etc., artificial sweetenings such as saccharin; sour agents such as citric acid, malic acid, ascorbic acid, etc.; suitable spices; condiments; and other natural matters and food additives such as sorbitol, dextrin, miller jelly, milk, fermented milk, vitamins, starch, alcoholic beverages, natural fruit juices and the like. The above-mentioned suspensions are then maintained in a mold accommodated in the space of a cube 5 to 30 mm on edge or when to be coagulated into a sphere, in a mold having a diameter of 5 to 30 mm. In this connection, a suitable shape, such as a sphere, ellipsoid, cube, strawberry-like shape or tomato-like shape, may be chosen.

Vessels for molding the candies may be made of various materials, and the molds may be heated in some uniform manner such as a boiling water bath, oven, etc. The heating temperature and the period of heating will vary with the size of the mold, the material of which it is made, etc. The gelling ratio is determined for each case.

The gelling ratio is the weight ratio of the gelled portion of each sample to the unheated suspensions used for the preparation of the sample. When the ratio corresponds to about 55 to 88 weight %, the product is a jelly-like food suitable for the present purposes. Such a product has an elastic gel skin and a liquid or pasty core. The process may be illustrated by the following examples:

Example 1: 45 g of polysaccharide Ps-B, 500 g of glucose, 5 g of gum arabic, 10 g of malic acid, suitable amounts of food colour and grape flavour and 500 ml. of water are admixed and homogenized using a homogenizer. The resulting mixture is filled into spherical moulding vessels of gun metal, 19 mm in diameter, and externally uniformly heated by steaming at about 100°C for about 60 seconds. Then, the vessels are immediately cooled in running water. The above procedure yields about 1,000 g of jelly balls which have an elastic gel skin and a liquid core. These jelly balls are resistant against 80 g weight plummet when measured by curd-tension meter.

Example 2: 50 g of polysaccharide PS-B, 250 ml of a concentrated fruit juice and 750 ml of water are evenly blended. The resulting suspension is filled into spherical moulding vessels of gun metal, 19 mm in diameter, and externally evenly heated by steaming at about 100°C for about 30 seconds, immediately followed by cooling in running water. The above procedure yields about 1,000 g of jelly balls which have an elastic gel skin and a liquid core.

Example 3: A suspension prepared in the manner described in Example 2 is maintained in rubber bladders in such a manner that jelly balls, 30 mm in diameter, will be obtained. The bladders are hermetically closed and heated in a boiling water bath for about 280 seconds, immediately followed by cooling in running water. The above procedure yields about 1,000 g of jelly balls which have an elastic gel skin and a liquid core.

Example 4: 50 g of polysccharide PS-B, 300 g of sucrose, 300 ml of brandy and 500 ml of water are admixed and homogenized using a homogenizer. The resulting mixture is filled into spherical moulding vessels of gun metal, 19 mm in diameter, and externally evenly heated by steaming at about 100°C for about 45 seconds, immediately followed by cooling in running water. The procedure yields about 1,100 g of jelly balls which have an elastic gel skin and a liquid core of brandy.

## Continuous Manufacture

P. Didelot, G. Lasserre, G. Letourneau and J.M. Sudan; U.S. Patent 3,908,032; September 23, 1975; assigned to General Foods France, France developed a continuous process for making soft candy which comprises the following steps: (1) quick concentrating to avoid formation of inverted sugar and forming a homogeneous mass which is free-flosing at high temperature and comprises sugar, glucose, fat, gelatin and water, (2) cooling the free-flowing mass to impart a paste consistency to it, (3) inducing formation of crystallization nuclei through the paste, (4) mixing, further homogenizing under pressure, and shaping into a paste web, (5) cooling the paste web to a substantially intermediate temperature below the temperature of the paste and the room temperature, (6) mixing, further homogenizing under pressure and extruding, especially in the shape of a rod of suitable size for packaging, (7) cooling the rod substantially to room temperature and (8) cutting the rod into suitably sized candy units.

The colouring matter, flavouring agents and acidulating agent can be added at any stage in the sequental steps, under such conditions that the product can be satisfactorily distributed through the mass so as to provide a homogeneous paste.

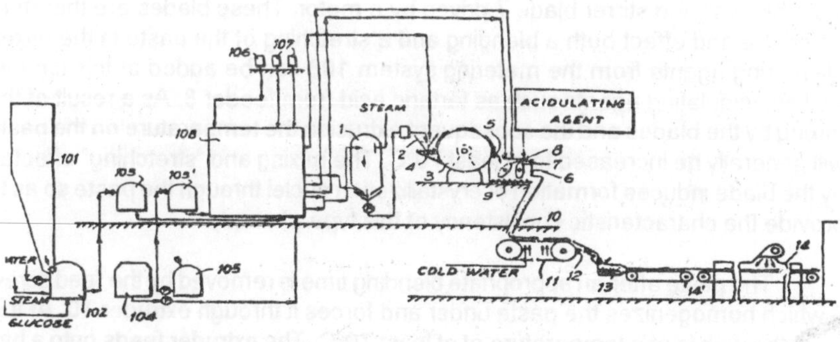


**Figure : Continuous Process for Manufacture of Soft Candy**

Sugar from a silo 101 is fed together with water, glucose and steam to dissolver 102. The water is metered by pump P. From the dissolver the solution is fed to stock tank 103. In mixer 105 a solution of gelatin and water is formed and fed to stock tank 103', fat is held in stock tank 104, colour is held in stock tank 106 and flavours in stock tanks 107. The solution or syrup of sucrose, and glucose, the fat, gelatin solution and the colouring and flavouring materials from the respective stock tanks are fed to volume metering system 108 which feeds the appropriate amounts of each component to the subsequent portions of the system. The gelatin solution, and a blend of sugar syrup and fat are fed to an appropriate rapid condensation apparatus preferably a thin film condenser.

In this condenser the mixture of sugar, glucose, fat, gelatin and water are concentrated to a paste of the desired concentration. Colouring agent can also be added prior to the concentrator. The concentration should be effected in a sufficiently short period to avoid formation of an excessive amount of invert sugar. In practice it has been found that this concentration should be effected in less than ten seconds. Other appropriate concentrators can be used but thin film concentrators give a particularly satisfactory result.

The concentrated paste discharged from the concentrator can be at a temperature of about 130°C at which temperature it has the consistency of a free-flowing paste. This paste is fed to a feeding chute 2 which discharged onto the external surface of a rotating drum 3. This drum can be cooled by a flow of water through the interior.

A doctor blade 4 can be provided to spread the paste and determine the thickness of the layer carried by the drum. The degree of cooling to be effected by the drum will be correlated with the conditions which will be later described for the mixer extruder but in general, the temperature will probably be dropped to approximately 70°C so as to provide a crystallization in the paste.

A doctor blade 5 at the other side of the drum strips the paste web from the drum and directs it to the mixer extruder 6. This mixer extruder preferably has a double wall and stirrer blade 7 driven by a motor. These blades are therefore off-centre and effect both a blending and a stretching of the paste in the mixer. Flavouring agents from the metering system 108 can be added at this time as well as acidulating agents such as tartaric acid from feeder 8. As a result of the mixing by the blades and the subsequent extrusion the temperature on the paste will generally be increased to at least 70°C. The mixing and "stretching" effected by the blade induces formation of crystallization nuclei through the paste so as to provide the characteristic consistency of this type of candy.

The paste after an appropriate blending time is removed by the feed screw 9 which homogenizes the paste under and forces it through extruder 10. At this point the web is at a temperature of at least 70°C. The extruder feeds onto a belt cooler 11 preferably cooled by cold water. The operation of this cooler is so controlled that the temperature of the web leaving this belt is substantially intermediate between the temperature at the exit of the first extruder and ambient temperature.

The web deposited on the best is stripped from the best by blade 12 and fed to further extruder 13 which can be an extruder of a conventional type. In this extruder the paste is further homogenized and blended by the feeder screw of the extruder and then forced through one or more orifice in the extruder preferably to be shaped into one or more rods which pass to further cooler 14 where the paste is completely cooled to ambient temperature. The rods are discharged from this belt to cutting machines 15 and thereafter the candy can be packaged and bagged.

## Fondant

Fondant type fillings for chocolate with natural or artificial flavourings such as rum, brandy, or fruit flavours tend to lose flavour rapidly if stored at room temperature. Although in factory storage it is possible to keep the product at reduced temperatures of 50° to 60°F and thus reduce flavour loss, it is not practical to maintain low temperature in distribution. Thus, most of the desirable flavour may be lost within a few weeks of leaving the factory.

J.A. Kitson; U.S. Patent 3,934,053; January 20, 1976; assigned to Canadian Patents and Development Limited, Canada has developed a flavoured fondant having improved flavour stability prepared by a process which comprises the steps of heating a sugars-containing mixtures to a temperature and for a period of time sufficient to cause formation of a sugar polymers base but insufficient to cause browning or caramelization, diluting the resultant sugar polymers base with hot water to a total sugars content of from about 85 to 95%, cooling the sugar polymers base and working to a smooth paste, and blending with the paste desired flavour and aroma essences. The required sugar polymers base is comprised essentially of oligo-saccharides and may be prepared from several different sugars and sugar-containing products such as sucrose, corn syrup, maltose, dextrose, maltodextrin, dextrin, the hydrol by-product of starch hydrolysate preparation, hydrogenated hydrol products, and mixtures thereof.

Hydrol is a common technical term utilized to describe the supernatent liquid remaining after separation of dextrose crystals from starch hydrolysates. Hydrol is a by-product from starch hydrolysates and contains dextrose and alpha-and beta-linked oligo-saccharides. For economic reasons it may be preferable to utilize hydrol or hydrogenated hydrol products in the starting mixtures.

The oligo-saccharides utilized for the flavour locking are prepared by heating the sugars-containing mixture to a temperature and for a period of time sufficient to cause formation of the necessary sugar-polymer stereo structures. This is preferably accomplished by adding a small amount of water to the mixture, bringing the mixture to a boil, increasing the temperature gradually to about 140° to 145°C, and holding it there for approximately five minutes.

Following formation of the oligo-saccharides stereo-polymers, hot water is added to the mixture to bring the total sugars content of the mixture to between 85 and about 95%. Preferably this is accomplished by cooling the mixture to less than about 120°C (usually approximately 90° to 110°C) and adding the water. The addition of water to the sugars syrup at this higher temperature is preferred since it has been found that it tends to drive off any undesirable flavours from the sugars resulting from any minor caramelization, although the tendency for the sugars to caramelize has been reduced by avoiding prolonged heating at higher temperatures. It has also been found easier to adjust the sugars content of the molten sugar mixture at this temperature since the syrup become quite viscous upon cooling.

The sugars syrup containing the oligo-saccharides is then cooled further to below 100°C, preferably to room temperature (or about 20° to 40°C) for the addition of the volatile food essences. Preferably, the essences are dissolved first in a binding agent, such as glycerin, of an amount sufficient to become about 0.5 to 10% of the final product. The binding agent may also be propylene glycol, polyethylene glycol, or mixtures thereof, and with glycerin. The binding agent acts as a solvent for both the sugars and the flavour compounds. The binding agent containing the flavour volatiles is then added to the cooled mixture containing the oligo-saccharide sugar polymers, and is stirred for sufficient time to achieve proper blending.

Where easily volatilized compounds are employed, it is necessary to mix the flavour essences with the glycerin or other binding agents at about room temperature or at as low a temperature as possible to minimize the loss of such compounds. For example, temperatures in the neighborhood of 50°C will result in significant loss in the case of delicate fruit flavours.

Example 1: The following mixture was formulated: 31.0% of glucose solids (dry); 2.5% of maltodextrins (10 to 25% dextrose content, preferably 10%); 64.0% of sucrose; and 2.0 to 5.0% (preferably 2.5%) of water. The mixture was heated to between 140° and 145°C and maintained at this temperature for 5 minutes. Hot water was added in portions equal to from 2 to 4% by weight of the molten sugar polymers mix.

The water must be hot, 60° to 80°C of higher, because cold water would set the polymer surface into a glass-like solid and further mixing would be impossible. The mixture was stirred continuously and the hot water added until a soluble solids level of from 85 to 95% (preferably no higher than 90%) was obtained. The mixture was then cooled to about 30°C before the following flavouring mixture was added thereto: 2.0% lemon oil; 2% glycerin; 2% ethyl alcohol; and 0.1% emulsifier. Addition of the foregoing and admixture thereof with the sugar polymers base was continued until the aroma of lemon oil was faintly apparent.

It was found that in the foregoing experiment, the percentages of the sugars could be varied widely as follows: 40 to 70% (preferably 60 to 70%) sucrose; 0 to 50% (preferably 0 to 10%) maltodextrins; and 10 to 50% (preferably 25 to 35%) glucose.

Example 2: A sugar polymers base was prepared as in Example 1, the soluble solids level being adjusted to between 85 and 90%. The mixture was cooled to 30°C and 2% water-soluble strawberry essence (10,000 fold) mixed with 1 to 2% glycerin was added. The mixing was continued until the strawberry aroma disappeared. An artificial strawberry flavour could also be used, instead of strawberry essence, if required.

Example 3: A sugar polymers base was again prepared as in Example 1, the soluble solids level adjusted to between 85 and 90% and the mixture cooled to about 30°C. After cooling, coffee essence (0.5%) and glycerin (0.5%) were added to the mixture.

The stability of the flavoured polymer candy fillings of this process is found to be good and it is possible, by using this process, to encapsulate flavouring materials at levels much higher than normally used for candy fillings. At lower encapsulation levels the flavour losses are still less than with conventional processes.

## Coating for Jujubes

Jujubes have the disadvantage of being badly protected against effects of the outside atmosphere even if they are packed in small bags which are more or less tight. In fact it is easy to notice that after a preservation period, a loss of the water and of the volatile flavourings on the surface of the jujubes occurs, which results in their progressive hardening.

J.E.M. Canonne; U.S. Patent 4,010,283; March 1, 1977; assigned to Soreat SA, Switzerland has deviced a coating method for improving preservation and over-aromatization of confectionery articles having a base of gum arabic which comprises moulding the articles in suitable molds having the desired shape, drying the articles and immediately refrigerating them at a low temperature to give them a rigid consistency, coating these refrigerated articles in at least one step by a varnish, subjecting the articles to fresh air at a temperature lower than 20°C to dry the varnish, and then coating with coats of sugar syrup dried thereon to constitute a sugar coating of a noticeable thickness.

The gum article used as a base is made according to the usual method of melting and flowing of a syrup of sugar and gum arabic or substitute with addition of flavourings and, if required, some tartaric or citric acid and glucose.

In the cases of formulas for pharmaceutical and dietetic use, the active principles are incorporated in this syrup. The gum article is then poured into starch molds of a suitable shape which permits obtaining confectionery products of various shapes, but generally in the shape of a truncated cone, cylinder or sphere. The articles which are obtained are then dried and refrigerated immediately at about 5°C in order to give them a rigid consistency, which is an important condition to obtain a coating of good quality. This coating is performed in a sugar coating centrifugal machine. The articles, then cold and of a given shape, are poured in one or several centrifugal machines in which they immediately have a coating, called "varnishing." with a varnish constituted or an alcoholic solution of edible shellac.

The shellac used is typically of a whitened and unwaxed quality found under the form of lemellas. This shellac comes from countries of the Far East and is made from secretions of certain insects on a variety of fig trees. The varnish coating must be very thick and, generally at least double that of the coating of the usual sugar-coated pill since its function is to stop, by an impassable barrier, the moisture and the flavourings contained in the core constituted by the gum article.

Besides, this coating forms, around the article, a rigid inseparable shell due to the hardness of the article which comes our from the refrigerated tunnel where there is a temperature within the ranges of a few °C, and lower than 5° or 6°C. This is a very important feature since it is necessary to prevent any subsequent contraction of the article, which could cause a cracking of the coating. Drying of the varnished shell should be done in the presence of fresh air and at a temperature lower than 20°C.

The sugar coating step properly so called is made with non-aromatized or non-flavoured syrup used for the first coating; this non-aromatized syrup then is replaced by an aromatized or flavoured syrup. The sugar coating step can be made either with a coloured or an uncoloured syrup, which may be added with a concentrated alcoholic solution of flavourings which may typically be within the range of 1 to 2% by weight of flavourings in the syrup. The syrup is sprayed and then dried in successive coatings. The first coatings and the last coating preferably use a mere sugar syrup without flavouring since they are above all protective and insulating coatings. However, the intermediary coatings which represent the major portion of the article are made with the flavoured or aromatized syrup. The coating is increased sufficiently to reach a weight which can be, for example, of 2 to 2.20 g for a basic core of 1.20 to 1.25 g.

## Gumdrops Containing Potato Starch

Various gelled confections take advantage of the ability of starch to form a gel in a system containing sucrose and corn syrup in addition to the starch. Exemplary of such confections are gem-centered candies, gum slices, gumdrops, jelly beans and the like. In making such gum confections it has been conventional practice to use an acid-modified, thin-boiling starch generally derived from corn or wheat. The earlier prior art batch-type procedures were very time-consuming and required a rather long boiling time in order to evaporate sufficient water so that the mixture could be poured into the forms in the moulding tray where, after holding for a period of one to several days, the confection was ready for planning or sanding. More recently, the proper amounts of water, sugar, syrup and starch have been cooked under pressure by steam injection or with a heat exchanger to reduce the cooking time and to enable the process to operate on a continuous basis. Regardless of the cooking method, the subsequent moulding procedures usually still involve holding the cooked syrup mix in the moulds for more than a day to obtain proper drying and gel formation. U.S. Patent 3,446,628 gives procedures for making gel confections in which starch is used as a congealing agent. The patent suggests that the moulding time can be decreased by the use of thin-boiling cereal starches which have been solvent extracted to reduce the content of fat below about 0.3% on a dry starch basis, but claims that potato starch cannot be used in the production of quick-setting gum confections, even though it is low in fat and contains the proper amount of amylose.

## HARD CANDIES

### Using a Tubular Evaporator to Make Toffee

In a well-know process, toffee is made with sugar, glucose, milk, fat, salt and flavouring and these ingredients are mixed to form a syrup. The syrup is then heated to about 200oF, while stirring, whereby the sugar dissolves in the moisture of the milk and the glucose. The next step is to place this processed mixture in an evaporator which comprises an open vessel surrounded by a steam jacket in order to drive off a desired amount of the moisture content. The process described enables batches of toffee to be produced. It should be noted that the mixture concerned is heat sensitive in that it will degrade if held for a significant period at elevated temperatures.

Similar difficulties have been found when toffee is produced in other ways, such as by continuous evaporation in a failing film evaporator. P. Antonelli and R.H. Seager; U.S. Patent 3,796,808; March 12, 1974; assigned to Tullamore SA, Switzerland propose a method of continuously evaporating a liquid from a heat sensitive liquid material, in which the material is passed through at least one passage having heated walls, the spacing between such walls being so small that the liquid vapour bubbles formed within the material serve to maintain a foam of vapour and material throughout the cross section of each passage.

As shown in Figure the heat exchanger comprises a cylindrical jacket 10 having steam inlet and outlet ports 11, 12. The jacket contains a nest of tubes 13 (55 in all) carried between end plates 14, 15 to which they are welded. The jacket is welded to the end plates. Annular plates 16, 17 serve to secure conical inlet and outlet nozzles 18, 19 to the ends of the jacket by way of flanges formed on the nozzles. The annular plates are bolted to the end plates. In this example, the tubes have an internal diameter of three-sixteenth of an inch and a length of three feet. The overall diameter of the jacket is four and one-half inches. These dimensions are suitable for material made up of the following constituents: 56.5% sugar/ glucose (1:1.2); 7% milk solids, nonfat; 20% fat; 0.5% salt; and 16% moisture.

Figure : Tubular Evaporator for Preparation of Toffee

a.

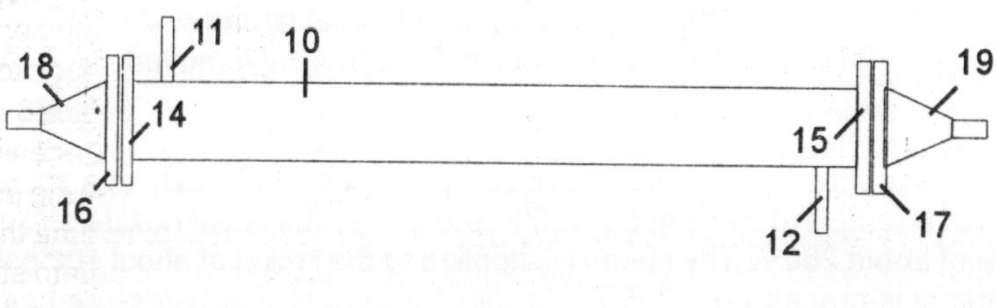


(continued)

**Figure : (Continued)**

*b.*

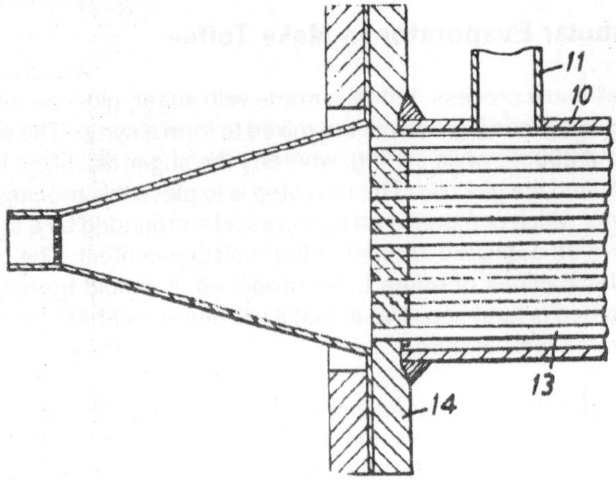


*c.*

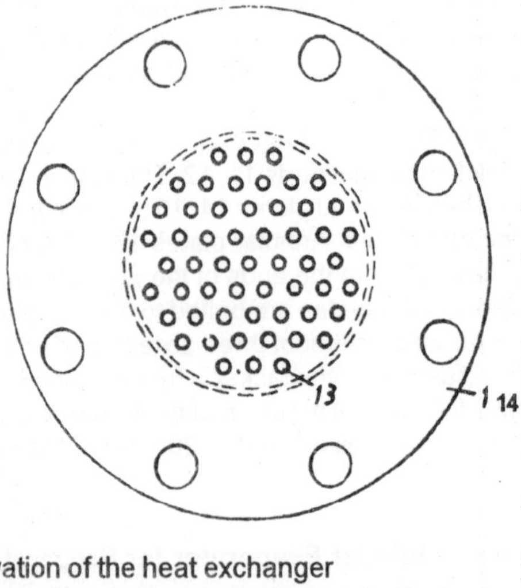


(a) Elevation of the heat exchanger
(b) Part sectional view along the longitudinal axis one end of the heat exchanger on an enlarged scale
(c) End elevation with the inlet nozzle removed

The mixture is fed by a gear pump into the inlet nozzle at a constant rate and at a temperature of about 180°F and leaves the outlet nozzle at a temperature of about 260°F. The steam is supplied to the jacket at about 100 psi and the material is processed at 8.5 lb per minute, the inlet feed pressure being about 40 psi, the material at the outlet being at atmospheric pressure. The material flows through each tube in less than one second.

The product is tested by the well-known “crack test” and the temperature of the material is adjusted to obtain the required characteristics of the product. The temperature is adjusted by varying the pressure of the steam supply by a suitable valve (not shown). The tube diameter is critical and a particular upper limit of diameter can be defined for a given set of condition, such that the flow which takes place within the tube is mass flow of steam and liquid mixture rather than the partial or completely separate flow of liquid film on the tube walls with steam flow along the tube centre, which would result from the use of a larger bore. In other words, the bubbles of vapour, in this instance steam, remain intact and do not separate from the mixture. By remaining intact the foam of steam and the remaining material is maintained throughout the cross section of each tube. Thus a considerable turbulence is formed within each tube, and bubbles of steam act in effect as pistons which sweep along the tube from and inlet to the outlet, cleaning the remaining material from the tube walls, so that there is no tendency to burn.

The mechanical construction is simple, there being no moving parts in the tubes to create unreliability. While the tubes are preferably all located in a common heating chamber, it is possible to surround each tube separately with its individual heating chamber. For most purposes in which moisture is evaporated from boiled sugar confectionery, the diameter of the tubes will be from 0.15 to 0.4 inch, with a length of 2 to 4 feet. The tubes may be made of glass, stainless steel, copper or other material.

While the process has been specifically described with reference to the removal of moisture from liquid mixtures of ingredients during the manufacture of boiled sugar confectionery, such as toffee, it is not restricted to this use. It can be applied to any process in which it is necessary to remove a liquid from a mixture in which the other ingredients of the mixture would degrade during the heating necessary to effect the evaporation to remove the liquid.

## Containing Low DE Starch Hydrolysate

Hard candy is a confection which has been formed into desired shape and size, and generally, is composed of sucrose and corn syrup with or without added flavour and colour. Most generally, hard candy contains less than about 2% by weight moisture. This low moisture content is necessary to provide the candy with reasonable storage stability. If the moisture content is significantly increased, the candy becomes sticky on the exterior. Such candy cannot be readily packaged in jars or similar containers since individaul candies will stick to each other, as well as to the walls of the container, making removal practically impossible.

Wrapping of candy having a moisture content above about 2% by weight similarly present problems. The wrapper of such candy typically adheres tenaciously to the candy. It is a common and frustrating experience not to be able to separate such candy from the wrapper. To avoid the various described problems, candy manufacturers process the candy to very low moisture contents, such as those well below 1% by weight. Such processing requires elevated temperatures, long cooking times, as well as the removal of water under vacuum. Long cooking times at elevated temperatures, however, cause the formation of colour in the product. This colour formation is a major problem in the manufacture of clear, white candy of good storage stability.

H.E. Horn and M.M. Godzicki; U.S. Patent 3,826,857; July 30, 1974; assigned to CPE International Inc. described a process which provides a hard candy having a relatively high moisture content, but excellent storage stability, improved resistance to moisture pick-up and which does not require stringent processing conditions, and which has a high gloss. These advantages are realized in a hard candy containing at least about 10% by weight of a starch hydrolysate having a D.E. (dextrose equivalent) from about 5 to 25 and a descriptive ratio of at least about 2.0 and containing from about 4 to about 8% by weight moisture.

The starch hydrolysates used in the formulas for making the hard candy are made by subjecting a source of starch to enzyme or acid treatment or a combination of both. It is important that the starch hydrolysate have a relatively low D.E. of say less than about 25 and most preferably in the range from 5 to 15. Starch hydrolysates of this type have been found to be excellent agents useful; in reducing moisture pick-up of normally hygroscopic edible foods whereas use of other hydrolysates having a D.E. substantially outside this range results in inferior hard candies which still show a tendency to entrap moisture, thus becoming sticky.

The starch hydrolysates preferred for use in the process are made by any number of specific methods. In one method a starch such as a waxy starch is treated with a single enzyme application of bacterial alpha-amylase. More specifically, an aqueous slurry of a waxy starch, having a solids content less than 50%, is subjected to the hydrolytic action of bacterial alpha-amylase under suitable conditions of fermentation to produce a starch hydrolysate.

The hydrolysate may be further characterized as having the sum of the percentages (dry basis) of saccharides therein with a degree of polymerization of 1 to 6 divided by the D.E. to provide a ratio greater than about 2.0. This ratio is referred to as the characteristic or descriptive ratio.

This product may also be made via a number of other routes. For example, a mixture of starch and water having a solids content less than 50% may be first subjected to the hydrolytic action of a bacterial alpha-amylase followed by a high-temperature heating step to solubilize any unsolubilized starch. Since this temperature tends to inactivate the enzymes, it is then necessary to cool the solubilized partial hydrolysate and subject it to a second hydrolysis by treatment with additional bacterial alpha-amylase to obtain the final starch hydrolysate.

A third method of making the preferred class of low D.E. starch hydrolysates consists of hydrolyzing a mixture of starch and water by the action of acid to reach a D.E. between about 5 and about 15. The partial hydrolysate is subsequently subjected to the action of bacterial alpha-amylase to obtain a starch hydrolysate having a D.E. of from about 10 to about 25. A particularly preferred starch hydrolysate useful in this process has the following specifications: moisture content about 5% maximum, D.E. 10 to 13, pH 4.5 to 5.5 at 10% solids, average bulk density 28 to 35 pounds per cubic foot.

In order to make the hard candy composition, it has been found necessary to intimately admix a sugar constituent, water, and the starch hydrolysate to obtain a homogeneous mixture which, when subjected to a heat treatment, forms a solution. The mixture is heated to an elevated temperature to form a solution and to drive off sufficient water to form a composition containing from about 4 to about 8% moisture. It is desirable to heat the mixture to a temperature of less than about 300°F, preferably from about 250° to about 300°F. At this point the solution is cooled sufficiently (to less than 240°F) to permit forming of a plastic composition (candy dough) so that it may be kneaded, pulled, molded or otherwise formed as in conventional hard candy manufacturing procedures. Upon cooling to room temperature, substantially nonhygroscopic hard candy is obtained that is typically characteristic of the treatment that it has received.

In a typical example, 30 parts of sucrose and 30 parts of 10 D.E. starch hydrolysate are mixed with 12 parts of water to which is added 40 parts of corn syrup. (All parts and percentages are by weight.) The ingredients are then heated to a temperature of about 270°F whereupon the substance exhibits a solids content of 95% and then the molten mixture is allowed to cool to about 200° to 220°F, thereby forming a plastic composition. the plastic composition is then moulded or otherwise treated and allowed to harden to form a hard candy of high moisture content and excellent resistance to moisture pick-up.

# Chapter - 24

# *Frozen Desserts*

## CREAM-TYPE PRODUCTS

### Frozen Thick Shake

The process described by R.P. Witzig; U.S. Patent 3,914,440; October 21, 1975; assigned to General Foods Corporation relates to the formulation and processing of frozen aqueous thick shakes which are characteristically possessed of ice particles and have a sufficient plasticity to permit the emulsion to be spooned or otherwise manipulated for mixing with milk or other like aqueous medium preparatory to stirring to form a shake of cold impact.

This kind of stabilized shake is made possible by the use in combination of xanthan gum, a soluble alginate and a polyvalent cation source which is operative to complex with the algin to form a water-insoluble alginate. Shakes so stabilized have been found to result in a product with improved texture, flavour and resistance to separation under abusive frozen food warehouse and distribution temperature conditions.

Whereas milk-solids algins of the type used in the ice cream industry (sodium, potassium or ammonium alginate) result in a slight improvement of texture and resistance to phase separation and whereas use of xanthan gum alone results in an icy texture and slight improvement also in resistance to separation, the use in combination of these two gelling agents under conditions operative to cause the algin to complex to an insoluble form imparts an optimum texture and resistance to phase separation under abusive storage conditions.

In formulating the shake, which will be understood to those skilled in the art as consisting of a mixture of discrete water ice crystals in a fat-phase and a sweetening sugar-phase that has been subjected to some degree of agitation and consequent overrun through air inclusion, a pasteurized batch containing the xanthan gum alginate stabilizer will be charged to a homogenizer at a pressure in excess of 3,000 psig and thereby reduce fat particles to as discrete a size as practical and most preferably to one having a high population of globules whose numerical majority is less than 50 μ. Among the major characterizing ingredients of the stabilizing composition are a corn syrup solids digest (enzymic) having a high dextrose equivalency, say, between 20 and 60, sucrose and a fat having preferably a sharp plastic range at about body temperature. These major characterizing agents will have added thereto other functional ingredients such as sorbitol and glycerol which further impart spoonability and a plasticizing property to the composition while also serving to significantly depress the product freezing point as ultimately packaged. The other characterizing ingredients of the composition will be flavouring and colouring.

Included in the water-soluble phase of the composition will be an amount of known sequestering salt, e.g., a monovalent cation salt such as an ammonium, potassium or sodium salt of an organic or inorganic acid such as sodium phosphate, sodium citrate which are also operative in controlling gelling alginate under the processing conditions used to prepare the shake; preferred sequestering salts are molecularly dehydrated phosphates like sodium hexametaphosphate and tetrasodium pyrophosphate.

Sodium alginate will be greatly aided in its functional effect by a source of polyvalent cations such as nonfat dry milk solids or sodium caseinates which provide a nutritious protein source and contribute to and support emulsification of the aqueous phase; alternatives to the dry skim milk solids and sodium caseinates will be the polyvalent salts or acid salts of organic or inorganic acids such as calcium gluconate, calcium tartrate, etc.

The fat preferably will be a hydrogenated nonlauric vegetable fat and typically one having a melting point of body temperature, say 100°F plus or minus 5°F, the solids index of the fat having a sharp plastic range when it achieves this temperature, at above 90°F and thus the solids index being rapidly reduced and providing a cooling effect on mouth feel when the product is eventually consumed.

In accordance with its more preferred aspects, xanthan gum will be employed at a level of approximately 0.1% of the total composition. Likewise, the alginate will be used preferably at a level of about 0.3%.

The shake system will preferably have a neutral pH in the order of 5.0 to 7.0 although lower pHs may be practical where certain fruit flavoured shakes are formulated and where algin gum functionality is fostered.

The weight percent of the sugar phase of the total composition is commonly in the range between 15 and 25%, solids of the fat base being 5 to 25% by weight of the total composition.

Example: In a typical processing operation the following formulation is employed:

| ***Ingredients*** | ***Parts by Weight*** |
|---|---|
| Water | 55.8 |
| Corn syrup | 23.8 |
| Wecotop A (plastic fat) | 8.9 |
| Sugar | 4.6 |
| Nonfat dry mix | 2.0 |
| Sorbitol | 2.0 |
| Glycerol | 2.0 |
| Xanthan gum | 0.1 |
| Salt (NaCl) | 0.2 |
| Tween Mos 280 VS | 0.1 |
| Sodium alginate | 0.351 |
| Tetrasodium pyrophosphate | 0.03 |
| Flavour | 0.3 |
| Colour | 0.003 |

Water at 140° to 150°F is added to a mix tank. Enzymatically converted corn syrup (33 DE) is added to the tank under continuous agitation whereafter fat maintained at 135° to 145°F in the liquid states is added followed by addition of the surfactant (Tween) emulsifier (mono-and diglycerides of an edible fat) and a polysorbate. With continued agitation freezing point depressants sorbitol and glycerol are added thereafter. At this point the mixture is an essentially emulsified mixture of fat and sugars in solution.

Thereafter the functional ingredients of this process are added as part of a dry mix, to wit, the sodium alginate and the xanthan gum together with sugar, non-fat dry milk solids, phosphate, sodium chloride, flavours and colours. These ingredients are mixed for a minimum period of five minutes or until the ingredients are all dispersed whereupon they are at a temperature of at least 140°F and not above 180°F. At this point, the liquid suspension is pasteurized under commercial sterilizing or pasteurizing conditions by being subjected to an elevated temperature of at least 160°F for a period in excess of ten minutes and ranging broadly between ten and twenty minutes depending upon the elevated pasteurizing temperature.

At this point, the batch is immediately charged to a two-stage Manton Gaulin homogenizer operating at a homogenization pressure in excess of 3,000 psig and typically in the neighborhood of 4,000 psig in the first stage and 500 psig in the second stage, thereby causing an emulsification of the fat globules to an extent such that the majority thereof may be viewed by spectral photometric means known to skilled art workers as less than 25 $\mu$ and a median particle size in the order of 10 $\mu$.

The homogenized emulsion formulation is immediately charged to a plate cooler wherein it is cooled to 35° to 50°F, preferably 40° to 45°F preparatory to being charged to a scrape surface heat exchanger wherein two conditions are achieved:

(a) the water in the emulsion is partially crystallized to produce dis crete water ice crystals in an amount (5 to 20%) sufficient to provide organoleptic cold impact in the final product (15%); and

(b) the material is caused to undergo a degree of overrun achieved by air injection into the scrape surface heat exchanger such that the product has an overrun between 5 and 25% and typically 10 to 15% of the original volume charged to the heat exchanger.

Generally, the formulation will typically have a freezing point ranging between 18° and 22°F, the optimal target being 19° to 21°F. The emulsion and shake produced by the heat exchange operation described herein will then be charged at a temperature below 20°F to a filler wherein the stabilized slush-shake system will be packaged and eventually frozen, say in a blast freezer which freezes the packaged composition to a centre temperature of 0°F or below.

The product so packaged can be distributed at wholesale and retail and will be uniquely characterized by its resistance to separation and the abusive storage temperatures which are commonly experienced and may range anywhere from 0°F to 40°F, the more common medium abusive temperature encountered being 10° to 15°F for frozen distribution.

## Home Frozen Dessert Requiring No Agitation

There are many difficulties inherent in the preparation of frozen desserts which are made by a process employing static freezing. Static freezing refers to the process step of freezing without concurrent agitation or aeration. Generally, frozen desserts made by static freezing do not compare in consistency and overall appearance to conventional frozen desserts made by the normal commercial process which involves agitation during the freezing process. Ordinary, if frozen dessert formulations are not agitated during freezing, large ice crystals are formed. Also, the fat base will tend to separate from the other components of the mix yielding a non-homogeneous product. Such results adversely affect texture, dryness, uniformity of appearance of the frozen dessert thereby affecting the overall quality of the product.

However, J.A. Hellyer, R.G. Kess and P. Seiden; U.S. Patent 3,949,102; April 6, 1976; assigned to The Procter & Gamble Company have discovered that a high quality frozen dessert can be convenientiy made in the home by employing the following method on next page:

**(A)** Making an emulsion by the steps of

(1) melting from about 0.5 to 18 parts of a first emulsifier selected from the group consisting of edible polyglycerol fatty acid esters and edible sorbitan fatty acid esters, with from 0.5 to 15% by weight of the first emulsifier of a second emulsifier which is an anionic surfactant,

(2) dispersing without aeration the melt of step (1) with high shear and cooling to below the crystal melting point of the melt into an aqueous medium of at least twice the weight of the melt; and

(3) emulsifying from 15 to 80% of a triglyceride fat or oil into the aqueous dispersion of (2); the emulsion having a water activity of less than 0.80;

**(B)** Mixing from 10 to 35% of the emulsion of step (A), from 10 to 35% of saccharides, from 7 to 18% of nonfat milk solids and from 35 to 65% of water;

**(C)** Aerating the mixture of step (B)

**(D)** Freezing the aerated mixture of step (C).

Additional ingredients such as stabilizers, flavours, colouring agents, etc. can be added to the frozen dessert product by incorporating the ingredients into the emulsion or the mixture of ingredients prior to or during the aeration step.

The resulting frozen dessert comprises from 7 to 18% milk solids, from 10 to 40% saccharides, from 0.2 to 2% of a primary emulsifier selected from the group consisting of edible polyglycerol fatty acid esters and edible sorbitan fatty acid esters, from 0.5 to 15% by weight of the primary emulsifier of a secondary emulsifier which is an anionic surfactant, from 45 to 65% water, and from 5 to 25% of a triglyceride fat or oil.

Polyglycerol esters suitable for use in the process have from 2 to 3 glycerol units metal salts of fatty carbosylates, sulfates, and sulfonates, half salts of dicarboxylic fatty acid esters and salts of fatty acid lactylates having from 8 to 20 carbon atoms in the anionic moiety.

Triglyceride fats or oils are employed in these frozen desserts to contribute to the smooth taste, minimize the formation of ice crystals, and to give the full, rich, creamy eating characteristic reminiscent of good commercial ice cream. The fat or oil contributes to the body and melting resistance of the frozen dessert and produces a smoothness of texture and consistency that is difficult to obtain by any other means. From 5 to 25% of fats may be used; the exact amount is not critical and can be minimized to obtain a low fat frozen dessert which might be desirable for dietary reasons. However, if the fat proportion of the frozen dessert is reduced, there must be a corresponding increase in the other ingredients contributing to the total solids content of the dessert in order that the frozen dessert product will have a solids content of from 35 to 55%.

Examples of suitable fats and oils include: cotton seed oil, soyabean oil, corn oil, peanut oil, olive oil, coconut oil, etc. These fats and oils may be partially or substantially hydrogenated to improve their melting behaviour and keeping quality. The nonfat milk solids which are used in the compositions of this process are the solids of skim milk and include proteins, mineral matter, and milk sugar.

The preferred saccharides for use in this process is sucrose; however, sucrose can be mixed with or replaced by other saccharides such as dextrose, fructose, maltose, and corn syrup in dry or syrup form or by artificial sweeteners such as saccharin, the cyclamates, etc. It has been found that the most desirable level of sweetness and texture may be obtained by employing sucrose in combination with a sugar which is less sweet such as dextrose, maltose or low-conversion corn syrup to obtain a relatively great proportion of sugar at a level of sweetness less that which would result from the use of sucrose alone.

The frozen dessert product may also contain additional ingredients such as lower chain monohydric and polyhydric alcohols, starches, gums or colloidal carbohydrate stabilizers, and alkali and alkaline earth metal salts of organic and inorganic acids. In addition, flavouring ingredients, pH buffering salts, antioxidants, and preservatives may be incorporated into the final dessert product. Additional emulsifiers may also be incorporated provided they do not cause instability of the primary emulsifier.

It is a particular advantage of this process that the ingredients can be conveniently to the consumer in such a way as to make it especially convenient for the consumer to make consistently good frozen dessert products. For example, it is contemplated that a manufacturer provide a kit of two packages for sale to the consumer. The first kit contains an emulsion made in accordance with step (A) of the process. In a preferred embodiment of the process, the preemulsion contains from 5 to 20% levulose, from 5 to 45% sucrose, from 2 to 6% of triglycerol monostearate, from 0.02 to 0.24% sodium oleate, from 30 to 60% of triglyceride fat having less than 10% solids at 37°C, from 0.01 to 0.25% of a stabilizer selected from the group consisting of xanthan gum, guar gum, hydroxypropyl cellulose, sodium carboxymethylcelloulose and from 5 to 25% water. The second packet comprises from 60 to 85% sugar and from 15 to 30% of nonfat milk solids.

It is contemplated that the consumer would purchase the two packets and then proceed to mix the ingredients of the two mixes with milk or water and then aerate by whipping with a home mixer and place in the freezing compartment of a home refrigerator or freezer and subject to static freezing.

Example: 58.3 g of triglycerol monostearate (Paniplus 504 from the Paniplus Company) was melted with 0.87 g of sodium oleate by heating to a temperature of 104°C. This melt was then placed in a stainless steel beaker with

767.4 g of high fructose corn syrup (Isomerose 100 from the Clintol Corn Processing Company) having a temperature of 60°C and subjected to high shear. The sheared mix was cooled to 32°C. Then 813.8 g of a triglyceride oil (Crisco Oil from the Procter & Gamble Company) at a temperature of 32°C was blended into the emulsifier-water dispersion and subjected to additional high shear. The resulting product water or milk, nonfat milk solids for use, when mixed with additional water or milk, nonfat milk solids and saccharides, to make frozen desserts having good eating quality characteristics, texture, appearance and flavour.

## Multipurpose Whipped Dessert

J.J. Jonas; U.S. Patent 4,012,533; March 15, 1977; assigned to Kraft, Inc. describes a multipurpose whipped dessert which may be consumed in the frozen state as an ice cream-type product, or alternately in the thawed state as a whipped topping.

Several embodiments are described: a unitary whipped and aerated frozen dessert prepared by whipping together an aqueous fat emulsion and an aqueous protein emulsion and freezing the aerated mixture; an unwhipped dessert mix in which a fat emulsion, dried or liquid, and a protein emulsion, dried or liquid, are packaged separately or in admixture and sold as a unit to the consumer who reconstitutes the dried emulsions, if necessary, and whips the two emulsions simultaneously in a suitable mixer; and an unwhipped protein emulsion, dry or liquid, which may be reconstituted, if necessary, mixed with a suitable whipped topping, for example, a thawed frozen whipped topping, and whipped to provide a multipurpose whipped dessert which can be consumed in the thawed state as a whipped topping or which can be frozen and consumed as an ice cream-type product.

A fat emulsion that is useful in forming this multipurpose whipped dessert has the composition in the table on the following page. All percentages are percent by weight unless specified otherwise.

| | *Percent* |
|---|---|
| Fat | 20-40 |
| Protein | 0.5-2 |
| Sweetener | 20-40 |
| Emulsifiers and stabilizers | 0.3-0.7 |
| Water | balance |
| Total solids | 40-60 |

The whipped topping formed from the topping emulsion, when whipped alone, should have an overrun of at least 180%, preferably between 190 and 240%, and a foam stiffness preferably between about 17 and 24 RVT units. Overrun is defined as (weight of unit volume of unwhipped mix/weight of unit volume of whipped topping - 1) x 100, and the foam stiffness measurement is defined as scale unit reading on a Brookfield viscometer equipped with a D-type spindle, run at a rotational speed of 25 rpm at 45°F, with heliopath suspension.

The fat component of the fat emulsion may be any edible triglyceride having desired organoleptic properties when incorporated in the multipurpose whipped dessert. Generally the fat is a hydrogenated vegetable oil, or blend of vegetable oils having a melting point within the range of 91° to 96°F.

The aqueous protein emulsion that is combined with the topping emulsion to provide a multipurpose whipped dessert has the following composition:

| | *Percent* |
|---|---|
| Fat | 0-15 |
| Protein | 3-10 |
| Carbohydrate | 20-30 |
| Emulsifiers | 0.05-0.20 |
| Stabilizers | 0.4-0.8 |
| Water | balance |
| Total solids | 30-40 |

The protein emulsion, when whipped alone to provide an aerated foam, which is referred to herein as a protein puree, has an overrun of at least 150%, preferably between 160 and 180%, and a low foam stiffness of at least 2.5 RVT units, preferably between 3 and 6 RVT units.

In a preferred embodiment, all or a major portion of the protein is derived from a milk source, and, more particularly, is derived from fresh cheese curd. The milk protein may be replaced by sodium caseinate or egg albumen. However, from an organoleptic point of view, and from a manufacturing point of view, it is generally preferred that a major portion of the protein be derived from a milk source. In the connection, the milk source may be whole milk, skim milk, nonfat dry milk, condensed skim milk or the like.

The fresh cheese curd may be cream cheese, creamed or uncreamed cottage cheese, or quark, which is an acid coagulated milk protein curd recovered by centrifugation. In as much as cottage cheese and quark have a particulate texture as obtained from the cheese-making process, these protein sources are homogenized to a smooth texture before admixture in the protein mix. While each of these fresh cheese curds provides a desirable protein puree, the presence of butterfat in cream cheese is considered preferable because of the improved organoleptic properties of the resulting whipped dessert.

In a preferred embodiment the cream cheese is processed to disrupt the body of the cream cheese before adding to the protein emulsion. This may be accomplished by subjecting the curd to shear as by mixing in a swept-wall heat exchanger prior to setting up of the cream cheese in the cheese-making process or by subjecting conventionally prepared cream cheese to chopping in a suitable chopper such as a Seydelman meat chopper prior to addition to the protein mix.

The protein emulsion further includes a mixture of stabilizers which includes at least two gums, one of which is from a marine source and one of which is derived from a vegetable source or a synthetic gum. A particularly desirable combination of gums is carrageenan, alginate, carboxymethylcellulose, and guar gum.

Example: A vanilla flavoured multipurpose whipped dessert was prepared with the following compositions for the finished product, fat emulsion, and protein emulsion, all data expressed as percentages by weight of the intermediates or it the finished product.

**Vanilla Flavoured Whipped Dessert**

| | *Finished Product* | *Fat Emulsion* | *Protein Emulsion* |
|---|---|---|---|
| | | *(percent)* | |
| Fortified skim milk* | 35.24 | - | 58.75 |
| Water | 19.18 | 47.10 | 0.57 |
| Soluble carbohydrates | 21.15 | 20.93 | 21.30 |
| Hydrogenated coconut fat (92°F) | 11.96 | 29.90 | - |
| Cream cheese | 8.59 | - | 14.31 |
| Sodium caseinate | 0.49 | 1.22 | - |
| Phosphate salts | 0.20 | 0.20 | 0.20 |
| Polyoxyethylene sorbitan monoester, sorbitan monostearate, lecithin | 0.21 | 0.52 | - |
| Propylene glycol monostearate, sodium stearoyl-2-lactylate in water (10% solids) | 2.10 | - | 3.50 |
| Gums: | | | |
| sodium alginate, carboxymethyl-cellulose | 0.26 | - | 0.44 |
| calcium carrageenan, guar gum | 0.11 | 0.07 | 0.13 |
| Flavouring and colourings | 0.51 | 0.06 | 0.80 |
| **Total** | **100.00** | **100.00** | **100.00** |

*1.0% NFMS and 1.5% condensed skim milk added.

The fat emulsion is prepared by melting the fat with the lecithin and fat-soluble colourings in a scraper agitated kettle. The sodium caseinate is added when the batch temperature is 135° to 140°F and the mixture agitated to ensure complete dispersion of the caseinate. The polyoxyethylene sorbitan monoester and sorbitan monostearate emulsifiers are added at 140°F, followed by the addition of hot water (140°F). The resulting oil-in-water emulsion is further agitated and the temperature raised to 150°F.

At this time, a dry blend of the phosphate salts, calcium carrageenan, guar gum, and the soluble carbohydrates is added. After complete dispersion of the dry additives, the emulsion is pasteurized for 20 minutes at 160°F. The flavourings are introduced after the completion of the pasteurization.

The fat emulsion is then homogenized in a two-stage homogenizer at 4,500 psig pressure in the first stage and at 500 psig in the second stage and then cooled in a plate cooler to 35° to 40°F. The fat emulsion is then held for 5 to 12 hours minimum time at 35° to 40°F to ensure proper fat crystallization. The ratio of crystalline to liquid fat is 80:20. 99.5% of the particles of the emulsion are smaller than 1.28 μ in the finished fat emulsion as determined by a Coulter counter.

The protein emulsion is prepared by heating the fortified skim milk to 120° to 125°F in a jacketed kettle under agitation. At 125°F, a dry blend of the soluble carbohydrates, calcium carrageenan, sodium alginate, carboxymethylcellulose, and guar gum is added to the milk, and after a proper dispersion is obtained, the phosphate salts are added. After the phosphate salts addition, homogenized cream cheese is dispersed in the heated liquid mixture. The mixture is then pasteurized at 160°F. The protein emulsion is then cooled to 80°F for the further addition of the hydrated emulsifiers and the flavourings.

After the fat and protein emulsions are prepared a blend of the two emulsions is prepared in a ratio of 60 parts of protein emulsion to 40 parts of fat emulsion. The resulting temperature of the blend is approximately 60°F. This blend serves as feed for the whipping equipment. The blending tank preferably is equipped with scraper blade agitators which are operated at slow speed to avoid air incorporation. The blend of the emulsions is composed of colloidal particles of which 87.12% are smaller than 1.28 μ.

Batch-wise whipping of the blend of emulsions is effected through use of a planetary mixer using a wire whip. A jacketed mixing bowl was used and slush ice was maintained in the jacket. At a medium speed setting, a whipped product having an overrun of from 150 to 200% was obtained in from 3 to 6 minutes. 37.19% of the colloidal particles are smaller than 1.6 μ.

For commercial production the whipping is carried out in a suitably designed continuous ice cream freezer. The air delivery system, the inlet pump and the outlet pump deliveries are synchronized to 164 to 180 gallons per hour finished product output with an inlet feed temperature of 63° to 64°F, and an outlet temperature of 46° to 50°F. Air pressure in the freezer is 24 to 25.5 psig. An overrun of 170 to 175% is achieved and 78.75% of the colloidal particles are smaller than 1.28 $\mu$. The density of the recovered foam is 92 to 94 grams per 8 fluid ounces which is equivalent to 3.25 to 3.32 pounds per gallon. The product is packed in suitable containers and frozen at -20oF for 24 hours. The whipped dessert is then stored at 0°F.

The whipped dessert can be consumed by spooning or scooping in the 0° to 10°F temperature range, in which case it simulates ice cream. It will hold its form without significant liquefaction and syneresis at room temperature for 4 to 6 hours. If the product is thawed at 35°F, its frozen structure gradually softens to a soft creamy consistency which is similar in texture and peak-forming capability to whipped topping for use on fruits, cakes, and may be used for various food recipes as is, or refrozen. The storability of the product in thawed state is 7 to 21 days.

Functionally, the whipped dessert differs from ice cream essentially because of its very slow melt-down, syneresis resistance, and refreezability. It differs from the conventional dessert toppings because these products, in the frozen state, are hard and nonspoonable. Its mouth feel, both in the frozen and thawed state is creamy, with none of the greasiness of toppings.

The storability of the product under programmed temperature cycling in the 0° to 25°F range is 3 to 4 weeks without significant ice crystal development. Conventional ice cream under the same conditions develops ice crystals in 4 to 7 days.

## COATING

### Chocolate

A very substantial proportion of all ice cream consumed reaches the consumer in the form of a small ice cream bar having a thin exterior coating of chocolate covering its surface. These bars are prepared by dipping the solid ice cream in a sweet chocolate liquid and then withdrawing it. The chocolate liquid solidifies at ice cream temperature forming a thin chocolate coating that covers the exterior of the ice cream bar.

In the usual commercial practice, the ice cream manufacturer prepares the ice cream bars and chocolate processors prepare chocolate liquids in finished form ready for immediate use in coating the ice cream bars. These liquids are shipped to the ice cream manufacturers in steel drums or in tank trucks, or tank cars.

Representative chocolate liquids suitable for coating ice cream bars are commonly prepared by stirring together cocoa powder, sugar, salt, vegetable oil, milk powder and lecithin with a vigor and for a time to produce a moderately stable dispersion of the solids in the vegetable oil. Chocolate liquids of this kind are manufactured and sold in very large volumes. While these liquids have been extensively used over a long period of time and yield an acceptable product, their use requires constant and expensive attention to cope with certain problems which arise out of inherent properties of the liquids.

When these liquids stand in storage, they tend to solidify at ambient temperature. If they are stored in drums, it is necessary to store the drums in a heated storage space in order to maintain the liquid in a sufficiently fluid form to permit it to be poured from the drums into the dipping vessel. If they are stored in large storage tanks, it is necessary to jacket the tanks and supply sufficient steam or hot water to the jacket to keep the liquids in fluid form.

During storage over the periods commonly experienced in commercial use of these materials, the solid components settle out of the vegetable oil forming heavy mud-like deposits in the bottoms of the containers. Where the container is a drum, it is necessary to subject the contents of the drum to agitation for considerable periods in order to put the solids back into reasonably uniform dispersion in the oil. Where the liquids are stored in larger tanks, it is necessary to supply continuous agitation to these tanks in order to maintain the solid components in suspension and so permit withdrawal of a reasonably uniform dispersion of solids in. Oil from the bottoms of storage tanks.

B.T. Warkentin; U.S. Patent 3,959,516; May 25, 1976; assigned to Shade Foods, Inc. has developed a chocolate composition for coating ice cream which completely does away with these problems. In his process, solid chocolate wafers having a softening point at about 100°F are supplied to the ice cream bar manufacturer instead of a finished dipping liquid. In order to prepare a chocolate dipping liquid, the manufacturer simply stirs the chocolate wafers into warm (110° to 130°F) vegetable oil. Approximately equal weights of the solid chocolate wafers and the warm vegetable oil are used in the preparation of the finished dipping liquid. The dipping liquid can be prepared in batches sized to accommodate a contemplated run and essentially no storage of dipping liquid is involved.

The solid chocolate wafers consist essentially of a macroscopically homogeneous mixture of about 12 to 24 parts by weight of cocoa powder or a mixtures of cocoa powder and chocolate liquor, 35 to 60 parts by weight of sugar, 20 to 32 parts by weight of hydrogenated vegetable oil, 0 to 10 parts by weight of low fat milk powder or whey powder or mixtures of the two, 0.3 to 0.7 part by weight of lecithin and from 0.2 to 0.5 part by weight of common salt. From 1.5 to 15 parts by weight of cocoa butter are contained, in the low fat cocoa powder and chocolate liquor used to supply the required cocoa content. The manufacture of solid chocolate wafers having a representative composition is described in the following example.

Example: 15.7 parts by weight of low fat cocoa powder (about 10% by weight cocoa butter content), 55.2 parts by weight of sugar, 10 to 16, preferably 14.1, parts by weight of hydrogenated vegetable oil, 0.27 part by weight of salt, 0.2 part by weight of vanilla and 0.46 part by weight of lecithin were placed in a milling paste mixer. The mixer is run until the mixture is ground into a smooth paste. The paste is passed through a stainless steel roll refiner which extrudes it as a thin layer. The layer is broken up and then mixed and heated with an additional 14.1 parts by weight of hydrogenated vegetable oil and run through a ribbon blender to reduce it to a liquid state.

The liquid is pumped into a heated high-speed mixing tank where it is mixed and further milled. The liquid is then pasteurized by heating to about 140°F and held at that temperature for about 15 minutes during which agitation is continued. The liquid product is then pumped into a storage tank from which it is fed onto a moving rubber conveyer belt. A depositing head squirts out small globs of this liquid mixture onto the moving belt which passes through a cooling tunnel where refrigerated air is circulated around it.

The globs solidify forming wafers which are carried out of the cooling tunnel and dropped into cartons. Wafers are about 1 inch in diameter and 3/8 inch thick. The wafers have an incipient softening point about 95°F and melt at 100° to 102°F. The wafers have an average weight of about 1/5 oz. They may be made larger, but should not exceed about 1 oz. in weight to facilitate weighing to close tolerances and facilitate melting and mixing during use to produce the finished dipping liquor. The wafers can be stored indefinitely without deterioration.

# Chapter - 25

## *Other Desserts*

### Smooth Custards

Custard powder is normally substantially composed of starch, which in order to form a custard sauce, whether eventually served hot or cold by the consumer, needs to be fully gelatinized by heat on the addition of hot milk with stirring. This preparation, however, has to be conducted with great care in order that a smooth, thick sauce of uniform texture without lumps is obtained. In the hands of an inexperienced person, this smooth texture may not be readily obtained, since the temperature of starch gelatinization may not be fully attained, and the starch powder may not be properly wetted out.

W.M. Mostyn, R.P. Verrall and B.C. Shrimpton; U.S. Patent 4,089,988; May 16, 1978; assigned to General Foods Ltd., England provide a process for the preparation of a dessert composition, a superior custard in dried granular and free-flowing form, which comprises admixing starch powder and sugar particles while spraying water in a controlled manner on the mixed particles to provide a moisture content of 13 to 18% by weight, granulating the moistened mixture, drying the resultant granules to a moisture content of 5 to 6% by weight, and grinding and screening the dried granules to a particles size of No. 10 to No. 36 British Standard Mesh. In hot liquid the granules form a uniform sauce.

Example: Dry ingredients in the following proportions were used: Coprn starch, 49.5%; pulverized sugar, 49.5% and minor ingredients (salt, colour, flavours), 1.0%.

The relevant aspects of the raw material specifications are:

***Corn starch:***

| | |
|---|---|
| bulk density | 52-60 g/100 cc |
| particle size | 1% max on 150 mesh screen |
| moisture | 10-12% wet basis |

***Pulverized sugar:***

| | |
|---|---|
| bulk density | 52 g/100 cc |
| particle size | 95% min through 60 mesh screen |

A 40 kilogram batch containing the ingredients in the above proportions was first sifted through a 40 mesh screen to remove oversize material then blended in a ribbon blender for 6 minutes. The blender was fitted with a 16 inch diameter ribbon rotating at 65 rpm. The blender was fitted with a variable speed drive, and, after the preliminary mixing operation, the rotation speed was increased to 200 rpm. This had the effect of fluidizing the mix, thus making the subsequent water dispersion most effective. Water was sprayed on over a period of 5 minutes via two Delavan-Watson Spraycone nozzles.

The water addition time was based on a desired wet mix moisture of 15% and a predetermined spray rate of 20 ml/min/kg of wet mix for a water pressure of 50 psig. After the water addition, the wet mix was further blended for 5 minutes (blender speed 65 rpm) to ensure total dispersion. The mix was discharged from the blender and fed at a rate of approximately 100 kg/hour in an Apex 52 Rach Rotary Wet Granulator, fitted with a perforated screen. The diameter of these holes was 0.097 inch.

The moist granules were collected in trays and dried in a proctor and Schwartz forced circulation dryer. The conditions employed in this dryer were: up through circulation, 125oF, 1 1/4 inch bed depth and the drying time, to a final moisture of 5% was 30 minutes. The dry granules were sized through 2 inch diameter crushing rolls, and then screened using both 10 and 35 mesh screens. The rolls were adjusted to ensure maximum recovery in the screening operation. Oversize material from the screen was recycled to the crushing rolls and fines, after milling, were stored for use in subsequent batches up to a level of incorporation of 25%. The actual level of fines produced from this batch was 21%.

The product produced in this manner was then made up as follows: A pint of milk was heated just to boiling, then removed from the heat. Immediately, 65 g of the granulated product was sprinkled on while stirring, and stirring was continued until the product had thickened to a smooth custard.

# Chapter - 26

## *Cocoa Butter*

### Extracting Cocoa Butter with Carbon Dioxide

W. Roselius, O. Vitzthum and P. Hubert; U.S. Patent 3,923, 847; December 2, 1975; assigned to Studiengesellschaft Kohle mbH, Germany have devised a method for the production of cocoa butter from cocoa nibs or cocoa mass whether or not the cocoa nibs are roasted or whether or not the material has been alkalized. The method is based on the observation that various gases, which are supercritical in respect of pressure and temperature constitute excellent solvents for cocoa fat. The gases are completely unobjectionable from the health point of view, i.e., are food acceptable.

Carbon dioxide is the preferred extraction medium, but other gases which may be used include nitrous oxide, vinylidene fluoride, octafluoropropane, fluoroform, ethane, ethylene, etc. The solvent should be purified before use. In a preferred method, which is illustrated in Figure 5.3, the procedur is as follows. Cocoa mass or crushed cocoa nibs are introduced without special pretreatment and without additions (e.g., lecithin in the pressing method) into the pressure tube 13 and the entire plant is first flushed free of air by means of $CO_2$.

The extrusion medium is then drawn by suction from the liquid gas tanks and the medium which in the first instance is still liquid, is forced by means of a pump into the heat exchanger 14, in which it is brought to supercritical conditions in rexpect of pressure and temperature. It the enters tube 13, passes thourhg the contents of the latter, and is thereby charged with cocoa fat in the form of a supercritical solution. The inlet and outlet apertures of the vessel are closed by metal filter discs (filter threshold 3 microns) so that the entrainment of particles of cocoa is not possible.

The charged supercritical gas phase is now expanded by means of a throttle valve 15 into the vessel 12 and it is ensured that the pressure falls to values lower than the critical pressure for $CO_2$ (~ 75.3 atm). The system thereby separates, i.e., the pure cocoa butter is separated. if the temperature is left at values slightly above the critical temperature for $CO_2$ (31.6°C), the fraction of water likewise entrained by the gas from the cocoa will not be separated from the mixture and will be further entrained by the current of $CO_2$, which is now free of extract.

The cocoa butter is thus practically free from water. In principle it should be observed at this point that a reduction of pressure and/or a raising of the temperature will lead to the sarne effect, i.e., the disintegration of the system, so that a number of varients of the method are conceivable. When the desired pressure and temperature conditons have been adjusted in the vessels, the flow of gas from the liquid gas tanks is stopped and the circuit closed. the valves 15, 16, 17, 18, 19 and 20 are for this purpose open and all others closed.

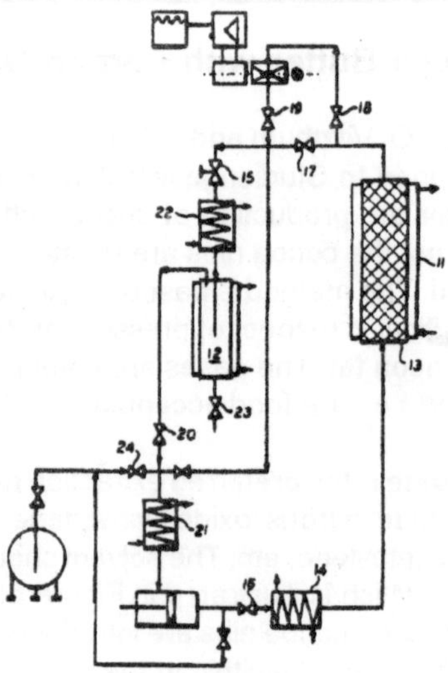


**Figure : Apparatus for Extraction of Cocoa Butter**

The gas leavening the vessel 12 is liquefiedl in the heat exchanger 21, delievered by the pump into the heat exchanger 14, in which it is brought to supercritical conditions again, and it passes as pure solvent back into the tube 13, and so on. Instead of the liquid gas pump it is also possible to use a compressor, in which case the liquefaction of the gas is not necessary. Which of the measures is selected will depend only ontechnical circumstances in the process, since in this case, other heat exchangers are necessary.

In practice a pressure above 100 atm gauge, and preferably between 200 to 400 atm gauge, is used. it is a particular feature of the method that in respect of temperature, it is only necesary to work slightly above the critical temperature of $CO_2$, preferably between 40o and 60°C. The heat exchangers 14, 21 and 22 will be connected together, thus leading to a procedure which is very advantageous in respect of energy, and therefore economical.

After completion of the processing, vessel 12 is first closed and all the gas contained in the remainder of the circuit is pumped back into the tanks. Valves 16, 15, 20, 23 and 24 are for this purpose closed, and all others are opened. Consequently practically no losses coour. A slightly yellowish cocoa butter is obtained which is completely free from particles of cocoa matter and which can be used without further filteration or other processing, while it is in every respect, including aroma, equivalent to a conventional press product of the highest quality. A feature of the method which should be emphasized is that the composition of the cocoa butter will not vary even if not all but only part of the cocoa fat is extracted.

If crushed nibs are used, the residue found in 11 will be a material which is unchanged in colour and structure and which can easily be further processed. When cocoa mass is used, a powdery or crumbly material is obtained which can easily be handled and the colour of which has been only slightly lightened. the nibs or masses which have undrgone extraction can therefore be further processed directly without other treatment.

## Flavour Enhancer for Cocoa

Many chocolate and cocoa foods and flavouring materials lack a certain flavour and aroma note, and this lack substantially detracts from their overall organoleptic impression. it has been found that one of these missing flavour notes is one which can be characterized as creamy, cocoa-like. this creamy, cocoa-like flavour and aroma note is supplied to chocolate, cocoa and other flavours according to the process developed by W.J. Evers, H.H. Heinsohn, Jr., B.J. Mayers, and E.A. Karoll; U.S. Patent 3,958,029; May 18, 1976; assigned to International Flavours & Fragrances, Inc. by the additon of 2,5-dimethyl-3-thioisovaleryl furan having the structure below.

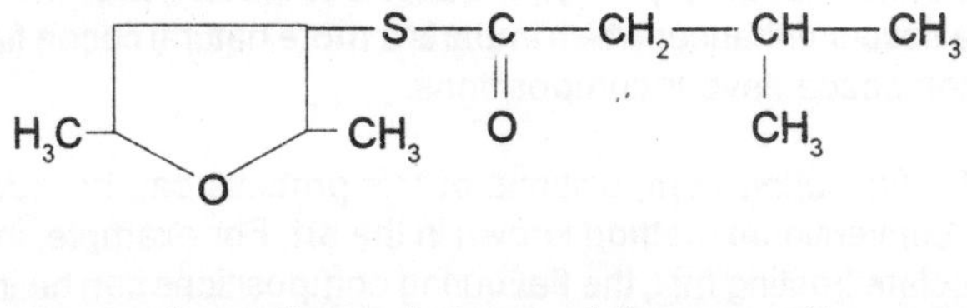

In many instances the optimum balance of flavour and/or aroma is obtained by utilizing a mixture of 2,5-dimethyl-3-thioisovaleryl furan and, in addition, phenyl alkenals, which are described in U.S. Patents 3,582,360, 3,754,038, 3,694,232 and 3,829,504. When mixtures of 2,5-dimethyl-3-thioisovalery furan and these aldehydes are used their proportions can be varied to suit the particular composition which is to be flavoured, enhanced, or otherwise altered and will depend upon whether the process is being utilized to enhance the flavour of a chocolate, cocoa, or other foodstuff which already has some desirable flavour and aroma characteristics or whether the entire flavour and/or aroma are to be supplied by the addition of a flavouring composition.

For example, it has been found when preparing cocoa flavours that a good blend is obtaine by using a mixture of 30 to 40% 2,5-dimethyl-3-thioisovaleryl furan; 40 to 50% of 5-methyl-2-phenyl-2-hexanal, about 3 to 7% of 4-methyl-2-phenyl-2-pentenal and from 3 to 7% of 2-phenyl-2-butenal. It will be understood that these ratios can be varied as necessary to enhance or forfity the flavour of the foodstuff. All parts, proportions, percentages and ratios are by weight, unless otherwise indicated.

The 2,5-dimethyl-3-thioisovaleryl furan can also be added directly to a food composition to alter, enhance, modify or impart flavour to the food composition. In the latter instance it is only necessary to make certain that it is thoroughly and uniformly distributed through the food.

It is preferred that the ultimate food composition contain at least about 50 parts per billion of the 2,5-dimethyl-3-thioisovalery furan based on total composition, and it is not generally desirable to use more than about 500 parts per million in the finished composition. Accordingly, the desirable range is from 80 parts per billion to 500 parts per million of the 2,5-dimethyl-3-thioisovaleryl furan. When 2,5-dimethyl-3-thioisovaleryl furan is added to the foodstuff in the form of chocolate, cocoa, or other flavour composition, the amount should be sufficient to impart the requisite flavour and/or aroma note to the composition so that the flavour and aroma will be balanced in the finished foodstuff. Accordingly, these flavouring compositions preferably contain from about 0.002 to 10% of the 2,5-dimethyl-3-thioisovaleryl furan.

When 2,5-dimethyl-3-thioisovaleryl furan is used in the formulation of chocolate flavouring material, it has been found especially useful to combine it with a vanilla flavouring agent and an alkyl acetate. Thus, the 2,5-dimethyl-3-thioisovaleryl furan can be combined with vanilla extract or other vanilla flavouring agent such as vanillin and with amyl phenyl acetate. Compositions containing this mixture provide a flavour enhancer which imparts a more natural cocoa flavour and aroma to imitation cocoa flavour compositions.

The flavouring compositions of this process can be added to the foodstuffs by conventional method known in the art. For example, in the preparation of a chocolate frosting mix, the flavouring compositions can be incorporated with the fat, sugar, thickeners, freshners, preservers and the like, and admixed in a conventional blender to obtain the desired consistency. Alternatively, the flavour material, together with any other liquids if desired, can be admixed with a carrier, such as gum arabic, gum tragacanth, carrageenan and the like, and spray-dried to obtain a particulate solid flavouring material. the preparation of 2,5-dimethyl-3-thioisovaleryl furan is described in detail in U.S. Patent 3,922,288; 3,872,111; 3,910.966; 3,873,731; and 3,917869.

Example: A panel evaluation (5 panelists) carried out an Royal instant chocolate pudding (Standard Brands, Inc.) containing 2,5-dimethyl-3-thioisovaleryl furan at a level of 80 parts per billion. The five panelists agreed that the 2,5-dimethyl-3-thioisovaleryl furan has a definite blending and rounding off effect on the pudding flavour. In addition, two of the panelists through that the 2,5-dimethyl-3-thioisovaleryl furan deepened the character of the cocoa itself and all five panelists agreed that the 2,5-dimethyl-3-thioisovaleryl furan improved the general flavour character of the chocolate pudding as compared to the same chocolate pudding without the 2,5-dimethyl-3-thioisovaleryl furan.

# Chapter - 27

# *Honey*

## Honey Product in Wafer Form

The process developed by R.D. Verner; U.S. Patent 3,879,567; April 22, 1975; assigned to Honey-Tein Products, Inc. related to the production of honey in a concentrated dry state which may be used in different forms to enrich foods with flavour and nutritional values or used in tablet and wafer form as a diet or food supplement. Figure 5.6 is a flow diagram for the manufacture of dried honey products in tablet and wafer form and is shown on the following page.

In accordance with this process, a honey-containing product comprising a dried composite of honey and a gelatinized starch material containing about 45% by weight of honey solids is utilized as the raw material. This product is disclosed in U.S. Patent 2,693,420 and is available commercially.

A mixture of approximately 280 pounds of the dried composition of honey and gelatinized starch and approximately 10 pounds of nonfat dried milk is mixed, screened and blended through a 12 to 14 mesh screen, and then granulated with approximately two gallons of distilled water and approximately two gallons of isopropyl alcohol. The granulated material is then placed in a tray and dried at approximately 45°C for a given length of time such as a 12-hour period, or it may be dried in the atmosphere for a longer period.

After drying, the material is blended to remove all lumps and milled and passed through a No. 3 screen with a 12, 13 or 14 mesh size. After passing thorough the screen the material is thoroughly mixed in a blender for approximately 20 minutes, then weighed.

Approximately 280 pounds of this material is then mixed with approximately 1,500 grans of magnesium stearate, which is added as a suitable lubricant, and this mixture is again mixed for approximately 5 minutes to form a uniform product. This product is then transmitted to tablet forming machine and compressed into suitable wafers or tablet, which are packaged for the consumer market.

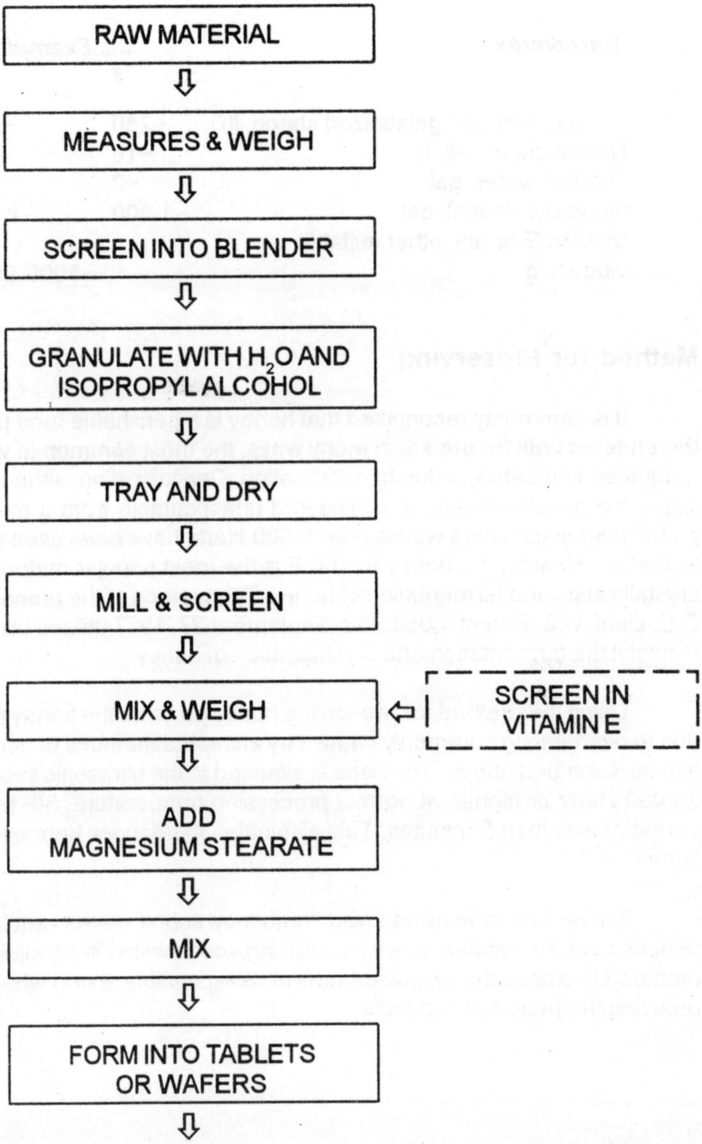


**Figure : Flow Diagram for making Honey Wafers**

If it is desired to add a vitamin to the wafer or tablet formed such as, for example, vitamin E, 8,000 to 9,000 grams of this vitamin may be added to the material after the drying step during the mixing and weighing step, as shown in the figure. The following products have been found to be commercially acceptable as chewable tablets.

| *Ingredients* | *......Example.......* 1 | 2 |
|---|---|---|
| Dried honey and gelatinized starch, lb | ~280 | ~260 |
| Nonfat dried milk, lb | ~10 | ~10 |
| Distilled water, gal | ~2 | ~2 |
| Isopropyl alcohol, gal | ~1,500 | ~1,500 |
| Vitamin E or any other suitable vitamin, g | | ~8000-9000 |

## Method for Preserving

It is commonly recognized that honey is a perishable food product. It can be rendered unfit for market in many ways, the most common of which are, fermentation and damage due to overheating. Crystallization, although it does not make the honey inedible, is considered unacceptable from a marketing viewpoint. In the past sound waves near 9,000 Herta have been used to inhibit crystallization. Heating the honey to 160°F is the most popular method of inhibiting crystallization and fermentation of honey. The method of the process devised by D.E. Liebl; U.S. Patent 4,050,952; September 27, 1977 utilizes ultrasonic sound to inhibit the fermentation and crystallization of honey.

Using the method for preserving honey protects the honey from damage due to overheating commonly caused by accepted methods of honey preservation as described above. The hone is exposed to the ultrasonic sound, 18,000 to 20,000 Hertz or higher, at normal processing temperature, 50° to 100°F, for a period of less than 5 minutes. This eliminates the danger from overheating the honey.

Earlier methods using lower frequency sound waves required exposure periods near 30 minutes as well as utilizing sound within the audible range. This method eliminates the disadvantages of using audible sound while significantly reducing the period of exposure.

# Chapter - 28

# *Chewing Gums*

## FORMULATIONS FOR LONGER-LASTING FLAVOUR AND SWEETNESS

### Addition of Monosodium Glutamate

Loss of flavour impact and sweetness in a flavoured chewing gum generally occurs after about 3 to 5 minutes of chewing. B.J. Bahoshy, C.E. Flynn and G.P. Malunis; U.S. Patent 3,897,566; July 29, 1975; assigned to General Foods Corporation have found, however, that the addition to the gum composition of gelatin-fixed monosodium glutamate is effective in extending the time period over which both sweetness and flavour are discernible. The term gelatin-fixed, as used herein, means uniformly distributing the flavour and sweetness extending material in a gelatin solution and then drying the resultant solution.

Gelatin fixation of the material may be achieved through a wide variety of processing methods. These methods may include freeze drying a mixture of gelatin and the material to be fixed, spray drying, drum drying, slab drying, oven drying, tray drying, pan drying, or other well-known drying techniques. Gelatin fixation may also be achieved through the use of other physical techniques such as coacervation, and other like methods. The gelatin which may be employed may be any of the grades and types of gelatin, including those obtained from tanner's stock, pigskin, and the like. The Bloom of the gelatin used is not critical and may vary widely, that is, anywhere from about 50 or less to as high as 250.

The amount of gelatin used in fixing the monosodium glutamate may vary widely subject to the necessity of using enough to effectively fix the component and the undesirability of using excessive amounts of gelatin which may adversely affect the texture of the finished gum product. Generally, it is found that within a gelatin-fixed particle the amount of material to be fixed may be anywhere from about 10 to 100% by weight of the gelatin without adversely affecting the gum product. The preparation of the chewing gums is achieved through conventional methods including a softening of the gum base through mixing, addition of sweetener, addition of the flavour extending compound, followed by addition of the flavouring materials and formation of the gum into suitable forms such as sticks.

## Addition of MSG plus Saccharin

Further work by B.J. Bahoshy, C.E. Flynn and R.E. Klose; U.S. Patent 3,903,305; September 2, 1975; assigned to General Foods Corporation has shown that, when saccharin is added to the monosodium glutamate (MSG) and fixed in gelatin, the gum has even greater lasting sweetness and favour. The total amount of the saccharin and monosodium glutamate mixture affective to achieve a significant flavour and sweetness extension in a chewing gum product is preferably between about 0.1 and 1.5% by weight of the final gum composition. The ratio of the two components may vary widely over the lower range of the preferred level of use of the mixture.

When higher levels of the mixture are employed, it is preferred to mix the two components such that the amount of saccharin does not exceed 0.5% by weight of the final gum composition. Use of saccharin above this level, while resulting in a flavour and sweetness extension, has been found to impart somewhat bitter after-taste to the gum product which may be undesirable according to one's preference. Preferably, the mixture should contain anywhere from about 0.05 to 1.0% of monosodium glutamate and about 0.05 to 0.5% of saccharin, percents by weight of the final gum composition. It is preferred to employ equal amounts of each component in the final product.

In order to measure the flavour and sweetness duration in a chewing gum, taste tests were conducted using trained personnel to evaluate the time versus intensity of flavour and sweetness. Panel members are given a stick of gum and asked to chew and record their values for flavour intensity at 30-second intervals. Comparisons of experimental gum samples are made against a sample of a control gum formulation and the time versus intensity values are used to assign a flavour duration value to each sample. For the purposes of the testing, flavour duration is defined as the chewing time in minutes for the gum flavour to become just barely detectable. Thus, flavour extension is the difference between the flavour duration of the control and the experimental sample.

Example 1: In order to evaluate the flavour and sweetness extension obtained through the use of the gelatin-fixed monosodium glutamate, gum samples were prepared from the following ingredients:

| *Ingredients* | 1 | 2 | 3 | 4 | 5 | 6 | 7 |
|---|---|---|---|---|---|---|---|
| | | | **Gum Sample** *(percent by weight)* | | | | |
| Chewing gum base | 23.993 | 23.993 | 23.993 | 23.993 | 23.993 | 23.993 | 23.993 |
| Sugar | 58.737 | 58.737 | 58.737 | 58.737 | 57.088 | 57.088 | 57.088 |
| Corn syrup, 46° | 14.245 | 14.245 | 14.245 | 14.245 | 14.245 | 14.245 | 14.245 |
| Glycerol | 0.749 | 0.749 | 0.749 | 0.749 | 0.749 | 0.749 | 0.749 |
| Flavour | 1.276 | 1.276 | 1.276 | 1.276 | 1.276 | 1.276 | 1.276 |
| Gelatin | 0.800 | 0.800 | – | 0.800 | – | 2.249 | – |
| MSG* | – | 0.200 | – | – | – | 0.200 | – |
| Gelatin-fixed MSG (20% MSG) | – | | 1.000 | – | – | – | 1.000 |
| Saccharin | – | | – | 0.200 | – | 0.200 | – |
| Gelatin-fixed saccharin (12% saccharin) | – | | – | – | 1.649 | – | 1.649 |

***Monosodium glutamate**

Gelatin fixation was achieved through slab-drying techniques. For Sample 3, 160 g of gelatin were mixed with 40 g of monosodium glutamate. The mixture was stirred into 800 ml of water, heated to solution, and poured into a tray in a layer of about 3/16 of an inch. The solution was cooled to about 40° to 50°F to form a firm gel which was cut into squares, dried at 100°F in a forced air oven, and ground for use in the gum formulation.

For the gum preparation, the gum base was softened for 10 minutes at 150°F in a mixer, the glycerol added and mixed for 10 minutes, and the corn syrup added as mixing continued for 10 minutes. The appropriate amount of MSG or saccharin or their mixture was blended with the sugar and added to the mixer in two portions with 10 minutes mixing after each addition. The flavour was then added, the gum was removed from the mixer, and then rolled and scored into sticks.

Example 2: The chewing gums prepared in Example 1 were evaluated by a taste panel for time versus intensity values from which a flavour duration value for each sample was obtained.

| *Sample No.* | *Description* | *Flavour Duration, min.* |
|---|---|---|
| 1. | Control 5.5 | |
| 2. | Unfixed MSG (0.2%) | 5.5 |
| 3. | Fixed MSG (0.2%) | 6.5 |
| 4. | Unfixed saccharin (0.2%) | 6.0 |
| 5. | Fixed saccharin (0.2%) | 6.0 |
| 6. | Unfixed MSG (0.2%) plus unfixed saccharin (0.2%) | 6.5 |
| 7. | Fixed MSG (0.2%) plus fixed saccharin (0.2%) | 8.0 |

It can be seen from the above values that the fixed MSG and fixed saccharin mixture extent the flavour in Sample 7 about 2.5 minutes over the control sample. This result is surprising in that the independent use of each fixed component results in an extension of only about 1 minute over the control sample. This synergistic effect makes possible the preparation of a chewing gum having a significant flavour extension over currently available products without having to use excessive quantities of each individual material.

## Special Order for Chewing Gum Manufacture

A typical chewing gum base in formulated from natural and/or synthetic gums or elastomers, hydrophilic plasticizers, ester gums (elastomer solvent and hydrophobic plasticizers), oleaginous plasticizers, fillers, emulsifiers, pigments and additives such as antioxidants, stabilizers or preservatives. Examples of natural gums or elastomers are natural rubber, chicle, balata, sorva, gutta percha, lechi caspi and jelutong. Example of synthetic gums or elastomers are polyisobutylene, isobutylene-isoprene copolymer and butadiene-styrene copoymer. The hydrophilic plasticizer is usually a synthetic resin, and examples of these are vinyl polymers such as polyvinyl acetate or partially hydrolyzed polyvinyl alcohol, or mixtures of the two. Ester gums function as elastomer solvent and as hydrophobic plasticizer.

The elastomer solvent is a rosin derivative such as dimerized rosin ester, or glycerol ester of polymerized rosin or a terpene resin, such as polymers of ß-pinene or x-pinene. The hydrophobic plasticizer includes esters of rosin and hydrogenated esters of rosin, such as the glyceryl esters of hydrogenated rosin or the glyceryl esters of partially hydrogenated rosin and the like. Fillers are optional and are usually inorganic materials such as $CaCO_3$, $MgCO_3$, $Al_2O_3$, talc and the like. The oleaginous materials like cocoa butter, hydrogenated vegetable oils, and waxes, such as petroleum waxes like paraffin waxes, as well as polyethylene waxes. Small amounts of an emulsifier such as fatty acid monoglycerides or diglycerides or triglycerides, e.g., glyceryl monostearate, propylene glycol monostearate may be used in preparing the gum. Inorganic pigments, e.g., TiO2, or organic pigments, e.g., copper chlorophyllin, carbon black, ß-carotene, Red No. 3, Blue No. 1, Yellow No. 5, or Yellow No. 6 may be used if desired to impart coloration to the gum. An antioxidant or preservative such as butylated hydroxyanisole or butylated hydroxytoluene may be used.

The term plasticizer as used herein includes masticatory substances which function as softening agents for the elastomers. The various ingredients are generally used in the following percentages by weight:

| ***Ingredient*** | ***Percent by Weight*** |
|---|---|
| Elastomer | 5-15 |
| Elastomer solvent | 5-20 |
| Hydrophilic plasticizer | 20-35 |
| Hydrophobic plasticizer | 5-15 |
| Oleaginous plasticizer | 15-25 |
| Emulsifier | 10-15 |
| Filler | 0-25 |
| Pigment | 0-05 |
| Additives | 0-02 |

In the process developed by C.W. Ehrgott and R.L. Roy; U.S. Patent Application (Published) B 583,712; February 10, 1976; assigned to Life Savers, Inc. the ingredients are separated into three groups. The first group comprises the natural or synthetic gums or elastomers, the elastomer solvent, and the additives. The second group comprises the hydrophilic plasticizer, hydrophobic plasticizer, filler and pigment. The third group comprises the oleaginous plasticizers and the emulsifiers.

The process is adapted to be carried out advantageously in batchwise or continuous manner, with the latter being preferred. Each group is preferably separately blended. The first group is then passed through a high intensity mixer, after which it is fed to an intermediate mixer, together with the second group of ingredients. The mixture of the first and second groups of ingredients is then fed to a rapid, efficient mixer, together with the third group of ingredients. However, it will be appreciated that each ingredient of the various groups of ingredients may be separately metered into its respective mixer without being previously blended. Furthermore, the various mixing operations carried out using the above mixers may be carried out using a single variable mixer.

The following is a description of a preferred method. The first group of ingredients, i.e., the elastomer, the elastomer solvent and additives is fed to a dry solids blender where a uniform mixing of the ingredients is obtained. From the blender, the mixture is fed to a feed belt which delivers the mixture in a predetermined amount by weight to a high intensity mixer. A high intensity mixer is one which effects a high degree of shear and in which a milling action is obtained due to small clearances between moving surfaces. The effluent from the high intensity mixer is a rubbery, completely homogenous product which has to undispersed elastomeric particles and which can be stretched into a translucent film. The second group of ingredients, i.e., the hydrophilic plasticizer, the hydrophobic plasticizer, fillers and pigments is fed to a second dry solids blender where a uniform mixing of the ingredients is obtained. From the blender, the mixture is fed to a feed belt which delivers the mixture in a predetermined amount by weight to an intermediate intensity mixer. An intermediate intensity mixer is one which provides less of a shearing action and more of a folding action because clearances between moving surfaces are greater. The effluent from the intermediate intensity mixture is a dough-like substance which can be stretched into a homogenous film which shows no individual particles. The effluent from the high intensity mixer is also bed to the intermediate intensity mixer where it is combined with the second group of ingredients.

The third group of ingredients comprising the oleaginous plasticizer and emulsifiers is fed to a dry solids blender. From the blender, the mixture is fed to a feed belt which delivers the mixture in a predetermined amount by weight to a rapid efficient mixer. A rapid efficient mixer is one which provides essentially no shearing action but a very rapid folding action. As the third group of ingredients enters the rapid efficient mixer, it is combined with the effluent from the intermediate intensity mixer which is also fed to the rapid efficient mixer. The effluent from the rapid efficient mixer is the finished chewing gum base which is then processed in conventional manner to obtain the final chewing gum product.

The foregoing sequence of mixing and blending has been found to be critical to the operability of this process. For example, if either the oleaginous plasticizer or the hydrophobic plasticizer is added to the first group of ingredients, a uniformly dispersed product cannot be obtained. Figure is a schematic flow sheet showing the process.

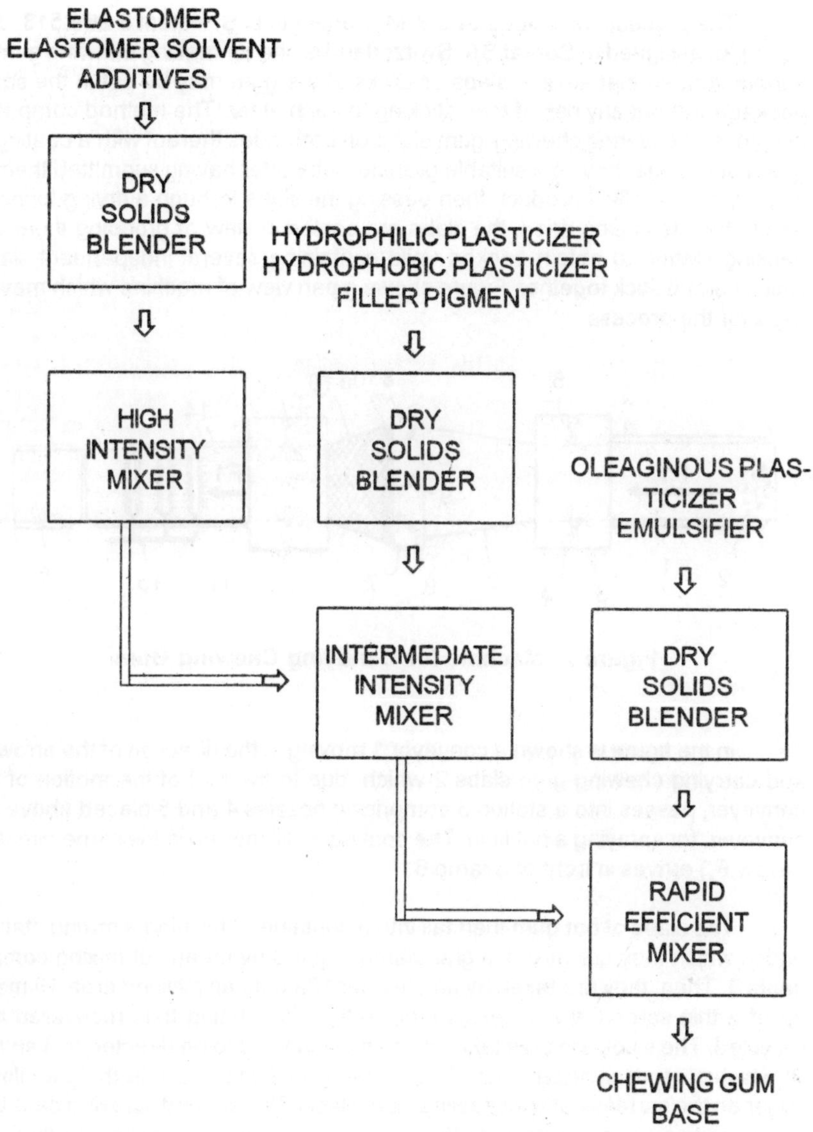


**Figure : Flow Sheet for Chewing Gum Manufacture**

## Candied Chewing Gum

The process developed by J.E.M. Canonne; U.S. Patent 3,969,513; July 13, 1976; assigned to Soreat SA, Switzerland is one for making chewing gum or bubble gum so that several slabs or sticks of the gum may be put in the same package without any risk of their sticking to each other. The method comprises the steps of covering chewing-gum slabs on both sides thereof with a coating of granulated sugar having a suitable granulometry after having submitted them to a spray of a hot fluid product, then passing the slabs through a drying tunnel in which, besides being dried, the slabs are cooled in view of grouping them in a packing station to obtain packed units containing several independent slabs, which cannot stick together. Figure shows a pan view of machine which may be used for the process.

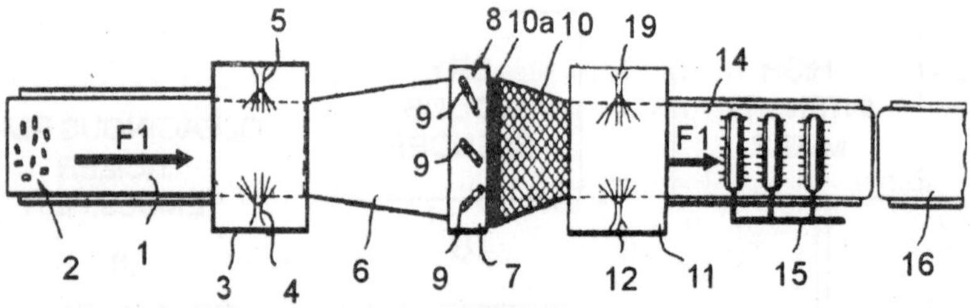


**Figure : Machine for Candying Chewing Gum**

In the figure is shown a conveyor 1 moving in the direction of the arrow $F_1$ and carrying chewing-gum slabs 2 which, due to the fact of the motion of the conveyer, passes into a station 3 comprising nozzles 4 and 5 placed above the conveyer, for spraying a hot fluid. The conveyer still moving in the same direction (arrow $F_1$) arrives in front of a ramp 6.

The slabs of hot gum then fall into a container 7 forming a mixing station, and in which they are mixed in granulated sugar 8 by means of mixing components 9. Then, they are taken by an elevator 10a onto an inclined area 10 made up of a thin screen, the excess sugar on the slabs being thus recovered and recycled. The slabs are then taken from the station 10 to be directed to a station 11 which comprises nozzles 12, 13 spraying a hot fluid so as to fix the granulated sugar on the surfaces of the chewing-gum slabs. This second spraying causes a slight melting on the surface of the sugar particles, which makes it easier for sugar to stick onto the slabs of chewing gum. The chewing-gum slabs are then placed on a conveyer 14 moving in the direction of the arrow $F_2$ passing under a drying station 15 and then onto a conveyer 16 which takes them to a packing machine. Since the slabs are coated with granulated sugar which is perfectly dry, they do not have any chance of sticking to each other. Though any kind of sugar can be used, it is also possible in this candying method to obtain an additional aromatization of the chewing gum by using a suitably aromatized sugar.

It is possible to first coat the chewing-gum slabs with an edible gluing liquid applied to the slabs in the form of a spray or of a hot aerosol, then to spray granulated sugar onto the chewing-gum slabs. Then, the slabs so coated are dried and cooled. As an edible gluing liquid product, there can be used a solution of honey molasses, syrup, gum arabic, etc.

## Freezing, Comminuting, and Heating

The process developed by K. Mochizuki and F. Yokomichi; U.S. Patent 4,000,321; December 28, 1976; assigned to Meiji Seika Kaisha, Ltd., Japan has as its particular object the preparation of chewing gum which is light in weight and low in specific gravity and which exhibits a soft chewing impression when it is chewed. This is accomplished by mixing a chewing gum base with the desired sweeteners, corn syrups, starches, flavourings or colorants in order to form a chewing gum composition which is thereafter refrigerated or cooled to a temperature below freezing to about - 15°C or lower. The refrigerated composition is then crushed or ground to obtain minute fragments which are heated to temperatures which cause them to adhere to form an integrated body.

Either of the following methods can be used to integrate the minute fragments or pieces of the mixture: (a) the refrigerated minute fragments or pieces may be warmed after an optional application of light pressure, if necessary by placing them in a mold or on a framed plate or by placing them on a conveyor belt or the like; or (b) the minute particles may be coated over pieces of edible materials which form centres, using a rotating coating device, such as revolving pan or drum, and thereafter, the coated materials may be warmed. By this process, there are obtained chewing gum products having a light weight, low specific gravity and a desirable homogeneous texture which exhibits a soft chewing impression when chewed.

A typical manufacturing process would be carried out as follows: after a chewing gum composition is refrigerated to below -15°C or even lower, and it is crushed or ground to form minute particles, the minute fragments or finely ground pieces are warmed to room temperature from the refrigerated state and they become cross-linked or self-adhered in order to form an integrated body which incorporates minute air bubbles in the spaces between the particles. This provides a chewing gum product having a light, soft chewing impression when chewed. A chewing gum product obtained by this process has a specific gravity of from 0.7 to 0.8 and this corresponds to about 50 to 70% of that of conventional stick chewing gums which lies between 1.2 and 1.3.

Example 1: A chewing gum composition was prepared by kneading 220 g of a chewing gum base obtained in a conventional manner together with 590 g of sugar, 70 g of glucose and 100 g of corn syrup. This chewing gum composition was cooled to a normal room temperature and cut into 10 mm cubes after rolling.

The cubes were then ground at a temperature of about - 15°C or even lower into a powder with the grain size of the order of all passing through a 325 mesh sieve. The powder was immediately layered into a mold of 2.5 cm long x 2.5 cm wide to 1 cm deep and then allowed to stand at 20°C for 2 hours to effect self-adhesion and integration. Thus, molded chewing gum of hexahedron shape was obtained by releasing from a mold of that shape.

Example 2: A chewing gum powder was prepared in the same manner as in Example 1. Jellies were molded into spherical particles of 2 g per particle in a room and kept at 10°C. 200 g of the chewing gum powder was sprinkled over the spherical jelly particles in a revolving pan to coat the same under temperatures kept below -10°C. After the coating was completed, 10 g of a gum solution prepared from corn syrup, sugar, gum arabic and water and 20 g of powdered sugar were sprinkled over the coated jelly particles and this process was repeated several times to assure uniform coating. The content of the mold was then emptied into a container and allowed to stand at 20°C for 10 hours to effect self-adhesion of the chewing gum matter and, consequently, integration. A chewing gum of a ball shape with jellied centres was obtained.

# Chapter - 29

## Extruded Sugar Product

In the process described by E.F. Glabe, P.W. Anderson, S. Laftsdis and P.G. Grothus; U.S. Patent 3,950,551; April 13, 1976; assigned to Food Technology, Inc., the starting material is a dehydrated sugary syrup in the form of dried flakes or ground flakes obtained by thin film drying of liquid aqueous syrups of honey, high fructose corn syrup, invert sugar, corn syrup, malt syrup, sorghum syrup and/or molasses in the presence of ungelatinized starch which is partially gelatinized in situ and/or in the presence of a soy protein.

In this process these products in the form of flakes or in the form of ground flakes, (i.e., a powder) are placed in a macaroni-type or spaghetti-type extruder machine. Water is mixed into the flakes (or powder) while the machine is operating so that a mixture is formed by a turning mechanism which also advances the mixture toward an extrusion die. The mixing is on a continuous basis. Optionally, a vegetable oil is added. The quantity of water used and the amount of oil used will effect the texture of the finished agglomerates.

Approximately 3% by weight of vegetable oil yields the ideal texture crispness in the finished agglomerates. Smaller amounts or larger amounts of oil may also be used with good effect depending upon the finished texture desired. The moistened oil-coated flakes are then processed through the extrusion barrel of the macaroni press and then through a die. The latter can be a macaroni-type die extruding a tube-shaped piece, or it can be a spaghetti die extruding a rod-shaped piece.

The length of the pieces ideally is approximately 1/8 inch, although this dimension can be varied. When a macaroni-type annular die is used the extruded products are tubular. When a spaghetti-type rod-shaped die is used, the extruded pieces have different configurations depending upon the diameter of the die aperture. Thus, a die aperture of 0.120 to 0.125 inch in diameter will give cut extruded pieces which are generally arcuate or curved in what can be described as a dish-shape. The agglomerates are then dried on a tray or conveyer drier so that they are in a more or less static condition, as distinguished from tumbling, at temperatures of 75° to 180°F. It is usually preferable to circulate warm dry air through and over the agglomerates until the moisture content is reduced to approximately 1.0 to 4.0% by weight.

Example: The starting material was a product composed of high fructose corn syrup solids, honey solids, partially gelatinized wheat starch, and hydroxylated lecithin in the form of dried flakes obtained by the general procedure of Example 1 of U.S. Patent 3,718,484 using the ingredients of Example V of the patent but without reducing the particle size in a hammer mill.

The flakes were placed in the dry materials mixer of a spaghetti extruder. Various amounts of water, or aqueous solutions of sugary syrups, with and without vegetable oil, were added to the flakes and mixed therewith for 10 to 15 minutes at room temperature (e.g., 70° to 80°F) and atmospheric pressure. The mixture was then fed to the barrel of the extruder where it was extruded by a screw feeder in approximately 1 to 5 minutes. The barrel of the extruder was water cooled to reduce the friction heat from the screw feeder as much as possible. The temperature of the mixture in this stage is usually 60° to 125°F, preferably 70° to 90°F. The diameter of the die orifice was 0.12 inch.

The extruded product was cut at approximately 1/16 to 3/16 inch intervals by a rapidly rotating knife just after emerging from the extruder die. The cut extruded agglomerates were then dried at temperatures within 75° to 180°F in a static condition on a tray drier to a moisture content of 1.0 to 4.0% by weight.

*The results were as follows:*

(a) With the addition of 15 parts of water per 85 parts of flakes and a drying temperature of 160° to 180°F for 4 hours, the product moisture was 1.5 to 2.0% by weight. The finished product was dry, very hard and tough in texture. There was some tendency to form lumps in the mixer but extrusion was good.

(b) The procedure was the same as in (a) except that 12 parts of water, 3 parts of oil and 85 parts of flakes were used & the product moisture was 1.0 to 2.0% by weight. The extrusion was good and the product character was excellent. The texture was crisp, not hard.

(c) The procedure was the same as in (a) except that 12 parts of water, 3 parts cotton seed oil, and 3 parts of a saturated solution of sucrose in water per 82 parts of flakes were used and the product moisture was 1.2 to 2.0% by weight. The product texture was very crisp and crunchy. The sweetness was greater than in the product from (b) and the general characteristics of the product were excellent.

(d) The procedure was the same as in (a) except that 6 parts water, 3 parts cotton seed oil and 6 parts sugar syrup (saturated solution of sucrose in water at 70° to 80°F) per 85 parts of flakes were used and the product moisture was 1.0 to 2.5% by weight. The taste was sweeter than that of the product from (c) and the product was crisp and very desirable.

(e) The procedure was carried out as in (d) except that liquid honey was substituted for the sugar syrup. The finished chips had a much stronger odour and taste of honey.

(f) The procedure was carried out as in (a) except that 6.0 parts water, 6 parts sugar syrup (sucrose), 3 parts dry granular sucrose and 3 parts cotton seed oil per 82 parts of flakes were used. The product was very sweet and very crisp and crunchy. The addition of the dry granular sucrose provides a coating of crystalline sugar on the outside of the finished chip thereby adding significantly to the crisp texture and the sweet taste.

(g) The procedure was carried out as in (a) except that 17 parts water and 3 parts cotton seed oil per 80 parts of flakes were used. The produce character was very hard and less crisp. The greater strength of this chip makes it more usable in certain applications in baking or in ice cream-making where the chip would come in contact with very wet doughs or with high-moisture-content solutions such as ice cream.

## LOW CALORIE SNACK

E. Farkas; U.S. Patent 3,821,428; June 28, 1974; assigned to General Foods Corp. has found that xanthan gum, commercially known as Keltrol, and dextrin work synergistically to produce a puffed product when baked. More specifically, when these two edible components are mixed with water to form a dough, allowed to stand for a period of hours and subsequently baked for a short period of time, an extremely aerated, freeze-dried-like structure is derived which closely resembles the standard gun-puffed cereals popcorn-like products.

Dextrin is well known in the art as being a starch gum produced by the incomplete hydrolysis of starch. Xanthan gum however, is a fermentation product of glucose and is commonly referred to as being a fermentation gum. The xanthan gum which is employed in this process may be illustrated by the Xanthomonas colloid produced by the bacterium, Xanthomonas campestris. By the process of fermentation, a long chain polysaccharides is formed which has a periodically repeating glucose-mannose-glucuronic acid configuration that is believed to be the key factor in its unique properties.

The production of xanthan gum is more fully described in U.S. Patent 3,507,664. An added feature of xanthan gum is that on an as is basis, i.e., on the basis of its 15% digestibility, xanthan gum has a caloric value of 0.5 cal/gm. A dry mix of xanthan gum and dextrin is first prepared, the ratios from 1:2 to 2:1, preferably about 1:1, and subsequently mixed with water. The amount of water needed usually ranges from 40 to 50% to prevent the formation of a too dry or too wet product. The paste is worked to a shiny, siringy, dough-like consistency. It is critical that the dough be allowed to stand for a period of at least 18 to 24 hours prior to baking for the desired degree of puffing to occur; otherwise the resultant product is puffed but wet, sticky and soon collapses. Xanthan gum and dextrin are not chemically incompatible as other gums would be and it is believed that this rather extended latent period is required for these two compatible gums to orientate their polymer structures and consequently exhibit their synergistic effects in causing this puffed, porous, freeze-dried-like structure to form. The dough is subsequently rolled out, cut, and baked for about 15 to 20 minutes in a 300° to 400°F oven. The higher temperatures for shorter periods have been found to be necessary for the puffing effect to take place.

Example: A dry mix of 50% xanthan gum and 50% dextrin was made and combined with water to form a 50% water-containing paste. The paste was worked like a very sticky dough in a mortar and pestle until it became stringly and shiny. It was covered and let stand for 24 hours. Subsequently, it was rolled out into a sheet of 1/8 inch thickness with some salt sprinkled on it.

One half inch squares were cut and place on a baking sheet and baked in the oven at 400°F for 15 minutes. They puffed up into fragile, crisp pillow shaped pieces that remained shiny and had a foam-like structure in the centre.

## HIGH PROTEIN CHOCOLATE SNACK

A high protein chocolate snack for use by the military, spacemen, campers, athletes, etc. has been developed by A. Rebane; U.S. Patent 3,901,966; August 26, 1975; assigned to Sandoz Inc. It contains 30 to 50%, preferably 40% chocolate, 15 to 30% protein and 0.5 to 2.5% calcium caseinate.

The chocolate portion normally consists of 15 to 25% milk chocolate and 15 to 25% dark chocolate. The milk chocolate contains at least 10% chocolate liquor according to the Federal Standards of Identity and the dark chocolate contains at least 15% chocolate liquor. The snack contains about 4.8 to 6.3% chocolate liquor in all.

The majority of the protein in the chocolate snack is provided by proteinaceous ingredients such as sodium caseinate, which contains about 90% by weight protein, and is present in the chocolate snack at levels of 10 to 20%, preferably 15 to 20%, and peanut butter which contains about 25% by weight protein and is present in the chocolate at levels of 15 to 20%. These proteinaceous ingredients comprise 25 to 40% of the contemplated chocolate snack. In addition to these ingredients, protein is also provided by the milk chocolate and dark chocolate which contains 7.5 to 8.0% protein based on the weight of the chocolate and by the calcium caseinate which is about 88% protein.

A sweetener such as sugar is used in the range of 10 to 15%; and corn syrup is also generally used at levels of 3 to 5% in the chocolate snack. In addition, vitamins and mineral which are compatible with the ingredients of the snack can also be added if desired to further enhance the nutritional value of high protein chocolate snack of this process.

A typical formulation and range of ingredients for the chocolate snack is as listed on the following page. This formulation provides chocolate snacks having a protein content between 15 to 30% by weight.

| *Ingredient* | *Percent Range* |
|---|---|
| Milk chocolate | 15-25 |
| Dark chocolate | 15-25 |
| Cocoa butter | 5-15 |
| Sodium caseinate | 10-20 |
| Calcium caseinate | 0.5-2.5 |
| Sugar | 10-15 |
| Corn syrup | 3-5 |
| Peanut butter | 15-20 |

*The process is carried out in accordance with the following steps.*

(a) Slowly heating a mixture which contains 15 to 25% milk chocolate, 15 to 25% dark chocolate and 5 to 15% cocoa butter to a temperature between 130° to 150°F and mixing until uniform.

(b) Cooling the mixture to a temperature of 80° to 100°F with continuous stirring.

(c) Adding 0.5 to 2.5% calcium caseinate and 25 to 40% proteinaceous ingredients.

(d) Stirring the mixture until uniform while maintaining the temperature between 80° to 100°F.

It is preferred that steps a, b, c, and d be carried out between 85° to 98°F. The sweetener and corn oil normally incorporated in the chocolate snack are usually added along with the peanut butter in the form of a peanut crunch in step c. Following step d, the melted composition, after mixing, can be formed into any of the conventional chocolate snack forms using standard techniques.

For example, the melted chocolate can be spread out in sheet as this as desired, chilled to about 45° to 70°F, preferably 65° to 70°F and then cut to the desired size and shape and packaged. Alternately, molds of various shapes can be filled with the melted chocolate, which can then be chilled to 45°F, after which the finished product is removed from the mold and packaged. The melted chocolate can also be extruded through a specific orifice, e.g., rod, ribbon, etc., cooled to 45° to 55°F in a cooling tunnel and packaged.

## EXPANDED CONFECTIONS

### For Fillings in Pastries

In three patents by J.H. Forkner; U.S. Patents 3,711,300, January 16, 1973; 3,779,772, December 18, 1973; and 3,782,966, January 1, 1974 food products composed of a wafer made of cooky or pastry dough containing an expanded confection filling are described.

In the first patent, a baked wafer is employed having characteristics compatible with the end product desired. This baked wafer may be any of many types of pie shells, cookies or crackers. Such products are made from various bakery doughs and batters. An expandable confection filling is then positioned adjacent the wafer. The filling material is not necessarily initially attached to the upper surface of the wafer because during subsequent processing an adhesive bond is formed. The assembly of water and expandable material is positioned within a tray which may be a metal tray used only for convenience in passing the assembly through subsequent processing operations, or preferably a tray in which the final product remains and which becomes all or a part of the final packages as, for example, a tray made of metal foil, foil lined or wax paper, or molded plastic. In the next step the entire assembly is subjected to heat for the purpose of softening the filling material.

In a typical instance such heating may serve to elevate the temperature of the filling to a temperature of the order of 100° to 120°F. Thereafter, a partial vacuum is applied to cause the filling to expand substantially. This step can be accomplished by use of conventional vacuum dehydrating equipment. Initially the shelf temperature of this equipment can be of the order of 180° to 240°F to effect the initial softening of the unexpanded filling as described above.

After such initial heating, a vacuum of the order of 28 to 29 inches of mercury column is applied with the shelf temperature being continue at a level of about 240°F for about 50 minutes and then reduced to a somewhat lower temperature within 150° to 80°F for the remainder of the cycle. Cooling at the end of the vacuum step (e.g., to as low as 80°F) serves to set the filling in its expanded form and this makes it possible to retain maximum expansion in the final product. During the above heat and vacuum treatment, the filling becomes firmly bonded to the upper contacting surface of the wafer and both the expanded filling and the wafer are dehydrated to a low moisture level of the order of 2% or less.

In carrying out this method, it is desirable to employ means for fixing the position of each wafer with respect to the tray before carrying out further processing. Also, assuming that the tray becomes all or a part of the final package, it is desirable that each wafer maintain a fixed position on the bottom of the tray. To effect such fixed location small amounts of viscous liquid material are applied between the wafer and the tray which will effect initial adhesion but which will provide a friable retention after processing.

A suitable material for this purpose is an expandable confection similar to the expandable filling employed but in liquid or semiliquid form. Small amounts of such confection in liquid form can be applied to areas of the tray bottom on which the wafers are deposited. It should be sufficient viscosity (e.g., concentration of 80 Brix) to provide the adhesion necessary to retain the cookies in place. During subsequent processing, such applications become cellular and are dehydrated, thereby forming a friable bond which is sufficient to hold the wafers in position within the tray during storage, handling and marketing, but which permits the consumer to remove the wafers and expand filling without difficulty.

In the second patent, a method for the manufacture of expanded confection products in which the confection material before expansion is made into the form of an aggregate of granules that are fused or bonded together to form a slug or wafer. This slug or wafer is heated to a plastic state and subsequently cooled. After cooling, the product is placed in contact with a mass of cooked dough, heated to soften the same followed by expanding with the aid of a partial vacuum. Various edible additives may be added to the granular material.

In general, the additives serve to modify the eating properties of the finished product, or they may add one or more flavours, or they may supplement or modify dietetic properties. One suitable type of additive is nut meats (e.g., almond, walnut, peanut, etc.) in particulate form. Another type is granules or small visible pieces of hard confection so formulated as not to be subject to expansion under vacuum.

Pieces of sweetened or unsweetened chocolate are examples of another type of material. Certain additives, such as malted milk or other milk solids or supplemental sucrose sugar can best be added in dry powdered form. In some instances, it is desirable to add 2 or more of such additives, whether powdered, particulate or both are intermixed and dispersed in the mass of discrete granules.

The base filling used in all the patents is the same. An example from the third mentioned patent is as follows:

Example 1: A conventional pie crust dough was prepared using 100 parts flour and 40 parts of shortening and with the usual formula and technique described in standard bakery cook books.

*The formulation of the filling was as follows:*

| ***Ingredients*** | ***Pounds*** |
|---|---|
| Dry corn sugar | 100 |
| Glucose syrup | 100 |
| Malt sugar | 30 |
| Granulated sugar | 50 |
| Hard fat (melting point 132°F) | 20 |
| Malted milk powder | 30 |
| Salt | 1 |

The above filling ingredients were blended together and added to the glucose, after the latter had been heated to boiling temperature. The moisture content was about 6%, being largely imparted by the glucose. During blending, heat was supplied to maintain the temperature at or near 212°F. Before the mix commenced to harden it was removed from the mixer and then sheeted to form sheets about 3/16 inch thick. The sheets were scored along lines extending at right angles to each other, the lines in one direction being 2 inches apart and in the other direction 1 inch apart.

These sheets were then permitted to cool and set at ambient room temperature (70°F) whereby they became brittle. Thereafter the temperature was reduced to about 60°F and the brittle sheets passed through a breaking roll to cause breakage along the score lines, thereby forming wafers each about 3/16 inch thick, 1 inch wide and 2 inches long. A sheet of the dough measuring about 3 inches wide and 4 inches long was placed on a baking pan and one of the wafers was placed on the central region of the dough sheet.

A top sheet of dough was then placed over the filling wafer and lower dough and trimmed off in such a manner as to provide a peripheral margin overlapping a peripheral margin of the lower sheet. The upper surface of the margin of the lower sheet was wetted to insure adhesion of the margins in baking and to avoid separation during the subsequent vacuum treatment. The pan containing this turnover or tart was then placed in an oven having an air temperature of 450°F and baked for a period of 8 minutes, during which time the dough was baked and the filling liquified. The pan and turnover were then transferred as rapidly as possible to the shelf of a vacuum dryer, the shelf having been preheated to 240°F. the vacuum dryer was then evacuated to a partial vacuum equivalent to 29 1/2 inches mercury column and maintained at that value for about 1 1/2 hours. The temperature of the turnover when the vacuum was first applied was about 200°F. At the end of this vacuum treatment the turnover was cooled to about 150°F over a period of about 15 minutes and thereafter the vacuum was broken and the pan turnover removed.

After cooling in ambient temperature, it was found that the filling had expanded several times its original volume, being of the order of a inch thick. The peripheral seams between the upper and lower margins of the dough were retained, and it was evident that the upper dough layer had been bulged upwardly during final expansion of the filling. A lesser bulge was evident on the lower plane.

The product in the foregoing Example 1 had sufficient strength to withstand packaging without breakage. The moisture content of the expanded filling and the baked dough was less than 2% and of the order of 1%. When consumed, it was found that the filling was crunchy or friable, which was attributed to its cellular structure and low moisture content. It was found that the product had good keeping properties when packaged in conventional laminated plastic film bags or containers capable of protecting the product from absorption of atmospheric moisture. In general the product was palatable and an attractive product for the consumer trade.

The baking operation for the foregoing Example 1 was carried out by use of a conventional kitchen oven. However, it was evident that the various operations carried out in Example 1 were amenable to automation and well adapted to commercial equipment.

Example 2: The same dough and filling formulas were used as in Example 1, however, the filling sheets were subdivided in their chilled brittle state to particles having a screen size of minus 8 mesh. This discrete confection filling was blended with malted milk powder and granulated sugar at ambient temperature in the ratio of 25% (of the weight of the confection filling) malted milk and 15% granulated sugar (by weight). This provided a combined average moisture content of 4% compared to 6% for the confection filling.

This mixture was then formed into wafers each measuring about 2 inches long and 1 inch wide and weighing about 15 g, by compression after softening by heating to 110°F. It was noted that fusion of the malted milk powder had served to attach it to the other material of the wafer. These agglomerated wafers were then used in the tars in place of the wafers used in Example 1. Because of the lower moisture content of the malted milk powder and granulated sugar which absorbed some moisture from the confection filling material, lateral flow of the wafer during heating and expansion was noticeably restricted.

This was attributed to the abutment-like effect of the malted milk in inhibiting spreading in contrast with the homogeneous filling used in Example 1. The restriction of lateral flow minimized leakage or flow of fused material from the perimeter seams of the tart. In the vacuum oven the filling expanded with even greater force than the material in Example 1, which is attributed to the lower moisture content and the added malted milk. This accentuated expanding force was evidanced by greater spread or bulging of the side walls of the tart with the force being so great as to provide a significant concave contour of the under dough as well as the more easily developed convex form of the upper dough. The final filling had a cellular structure that was finer and more uniform than Example 1. The filling was sweeter due to the presence of the malted milk. The malted milk retained the general distribution pattern that it had before expansion, and its characteristic flavour was more apparent than was provided by the hcmogeneous mix of malted milk with other ingredients like corn sugar.

It was noted in connection with Example 2 that additional edible additives could be used with the discrete filling, thus producing a variety of products. Particular materials which were added included dried meat and shrimp, cocoa, nuts, granular dry cheese and various powdered vegetables, and soya products.

## Special Packaging

In another patent in the series by J.H. Forkner; U.S. Patent 3,989,853; November 2, 1976, the process of manufacturing the expanded confection includes its packaging. In general, the method comprises manufacturing a product including a package or bag containing an expandable confection and having one or more vent openings or perforations. Shortly before or at the time a retail establishment sells such products to the consumer trade, the confection is expanded within the bag while the vent is open, and then the vent may be closed when expansion is completed. In one embodiment the vent is closed or opened by use of a seal tab or strip that is secured to the bag and adapted to be adhesively applied over the vent. A view schematically illustrating the filling and sealing operations is shown in figure.

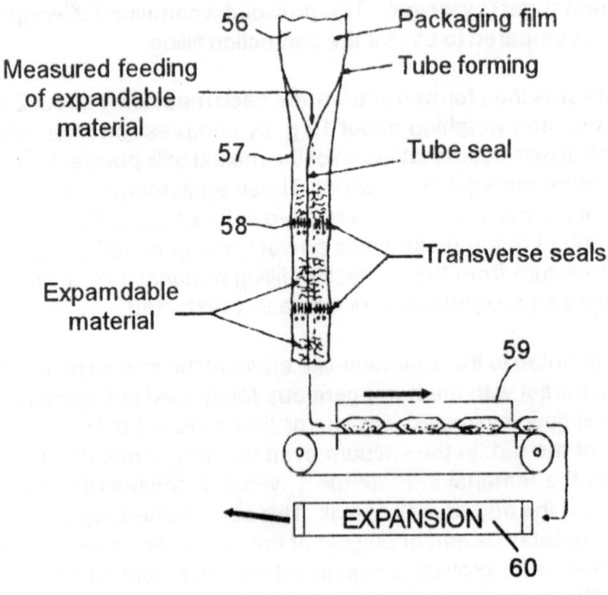


**Figure : Special Packaging for Expanded Confection**

## Bonded to Ice Cream Cone

It is known that certain confections can be greatly expanded in volume by heating to soften the same, followed by applying a partial vacuum. Certain sugars present in most commercial confections impart expandable properties, such as the solids of corn syrup (containing dextrose, maltose and dextrins), refined corn sugar (dextrose), malt syrup, malt sugar, hydrolyzed cereal solids of low dextrin equivalency (e.g., DE 15-35), and confections like peanut brittle which include such sugars. Various U.S. patents disclose such expanded products and method for their manufacture.

By this process, J.H. Forkner; U.S. Patent 4,104,405; August 1, 1978 has produced an expandable confection which is consumed with an added frozen dessert. In general, the product consists of a shell comparable to an ice cream cone or cone which has an expanded confection bonded to the peripheral surface of the head of the shell in such a manner that a scoop of ice cream or other frozen dessert may be applied upon the head and in the space generally surrounding the confection.

The product shown in figure a consists of a shell 10 which in this instance is a conventional ice cream cone made of sweet dough or batter and which has sufficient strength for handling but is friable and edible. The upper annular portion of greatest diameter may be referred to as the head of the shell. Surrounding and extending upwardly from the head of the shell there is an expanded annular mass 12 of confection which is bonded to the outer peripheral surface of the shell. It will be seen that the interior of the head portion is open for receiving a scoop of ice cream or other frozen dessert. A plurality of such products can be nested and packaged in nested form for storage and distribution. Because the expanded confection mass 12 extends about and is bonded to the peripheral surface of the head of the shell, preferably protruding above the rim of the cone, it does not interfere with placement of a scoop of ice cream upon the head in the manner conventionally followed in dispensing ice cream cones. Likewise, when the ice cream or other frozen dessert is applied, it contacts only a minor part of the expanded mass, thus limiting any tendency for moisture from the ice cream or other frozen dessert to be rapidly absorbed by the expanded mass, which would cause collapsing of the expanded confection.

Assuming that the expanded mass has the characteristics desired, portions of the mass can be broken away as the frozen dessert is consumed without causing the remaining portions of the expanded mass to break or fall away from the shell. The breakaway may involve severance from the walls of the shell or may include removal of the adjacent portion of the friable shell.

Assuming that two types of source confections are employed, one material has a relatively high moisture content, as for example from 10 to 20%. Also it contains in its formulation gel-forming and film-forming ingredients, such as gelatin, albumen, or natural gums, singly or in combination. In addition, it is desirable that this confection be aerated during its manufacture, as by a whipping operation in which air is beaten into the mix. A confection possessing all of these characteristics is commercial marshmallow, which in a typical instance has moisture content of the order of 15 to 20% and about 1.5 to 2.25% of gel-forming ingredient (e.g., gelatin); it also contains a relatively high percentage of corn solids (e.g., 40% or more) which imparts expandability.

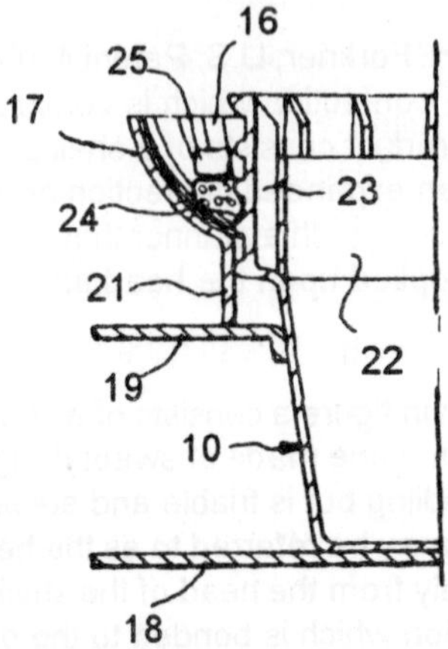


**Figure : Expanded Confection Bonded to Ice Cream Cone**

While the moisture content of commercial marshmallow may generally range from 15 to 20%, it may be processed to have a lower moisture content 9e.g., 10%). Marshmallows or marshmallow drops are manufactured and sold in various sizes, including a size of the order of 1 inch in diameter and rounded or with rounded corners, and a size commonly referred to as miniature marshmallows, about 1/2 inch in diameter and similarly shaped.

The other source confection which can be used in combination with the first named confection is what is commonly known as hard candy. Hard candies have relatively low moisture contents ranging for example from 1 to 2%. They also have a substantial content of corn sugar solids (e.g., 40% or more) which impart expandable properties.

Because of their different formulations and moisture contents, equal weights of the two source confections referred to above, under comparable conditions of temperature, time and applied vacuum, will expand differently. The first high moisture content source confection will expand to a much greater volume than the hard candy.

The procedure described above can be carried out by use of an assembly as shown in figure. In this instance means is associated with the head portion of the shell which forms an annular mold space surrounding the head. In this instance the means consists of an annulus 16 which can be made of inexpensive material such as waxed paper, foil or foil laminate. The paper preferably is fluted or corrugated, because such paper can be more readily stripped from the expanded confection mass. In the instance the annulus flares outwardly and upwardly, while the lower end fits snugly about the head of the cone. Immediately surrounding the paper annulus there is an annular supporting member 17 which can be made of suitable material and which serves to support and maintain the paper annulus in place.

Preferably this member is made of material of poor heat conductivity, such as a plastic material or cellular fiber blended with a plastic resin. In figure it is assumed that the shell 10 together with other 5 like shells, is retained within a rack which may include the bottom plate 18 which supports the shells, with the plate 19 having openings which accomodate the shells. The lower annular extension 21 of the member 17 is shown resting upon the plate 19. The type of cone or shell illustrated also is provided with an inner annular wall 22 which is connected to the outer wall of the head by the webs 23.

The source confection is introduced into the mold space between the paper annulus and the head of the shell. Assuming use of the two types of confection, the high moisture content confection pieces 24 are deposited in the lower end of the mold space, and thereafter hard candy pieces 25 are deposited on top of the first confection. Assuming that the first confection is commercial marshmallow, it is preferred to use a commercial form of marshmallow that has been cured, and in addition, to have it in relatively small pieces.

These pieces may range in size from 1/16 to 1/8 inch and may be produced by subdividing larger pieces of cured marshmallow. The hard candy 25 is in the form of pieces such as are commonly known as candy bits or candy pillows. For example, such pieces may be about 1/2 inch long, 3/8 inch wide, and 3/8 inch thick at the centre, alhough other sizes can be used.

The proportions by weight of the high moisture content confection and the hard candy can be varied in accordance with the type of final product desired. However, it is preferred to utilize a quantity of the high moisture content confection by weight which is greatly less than the amount of hard candy used. By way of example, the amount by weight of hard candy used can be from 5 to 20 times the weight of the high moisture content confection. In a typical instance, 1 g of the high moisture content confection can be used together with 9g of the hard candy.

Both confections are distributed about the head of the shell, although the pieces may or may not be in direct contact with each other. Expansion results in areas of direct contact between the expanded hard or low moisture content candy pieces. In addition to utilizing the pieces of hard candy as described above, it is preferable to utilize hard candy bits or pillows which have bands or areas of bright colour on their surfaces. Typical colours are red, yellow, green and the natural white of the candy. Some pieces may be malted milk balls or fragments thereof which have not been expanded.

After introducing the confections into the mold space provided by the paper annulus 16, the assembly is in condition for proceeding with heating and expansion. While it is possible to heat in hot air as provided by a conventional hot air oven, the confections preferably are heated by exposing their upper surfaces to downwardly directed radiant heat. A cooking broiler provided with overhead radiant heating elements is suitable for this purpose. Heating is continued for a relatively short period of the order of from 1 to 5 minutes.

During this time the directly exposed surfaces of the candy bits are rapidly heated to a temperature sufficiently high (e.g., 16° to 25°F) to make them fluid or semifluid. Also the interiors of the candy pieces are heated sufficiently (e.g., 120° to 160°F) to soften them to an extent sufficient for expansion. In addition, some heat penetrates the lower mass 24 of the high moisture content confection to elevate its temperature to an extent sufficient for controlled expansion (e.g., 100° to 120°F). Thus this type of heating provides different temperature levels for different portions of the hard candy and different average temperatures for the hard candy which is directly exposed to radiant heat and the underlying marshmallows which are completely or partially shielded from direct exposure by the hard candy.

Following heating as described above, the assembly is immediately placed in a vacuum chamber, and by means of a suitable vacuum pump the pressure within the chamber is progressively reduced to an end partial vacuum corresponding to 29 inches mercury column. By the time the vacuum reaches a value of about 15 inches mercury column. Initial expansion of the first confection 24 occurs without, however, any appreciable expansion of the hard candy.

Initial expansion of the moisture content confection tends to push or boost the hard candy upward, with the hard candy pieces being more or less adhesively secured to the high moisture content confection due to fusion of their outer surfaces. As the vacuum increases, the high moisture content confection continues to expand, and at the same time the hard candy expands over the upper surface of the expanded high moisture content confection. During the expansion just described, a substantial amount of heat transfer occurs from the hard candy pieces, which are at a higher average temperature and represent a greater weight, to the underlying high moisture confection, which is at a lower average temperature and of lesser weight, assuming that differential heating is employed as previously described. This heat transfer plaus a part in the removal of moisture from the high moisture content confection or, in other words, in dehydrating the expanded marshmallow type of confection to a point where at the end of the expansion operation this entire expanded mass has sufficient strength and stability to inhibit collapsing when the vacuum is broken. Also the overall low moisture content attained (e.g., average 1 to 15%) promotes production of a final expanded mass which is friable, crunchy and edible as desired.

# Chapter - 30

## *Project Profiles*

- *Automatic Biscuit Making Plant*
- *Bread Plant*
- *Confectionery Industry*
- *Dairy Farm To Produce Milk*
- *Dairy Products and Milk Packaging in Pouches*
- *Fruits and Vegetables Drying by Freeze Drying Method*
- *Instant Noodles*
- *Mineral Water*
- *Palm Oil Production*
- *Pasta Products*
- *Pickles and Murabbas*
- *Processed Foods*
- *Roller Flour Mill*

# Automatic Biscuit Making Plant

| | | |
|---|---|---|
| 1. | **Capacity** | 5 MT/Day |
| | | **Rs. in Lacs.** |
| 2. | **Land & Building**<br>(Area covered 800 sq. mtr.) | 16.95 |
| 3. | **Plant & Machinery**<br>(Rotary Moulding & Cutting M/c., Mixing M/c., Flour Shifter, Electric Oven, Automatic Biscuit Packaging M/c. | 44.07 |
| 4. | **Other Fixed Assets**<br>(Office Equipment, Furniture, Installation Cost for Water, Electricity & Pre-operative & Preliminary Expenses) | 4.80 |
| 5. | **Fixed Capital**<br>(Land & Bldg. + Plant & Machinery + Other Fixed Assets) | 65.82 |
| 6. | **Raw Materials/Month**<br>(Wheat flour, Vanaspati, Sugar, Baking powder, Milk, Salt, Yeast, Wrappers, etc.) | 22.10 |
| 7. | **Salary & Wages/Month** | 1.09 |
| 8. | **Utilities & Overheads/Month**<br>(Power Consumption, Water Consumption, Stationery, Postage, Telephone, Advertisement, Conveyance & Transportation, Administrative & Miscellaneous expenses) | 1.57 |
| 9. | **Total Working Capital/Month**<br>(Raw Material + Salary & Wages + Utilities & Overheads) | 24.77 |
| 10. | **Total Capital Investment**<br>(Total Fixed Capital + Total Working Capital for 3 months) | 140.13 |
| 11. | **Cost of Production/Annum** | 340.18 |
| 12. | **Turnover/Annum** | 450.00 |
| 13. | **Profit** | 110.00 |
| 14. | **Rate of Return** | 78.36% |
| 15. | **Break Even Point (B.E.P.)** | 33.67% |

# Bread Plant

| | | |
|---|---|---|
| 1. | **Capacity** | 10,000 Loaves/Day |
| | | **Rs. in Lacs.** |
| 2. | **Land & Building**<br>(Area covered 1800 sq. mtr.) | 28.50 |
| 3. | **Plant & Machinery**<br>(Flour shifter, Water measuring tank, Dough kneading machine, Rounder, Moulder, Travelling oven, Trolleys, Baking pans & lids etc. | 25.00 |
| 4. | **Other Fixed Assets**<br>(Office Equipment, Furniture, Installation Cost for Water, Electricity & Pre-operative & Preliminary Expenses) | 6.00 |
| 5. | **Fixed Capital**<br>(Land & Bldg. + Plant & Machinery + Other Fixed Assets) | 59.50 |
| 6. | **Raw Materials/Month**<br>(Wheat flour, Salt, Sugar, Milk powder, Yeast, Shortening, Wrappers, etc.) | 27.48 |
| 7. | **Salary & Wages/Month** | 0.92 |
| 8. | **Utilities & Overheads/Month**<br>(Power Consumption, Water Consumption, Stationery, Postage, Telephone, Advertisement, Conveyance & Transportation, Administrative & Miscellaneous expenses) | 0.89 |
| 9. | **Total Working Capital/Month**<br>(Raw Material + Salary & Wages + Utilities & Overheads) | 29.52 |
| 10. | **Total Capital Investment**<br>(Total Fixed Capital + Total Working Capital for 3 months) | 89.00 |
| 11. | **Cost of Production/Annum** | 381.42 |
| 12. | **Turnover/Annum** | 414.00 |
| 13. | **Profit** | 32.57 |
| 14. | **Rate of Return** | 36.59% |
| 15. | **Break Even Point (B.E.P.)** | 53.16% |

# Confectionery Industry (Toffee & Candy)

| | | |
|---|---|---|
| 1. | **Capacity** | 1 Ton/Day |
| | | **Rs. in Lacs.** |
| 2. | **Land & Building**<br>(Area covered 500 sq. mtr.) | 12.37 |
| 3. | **Plant & Machinery**<br>(Homogenizer, Steam & vacuum pans, Drop cutting machine, Pulling machine, Toffee cutting machine, Revolving comfits pan, Tableting machine, Wrapping and packing machine etc.) | 8.30 |
| 4. | **Other Fixed Assets**<br>(Office Equipment, Furniture, Installation Cost for Water, Electricity & Pre-operative & Preliminary Expenses) | 1.85 |
| 5. | **Fixed Capital**<br>(Land & Bldg. + Plant & Machinery + Other Fixed Assets) | 22.52 |
| 6. | **Raw Materials/Month**<br>(Sugar, Milk, Corn syrup, Invert sugar, Flavours, Colours etc.) | 5.22 |
| 7. | **Salary & Wages/Month** | 0.63 |
| 8. | **Utilities & Overheads/Month**<br>(Power Consumption, Water Consumption, Stationery, Postage, Telephone, Advertisement, Conveyance & Transportation, Administrative & Miscellaneous expenses) | 045. |
| 9. | **Total Working Capital/Month**<br>(Raw Material + Salary & Wages + Utilities & Overheads) | 6.30 |
| 10. | **Total Capital Investment**<br>(Total Fixed Capital + Total Working Capital for 3 months) | 41.44 |
| 11. | **Cost of Production/Annum** | 86.69 |
| 12. | **Turnover/Annum** | 105.00 |
| 13. | **Profit** | 18.30 |
| 14. | **Rate of Return** | 44.17% |
| 15. | **Break Even Point (B.E.P.)** | 47.46% |

# Dairy Farm to Produce Milk

| | | |
|---|---|---|
| 1. | **Capacity** | 700 ltr./Day |
| | | **Rs. in Lacs.** |
| 2. | **Land & Building**<br>(Area covered 1 acre) | 27.87 |
| 3. | **Plant & Machinery**<br>(Pasteuriser, Boiler, Filter, Storage Tank, Milk Reception Tank, Homogenizer, Milk Cans, Automatic Pouch Filling & Sealing Machine etc.) | 2.40 |
| 4. | **Other Fixed Assets**<br>(Office Equipment, Furniture, Installation Cost for Water, Electricity & Pre-operative & Preliminary Expenses) | 8.60 |
| 5. | **Fixed Capital**<br>(Land & Bldg. + Plant & Machinery + Other Fixed Assets) | 38.87 |
| 6. | **Raw Materials/Month**<br>(Cattle Feed, Pouches etc. | 0.55 |
| 7. | **Salary & Wages/Month** | 0.32 |
| 8. | **Utilities & Overheads/Month**<br>(Power Consumption, Water Consumption, Stationery, Postage, Telephone, Advertisement, Conveyance & Transportation, Administrative & Miscellaneous expenses) | 0.22 |
| 9. | **Total Working Capital/Month**<br>(Raw Material + Salary & Wages + Utilities & Overheads) | 1.09 |
| 10. | **Total Capital Investment**<br>(Total Fixed Capital + Total Working Capital for 3 months) | 42.00 |
| 11. | **Cost of Production/Annum** | 24.66 |
| 12. | **Turnover/Annum** | 35.28 |
| 13. | **Profit** | 10.61 |
| 14. | **Rate of Return** | 25.29% |
| 15. | **Break Even Point (B.E.P.)** | 57.18% |

# Dairy Products & Milk Packaging

| | | |
|---|---|---|
| 1. | **Capacity** | 1390 kg./Day |
| | | **Rs. in Lacs.** |
| 2. | **Land & Building** (Area covered 1500 sq. mtr.) | 34.75 |
| 3. | **Plant & Machinery** (Pasteuriser, Boiler, Vacuum Pan Evaporator, Storage Tank, Fermenting Tank, Churner, Tray Dryer, Automatic Pouch Filling & Sealing Machine etc.) | 24.11 |
| 4. | **Other Fixed Assets** (Office Equipment, Furniture, Installation Cost for Water, Electricity & Pre-operative & Preliminary Expenses) | 5.05 |
| 5. | **Fixed Capital** (Land & Bldg. + Plant & Machinery + Other Fixed Assets) | 63.91 |
| 6. | **Raw Materials/Month** (Milk, Chemicals for Butter, Paneer etc., Hydraulic Acid, Cans, Polythenes, Packets & Corrugated Boxes etc.) | 22.70 |
| 7. | **Salary & Wages/Month** | 2.23 |
| 8. | **Utilities & Overheads/Month** (Power Consumption, Water Consumption, Stationery, Postage, Telephone, Advertisement, Conveyance & Transportation, Administrative & Miscellaneous expenses) | 2.14 |
| 9. | **Total Working Capital/Month** (Raw Material + Salary & Wages + Utilities & Overheads) | 27.07 |
| 10. | **Total Capital Investment** (Total Fixed Capital + Total Working Capital for 3 months) | 145.00 |
| 11. | **Cost of Production/Annum** | 362.00 |
| 12. | **Turnover/Annum** | 418.50 |
| 13. | **Profit** | 56.65 |
| 14. | **Rate of Return** | 39.04% |
| 15. | **Break Even Point (B.E.P.)** | 51.15% |

# Fruits & Veg. Drying by Freeze Drying Method

| | | |
|---|---|---|
| 1. | **Capacity** | 500 kg./Day |
| | | **Rs. in Lacs.** |
| 2. | **Land & Building** (Area covered 2 acre) | 27.50 |
| 3. | **Plant & Machinery** (Washing machine, Peeling machine, Blanching machine, Storage tank, Freeze drying machine, Boiler, Pouch packing machine etc.) | 116.07 |
| 4. | **Other Fixed Assets** (Office Equipment, Furniture, Installation Cost for Water, Electricity & Pre-operative & Preliminary Expenses) | 20.00 |
| 5. | **Fixed Capitl** (Land & Bldg. + Plant & Machinery + Other Fixed Assets) | 163.57 |
| 6. | **Raw Materials/Month** (Fruits, Vegetables, Chemicals as potassium, metabi-sulphite etc.) | 2.89 |
| 7. | **Salary & Wages/Month** | 0.42 |
| 8. | **Utilities & Overheads/Month** (Power Consumption, Water Consumption, Stationery, Postage, Telephone, Advertisement, Conveyance & Transportation, Administrative & Miscellaneous expenses) | 1.13 |
| 9. | **Total Working Capital/Month** (Raw Material + Salary & Wages + Utilities & Overheads) | 4.44 |
| 10. | **Total Capital Investment** (Total Fixed Capital + Total Working Capital for 3 months) | 176.90 |
| 11. | **Cost of Production/Annum** | 115.67 |
| 12. | **Turnover/Annum** | 157.50 |
| 13. | **Profit** | 41.82 |
| 14. | **Rate of Return** | 23.65% |
| 15. | **Break Even Point (B.E.P.)** | 62.53% |

# *Instant Noodles*

## INTRODUCTION

Instant noodles is a ready to cook and serve snack food which has become very popular in India in the recent years after its introduction on mass scale of M/s. Food Specialities Ltd., New Delhi under the brand name "Maggi".

The manufacture of instant noodles in Japan was developed in 1952. Today nearly 8,000 million packs per year are produced for domestic and expor use. Meanwhile noodle manufacturing machines have become fully automatic compact with high speed and effectiveness.

Instant noodles are manufacture in two kinds, namely, seasoned noodles and plain noodles with a soup bag. The former must contain a seasoning liquid and highly humid glutinous wheat is used to prevent weakness is stickiness. The latter requires a white colour as its first prerequisite rather than stickiness. Thus wheat powder containing ash content of 0.3 - 0.45% is used as the raw materials.

Alongwith the main material of wheat powder, carbonic salt water, common salt, soft water and other additives are required for the mixture. Carbonic salt water, $K_2 Co_3$ or $Na_2 Co_3$, is also an important additive, giving the noodle special stickiness, elasticity, smoothness and good taste.

Salt water gives homogeneity and regulates the stickiness of the noodle as well as adding salty taste to the noodles. The necessity of the other ingredients also goes without saying.

# TECHNOLOGY AND PROCESS DESCRIPTION

## Mixing of Raw Materials

Mixing or compounding wheat powder and additives (powder state) or their solution are the most important factor to decide the quality of the dough (paste state). The additives in the wheat powder are dissolved in carbonic salt solution or common salt solution or are dispersed in emulation state. In the case of mixing time of 10 to 15 minutes is supposed to be taken, a special cooling device is needed, for, in such cases temperature rises by interpowder friction, has bad influence on wheat protein. The quantity of water as well as of the salt must be changed in summer and winter season, as the viscosity is influenced by atmospheric temperature. Thus a large amount of water, as well as long mixing time is necessary in winter, and it is better to take some maturing time of 15 to 30 minutes.

## Dough Sheet Making

In the process thin dough sheets are made by means of press rollers. Two dough sheets processed through 2 pairs of rollers, where 2 dough sheets are pressed together into one sheet. Meanwhile the dough sheets are made thinner, finally to save 15 min. During these several rolling processes, the dough sheet gain in stickiness and smoothness.

The sheet is oriented only one direction (longitudinal) being advantageously different from that of hand operation of orientation into two directions (longitudinal and lateral).

## Cutting (Strip Cutting)

A cutting roller is provided to make the noodle strip.

## Measuring

The weight of one portion is calculated in consideration of the dough making conditions, dough thickness and width of dough. Generally speaking, measure cutting is done at the front or the rear side of the cutter according to the user's convenience (Recently cutting at the outlet of the steaming tunnel has become more popular).

## Steaming

In the steaming tunnel, the protein in the dough is changed into alpha protein by steam heating, that is to say, deterioration with heat. The deterioration causes the strips to become more sticky and smoother than before. The quality of noodles is affected by this steaming technique. At first, wet steam is used to give humidity homogeneously to the noodles and at the last stage dry steam is used for alphanization. More than 90% content of alpha protein can be attained in one minute under the condition of steam pressure 1.5 - 2.5 kg. $cm^2$.

## Casing

After measure cutting, cut noodle strips are made curled (often performed at the rear side of the strip cutting machine) and put into cases for easy complete frying and to prevent deformation during frying. There are several types of cases, such as circular, square and eliptic. The cases are fitted on a net conveyor.

## Frying

The purpose of frying is to eliminate moisture in the noodles, to secure a permanent form, and to promote the alphanization process. The structure of fried noodles is the so-called swelling type, as against the simply dried noodles. Accordingly, the former is edible instantly by pouring boiled water over them or boiling them in water, for a few minutes. This is the most advantageous feature of the fried noodles. The temperature of frying oil generally lies between 140°C and 150°C. It is necessary to control the oil temperature to a high level at the beginning and gradually lower it at the end, or else the noodle will become spotted undesirably. Frying time is 1 to 1.5 minutes. As to the oil, lard is recommended for better stability against acidification than vegetable oil.

## Cooling

Fried noodles (above 100°C) shall then be cooled by cooling air to solidify the lard oil fixed on the surface of the strip noodles, after which they are packed in cellophane bags. If they are packed while still hot, the quality will be changed. Especially, when soup powder bags are attached, degradation of soup quality will be unavoidable and melted lard oil will adhere to the inside of the bag.

## Inspection and Packing

The Cooled products are inspected as to weight, from the colour, before packing.

## PROCESS FLOW CHART

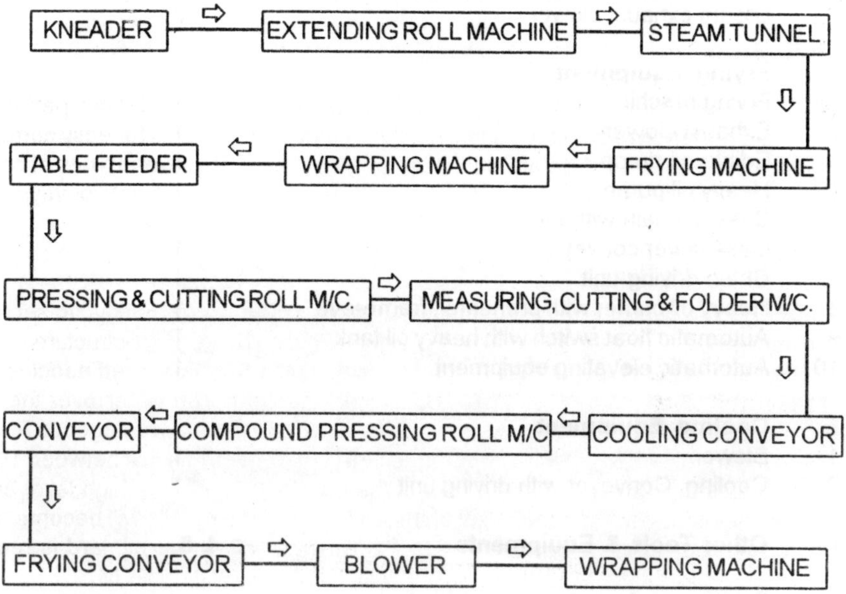


## PLANT CAPACITY

The unit may apply for an industrial approval for a plant to manufacture 3000 M.T.A. of instant noodles.

## PLANT AND MACHINERY

Various machinery and equipment required for the manufacture of instant noodles are as follows :

| | *Description* | | *Set* |
|---|---|---|---|
| **A.** | **Noodle making equipment** | | |
| 1. | Kneader | : | 2 |
| 2. | Table feeder | : | 1 |
| 3. | Compound pressing roll machine | : | 1 |
| 4. | Extending roll machine | : | 1 |
| 5. | Pressing & Cutting roll machine | : | 1 |
| **B.** | **Steaming & Measuring Cutter Equipments** | | |
| 1. | Steam tunnel | : | 1 |
| 2. | Conveyor | : | 1 |

| | | | |
|---|---|---|---|
| **C.** | **Measuring, Cutting & Folding Machine** | | |
| 1. | Steam exhaust blower | : | 2 |
| **D.** | **Frying Equipment** | | |
| 1. | Frying machine | : | 1 |
| 2. | Exhaust blower | : | 1 |
| 3. | Edible oil pump | : | 1 |
| 4. | Heavy oil pump | : | 1 |
| 5. | Special chain with case | | |
| 6. | Case cover conveyor | : | 1 |
| 7. | Chain driving unit | : | 1 |
| 8. | Heavy oil burner with preheater, frame-eye | : | 1 |
| 9. | Automatic float switch with heavy oil tank | : | 1 |
| 10. | Automatic elevating equipment | : | 1 |
| **E.** | **Cooling Equipment** | | |
| 1. | Blower | : | 1 |
| 2. | Cooling, Conveyor with driving unit | : | 1 |
| **F.** | **Other Tools & Equipments** | : | **L.S.** |

Total cost of machinery and equipments both imported and indigenous shall be Rs. 60 lakhs.

## RAW MATERIALS

The main raw material and consumables required for the manufacture of instant noodles are wheat flour refined vegetable cooking oils, sodium bicarbonate and eggs etc.

*Percentage Compositon:*

| | |
|---|---|
| Flour | 73.3% |
| C.M.C. | 0.33% |
| Sod. Polyphossphate | 0.1% |
| Common Salt | 0.8% |
| Edible Colour | 0.03% |
| Soup | 5.5% |
| Lard | 15.5% |

## INFRASTRUCTURE AND FACILITIES

| | | | |
|---|---|---|---|
| 1. | Land | : | 10,000 sq. metres |
| 2. | Building | : | 1,800 sq. metres |
| 3. | Power/Electric load | : | 300 KVA connected load |
| 4. | Steam | : | 400 Kg/hr. |
| 5. | Heavy Oil | : | 80 Kg/hr. |

## ESTIMATED COST OF PROJECT

Total cost of the project with a capacity to manufacture 4000 TPA of instant noodles is estimated at Rs. 172 lakhs. Various details are as follows :

| | | | (Rs. in lakhs) |
|---|---|---|---|
| 1. | Land and Site Development | : | 5.00 |
| 2. | Buildings | : | 27.00 |
| 3. | Plant & Machinery | : | |
| | (a) Imported | : | 50.00 |
| | (b) Indigenous | : | 10.00 |
| 4. | Miscellaneous fixed assets | : | 10.00 |
| 5. | Technical know-how | : | 10.00 |
| 6. | Preliminary and preperative expenses | : | 20.00 |
| 7. | Contingencies | : | 10.00 |
| 8. | Margin money for working capital | : | 30.00 |
| | **Total** | **:** | **172.00** |

## SUGGESTED MEANS OF FINANCE

*The project may be financed as suggested below :*

| | | | (Rs. in lakhs) |
|---|---|---|---|
| 1. | Long term loans from financial institutions | : | 115.00 |
| 2. | Equity capital | : | 57.00 |
| | **Total** | **:** | **172.00** |

# MANUFACTURERS/SUPPLIERS OF PLANT AND MACHINERY

## A. Overseas

1. **Emiul Lihotzky Maschinenfabric -V-**
   Postfach 1165,8350 Platting (Bay)
   West Germany

2. **Gaung Hwang Trading Co. Ltd.**
   440 Chengteh Road Taipei,
   Taiwan

3. **Sen Yuan Iron Works**
   6, Alloy 26, Lane 49
   Hsinsheng Road, Yuanlin
   Taiwan

4. **Teriet (n.v. machinefabrik tarlet)**
   Oostzeestraat 6,7202 CM Zutphen-
   P.O. Box 62,7200 AB Zutphen
   Netherland

## B. Indigenous

1. **Somani International Corporation**
   1810. Makers Chambers V
   Nariman Point
   Mumbai - 400 021

2. **KST Foods & Services (P) Ltd.**
   7-87, Vishnu Prashad Mahant Road,
   Vile-Parle,
   Mumbai - 400 005

3. **Parekh Corporation**
   59, IM Merchant Road,
   P.B. No. 5036,
   Mumbai - 400 009

# *Mineral Water*

## INTRODUCTION

Potable spring waters containing, sulphur iron, magnesium and other mineral salts occuring in certain regions are claimed to be beneficial to human metabolism. They occur in specific and widely scattered locations best known of which are white sulphur springs (Virginia) Hot Springs (Arkansas), Saragoga Springs (New York) Vichy (France Baden Baden (Germany) and U.S.S.R. The therapitic value of such waters is questionable carbonated mineral waters also contain lithium salts

Mineral water can be safely defined as potable water. Containing the necessary mineral nutrients required by the body and beneficial to human metabolism

Water Supplies and Their Impurities

Natural fresh water supplies are derived indirectly from the oceans; clouds form by solar evaporation and the winds move the moisture overland to precipitation as rain, snow or hail. The water flows over the surface or percolates into the ground excess water flows back to the oceans completing the hydrological cycle

Water supplies are classified as surfaces supplies and underground waters. Surfaces waters are rivers, lakes, creeks, ponds, and reservoirs, wells and springs are the sources of underground water

Water vapour in clouds is generally pure but gathers dust and gases when it reaches the earth suspended organic matter and soil turbidity are picked up. Minerals are leached from the soil and rocks and organic matter is added from municipal and industrial wastes and decaying vegetation. Well waters usually are free of suspended materials and organic matter due to filteration through the earth. Surface waters are generally low in mineral content but relatively high in suspended and organic materials

*Major Impurities in water*

The major impurities in natural water supplies are listed in Table-W-8. Most surface waters contain 50-250 ppm. Dissloved salts. Well waters contain 150-500 ppm. Water from the great Laks contains about 150 ppm total dissolved solids TDS

Drinking water standards (1962) published by the American Public Health Association are given in Table unrex Head specification

## TABLE-W-8 MAJOR IMPURITIES IN WATER

| Ionic and Dissolved | | Noion and Undissolved | Gaseous |
|---|---|---|---|
| Cationic | Anionic | | |
| Calcium | Bicarbonate Alkalinity | Turbidity, mud dirt silt | Carbon dioxide Nitrogen |
| Magnesium Sodium | Carbonate Hydroxyl | Organics* | Oxygen |
| Potassium | Sulfate | Colour* | Hydrogen Sulfide |
| Ammonium | Chloride | Microogranisms | Ammonia |
| Iron | Nitrate | Algae | Methane |
| Manganese | Phosphate Silica Fluoride Organics* Colour* | Bacteria Oil Metal Oxides and hydroxides | |

* Organic materials may be suspended or dissolved, ionic or nonionic.

## MANUFACTURING PROCESS

*The basic Manufacturing process consists the following steps.*

1. Filteration
2. Demineralisation
3. Blending with Salts & Gases
4. Quality Control & Testing
5. Bottling
6. Packing
7. Despatching

## PROCESS OF MANUFACTURE OF MINERAL WATER

### Bottle filling and packing

After filling the quality mineral water in Bottles the same are packed in cardboard boxes each containing 10 bottles

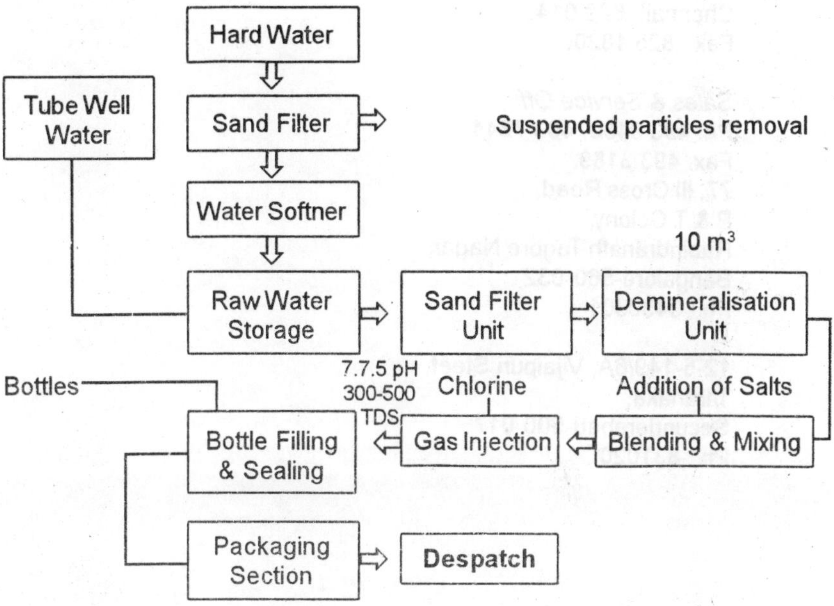

## DE MINERALISATION UNIT

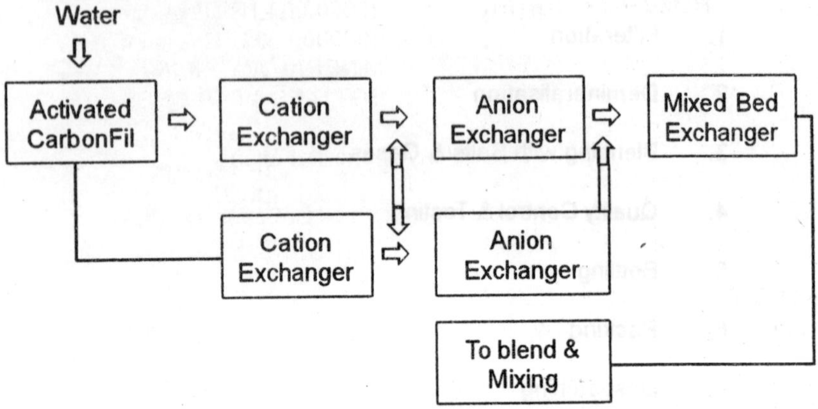


## COMPLETE PLANT & MACHINERY SUPPLIER

**M/s. Mansel Equipments Pvt. Ltd.,**
*Regd. Off:*
8, Masilamani Road,
Balaji Nagar,
Chennai - 600 014.
Fax : 825 1820.

*Sales & Service Off:*
Ph: 493 9450, 493 7844
Fax: 493 3189.
77, III Cross Road,
P & T Colony,
Rabindranath Tagore Nagar,
Bangalore-560 032
Ph : 3430301

12-5-149/6A, Vijaipuri Steet,
Taranaka,
Secunderabad-500 017
Ph : 831020

# PLANT ECONOMICS

Rated Plant Capacity = 20000.00 LTR/Day
= 6000000.00 LTR/Annum
MINERAL WATER IN BOTTLES & POUCHES

(1) 10,000 Bottles/day of one litre each

(2) 20,000 Pouches/day of half litre each

## LAND & BUILDING

(Total land area required 1200 sq. mtr.) **Rs. 24,00,000.00**

## PLANT & MACHINERY

1. M.S. sand filters
2. Dimineralization Unit Activated carbon Filter FRP PVC lined
3. Anion Exchanger FRP lined
4. Cation Exchanger FRP PVC lined
5. Mixed Bed Exchanger FRP PVC lined
6. Piping, valves, Accessories Insturmentation, pumps, blowers
7. Chemical Tanks
8. Mis. Tools & Spares and lab.

*Testing equipment*

9. S.S. Mixing Tanks-Cap 5M3 with agitator with 5 HP. Motor
10. Chlorination for Cl2 injection
11. Carbon dioxide injection equipment
12. FRP lined storage tanks (5 M3)
13. M.S. Tanks
14. Automatic Bottle filling and sealing unit
15. Laboratory testing and a quality control equipment
16. Pumps
17. Valves, piping & instrumentation
18. Tools, jigs & Fixtures
19. Automatic Pouch filling machine
20. Miscellaneous

**TOTAL** **Rs. 56,40,000.00**

## OTHER FIXED ASSETS **Rs. 8,64,000.00**

## FIXED CAPITAL

| | | |
|---|---|---|
| 1. | Land & Building | Rs. 24,00,000.00 |
| 2. | Plant & Machinery | Rs. 56,40,000.00 |
| 3. | Other Fixed Assets | Rs. 8,64,000.00 |
| | **TOTAL** | **Rs.89,04,000.00** |

## TOTAL WORKING CAPITAL/MONTH

| | | |
|---|---|---|
| 1. | Raw Material | Rs. 19,73,700.00 |
| 2. | Salary & Wages | Rs. 45,625.00 |
| 3. | Utilities & Overheads | Rs. 61,000.00 |
| | **TOTAL** | **Rs.20,80,325.00** |

## TOTAL CAPITAL INVESTMENT

| | |
|---|---|
| Total Fixed Capital | Rs. 89,04,000.00 |
| Total Working Capital for 3 Months | Rs. 62,40,975.00 |
| **TOTAL** | **Rs. 1,51,44,975.00** |

## TURN OVER/ANNUM

1. By Sale of 30 lakh Mineral Water Bottles
2. By Sale of 60 Lakh Mineral Water Pouches

**TOTAL** **Rs.4,05,00,000.00**

**PROFIT = RECEIPTS - COST OF PRODUCTION**
= 4,05,00,000.00 - 2,98,03,794.50
= 1,06,96,205.50

**PROFIT SALES RATIO** = Profit/Sales x 100 = 26.41 %

**RATE OF RETURN** = Operating profit / T.C.I. x 100 = 70.63 %

**BREAK EVEN POINT (B.E.P.)** = 33.35 %

# Palm Oil Production

## INTRODUCTION

Palm oil is a constituent of the fruit-pulp of oil palms and is used in the manufacture of soap, candles, and for colouring and scenting ointments. Bleached or slightly hardened it serves also as a raw material for the production of margarine and baking fats.

The palm oil is produced by extraction from the reddish-to-orange pulp of the ovoid shaped fruits which grow on stalks in fresh fruits bunches (FFB) on the oil palms. Pure oil and kernel are the main final products besides minor quantities of solids which are used for animal feed and fertilizers. Shell and dry fibres are used within the palm oil processing line for fuelling the steam boiler.

## TECHNOLOGY AND PROCESS DESCRIPTION

### 1. Reception of Raw Material

The FFB are brought from the field to the mill by means of trailors or trucks which pass a weighbridge (for quantity control of the incoming FFB and the outgoing product as well). After weighining the bunches are dumped on the storage area, which is either a concrete floor or a raised unloading ramps (in small scale plants). Depending upon the type of sterilizer and the capacity of the plant filling of sterilizer baskets or cages is carried out by hand or by suitable system (gravity, loaders etc.). In large plants unloading hopper or specially designed reception systems are applied.

### 2. Sterilizing

In this section the fruit bunches are submitted to direct steam at a pressure of approx. 3 bar over a period in the range of 3 - 60 minuts depending on the weight/size of the bunches.

*Sterilization is carried out with the following objective in view :*

- Prevention of any further rise in F.F.A. (free fatty acid content) due to enzyme action by inactivation of these lipolytic

- Facilitation of mechanical stripping. To loosen the fruits from the bunches, sufficient moist heat must penetrate to the point of attachment of the fruits to the stalk.

- Modification of the colloids of the pericarp and stalk in a way that de-oiling of the fruit solids is favoured in teh following pressint phase. This applies both to the fibre solids and to the solids in crude oil which are deoiled in the clarification section.

- Pre-conditioning the nuts to minimize kernel breakage during both pressing and nut cracking. Adequate sterilizationpermits sufficient heat penetration to cause a high percentage of the kernels to become detached from the shell. (This process of loosening the kernels is continued in the nut silos and must be completed before the nuts are cracked if "split nuts" are to be avoided).

Vertical type sterilizers used in small scale plants are with a limited volume while for large scale plants sterilizers employed are big and of horizontal type and for continuous sterilization process.

## PROCESS FLOW CHART

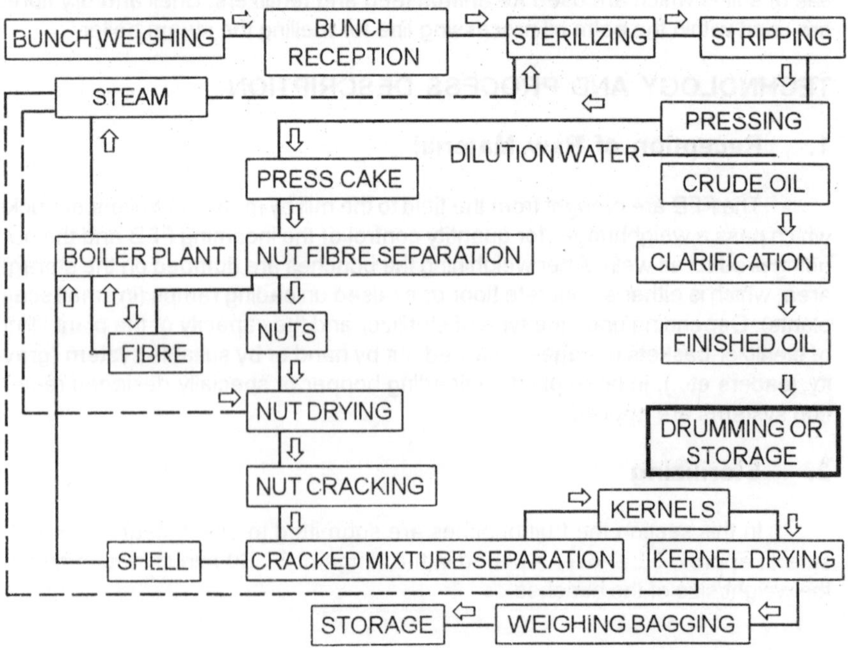

## 3. Stripping

After sterilization of the complete FFB, the fruits are separated from the bunch stalks in the stripping station. No palm oil is contained in the calyx leaves and the stalks of the FFB, but during sterilizing and stripping some oil is absorbed by them. As far as the calyx leaves are concerned the absorbed quantity is unimportant since they will be pressed alongwith the fruits. They could be screened off before, however, their presence has been found helpful to improve the press fibre de-oiling. The bunch stalks, on the other hand, cannot be pressed and it is important, therefore, to keep the amount of oil transferred to them to a minimum and to care that no significant quantity of residual fruit remains attached.

## 4. Digesting

After the bunches have been stripped, the sterilized fruit are reheated together with the accompanying calyx leaves and thus the pericarp is loosened from the nuts and prepared for pressing. This is achieved in steam heated vessels (digesters) provided with a rotating shaft towhich stirring arms are attached.

## 5. Pressing/Oil Extraction

Pressing is the most usual method of extracting crude palm oil from digested palm fruit. Other methods are centrifuging and the wet processs. Modern types of presses with highest efficiency are continuously operating double screw presses, in which two parallel screws are running side by side in a common perforated presscage. the position of a double cone is controlled hydraulically in order to achieve constant cone pressure applied to teh fruits. Such pressess can be rated for different through puts at different screw speeds depending upon the various types of fruits. During the pressing operation, the press cylinder will be flushed with hot water the rate of which is determined by the rate of crude oil. Usually the water to oil ratio is 1 : 1.

## 6. Clarification and Storage

The crude oil obtained by pressing, centrifuging or by the wet processes contains varying amount of water together with impurities consisting of vegetable matter which is partly dissolved in the water and partly forms insoluble solids. Oil is now pumped through direct steam heater to a settling tank. Water contents are reduced to 0.2% and then oil moves to pure oil storage tank.

*Simultaneously the kernel recovery is carried out by various steps as:*

a) Nut drying
b) Nut cracking
c) Kernel separation and drying

## CAPACITY

The suggested capacity of the plant for producting palm oil is crushing 24 tonne of FFB per (8-hours) shift which is ideal one for extracting palm oil.

## PLANT AND MACHINERY

| | | | |
|---|---|---|---|
| 1. | Fruit bunch elevator | : | 1 unit |
| 2. | Sterilizing plant with 4 baskets | : | 1 unit |
| 3. | Stripping plant including stalk in incinerator | : | 1 unit |
| 4. | Extracting station including digester & screw press | : | 1 unit |
| 5. | Clarification plant including settling tanks & re-heaters | : | 1 unit |
| 6. | Oil storage tank with drum & lorry filling equipments | : | 2 nos. |
| 7. | Weighbridge 30 TPD cap. | : | 1 no. |
| 8. | Kernal plant with equipments for nut/fibre separation | : | 1 unit |
| 9. | Steam generation unit 1000 kg./hr. cap. | : | 1 no. |
| 10. | Miscellaneous tools, equipments & elevators, conveyors, instruments, pumps etc. | : | 1 lot |

Total cost of machinery and equipments is Rs. 100 lakhs.

## RAW MATERIAL

Fresh fruit bunches : 7300 TPA
(FFB of Palm tree)

## INFRASTRUCTURE AND FACILITIES

| | | | |
|---|---|---|---|
| 1. | Land | : | 5000 sq. mts. |
| 2. | Building | : | 750 sq. mts. |
| 3. | Power/electrical load | : | 560 kwh/day |
| 4. | Water | : | 40 m$^3$/day |
| 5. | Steam | : | 13 tonnes/day |
| 6. | Manpower | : | 40 nos. |

## ESTIMATED COST OF THE PROJECT

| | | | (Rs. in lakhs.) |
|---|---|---|---|
| 1. | Land & Site Development | : | 2.00 |
| 2. | Building | : | 13.00 |
| 3. | Machinery & Equipments | : | 100.00 |
| 4. | Miscellaneous fixed assets | : | 20.00 |
| 5. | Preliminary & pre-operative exp. | : | 10.00 |
| 6. | Contingencies | : | 15.00 |
| 7. | Margin money for W/C | : | 25.00 |
| | **Total** | : | **185.00** |

## SUGGESTED MEANS OF FINANCING

*The project may be financed as suggested below :*

| | | | (Rs. in lakhs.) |
|---|---|---|---|
| 1. | Long term loan from financial institutions | : | 138.00 |
| 2. | Equity capital | : | 47.00 |
| | **Total** | : | **185.00** |

## SUPPLIERS OF PLANT AND MACHINERY

### A. Overseas

1. **Zimmermann & Tansen Gmbh**
   Bereich Usine de Wecker
   Postfach 102254, 5160 Duren
   Federal Republic of Germany

2. **Stork Amsterdam BV**
   P.O. Box 3007,
   1003 AA Amsterdam,
   The Netherlands

3. **Speichim**
   Parc St. Christophe
   95864 Cergy-Pentoise Cedex
   France

4. **Fives - Call Babcock**
   B. P. 2047,
   5015 Lile Cedex,
   France

# *Pasta Production Plant*

## INTRODUCTION

Pasta is commonly made by kneading Semolina or wheat flour and water. Other substances can be added to modify the pasta. Egg, gluten and casein are often used to modify the composition of the paste; spinach, tomatoes and carrots are used to alter the taste.

It is possible to use raw materials other than semolina or wheat flour. Using locally available raw materials such as cassava or maize would make the use of semolina or wheat flour unnecessary, and would produce a pasta more adapted to the taste of local people. This profile concentrates on a long pasta obtained from a laminated pasta cut length-wise.

## TECHNOLOGY AND PROCESS DESCRIPTION

The manufacturing of pasta is basically quite simple, but requires a high degree of cleanliness and perfectly adjusted machines.

*The stages involved are :*

1. Raw material purification
2. Kneading and homogenization which takes place in a mechanical kneader.
3. Pressing and drawing, which gives the pasta the desired shape by pushing it through the dies of a mould. Pressing can be done by a screw press, a hydraulic press or a three phase continuous press, which carries out all three operations of kneading, homogenization and drawing.
4. On leaving the machine the pasta is cooled by ventilation. For long pasta, the pasta is delivered onto rods called "Canes", and then taken to the driers.
5. Drying evaporates the excess water from the pasta, and must follow immediately after the drawing & pressing phase. There are three phases.

(a) Pre-drying: Surface evaporation removing 30-35% of water.
(b) Softening: Pasta is left to re-establish a moisture balance.
(c) Final drying: Reduces the moisture content to a normal 12-13%. Long pasta is dried in "Cane driers" and

6. Packaging takes place after the pasta leaves the driers. Carton boxes of about 250 grams are commonly used.

## PROCESS FLOW CHART

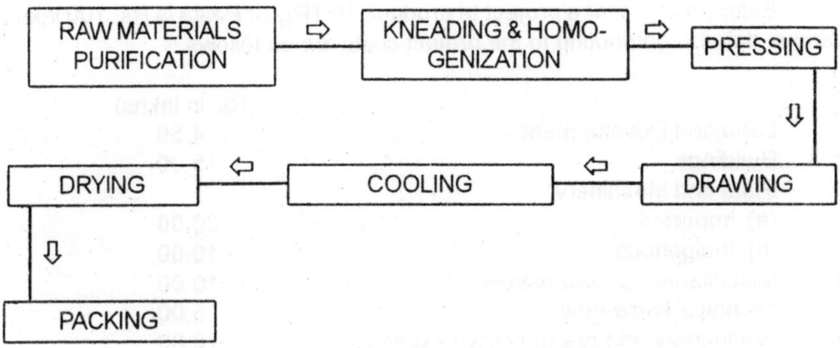


## PLANT CAPACITY

Suggested capacity of a plant to produce pasta products is 1200 TPA.

## PLANT AND MACHINERY

| | | | |
|---|---|---|---|
| 1. | Mechanical kneader | : | 2 nos. |
| 2. | Calendering machines | : | 2 |
| 3. | Longitudinal cutters | : | 2 |
| 4. | Cane loading gear | : | 2 |
| 5. | Cane-driers (electric) | : | 2 |
| 6. | Packaging unit | : | 1 |
| 7. | Cooking unit | : | 1 |
| 8. | Miscellaneous tools and equipments | : | L.S. |

Total cost of the machienry both imported and indigenous is Rs. 40 lakhs.

## RAW MATERIALS

Semolina/Wheat/Corn flour : 2600 Tonnes per annum.

## INFRASTRUCTURE AND FACILITIES

| | | | |
|---|---|---|---|
| 1. | Land area | : | 4000 sq. mts. |
| 2. | Building | : | 1000 sq. mts. |
| 3. | Power/Electric load | : | 50 KVA |
| 4. | Water | : | 1500 KLA |
| 5. | Manpower | : | 30 nos. |

## ESTIMATED COST OF PROJECT

Estimated cost of a project to produce 10 TPD of Pasta is Rs. 100 lakhs. Various details contributing to the project costs are as follows :

| | | | (Rs. in lakhs) |
|---|---|---|---|
| 1. | Land and Development | : | 4.50 |
| 2. | Buildings | : | 15.00 |
| 3. | Plant and Machinery | | |
| | (a) Imported | : | 30.00 |
| | (b) Indigenous | : | 10.00 |
| 4. | Miscellaneous fixed assets | : | 10.00 |
| 5. | Technical know-how | : | 5.00 |
| 6. | Preliminary and pre-operative expenses | : | 10.00 |
| 7. | Contingencies | : | 5.50 |
| 8. | Margin money for working capital | : | 10.00 |
| | **Total** | : | **100.00** |

## SUGGESTED MEANS OF FINANCE

*The project may be financed as suggested below:*

| | | | (Rs. in lakhs) |
|---|---|---|---|
| 1. | Long term loans from financial institutions | : | 67.00 |
| 2. | Equity capital | : | 33.00 |
| | **Total** | : | **100.00** |

# MANUFACTURERS/SUPPLIERS OF PLANT & MACHINERY

## A. Overseas

1. **Emil Lihotzky Machinenfabrik -v-**
   Postfach 1165,8350 Platting (Bay)
   West Germany

## B. Indigenous

1. **Aswini Marketing and Services**
   54/18, 1st floor, 8th floor, Main Raod,
   Jayanagar, Bangalore - 560 011

2. **KSJ Foods & Services P. Ltd.**
   C/o. 7-87, Vishnu Prasad Mahant Road,
   Vile Parle, Mumbai - 400 005

# Pickles & Murabbas etc.

| | | |
|---|---|---|
| 1. | **Capacity** | 100 kg./Day |
| | | **Rs. in Lacs.** |
| 2. | **Land & Building**<br>(Area covered 500 sq. mtr.) | 7.15 |
| 3. | **Plant & Machinery**<br>(Working table, Aluminium trays, Storage & Fixing tanks, Lemon halving machine, Bottle washing machine, Wooden baskets, Fruits & Vegetable slicers, Cooking pan, Gas cylinder with burner etc.) | 3.53 |
| 4. | **Other Fixed Assets**<br>(Office Equipment, Furniture, Installation Cost for Water, Electricity & Pre-operative & Preliminary Expenses) | 1.50 |
| 5. | **Fixed Capitl**<br>(Land & Bldg. + Plant & Machinery + Other Fixed Assets) | 12.18 |
| 6. | **Raw Materials/Month**<br>(Mango, Lemon, Cauliflower, Salt powder, Chillies, Turmeric powder, Saunf, Saunth, Spices, Amchur, Rai etc.) | 0.54 |
| 7. | **Salary & Wages/Month** | 0.13 |
| 8. | **Utilities & Overheads/Month**<br>(Power Consumption, Water Consumption, Stationery, Postage, Telephone, Advertisement, Conveyance & Transportation, Administrative & Miscellaneous expenses) | 0.47 |
| 9. | **Total Working Capital/Month**<br>(Raw Material + Salary & Wages + Utilities & Overheads) | 1.14 |
| 10. | **Total Capital Investment**<br>(Total Fixed Capital + Total Working Capital for 3 months) | 13.32 |
| 11. | **Cost of Production/Annum** | 17.50 |
| 12. | **Turnover/Annum** | 21.12 |
| 13. | **Profit** | 3.62 |
| 14. | **Rate of Return** | 27.17% |
| 15. | **Break Even Point (B.E.P.)** | 64.82% |

# Processed Food

| | | |
|---|---|---|
| 1. | **Capacity** | 10 ,000 Bottles/Day |
| | | **Rs. in Lacs.** |
| 2. | **Land & Building** (Area covered 1200 sq. mtr.) | 30.08 |
| 3. | **Plant & Machinery** (Hammer mill, Neutralising vessel, Filteration press, S.S. Lining mixers, Storage Tanks, Clarification vessels, Cooling/ Conditioning unit, Spray drier, Boiler etc. | 23.31 |
| 4. | **Other Fixed Assets** (Office Equipment, Furniture, Installation Cost for Water, Electricity & Pre-operative & Preliminary Expenses) | 5.50 |
| 5. | **Fixed Capital** (Land & Bldg. + Plant & Machinery + Other Fixed Assets) | 60.89 |
| 6. | **Raw Materials/Month** (Fruits, Sugar, Citric acid, Glass bottles etc.) | 12.22 |
| 7. | **Salary & Wages/Month** | 1.14 |
| 8. | **Utilities & Overheads/Month** (Power Consumption, Water Consumption, Stationery, Postage, Telephone, Advertisement, Conveyance & Transportation, Administrative & Miscellaneous expenses) | 1.66 |
| 9. | **Total Working Capital/Month** (Raw Material + Salary & Wages + Utilities & Overheads) | 15.30 |
| 10. | **Total Capital Investment** (Total Fixed Capital + Total Working Capital for 3 months) | 106.79 |
| 11. | **Cost of Production/Annum** | 215.14 |
| 12. | **Turnover/Annum** | 300.00 |
| 13. | **Profit** | 84.85 |
| 14. | **Rate of Return** | 79.45% |
| 15. | **Break Even Point (B.E.P.)** | 35.32% |

# *Roller Flour Mill*

## INTRODUCTION

Roller Flour Mill will have facility to produce, maida, sooji, atta and bran. These products will be sold as per the guidance issued for Food and Civil Supplies Department of the concerned state.

Flour mill consists of following machineries as blender, sievs, breakrolls, smooth steel reduction, rolls aspirators, conveyors water washers etc.

Flour is classified according to the amount of grain included in the final product into graham flour which contains the entire grain. Whole wheat flour all in grain except about half of bran and straight bed flour results when all the ban is removed early in the grinding process.

## MANUFACTURING PROCESS

*Processing of wheat involves three main stages as given below :-*

a) Cleaning, Washing and Conditioning

b) Milling of wheat into flour.

c) Packaging & Despatch.

The milling process breaks open the wheat kernel and reduces the particles formed so as to separate the outer and inner portions of the kernal. Bran and germ are almost completely separated from the white interior portions in the milling of refined flour.

When the entire kernal is ground and no separations are made, the product is whole white flour. The following steps are involved in milling wheat. Wheat selection, blending sieving, purifying, reducing classifying, and some combination of maturing bleaching and diastatic or enriching treatment of the flour. It is not necessary that all these operations be performed is every flour mill. But either these operations are performed as such as or combination of these operations to serve the same purpose performed in the flour mills.

## FLOUR BY-PRODUCTS:

Flour by products divided from the outer coverings of the wheat grain separated in extraction of the flour from the grain, consist of bran (coause or fine according to the state of subdivision and how much adhering endosperm is attached) the finer more floury outer coverings called middlings. The composition of such products many vary considering depending on the wheats used and the amount of endosperm present Table below gives the general composition of these by products mainly used in live stock feed.

## PROCESS FLOW SHEET

Conveyor

⇩

Sieves

⇩

Disc Separator

⇩

Magnetic Sepkarator

⇩

Washer

⇩

Conditioner

⇩

Aspirator

⇩

Breaking System

⇩

Plan Sifter

⇩

Paired Roller Grinders

⇩

Classifier

⇩

Flour

# ROLLER FLOUR MILL MACHINERY SUPPLIER

1. **A.T. Moshin & Co.,**
   71-A, Netaji Subhash Road,
   Calcutta-700001.
   Ph: 033-256277

2. **Ajit Industrial Trading Co.,**
   Dhebar Road (S),
   Behind 'Atika',
   Rajkot-360002.
   Ph: 0281-82423

3. **Bansal Flour Mill Engineers,**
   4/5-B, Asaf Ali Road,
   New Delhi-110002.
   Ph: 011-3264041

4. **Hyderabad Roller Flour Mills Co Ltd.,**
   Opp. Moulali Rig Station,
   Moula Ali,
   Hyderabad-500040.
   Ph: 040-852334

5. **Rollflute Industries,**
   34, Vaidyanatha Mudali Street,
   Tondiyarpet,
   Chennai - 600 081.
   Ph: 044—555108

6. **Suri Engineers Pvt. Ltd,**
   Plot No. 4/4, I.D.A. Area,
   Nacharam,
   Hyderabad-501507.
   Ph: 040-852489

## PLANT ECONOMICS

Rated Plant Capacity = 50.00 MT/Day
= 15000.00 MT/annum
ROLLER FLOUR MILL

### LAND & BUILDING

(Open Land required 2000 sq.mtr.) Rs. 24,00,000.00

### PLANT & MACHINERY

1. FOR CLEANING SECTION:- Reel Machine
2. Aspirator Separator
3. Scourer Machine
4. Washer Whitter Machine
5. Brush Machine
6. Carter Disc seperator
7. Spray Damper
8. Low Pressure Fan
9. Dust cyclene with air seal
10. Elavator system
11. Warm conveyor
12. Fabrication Material
13. Roller Mill complete in all respects
14. Plansifter having 8 section and 16 sieves
15. Double Deck purifier
16. Bran Finisher
17. Bleacher
18. Entolator
19. Low Pressure Fan with cyclone and air seal
20. High Pressure Fan
21. Dust Collector
22. Low Pressure Fan for Dust collector
23. Warm Conveyor
24. Pneumatic systmatic comple in all respects with Pneumatic cyclones, Feeders, Air seal, G.I. lifts, etc.
25. Fabrication Material Required for erection like nylon, Boolting cloths, Reduction Gears and Misc.
26. V. Belts, Nuts and Bolts, Hareware etc.
27. Electric Motor 15 HP
28. Silo Bim

TOTAL Rs. 34,50,500.00

## FIXED CAPITAL

| | | | |
|---|---|---|---|
| 1. | Land & Building | Rs. | 24,00,000.00 |
| 2. | Plant & Machinery | Rs. | 34,50,500.00 |
| 3. | Other Fixed Assets | Rs. | 90,000.00 |
| | **TOTAL** | **Rs.** | **59,40,500.00** |

## TOTAL WORKING CAPITAL/MONTH

| | | | |
|---|---|---|---|
| 1. | Raw Material | Rs. | 69,10,000.00 |
| 2. | Salary & Wages | Rs. | 1,32,480.00 |
| 3. | Utilities & Overheads | Rs. | 67,600.00 |
| | **TOTAL** | **Rs.** | **71,10,080.00** |

## TOTAL CAPITAL INVESTMENT

| | | |
|---|---|---|
| Total Fixed Capital | Rs. | 59,40,500.00 |
| Total Working Capital for 3 Months | Rs. | 71,10,080.00 |
| **TOTAL** | **Rs.** | **1,30,50,580.00** |

## TURN OVER/ANNUM

1. By selling Maida 9000 MT
2. BY selling Atta 3000 MT
3. By selling Suji 2250 MT
4. By selling wheat Bran 750 MT

**TOTAL** **Rs. 9,37,50,000.00**

**PROFIT = RECEIPTS - COST OF PRODUCTION**
= 9,37,50,000.00 - 8,91,75,212.60
= 45,74,787.40

**PROFIT SALES RATIO** = Profit/Sales x 100 = 4.88 %

**RATE OF RETURN** = Operating profit / T.C.I. x 100 = 35.05 %

**BREAK EVEN POINT (B.E.P.)** = 51.28 %

# Chapter - 31

## *Directory Section*

*Plant and Machineries Suppliers & Manufacturers of :*

- Bakery
- Confectionery
- Dairy and Milk Processing
- Food and Beverages Machines
- Form-Fill-Seal and Packaging Machineries
- Ice Cream Making Machines
- Pasta Products Making Machines
- Processed Fruits and Vegetables
- Refrigeration and Kitchen Equipments
- Snack Food Making Machine

## Manufacturers & Suppliers of Plant and Machineries

**Suan Scientific Instruments & Equipments**
Deals in exporting and supplying various range of food processing machinery such as noodle making machine, noodles drying machine, pre processing equipment, automatic chowmin making machine, fish feed/poultry feed making machine and universal mill.
Address: P-814, Ground Floor, Block-A, Lake Town, Kolkata - 700 089, India
Phone: +(91)-(33)-25342047
Fax: +(91)-(33)-25213743
Mobile: +(91)-9433263575/9903872341

**Pharma Seals**
Leading manufacturers and exporters of food processing machinery including ROPP capping machines, bottle valve crimping machines, turn tables for bottle unscrambling, volumetric liquid filling machines, vial crimpers and tube sealing machines.
Address: Salvi Chawl, Gala No 4, Somwar Bazar, Malad West, Mumbai - 400 064, India
Phone: +(91)-(22)-28810648
Mobile: +(91)-9821410365

**Chetan Agro Industries**
Engaged in exporting and supplying of food processing machinery such as bread cutting machines, wafer cutting machine, gravy making machine, pulpier machines, dry fruits cutting machine, powder making machine and crown cooking machinery.
Address: No. 108, Atul Complex, Gondal Road, Opposite Bombay Hotel, Rajkot - 360 002, India
Phone: +(91)-(281)-2461781
Fax: +(91)-(281)-2461781
Mobile: +(91)-9825216014/9825216014

**Good Earth Engineering Industries**
Engaged in supplying and manufacturing of food processing machinery vibratory screens, vibratory feeder screens, vibration simulator machinery, vibratory feeders, vibrating tables, separation equipment and packers.
Address: No. 6, Tarun Plastic Industrial Estate, Mogra Village Road, Andheri East, Mumbai - 400 069, India
Phone: +(91)-(22)-28200559/26833189
Fax: +(91)-(22)-26840346
Mobile: +(91)-9820268595

**Honey Combb Products**
Manufacturer and exporter of food processing machinery, milk heating machinery, potato peeler machinery, wafer slicer machinery, dough kneading machinery, khakhra roasting machinery, oil extracting machinery and roti making machinery.
Address: A-14, Mahalaxmi Industrial Estate, B/h, Maruti & Shivshakti Estate Opposite Kirti Tools, Phase - 1, G I D C, Vatva, Ahmedabad - 382 445, India
Phone: +(91)-(79)-25830342
Mobile : +(91)-9825096342

**Dynamech Engineers**
Manufacturer and exporter of food processing plant and food processing machinery such as sev extruder, dough kneader, oil extracter, automatic frying system, potato peeler, potato slicer, centrifugal dryer, banana slicer and chana jor pressing machinery.
Address: 214, Palsikar Colony, Indore, Madhya Pradesh - 452 001, India
Phone: +(91)-(731)-2364890
Fax: +(91)-(731)-4036004
Mobile : +(91)-9893078979
Website: www.dynamechengineers.com

**Trident Engineers, India**
Leading manufacturer and exporter of food processing plants, food processing machinery, food processing appliances, industrial food processing machine, commercial food processing equipment, commercial grinder and commercial batter mixer.
Address: SF 93 / 3, Revenue Nagar (Opposite Cri Chola Pumps) Sathy Road, Saravanampatti (North), Coimbatore, Tamil Nadu - 641 035, India
Phone: +(91)-(422)-6455976/6455922
Mobile: +(91)-9500988123/9500988121
Website: www.tridentengineers.com

**Pawar Engineering Works**
Manufacturers and exporters of all types of food processing machinery, plastic food processing machinery that includes high speed mixer, plastic scrap grinder, plastic granulator and plastic extrusion machinery.
Address: 5, Shramlaxmi Udyog Bhawan, Plot No. 9 C, Moti Udyog Nagar, Ramchandra Lane Extension, Katchpada, Malad (West), Mumbai - 400 064, India
Phone: +(91)-(22)-28831693
Fax: +(91)-(22)-28827227
Mobile : +(91)-9892123373

**Muez Hest India Private Limited ISO 9001:2008**
Exporter and supplier of food processing machinery and food processing equipment such as winterization machinery, deodorization machinery, dewaxing machinery, dry fractionation machinery, industrial hardening machinery and inter-esterification machinery.
Address: 231, Blue Rose Industrial Estate, Near Cable Corporation Western Express Highway, Borivali (E), Mumbai, Maharashtra - 400 066, India
Phone: +(91)-(22)-28701752/28541758/ 28541758
Fax: +(91)-(22)-28701752/28544826
Mobile : +(91)-9324610477

**Able Manufacturers**
Able Manufacturers deals in supplying and manufacturing food processing machinery, food processing equipment, flaking machines, industrial flanking machines, food processing mixers, vegetable slicers, vegetable cutters, chemical equipment, crystallizers.
Address: 12-2-799/2, G - 2, Jandar Nagar, Mehdipatnam, Hyderabad - 500 028, India
Phone: +(91)-(40)-65974111
Fax: +(91)-(40)-23510373
Mobile : +(91)-9849271975
Website: www.processmachines.com

**J. K. Group Of Industries**
Exporters and manufacturers of food processing machinery like corn grinding mill, danish type flour mills, rice huller and rice huller with polisher. Also supplies diesel engines like lister type diesel engine, kirloskar type diesel engine etc.
Address: E/5, Bhaktinagar Industrial Estate, P. O. Box 577, Rajkot - 360 002, India
Phone: +(91)-(281)-2362842/2363381/ 2363382
Fax: +(91)-(281)-2362477
Mobile : +(91)-9824231042/9825069696

**Hindustan Equipment Company**
Manufacturer and exporter of food processing plants, food processing machinery, four burner range, chinese range, deep fat fryer, portable griller, stainless steel salamander, pizza assembly unit, back bar counter and ultra cool machines.
Address: 1507, Aljamiat Building, Qasimjan Street Ballimaran, New Delhi - 110 006,
Phone: +(91)-(11)-32987902/23973981
Fax: +(91)-(11)-23912532
Mobile : +(91)-9810870976/9810019762

**Mangal Machines Private Limited**
Deals in manufacturing and supplying of food processing machinery such as flour sifter machinery, sugar grinder machinery, cream mixer machinery and biscuit packing machines.
Address: Old Factory Area,
Patiala - 147 001, India
Fax: +(91)-(175)-2360180/5003358
Mobile : +(91)-9357002223
Website: www.mangalmachine.com

**Dolphin Engineers**
Engaged in manufacturing and supplying of food processing machinery, food processing plants, pulse processing plants, multiple pulse processing plants, grain processing plants, rice processing machines. Also supplies pulverizers and precleaners.
Address: Kalyan-Bhiwandi Road Kon (Kalyan), Mumbai - 421301, India
Phone: +(91)-(2522)-280316/280646
Fax: +(91)-(2522)-80316
Mobile : +(91)-9820253033/9820054756

**Master Food Tech**
Supply and manufacture of food processing plants, ice cream plant machinery, ice plant machinery, brine chilling plant equipment, deep freezer plant equipment, cold storage plant, mushroom plant, dairy plant and industrial food processing plant.
Address: S. No. 232/2, Pune Nasik Road, Atlas Compound, Opposite Rupee Co.Op. Bank, Bhosari, Pune - 411 039, India
Mobile : +(91)-9822027910

**Sehgal Exports**
Manufacturers and suppliers food processing plants, biscuit making machinery, biscuit dough mixing machinery, biscuit dies, sand-witching machinery, cream biscuit making machinery, sugar grinding machinery, roti making machinery, biscuit cutting rollers.
Address: D-4, Focal Point, Patiala - 147 001
Phone: +(91)-(175)-2232647
Fax: +(91)-(175)-5004642
Mobile : +(91)-9815480042/9216908342

**Troika Processes Private Limited**
Manufacturer and exporter of food processing plants including vegetable oil plant and machinery, rice bran processing plants, hydrogenation plants, oil milling plants, solvent extraction plants, cattle feed plants and soya bean processing plants.
Address: 6th Floor, Embassy Centre, Nariman Point, Mumbai - 400 021, India
Phone: +(91)-(22)-22834429/22834334
Fax: +(91)-(22)-22823778

**Packaging Solution**
Engaged in manufacture and export of food processing plants and machinery like cooking kettles, pulp extraction machinery, pickle making equipments, papaya cubes equipments and vegetable dehydration equipments.
Address: 8/287, Sec-3, Rajendra Nagar, Sahibabad - 201 005, India
Mobile : +(91)-9310252152/9818293306
Website: www.packaging-solutionsindia.com

**Kalina Engineering Private Limited**
Engaged in manufacturing and supplying of food processing plants, food processing machinery like food mixers, food processing mixers, agitators etc.
Address: Unit no. 34, Surya Kirti Industrial Estate, No. 02, Chinchpada, Vasai East Vasai East, Vasai, Maharashtra - 401 208
Phone: +(91)-(22)-28049770
Fax: +(91)-(22)-28045840
Mobile : +(91)-9869214569
Website: www.chemicalequipmentindia.com

**NETZSCH Technologies India Pvt. Ltd.**
Manufacture food processing machinery, food pump, industrial food pumps, bh hygienic pump, sh hygienic pump, mini bh hygienic pump, sh plus hygienic pump, sa aseptic pump, mc pumps and industrial pumps.
Address: No. 39, 2nd Street Spartan Nagar, Mogappair, Chennai - 600 037, India
Phone: +(91)-(44)-42965163/42965100
Fax: +(91)-(44)-42965150
Mobile : +(91)-9841884907/9840288098

**Mahesh Eng. Works**
Manufacturer of food processing machinery, farsan making equipment, dairy equipment, milk cream separator, butter churner, electric butter churner, milk analyser, milk processing plant, turnkey dairy plant, milk pasteurizers.
Address: No. 1, Modi Estate, Near Mahakali Temple, Dudheswer Road,
Ahmedabad - 380 004, India
Phone: +(91)-(79)-25626688
Fax: +(91)-(79)-25626688
Mobile : +(91)-9825336443
Website: www.milkycreamseparator.com

**Basant Products (India)**
Exporter and manufacturer of agricultural machinery like wheat threshers, seed drills, food processing machinery, maize shellers, processing machines and cream separators.
Address: C- 46, Foundry Nagar,
Hathras Road, Agra - 282 006, India
Phone: +(91)-(562)-2242690
Fax: +(91)-(562)-2240765
Mobile : +(91)-9997408448/9837005782

**Shree Engineering**
Engaged in manufacturing and supplying of food processing machinery like bakery machinery, automatic bakery machinery, semi automatic bakery machinery and manual bakery machinery etc.
Address: Flat No. 7, Om Shakthi Nagar,
Bharathi Street, Chinnavedampatti,
Ganapathy, Coimbatore,
Tamil Nadu - 641 006, India
Phone: +(91)-(422)-2669726/2669729
Fax: +(91)-(422)-2666276
Mobile : +(91)-9843411156/9842285512

**Mathesis Engineers Private Limited**
Exporting agricultural and post harvest agro machinery, chemical process plant equipment and machinery, chemical plant machinery, agro machinery, post harvest machinery, extruded snack foods, food processing machinery , dryers and fine chemicals.
Address: Plot No. B -35, Bhel - A. I. E.,
Ramachandrapuram, Hyderabad - 500 032
Phone: +(91)-(40)-23020628/23022298
Fax: +(91)-(40)-23027859
Mobile : +(91)-9885245680

**The Scientific Apparatus Company**
Engaged in exporting and manufacturing of food processors, automatic food processing machinery, industrial food processing machinery and food processing machinery.
Address: No. 40 - A, Chaulpathy Road, P. O. Beleghata, Kolkata - 700 010, India
Phone: +(91)-(33)-23707036
Mobile : +(91)-9830407351/9874746448
Website: www.pharmachemfood.com

**The Bombay Engineering Works**
Suppliers and exporters of pressure vessels, industrial pressure vessels, commercial pressure vessels, pneumatic pressure vessels. Also offer pharmaceutical machinery, cosmetic machinery, food processing machinery, octagonal blender, tube filling machine.
Address: Unit Nos. 12, Navyug Industrial Estate, Tokersey Jivraj Road, Sewree West, Mumbai, Maharashtra - 400 015
Phone: +(91)-(22)-24137094/24135959
Fax: +(91)-(22)-24135828
Mobile : +(91)-9821042408
Website: www.pharma-machinery.co.in

**Orange Sorting Machines (India) (P) Ltd.**
Engaged in manufacturing and supplying of food processing machinery like color sorting machines, food grain color sorting machines, automatic color sorting machines, rice color sorting machines and semi automatic color sorting machines.
Address: SF No. 90/3, Adhavan Industrial Estate, Athipalayam Road,
Chinnavedampatti, Coimbatore - 641 049
Phone: +(91)-(422)-4528888/4528899Fax: +(91)-(422)-4528899
Mobile : +(91)-9443259127/9443159596
Website: www.sortingmachine.in

**Shree Biocare India**
Supplier and exporter of food processing machinery, fermentation equipment, pilot scale fermentor, lab scale fermentor, microbiology fermentor, pharma fermentor, biofertilizer fermentor, production scale fermentor and refurnishing fermentor.
Address: No. 28, Hariom Nagar-I,
Motera Road, Sabarmati, Ahmedabad,

Gujarat - 380 005, India
Phone: +(91)-(79)-40084116
Fax: +(91)-(79)-40084116
Mobile : +(91)-9898999146/9033025502
Website: www.fermentorsolution.com

**BHARAT REFRIGERATIONS PVT LTD.**
Manufacture and supply food processing machinery such as ice candy tanks, lolly tanks, bulk milk coolers, cold rooms, truck refrigeration, blast freezers, water coolers, water cooled chillers and air cooled chillers.
Address:21/A, Kanniappan Street, Shanthi Nagar Ramapuram, Chennai - 600 089
Phone: +(91)-(44)-22495959/22495969
Fax: +(91)-(44)-22494236
Mobile : +(91)-9840020026
Website: www.coldroomindia.com

**Shree Hari Enterprise**
Engaged in supplying of a wide range of kitchen equipments that includes atta kneaders, food processing machinery and vegetable cutters.
Address:No. 40, Jimmy Towers, Opposite Swaminarayan Gurukul, Gondal Road, Rajkot - 360 002, India
Phone: +(91)-(281)-2362775
Fax: +(91)-(281)-2362775
Mobile : +(91)-9426711006

**Forsberg Agritech India Private Limited**
Manufacturers and exporters of food processing machinery, industrial food processing machinery, seed processing machinery, seed cleaning machinery, seed grading machinery and granular separation machinery for food and industrial applications.
Address:No. 123, GIDC, Makarpura, Vadodara - 390 010, India
Phone: +(91)-(265)-3098131/3098127/2649151
Fax: +(91)-(265)-2649151
Mobile : +(91)-9825095588

**Kumar Metal Industries Private Limited**
Supplying and manufacturing food processing plants which includes flaking machines, oil mill flaking machines, oil bearing cellular flaking machines and food processing machinery.
Address: 101, Kakad Bhavan, 30th Road, Opp. Gaiety Galaxy Cinema, Bandra (West), Thane, Maharashtra - 400 050, India
Phone: +(91)-(22)-26441667/26441664/26441663/26427982
Fax: +(91)-(22)-26428136
Website: www.solvent-extraction-plant.com

**Shri Yash Fabricators & Consultancy**
Manufacturing and exporting of food processing equipments such as food processing machinery, industrial food processing machines, rotors, food processing plant equipments, durable rotors, robust rotors.
Address:Sector- D, Plot No. D2, Sanwer Road, Indore - 452 010, India
Phone: +(91)-(731)-3299588
Mobile : +(91)-9425314138/9713618838
Website: www.shriyashfabricators.com

**Harvest Pumps (ISO 9001:2000)**
Manufacturers, suppliers and exporters of food processing plants, food processing machinery, food processing equipment, homogeniser for fruit juice and fruit juice homogeniser.
Address: 16-A, Sarathi Nagar, Nandha Nagar Road, Singanallur, Coimbatore, Tamil Nadu - 641 005, India
Phone: +(91)-(422)-2580712/2580835/4348040
Fax: +(91)-(422)-2580712
Mobile : +(91)-9843057871
Website: www.homogenisers.net

**Goyum Screw Press (Oil Refinery Division)**
Manufacturer, supplier and exporter of food processing plants, food processing machinery and food processing equipment like crystallizer, bleacher, deodorizer, neutralizer, scrubber, reaction vessels for bio diesel.
Address: Plot No. 324/2, Industrial Area- A, Ludhiana, Punjab - 141 003, India
Phone: +(91)-(161)-4633180
Fax: +(91)-(161)-2230380
Mobile : +(91)-9915065000
Website: www.vegetableoilrefinery.net

**Bright International**
Engaged in the manufacturing and supplying of food processing machinery like food steamers, food steamers stock pots, shallow

food steamers, pasta food steamers, coffee warmers and stainless steel coffee warmers.
Address: 30/106, Laxmi Krupa Building, L.T.Colony Road, Dadar East, Mumbai, Maharashtra - 400 014, India
Phone: +(91)-(22)-24162345/24162266
Fax: +(91)-(22)-24162266
Mobile : +(91)-9892230348/9324593106
Website: www.aceroinoxidable.co.in

**S. R. Industries**
Manufacturers, exporters and suppliers of industrial machinery that includes food pumps, stainless steel food pumps, food processing pumps, industrial food pumps, dairy processing pumps and meals processing pumps.
Address: Gala No. 3 C, Ambamata Industrial Estate, B. P. Cross Road, No. 5, Jai Ambe Road, Near Ram Mandir, Bhayander East, Thane - 401 105, India
Phone: +(91)-(22)-28044062/28043163
Fax: +(91)-(22)-28044062
Mobile : +(91)-9869051432

**Saifco Agrotech Engineers**
Supplying and manufacturing of agricultural equipment, vibro separator, dry-d-stoner machine, drum sieve machines, rotary separator, food processing machinery, flour mill machines and rice mill machines.
Address:D - 103, Sector - 10, Noida - 201 301, India
Phone: +(91)-(120)-4337841
Mobile : +(91)-9717814200

**Veendeep Oiltek Exports, Navi Mumbai**
Manufacturer and exporter of food processing plants, food processing machinery and food processing equipment like crystallizer, bleacher, deodorizer, neutralizer, scrubber, reaction vessels, edible oil plants etc.
Address: No. A-67, MIDC, Taloja, Mumbai, Maharashtra - 410 208, India
Phone: +(91)-(22)-27402073
Fax: +(91)-(22)-27402078/25283875
Mobile : +(91)-9769315466/9769315463
Website: www.veendeep.com

**K K Industries, Ghaziabad**
Supplying and manufacturing food processing machinery which includes biscuit machines, biscuit making machines, biscuit plant machines and industrial biscuit machines along with precision job works and cast nylon products.
Address:248 A, Patel Marg (BHONJA), Ghaziabad - 201001, India
Phone: +(91)-(120)-2834097
Mobile : +(91)-9810777035

**Softel Machines Limited**
Suppliers of food processing machinery like domestic flour mill, hand blender, electric hand blender, electrical juicer, soda maker, ice cream maker, flour kneader, mixer grinder, electric grinder and sandwich maker.
Address: Plot No . 69, Sector No. 1-A, Gandhidham - 370 201, India
Phone: +(91)-(2836)-329679
Fax: +(91)-(2836)-222830
Mobile : +(91)-9426217227
Website: www.softelindia.com

**Tirth Engineering**
Deals in manufacturing and supplying of food processing machinery which includes namkeen machines, chakli machines, die cutting machines and papad dough kneading.
Address:S. No.- 81/1, NDA Road, Near Vishnu Malti Ind. Area, Shivane Goan, Pune - 411 023, India
Phone: +(91)-(20)-65206932/65206933
Fax: +(91)-(20)-25294102
Mobile : +(91)-9552580293/9552580294

**Sai Engineers & Machineries (P) Ltd.**
Engaged in export and manufacture of food processing plants, food processing machinery, sugar plants, industrial sugar making plants, sugar making machinery, sugar making mill plants and replaceable sugar mill making plants.
Address: No. A-23, M. I. D. C, Ahmadnagar - 414 111, India
Phone: +(91)-(241)-2777282
Fax: +(91)-(241)-2778492
Mobile : +(91)-9422220982/9890077282

**Sai Teja Engineering Works**
Manufacturing and exporting of food processing machinery like lab ovens, pulverizes, sifters, homogenizes, multi mills, metal food processing machines, steel food processing machines, stainless steel food processing machines and mild steel food machines.
Address: Shed No. 12,
Gajularamaram Road, Vivekanada Nagar,
Hyderabad - 500 055, India
Mobile : +(91)-9347231032

**Sunrise Process Equipments**
Manufacturing and supplying of food processing machinery like dairy tanks, diary storage tanks, food product storage tanks, metal food product storage tanks, steel storage tanks, stainless steel storage tanks and mild steel storage tanks etc.
Address: A-102, Shree Rameshwar Tower,
Shimpoli Road, Borivali West,
Mumbai - 400 092, India
Phone: +(91)-(22)-28993705/28993706/28993707
Fax: +(91)-(22)-28993705
Mobile : +(91)-9821226682

**Process Masters Equipment [I] Pvt. Ltd.**
Providing turnkey projects for food processing machinery, fruit processing machinery, vegetable processing machinery, mango processing line, pineapple processing line, frozen vegetable line, tomato processing line.
Address: Plot No. 37/1, Block F-II,
M. I. D. C. Pimpri, Pune - 411 018, India
Phone: +(91)-(20)-27443648
Fax: +(91)-(20)-27443647
Mobile : +(91)-9822841126/9822841127

**Ambica Engineering Equipment**
Deals in manufacture and export of pressure vessels, vibrating screens, centrifuges, chemical processing machinery, accufeed systems, diary equipments, material handling equipments and food processing machinery.
Address: No. 986/18/B, Diamond Park,
G. I. D. C., Makarpura, Vadodara - 390 010
Phone: +(91)-(265)-3043182
Mobile : +(91)-9824531122/9825372189

**Engineering Group, India**
Engaged in manufacturing and supplying of industrial machinery such as food processing machinery, pharmaceutical machinery, bottling machinery and tablet making machinery etc.
Address: Plot No. 87, Opposite Modern Public School, Near Apar Nursing Home,
Jeewan Park, Uttamnagar, Delhi - 110 059
Phone: +(91)-(11)-65486527/64529627
Fax: +(91)-(11)-25644399/42697427
Mobile : +(91)-9811427627/9310924399
Website: www.engineeringgroupindia.com

**Jaya Impex**
Exporters and supplier of food processing plants that includes crystal sugar plants, sugar factory plants, sugar plant spares and industrial sugar plants. Also deals with colorful empty gelatin capsule, pharmaceutical machines and workshop machinery,
Address:16, Gokul Regency II,
Thakur Complex, Kandivali (East),
Mumbai - 400 101, India
Phone: +(91)-(22)-28544176/28544177
Fax: +(91)-(22)-28543451/66781688
Mobile : +(91)-9820063823/9820067284

**Jamal Engg. Works**
Supplier and manufacturer of food processing machinery like bakery machinery, rusk slicing machinery, vertical rusk slicing machinery, cream mixers, automatic cream mixers, flour mixers and compact flour mixers.
Address: 245/20, Kailash Colony,
Near iti Gate, Sonipat - 131 001, India
Phone: +(91)-(130)-2200872
Mobile : +(91)-9896350438

**Atlas Machine Tools**
Dealing and supplying of food processing equipment such as food processing machinery, industrial food processing machinery and simple configuration food processing machinery.
Address: Atlas House, Kunnathurmedu,
Palakkad - 678 013, India
Phone: +(91)-(491)-2535669/2539870/2536017
Fax: +(91)-(491)-2539870
Mobile : +(91)-9447039870

**Innovative Engineers**
Supplying and manufacturing food processing machinery such as rotary head extruders, flavour drum machines, flavor applicators, vertical mill mixers, slurry preparation machines, form fill seal machines and powder seal machines.
Address:G - 245, Sector - 63,
Noida - 201 307, India
Phone: +(91)-(120)-4347775
Fax: +(91)-(120)-4347775
Mobile : +(91)-9871374601/9891280158

**Shruti Icemac Engineers**
Manufacturing, supplying and exporting food processing machinery such as soft ice cream plants, industrial ice cream machines, electric ice cream machines and automatic ice cream machines.
Address:No. 107, Rajshree Industrial Estate-2, Chitalsar Manpada, Ghodbunder Road,
Thane West, Thane - 400 607, India
Phone: +(91)-(22)-25896580
Mobile : +(91)-9820141567

**Forsberg Agritech (INDIA)**
Supplying and manufacturing food processing machinery such as industrial rice mill machines, agriculture rice mill machines, metallic rice mill machines and small rice mill machines.
Address:123, GIDC Estate, Makarpura
Baroda, Vadodara - 390 010, India
Phone: +(91)-(265)-2636752/6590584
Fax: +(91)-(265)-2638583
Mobile : +(91)-9825072483

**Ecowatech Pvt. Ltd**
Engaged in manufacturing and exporting of industrial machinery such as industrial machines, pharmaceutical machinery, food processing machinery and chemical process machinery.
Address:No. 144, Pilaiyar Koli Street,
Vadapalani, Chennai - 600 026, India
Phone: +(91)-(44)-24846465/24846465
Mobile : +(91)-9952909169

**Shri Ram Engineering Company**
Supplying and manufacturing food processing machinery such as scourer machines, chakki heavyduty, destoners, rawa purifier, drum sieve machines, intensive dampener and mini classifiers- baibro seprators.
Address:Near Central Bank, Chaubepur,
Kanpur - 208 004, India
Phone: +(91)-(511)-2282729
Fax: +(91)-(511)-2282729
Mobile : +(91)-9415405372/9198029658

**Flavorite Technologies Private Limited**
Deals in manufacturing and exporting of industrial machinery, industrial food processing machinery and precision engineered industrial food processing machinery.
Address:Khasara No. 50 / 1,
Patwari Halka - 28, Village Tillore Khurd,
Indore - 452 020, India
Phone: +(91)-(731)-4046509
Fax: +(91)-(731)-4040953
Mobile : +(91)-9425052469

**D E Bright International**
Supplying and exporting industrial machinery such as cold storage, refrigerant cooling coils, evaporating cooling coils, condensing & cooling coils, cooling towers, ice plants, chilling units and food processing machinery.
Address:Unit No. 04, Kamal Estate,
Opposite Hindsaurastra Industrial Estate,
Ibi House Road, Marol Naka, Andheri East,
Mumbai - 400 059, India
Phone: +(91)-(22)-28524572
Mobile : +(91)-9820700411

**Sterling Marketing & Services**
Dealing and supplying of food processing machinery such as digital coffee machines, coffee vending machines, coffee machines, digital bubble top coffee machines, instant coffee machines and natural coffee machines.
Address:No. 23, 1st Floor, Sarbati Complex,
Jwala Heri Market, New Delhi - 110 063,
India
Mobile : +(91)-9810352014/9910352014

**Mitsun Engineering, Vadodara**
Manufacturer and exporter of chemical processing plants, chemical processing machines, chemical processing equipments, oil mill machinery, seed cleaning machinery, food processing machines and plants, detergent powder, cake and soap plants.
Address:FF-107, Silver Coin, Shrenikpark Char Rasta, Akota, Vadodara - 390 020, India
Phone: +(91)-(265)-2352802/2352805
Mobile : +(91)-9824083532
Website: www.mitsunengg.com

**Kwality Engineering Corporation, India**
Manufacturers and suppliers of food processing machines, food making machinery, food mixing machine, food mixing machine with bottom entry agitator, high speed mixers, planetary mixers. Also supply distribution column, agitators, ss vessels and ss tanks.
Address: Plot No. 198, Sector 1 Vasai Taluka I. E. Gauraipada, Thane,
Maharashtra - 401 208, India
Phone: +(91)-(250)-6417968
Mobile : +(91)-9324623556

**Saka Engineering Systems Private Limited**
Engaged in supplying food processing plants and machinery such as dryer that includes spray dryer, flash dryer, co-current direct-heat rotary dryer, rotary dryer, fluid bed dryer and spin flash dryer.
Address:396/8 Santosh Park Kundan Nagar,Mumbai Pune Highway,
Dapodi Pune, Pune - 411 012, India
Phone: +(91)-(20)-30710416
Fax: +(91)-(20)-46720074
Mobile : +(91)-9924911228/9561094128

**Adarsh Fabricators, Faridabad**
Exporting and supplying food processing equipments, sieving machine, farm machinery, swing grader farm machinery, automatic swing grader machinery, commercial farm machinery, heavy duty farm machinery and agricultural farm machinery.
Address:No. 212, Sector-24,
Faridabad - 121 005, India
Phone: +(91)-(129)-4024585
Mobile : +(91)-9810072359
Website: www.shotblastingindia.com

**Novatech Process Equipments (P) Ltd.**
Manufacturers, exporters and suppliers of miscellaneous plants & machinery such as process equipments, food process equipments, industrial process equipments, chemical process equipments and pharmaceutical process equipments.
Address:601, Building No. 1, Pushpamangal Complex, Near Babubhai Petrol Pump, Old Agra Road, Mano Pada, Thane West,
Ambarnath - 400 601, India
Phone: +(91)-(22)-25478864/25478865-66
Fax: +(91)-(22)-25478868
Mobile : +(91)-9320553351

**Goldin (India)Engg.Co**
Manufacturing food processing machines, post harvest processing machinery, agro processing machinery, sunflower cleaning machinery, maize cleaning machine, grain pre cleaners, seed pre cleaners, screen air separator and seed fine cleaner grader.
Address: No. 10/11, B. I. D. C. Estate, Gorwa Alembic Road, Gorwa, Vadodara - 390 023
Phone: +(91)-(265)-2291540/2284120
Fax: +(91)-(265)-2291540/2284120
Mobile : +(91)-9824240130/9824160180

**Fabcon India**
Manufacturer and supplier of flour mill, flour mill machine, flour milling equipment, food processing equipment, wheat processing machinery, grain processing machinery, agricultural processing machinery, flour mill machine and roller mill plants.
Address: No. 89/1, Dharmutalla Road,
Salkia, Howrah - 711 106, India
Phone: +(91)-(33)-26555354/26559010
Mobile : +(91)-9433011309/9830948562

**Technocraft, Belgachia**
Supplier and manufacturer of feeding machines, industrial machinery, separating machine, sheet cutting machine, separate impurities cutting machines, food processing cutting machine, grains cutting machine and cereals cutting machine.
Address: 5 B Kundu Lane, Belgachia,
Kolkata - 700 037, India
Phone: +(91)-(33)-25765831
Mobile : +(91)-9830214207

**Akshar Industries**

Manufacturing a range of ice cream machinery, ice cream machinery parts, bakery oven, candy machine, chocolate machine, confectionery equipment, food processing equipment and chocolate coating machine.

Address: 94-C, Shankar Estate, Near Reva Bhai Estate, C.T.M Amraiwadi,
Ahmedabad - 380 026, India
Phone: +(91)-(79)-25860149
Mobile : +(91)-9327060160/9375260160

**Sree Balaji Industries, Coimbatore**

Engaged in supplying of rice polishers, rice mill machinery, food processing equipments, vibro destoner food processing equipments, trouble free food processing equipments and pollution free food processing equipments.

Address:20, Ishwar Trade Center, Dr. Nanjappa Road, Grey Town, Coimbatore - 641 018, India
Phone: +(91)-(422)-2307811/2301598/4393763
Fax: +(91)-(422)-2301598
Mobile : +(91)-9443378106

**Maruti Machines Pvt. Ltd.**

Supplier of food processing equipments, bakery machinery, biscuit making machines, candy machines, confectionery machines, dairy processing plants, fruit processing equipments, mineral water plants, snack machines and vegetable dehydration plants.

Address:B - 23, Ambica Industrial Estate,
Ambica Nagar, Odhav,
Ahmedabad - 382 415, India
Phone: +(91)-(79)-22975760/22874026
Fax: +(91)-(79)-22874026
Mobile : +(91)-9879599554/9879798821

**Industrial Equipments Co.**

Manufacturing and exporting of food processing equipments, precision food industry machinery, food industry machinery, customized food processing equipments and industrial food processing equipments.

Address: MIDC, Plot No. E7/8, Bhosari,
Near NARI., Pune - 411 026, India
Mobile : +(91)-9696373874

**Sadas Engineering Works**

Manufacturing and exporting bakery equipments, bakery machinery, dough kneaders, food processing equipments, frying equipments, idli makers, meat grinders, noodle machines, potato peelers and popcorn machines.

Address:No. 157, New Scheme Road,
Papanaikan Palyam, Coimbatore - 641 037
Phone: +(91)-(422)-2210950
Mobile : +(91)-9788260997/9360331250

**B. B. Investment Casting**

Manufacturer and supplier of Machined Components like Casting For Food Processing and Casting For Machinery Parts & Ortho Implants. Also offering Casting For Pumps, Casting For AutoMobiles and Casting For Valves

Address: A / 2205 - 2206, Road - A, G. I. D. C. Metoda, Kalawad Road, Rajkot - 360 021
Phone: +(91)-(2827)-287897
Fax: +(91)-(2827)-287818
Mobile : +(91)-9925208050

**Hydro Services**

providing services like equipment services, machinery services, plants services, food processing services, food processing plants services, processing services, after sales services and research services.

Address:No. 93, Nanjunda Reddy Building,
Konena Agrahara, Old Air Port Road,
Bengaluru - 560 017, India
Phone: +(91)-(80)-66496228
Fax: +(91)-(80)-25227181
Mobile : +(91)-9945327607

**Manu Enterprises, Chennai**

Manufacturer and exporter of industrial process equipment, electrical process equipment, friction equipment, Simple cluster equipment, cosmetics machinery, dispersing equipment and food processing mixers.

Address: No.11, Reddy Street,
Madurametttupalayam, Puzhal,
Chennai - 600 066, India
Phone: +(91)-(44)-25376812/26591397
Fax: +(91)-(44)-26591397
Mobile : +(91)-9840295194

# ALL FOLLOWING PROJECT REPORTS ARE READILY AVAILABLE

## PAINT, ENAMEL, SOLVENTS, THINNERS, INKS & VARNISH

PAINT, ENAMEL, SOLVENTS, THINNERS, INKS & VARNISH

- Acrylic Emulsion Paints
- Acrylic Cement Paint (Dry Powder)
- Aluminium Paint
- Automobile Paints
- Ball Point Pen Refill Ink
- Bituminious Road Emulsion
- Bitumen
- Bituminious Felts For Water & Damp Proofing
- Bituminious Road Emulsion Rapid Medium & Slow Setting
- Buffing & Polishing
- Cement Paint For White & Grey Cement
- Dispersant
- Dry Distemper
- Dry Distemper & Cement Paint
- Duplicating Ink Black For Gestner Duplicator
- Emulsion Paints (Water Based)
- Hammertone Paint
- Insulating Varnish & Wire Enamel
- Iron Oxide Pigments
- Insulating Varnish (Poly Vinyl Butyral Based, Ffc Grade)
- Lime Colour (Cement Colour)
- Synthetic Red Oxide For Floorings
- Solvent & Thinners
- Marking Inks (Water Proof)
- Metal Naphthanate (As Drier For Paints)
- N.C.Putty
- Offset Printing Ink
- Oil Bound Distemper Paint
- Paint Brushes
- Paint Manufacture For Rolling Coating Of Aluminium And Steel Coil
- Paint Removers
- Paint Industry
- Paint & Varnish
- Picture Varnish
- Powder Coating Paint
- Printing Inks (Offset,Flexo & Roto Gravure)

- Primer Paint & Enamel Paint
- Putty & Water Proofing Paint
- Printing Inks (Flexo-Graphic Ink)
- Putty (Metal Casement)
- Red Oxide Primer (Anti Corrosive)
- Refrectory Paint (Graphite Based)
- Screen Printing Inks
- Silk Screen Printing Ink Formulation For Plastic, Paper, Cloth
- Stamp & Pad Ink
- Stoving Paint
- Spirit Soluble Maleic Resin
- Texture Paint
- Thinners And Its Allied Products
- Toner Ink
- Varnish Thinner (Solvent)
- Vacuum Metallizing Lacquers
- Wood Primer

## PHARMACEUTICAL, DRUGS, AYURVEDIC/HERBAL COSMETICS & MEDICINES, HOMOEOPATHIC MEDICINES, HOMOEOPATHIC MEDICINES, DISPOSABLE SYRINGE, DENTAL COLLEGE & FINE CHEMICALS ETC.

MEDICINES, HOMOEOPATHIC MEDICINES, DISPOSABLE SYRINGE, DENTAL COLLEGE & FINE CHEMICALS ETC.

- Aromatic Pills
- Alumina From Bauxite
- Aspirin
- Ayurvedic Pain Balm Ointments
- Ayurvedic Churan And Tablets
- Ayurvedic Tablets (Hajmola Type)
- Ayurvedic/Herbalpharmacy
- Ayurvedic Sherbats
- Ayurvedic Products
- Bulk Drugs (E.O.U)
- Blood Bags
- Calcium Gluconate
- Capsule, Tablet & Injection With Modern Instruments
- Cashew Feni
- Chloroquinone Phosphate (Bulk Drugs)
- Clinical Thermometer
- Dental Clinic
- Dental College
- Dental Grade Eugenol
- Dextrose Monohydrate, Liquid Glucose
- Dehydrated Onion & Onion Powder
- Dextrose Powder (Anhydrous From Starch)
- Dextrose Saline Solution
- Distillery (I.M.F.L)
- Disposable Needles For Syringes
- Disprin
- Distilled Water
- Empty Hard Gelatine Capsules
- Fairness Cream
- Filling & Packing Of Capsules
- Glucose - D - Powder
- Glycerine
- Hair Colour Mate (Formulations And Process Only)
- Herbal Cosmetics
- Herbal Shampoo
- Herbal Shampoo And Cream
- Herbal Hair Oils (Ayurvedic)
- Homoe & Bio-Medicines With Mother Tincture
- Homoepathic Medicines
- Hypodermic Needles
- I.V. Fluids
- Ibuprofen
- Infusion & Transfusion Sets (I.V. Set)
- Injectable For Pharmaceuticals
- Injection Ampoules Packaging Box
- Integerated Surgical Cotton
- Ice Making Plant
- Ice & Cold Storage
- Lactose & By Products Processing From Milk
- Lichen (Jatamansi Charila)
- Liquid Glucose And Its By-Products
- L-Lysine Monohydro Chloride
- Liquid Glucose From Potatoes
- Medical College
- Methanol (Hpcl Grade)
- Nicotine From Tobacco Waste
- Ointment-Ayurvedic (Yellow & White)
- Pharmaceutical And Food Grade Gelatine
- Pharmaceutical Industry (Tablets, Capsules, Liquid, Gel, Ointment Powder Injectable)
- Pharmaceutical Unit (Eou) With Formulations, Injectables, Etc.
- Pyridine & Derivatives
- Salt (Iodized Salt)
- Saline & Injection Water
- Saline Water & Dextrose Solution (I.V.Fluid In Plastic Bottles)
- Sorbitol
- Starch (Maize)
- Surgical Adhesive Plaster
- Surgical Bandages
- Surgical Gloves
- Surgical Cotton
- Surgical Cotton And Bandage
- Synthetic Camphor Powder
- Tablets & Capsules
- Tissue Culture
- Tincture From Rectified Spirit
- Trimethopime
- Veterinary College With Hospital
- Veterenary Medicines (Only Formulations)
- Vitamin 'C', Sorbitol' Anhydrous Dextrose, Starch

# MULTIPLE PROJECT REPORTS IN CD-ROMS

## 42 HOSPITALITY, BUILDING MATERIALS, POWER, STEELS, ALCOHOL & OTHER FOOD PRODUCTS. ₹ 18000/-

ALCOHOL FROM RICE STRAW, ALCOHOL FROM MOLASSES, ALCOHOL FROM POTATOES, AUTOMATIC BRICK PLANT, AMUSEMENT PARK CUM WATER PARK, BRICKS BY CHEMICAL TREATMENT WITHOUT DRYING, BIOFERTILISER , BEER PLANT (E.O.U.), COUNTRY LIQUOR, COLD STORAGE, CORRUGATED SHEET BOARD & BOXES , CORN FLAKES , CHILDREN RECREATION CENTRE, ETHANOL (BIOFUEL) FROM MOLASSES, HONEY PROCESSING AND PACKAGING, HOTEL INDUSTRY (FIVE STAR), INDIAN MADE FOREIGN LIQUOR, JATROPHA (BIO-DIESEL) CULTIVATION & EXTRACTION, MUSTARD OIL , MINI STEEL PLANT/ M.S. INGOTS BY INDUCTION FURNACE, MOTEL/SMALL HOTEL ,MINERAL WATER , MUSHROOM GROWING AND PROCESSING WITH AIR CONDITION, OXYGEN GAS PLANT, PRE-FABRICATED BUILDINGS , PCC SOLID POLE WITH REINFORCEMENT (NOT CIRCULAR), READY TO EAT PROCESSED COOKED FOOD , RECTIFIED SPIRIT FOR POTABLE ALCOHOL, INDUSTRIAL ALCOHOL & MEDICAL ALCOHOL, READY MIX CEMENT CONCRETE, RECTIFIED SPIRIT FROM RICE/PADDY STRAW , READY TO EAT RETORT PACKED FOOD, RICE MILL , SEEDS GRADING AND PROCESSING , STONE CRUSHER, SPECIAL ECONOMIC ZONE (SEZ), SOYABEAN PRODUCTS ,SPONGE IRON, SOLAR POWER PLANT, STEEL ROLLING MILL (SARIYA), THREE STAR HOTEL, UREA FERTILIZER PLANT, WIND ENERGY POWER PROJECT

## 16 MULTI CRORES PROFITABLE PROJECTS (From 50 Crores & Above)

**Price of this CD : ₹ 20,000/-**

CASEIN FROM MILK, CHROME BENEFICIATION PLANT, HOSPITAL (100 BEDS), IRON ORE MINING AND MANUFACTURE OFSPONGE IRON, MULTIPRODUCTS, PORTLAND CEMENT PLANT, PAPER PLANT, RESIDENTIAL COMPLEX (TOWNSHIP), ROLLING MILL WITH INDUCTION FURNACE, SUGAR PLANT, SPONGE IRON FROM IRON ORE, STEEL PLANT (BILLETS) BASED ON INDUCTION FURNACE, STEEL TRANSMISSION LINE TOWER & HOT ROLLING MILL, SODIUM TRIPOLY PHOSPHATE, TYRES, TUBES & FLAP (MOPED TO TRUCK), UREA FERTILIZER PLANT

## 9 WHEAT AND WHEAT PROJECTS ₹ 16000/-

AUTOMATIC BISCUIT MAKING PLANT, AUTOMATIC BREAD MAKING PLANT, ATTA, MAIDA, SUJI & WHEAT BRAN (ROLLER FLOUR MILL (MINI FLOUR MILL), BAKERY UNIT, ROLLER FLOUR MILL (FLOUR MILL), MINI FLOUR MILL (MAIZE, SORGHUM, MILLET), MINI FLOUR MILL (ATTA), PAPER FROM RICE HUSK & WHEAT HUSK, WHOLE WHEAT PORRIDGE (DALIA).

## 19 MULTI CRORES PROFITABLE PROJECTS (From 1 Crore To 10 Crores Projects)

**Price of this CD : ₹ 20,000/-**

ALCOHOL FROM BROKEN RICE, AUTOMATIC BRICK PLANT, BATTERY-OPERATED THREE WHEELER, BIOFERTILIZER, BUTYL RUBBER FOR THE MANUFACTURE OF TUBES FOR TRUCK AND CAR TYRES, CORRUGATED SHEET BOARD & BOXES (PRINTED AND LAMINATED), COMPUTER SOFTWARE DEVELOPMENT AND CALL CENTRE, CONSTRUCTION CHEMICALS, DEHYDRATION OF ONION AND GARLIC, DEHYDRATION OF FRUITS AND VEGETABLES BY IQF TECHNOLOGY, FERRIC ALUM, GUAR GUM POWDER FROM GUAR SPLIT, INTEGRATED UNIT OF DAIRY, FARMING MILK COLLECTION & PROCESSING, FISH FARMING, POULTRY FARMING & HATCHERY, KATHA & CUTCH, MINERAL WATER CUM PET BOTTLE MANUFACTURING UNIT, PRODUCTION OF BIO-OIL FOR POWER GENERATION FROM COFFEE HUSK, PVC PIPE AND FITTING, SOLAR POWER (ENERGY) PLANT, TMT STEEL BARS

**E-Mail :** eiriprojects@gmail.com , eiribooks@yahoo.com

**ENGINEERS INDIA RESEARCH INSTITUTE** Mobile : 9811437895, 9811151047

4449, Nai Sarak, Main Road, Delhi - 110 006 (INDIA) Ph. 91-11- 23918117, 23916431, 23947058